THE ENCYCLOPAEDIA OF WOMEN'S STUDIES

THE ENCYCLOPAEDIA OF WOMEN'S STUDIES

(In Two Volumes)

(Vol. 2)

GIRIRAJ SHAH

GYAN PUBLISHING HOUSE
NEW DELHI-110002

The Encyclopaedia of Women's Studies

Rs. 1800 (Set)

ISBN: 81-212-0474-7 (Set)
81-212-0476-3 (Vol. 2)

Published in 2008 in India by
Gyan Publishing House
5, Ansari Road, Darya Ganj,
New Delhi-110002
Phones : 23282060, 23261060
Fax : 011-23285914
E-mail: books@gyanbooks.com
Website: www.gyanbooks.com

Laser Type Setting by: Rudra Computer Graphics, Delhi
Printed at: Vishal Kaushik Printers, Delhi

Contents

Vol. 2

36.	Amendment of Dowry Prohibition Act	377
37.	Wife-Beating Syndrome	382
38.	Happy Endings Through Mediation	404
39.	Dowry—the Scourge	416
40.	Dowry—Divorce	428
41.	Dowry—Deaths	451
42.	Giving in to the Unceasing Demands Does not Stop the Torture	460
43.	Divorce	474
44.	Today's Family	480
45.	Women and Crime	486
46.	Crime by Women	492
47.	Women, Crime and Punishment	511
48.	Handling of Women Criminals	519
49.	Women in Jails	523
50.	Police and Crime Against Women	535
51.	Law Enforcement and Women Police	545

52. Women Police 555
53. Women Cops 565
54. 'Women Police Face a Tremendous Bias' 576
55. Battle for Prestige 583
56. All Women Police Force 591
57. Role of Women in Army 602
58. Regiments of Women 610
59. A Feminine Touch 618
60. Policing by Women Police in Foreign Countries 622
61. The Changing Pattern of Women in Indian Society 632
62. Rise of Woman Power 637
63. Women's Lib in Asia 650
64. Extensive Benefits to Women 654
65. Women Against Women 671
66. Women's Rights Can't be Won at Cocktail Parties 678
67. Rights Writing—Kali for Women 690
68. Do Women Need Part-Time Jobs? 695
69. Mahila Yojna Announcement Available 698
70. Harnessing Women Power 700
71. Work for Women: Need for Reviewing EGS 716
72. Role of Women in Agriculture 725
73. Women in India: Law and Reality 748
74. Sweating for Freedom 752
75. Women and Population 759

76. Indian Women—Endangered Species 766

77. Demography: The Declining Sex Ratio 787

78. Female Foeticide: Undemocratic 793

79. Female Foeticide: Census Pointers 798

80. Are Women Indifferent to Health? 802

81. Women.The Key to Family Planning 810

82. Complex Problem that Women Face Today 814

83. Tribal Women's Power 821

Index 828

"Like, this time, I was busy and didn't wash the clothes at once". Officer (writing this down with great satisfaction) : "I knew there must be some reason:"

Here, the woman's own perception that beating his wife is her husband's habit was transferred by persistent questioning to an external cause–a result of her lapse. The absurdity of this cause finding exercise becomes clear when we consider the horror with which a woman would be viewed as one who beats up her husband for not earning enough or for refusing to help take care of children while she cooked for the family, or even for getting drunk.

Husbands can cultivate and sustain 'habits' of beating up wives only because society considers such habits more or less appropriate. A wife is beaten because she is beatable—society, while not openly approving wife beating, condones it : "After all, she is his own wife: " A man who indulged in a habit of beating his neighbours' wives would soon find it too costly a practice to continue.

A man's own wife is available as an outlet for violent tendencies. In the very apt phrase used by one battered wife, " My husband used me as a punching bag." Many wives are advised to and actually attempt to reform husbands by 'Understanding' their violent misbehaviour, trying to find excuses and justifications for it—he must be frustrated at work, he had an unhappy childhood etc. The assumption behind such attempts at understanding is that the wife exists for the husband's convenience, physical and mental.

Most important, a wife is beaten if, when and because the husband knows she has no option but to endure, no other place to go, and hence no way to resist violence. This is where the role of her own family becomes crucial.

In a typical report of a young wife driven to burn herself to death, the Indian Express of April 4,1989, quoted the victim's brother........ "they used to threaten to throw her out. And we persuaded them to take her back. " The woman (who happened to be employed in a government office) is like a useless object which is to be thrown out or taken back depending on the deal her male relatives strike. The only statement by the woman quoted in the report is "All they wanted was my death". In committing suicide, she saw herself as fulfilling her husband's and in-laws' wish.

The question arises, however, as to whether the parents and brothers of such a woman really want her to live, when they 'persuade' her violently abusive in-laws to 'take her back'. When counselling victims of marital violence over the years, we have met innumerable parents and brothers who wished us to help them in their efforts to 'persuade' violent husbands to 'take' their wives back. We have met very few who tried to persuade the woman not to endure violence, and unequivocally assured her of their support.

In almost all wife murder cases, the death is preceded by a process of the woman's repeatedly returning to the parental home and repeatedly being sent back to the marital home after negotiations. This shunting back and forth is the single most common pattern perceptible in marital violence cases in our society. Each time the woman is forced to return to her marital home without the conditions having altered in her favour, she is more demoralised and therefore more vulnerable to violence. Often, the process is abruptly terminated when her death follows and apparently successful reconciliation effort, 'reconciliation' being commonly defined as the husband's condescending to take her back.

Take the example of Santosh of Dhansa village, Haryana. She visited the Crimes Against Women (CAW) cell, Delhi, on February 10, 1989, along with her parents and brother, and complained that the husband Jagdish was maltreating her and having an affair with another woman. A few days later, the cell, arranged a 'reconciliation', Jagdish signed an agreement not to maltreat her, and Santosh's brother also signed the agreement. On February 29, Santosh was murdered by Jagdish. The agreement was clearly worth little more than the paper it was written on as it did not confer on Santosh any power, and left her just as helpless as she was before.

Yet, parents and brothers knowing the high risks involved, continue to value the marriage above the woman's life and continue to pressurise their daughters to return to their husbands. In one memorable instance, we were visited by three brothers, wealthy Haryana landowners, who boasted belligerently of their power, influence and ability to get people murdered with police connivance, yet wanted help to 'reform' their sister's husband who for years had been severely maltreating her–grabbing her salary, visiting her only to batter her, frequently locking her out of the tiny room in a slum where she was forced to live. These men were not willing to divert some part of their wealth to helping their sister out of this marriage but instead put all their efforts into persuading a brutally violent man to 'keep' her with him.

Parents will go to extraordinary lengths, both in terms of self abasement and of bribery, in order to persuade a violent son-in-law to keep their daughter with him. At the CAW cell, the mother of a woman who had been beaten and thrown out be her husband, expressed this parental sense of priorities : 'I told my son-in-law that I was ready to eat his shit if only he could keep my daughter. In our family, divorce is unknown. I pleaded with him with folded hands and asked them not to talk of divorce." One can imagine to what lengths such parents would expect the daughter to go, in order to stay married. As one brother put it : "My sister's husband slaps her in front of us. We do not say a word. ....It is a family affair-let them settle it."

In almost every case of wife-murder the parents who knew in advance that their daughter was exposed to violence, and, often, even knew that her life was in danger. Decisive intervention on their part was all that was required save her life. But they continued to behave like the monkeys who see, hear and think no evil until, after the daughter's death, when they react with a posture of bewildered and helpless innocence : "We never thought it would go so far." In almost all cases where parents set a high enough value on their daughter's life to recall her, her life is saved. The decisive difference between life and death thus lies in the woman's parents' hands. This is true, regardless of the social and economic standing of the parents. Shakila Bano, daughter of a poor labourer, survived severe burns and built a new life, primarily because of the determination of her father, Ahmed, to stand by her. Shakila's natal family ate one meal a day so that she could have a proper diet while undergoing treatment; her father used to wheel her all the way from home to hospital every day, as he could not afford other transport; her brother discontinued his studies and took up a job to contribute to expenses : and the family postponed building another room in their tiny tenement, so that she could be treated and the legal case be fought. Shakila today has recovered not only her health and her will to live but also her confidence. Ahmed refused to let her go back when her husband started writing tender letters to her in order to get her to withdraw the case.

At the other end of the social scale, Amita Sharma, an MBBS, MD, after three years of suffering extreme humiliation and cruelty at the hand of her MBBS husband, during which she frequently considered suicide and was also threatened with death by him, finally managed to leave and make an independent life for herself and her daughter, primarily because of the support of her sister and her old, retired father. When she was in a village of Rajasthan, a captive of her husband, writing despairing letters to her father in Delhi, he went around mobilising support for her, including coming to Manushi for advice and constantly advised her to break away. Even while she hesitated to do so, she was always aware that the option was open to her, until she finally took it. To know that the option exists is crucial for a woman's survival.

A culture in which wife torture and wife murder are widely prevalent is one in which women's lives are devalued. It would be a mistake to think that it is only a woman's in-laws who devalue her, while her parents value her highly. Daughters in our society are not valued much higher than are daughters-in-law. That is why the common reformist programme which hopes to persuade in-laws to treat daughters-in-law like daughters, is inadequate to counter marital violence. A woman become vulnerable to marital violence precisely because she is transformed from a daughter into a daughter-in-law under circumstances over which she has little control. And her parents are equally active participants in this process of divesting her of control, by getting her married without her actively being involved in the decision making.

Also, the whole upbringing of a woman contributes to making her helpless to resist violence. The process of bringing her up with only marriage in view as her life's aim is the process of developing her not as an individual but as a wife, a service object. It is a woman's parents who thus play the crucial role in crippling her or strengthening her, in the formative years of her life. The heavily differential up-bringing given to sons and daughters prepares the latter for dependence and abuse. How many parents spend even half the amount that they spend on her marriage, in equipping the daughter with her own resources, with her own house, means of transport, bank account? They will much more willingly get a car for the son-in-law than a scooter for the daughter, pay for his education abroad than for hers, set up his business than hers. A woman who has been truly equipped socially, economically and psychologically for independence, by her parents (as very few are) will not need to submit to maltreament by in-laws.

It is not a coincidence that the same communities and regions where female infanticide was once prevalent, and where severe discrimination against daughters is still prevalent (as seen in the higher mortality rates of girl children as compared to boys, in the low sex ratio, and in the avid desire for amniocentesis followed by abortion of female foetuses) are precisely those where wives are most devalued and oppressed. These are communities where it is common for a wife to be harassed, abandoned even killed, if she produced only girls. Thus, daughters are just as powerless as are daughters-in-law. Both are perceived as dispensable, although the forms of violence inflicted on each differ.

It is not just the dowry which is rapidly spreading to regions and communities where it was not practised earlier. It is the hegemonic culture of extreme forms of wifely subservience accompanied by belligerent forms of son preference, which is spreading. This is reflected in the changing sex ratios–several areas of the country, especially in the south, which had a relatively higher sex ratio, are gradually sliding backward in this respect.

It is simplistic to attribute to spread of dowry to growing greed springing from a materialist or consumer culture. Rather, it is a symptom of the growing devaluation of women's lives. Anti-dowry campaigners have often confused the issue by making it out to be a case of greedy in-laws versus helpless parents. This categorisation makes little sense since the two categories invariably overlap. Most parents of girls also have sons and daughters-in-law. Sometimes, the overlapping of the two categories is visible in a dramatic form, as in the case of Arveen Kaur's in-laws whose own daughter had died of burning in her husband's home. Parents and in-laws of a woman share common assumptions. The assumption (that her life is of worth only as a serviceable object for her husband) is the real killer of women rather than dowry.

It is most essential, therefore, to alter the assumptions our society makes about women's lives, as inherently inferior expendable, having no indisputable rights in their natal homes, but intended only to live subsumed in the interests of husband and sons. Only when these assumptions change, when parents begin to equip their daughters, like their sons, to have an independent existence in their own right, an identity and life that is primary, and inalienable rights in their natal homes, can we expect more women to be able to resist marital violence before it escalates to the point of murder.

Steps to Combat Discrimination against Women

The only effective way to strengthen women's position in their husbands' families is first to strengthen their position as daughters. Parents' desperation to get rid of daughters leads them to push them into humiliating marriages and insist that these be kept going at any cost. This desperation gives the husbands power to tyrannise and subjugate the wives endlessly. The justification given by parents is that bringing a daughter back will involve imposing a life long burden on her brothers. Yet, they would rather pay lakhs to a son-in-law to keep this 'burden' off their shoulders. These extortionist payments are further used as an excuse to deny her a share in the parental property.

The disinheritance of women is what makes them appear a burden. Even after the passing of the Hindu Succession Act which ostensibly provided equal inheritance rights to women, daughters are seldom given a share in parental property. The two devices used to ensure this are :

1. Fathers invariably will away all their property to sons.

2. In cases where the father dies without leaving a will, the daughters are pressured to sign away their rights in favour of their brothers. In any case, few women have the resources to fight legal battles to claim their share. Thus, in the few cases that sisters demand their share, it is invariably their husbands who push them to do so. The net effect is the property then effectively passes from the woman's brothers to her husband.

The following steps would help combat this systematic discrimination against and disinheritance of woman :

1. Amendment of property laws in such a way that any will which disinherits daughters in favour of male heirs is not treated as a valid document.

2. Any document by a women signing away her rights in favour of brothers or husband is not treated as legally valid.

3. Legally establish the concept of joint matrimonial property whereby any property acquired by husband and/or wife during the cause of the marriage, is con-

> sidered the joint property, and in the event of a separation, is divided equally between them with the provison that if there are children, the wife must get custody of them and will be entitled to the matrimonial home since she has to bring up the children. If she is not earning, the husband must pay for her and the children's support, and if she is earning, he pays proportionately for the children's support.

This would ensure that a woman gets her share in parental property but cannot be deprived of it by her husband and in-laws. On the other hand, she will also acquire a right in her marital home, and cannot be beaten out of there without independent means of support.

36

Amendment of Dowry Prohibition Act

The Dowry Prohibition Act has been variously described as a negative, limited, penal and the impractical Act, one which failed to achieve its objective. The definition of the word 'Dowry' itself under Section 2 of the Act sees dowry as 'any property or valuable security' given or agreed to be given at or before the marriage, as 'consideration for the marriage of the parties.' Any presents given at the time of marriage, unless made as a consideration for marriage, will not be termed as dowry. The phrase 'in consideration of marriage' has also provided much indignation.

The Act provides both the giver and the taker of dowry, which, in effect, means that the courageous parents who protest against the son-in-law who demands more than the dowry given to him, will be signing his own arrest warrant. In Indian society those who give dowry are victims of tradition, who face harshest form of social ostracization if they desist, must they be treated on par with those who exploit such fears and customs.

The other forms of sexual crimes extending to the definition of perversion are commonly defined as sadesion, masodism, fetishcheons, transvestism or eonim. In some advanced countries like Sweden women are much more vulnerable to sexual assaults because being "hustled", "touched up" or treated as "Sex Objects". At times they might compliment a woman 'she's got big knockers' (breats) or 'she's a game'. Men tease women, wolf, whistle, ogle and try to touch them.

Obscure Laws—Legal Reforms

Mr. Y.V. Chandrachud, Chief Justice of India, stressed the need for steps to improve the moral tone of the society as no amount of tempering with the law or piecemeal amendments would help protect womens' honours, dignity and rights. Social therapy to cure the mind of the men who indulged in the crime was the prime need of the hour. The main lacunas lie in the law itself which is based on the western prudence and the basic principle. There are the legal systems which lay down responsibility for the guilt on the accused for prosecution. While it may be good in many other cases but in cases when the protector becomes killer, there is no reason why certain presumptions, circumstantial evidence and the question of burden of proof should rest on the accused. It is absolutely necessary that to take the case of a wife under auspicious circumstances, the guilt of the husband should be automatically pursued unless the circumstances themselves are obviously against it. Legal safeguards as envisaged under Section 317 should be introduced which lays full responsibility on the parents for the care of their children. There should be a similar presumption in suicide case which should be treated as forced death to be dealt with under Section 306 IPC. Punishment should be deterrent.

The Obscenity Laws

The law relating to the publication of obscene literature, selling, distributing, exhibiting is embodied in Section 292 of the Indian Penal Code and that such an offence is punishable with two years' imprisonment and with a fine which may extend to Rs. 2000/- only in case of a first conviction, the penalty and fine being more stringent in case of subsequent conviction.

A person who makes or produces or has in his possession any obscene book for the said purpose, would also be guilty of obscenity. So also is anyone who advertises or receives profits from a premises which put obscene matters or objects into circulation.

Strangely enough, the law relating to obscenity in England on which the Indian Law is based began with the working prauls of Sir Charles Ledly in criated and nude, the act though obscene, would be covered by Section 294 of the IPC which makes it an offence to do an obscene act in public to the annoyance of others. Neither English nor Indian laws define obscinity though both lay down exacting standards as to what will be obscenity. The test was evolved in RUS HICHBU in 1868 in England. The care arose out of an attack on the Catholic Churches and its practice of resorting to confessions in a book which was considered a blatant instrument of propaganda for the Protestant Society. The test laid down by Cockhem (Chief Justice) was whether the tendency of the matter charged as obscenity is to deprive and corrupt those whose minds are open to such immoral influences.

The Hichelin test was endorsed by the Supreme Court of India in Ranjit Udeshi's case in 1965 when they had to consider whether D.H. Lawrence notes 'Lady Chatterley's Lover' was obscenc. The Supreme Court held it was so and "the allegations with sex are not a legislativc embroidery but they cover, the only attractions to the common man". The test endorsed by the Supreme Court has now been statutorily embodied in Section 292 of the IPC by an amendment in 1969 to confirm to the provisions of the Obscene Publication Act of 1959 in England.

The test to determine obscenity is necessarily dependent on the moral values in a Community at a particular time. What was considered obscene a few years ago may well be innocuous today.

Inspite of so much legislation about crime against women, it has been felt that the law enforcing agencies have been somewhat dragging their feet in registering and processing such cases. The police should no doubt proble more vigorously the cases concerning death of a newly married woman.

Preventive Measures Against Sexual Crimes

It is proper to seek to protect children from the sexual depridations of adult sexual perverts. The increased police awareness and concern about the problem of rape is an example of the effectiveness of these efforts. Some felt that rape is a "backlash" to 'liberated' women. Rape is the only crime which involves a role reversed between the accused and accusor, thereby placing the victim on trial. The victim usually a female must prove her innocence. Rape is in fact the most traumatic form of victimisation in which the subject survives after gruesome ordeal of producing an imperishable cascade of evidence.

Preventive measures to guard the dignity and honour of women must be taken in right earnest. I can only suggest few steps which may bring out some reform in the contemporary situation.

Legal enforcement—Police should enforce the laws in right earnest and with all sincerity.

Preventing prostitution—Preventing prostitution by law enforcement resource is normally a fruitless effort to promote moral virtue is once again wasteful and socially injurious.

Introducing personal security system—Parents should make their own security arrangements for the protection of their childern.

Social fightout against sexual offenders—Public must also raise a voice against all sexual offenders and socially ostracise them.

Role of the Press—Press can also give wide publicity against the crime of sex offenders so that maximum humiliation is caused to the sex offenders.

Printing and publication of sexy magazines with photographic material must be controlled so that vulgarity does not creep in the young and impressionable minds.

Introducing jury system—Besides introducing jury system, woman juries must be introduced in order to streamline judicial system.

Age of consent—It has also been suggested that the age of consent be raised to 18 from 16 in cases of rape. Originally in 1891, it was 10 years and was raised to 12 in 1925 and 16 in 1949.

Oneness of proof—The oneness of proof must be on the accused instead of being in the prosecutrix. At present, it was on the prosecutrix to prove that she was not the consulting party to the rape.

Role of women organisations—The woman organisations can play significant role by taking up the cases of raped women. If this was done hundreds of hundreds unreported cases would come to light.

Role of judiciary—Justice Krishna Iyer has rightly pointed out that no law could be effective unless the judges are awakened to their social responsibilities and given prudence to judge the crime without going by the outdated definition given in the Indian Penal Code. There was need for the conscience and we must liberate the law from interpretation shackles.

The proceedings of rape cases should be held in camera.

Changing moral line of the society—Incest is no longer a taboo. To be sexual is no longer a crime. Adultery, wife swapping and prepuberty sex are only 'natural'. A new trend is sweeping in western society. Will it lead to an abolition of the institution of marriage? All the questions are rocking the minds of social ushers and reformers.

Today in elitist western society, the traditional marriage and the sense of deep emotional involvement is on the way out. Today the boys and leshians have their own organisations.

37

Wife-Beating Syndrome

Marital violence has been by and large a feature of family life to which society has usually turned a blind eye. Marital violence is symptomatic of the more general oppression of women in patriarchal society. Millions of women suffer this quietly and silently. Physical force, verbal abuse, persistence born out of violence not necessarily extreme, continually pushing, shoving, making the woman a door-mat, make out a case of marital violence. Researched reasons broadly appear to be alcoholism, poverty, maschocism, psycho-sexual problems, unemployment, immaturity, illness, upbringing, high expectations and different levels of tolerance-each relationship having its own standards.

Marital violence is largely a hidden phenomenon and the marriages concerned are not easily identifiable. As a general rule, studies indicate that such violence is rampant in developing as well as developed societies. It is stated that in England and the United States as many as one in three marriages experience episodes of violences, 41 per cent experience their first violent attack within six months after the wedding, another 25 per cent are hit within the next two years, making a total of

84 per cent affected by marital violence within the first three years of marriage.

Privacy protects intimacy but it weakens social control, and weakening social control fosters freedom to be more deviant. Not only are the battered wives likely to want their marriage to continue for the sake of privacy and security, but it is only later on, as the violence gets worse that they look out for external aid to challenge the man's use of violence. If appropriate help is not found easily at the early stages of reporting, women tend to give the search for it until there is an emergency.

We have yet to evolve social systems of intervention prior to reaching the final punitive authority-the police. In our system institutional social welfare agencies have yet to make a credible breakthrough in a systematic way. So far one only sees the police as an agency of first and last resort. With a totally male-oriented police, women are reluctant to go to the police stations and report for help at the early stages. On occasions when they do so, response to such acts of violence is grossly inadequate in terms of the need for support and quality of service.

Police is known to have disposed of such instances "rather domestic" and "priorities of the police being cognisable crime and not social work". We have a case example of systems available in England, where there is a system of Health Visitors calling on the families regularly, the primary concern being welfare of children. Since the Health Visitors are regular visitors to the families, they do detect cases of marital violence at the initial stage itself. After detection, they play a specialist liaison role crossing the frontier between medicine and social work and very often act as the general practitioner go-beyond, in this respect.

There are solicitors to provide free legal aid to the victims of marital violence. There is a system of "Green Form Scheme" under the legal Aid Act 1974, where the legal aid scheme allows a solicitor to give advice and assistance in the application of

English Law to anybody, in particular circumstances, which has reason in relation to the person seeking the advice. The solicitor completes the Green Application Form to claim reimbursement from the Legal Aid Fund, hence, the Green Form Scheme. Psychiatrists are also available as an institutional help to women in distress requiring counselling.

Experience of Indian conditions reveals that in situations when no help is forthcoming, the woman is left with no alternative but to remain a door-mat or bring in major changes in her personality for the sake of security and welfare of her family, primarily children, or take the extreme step of suicide. In 1982 Delhi police alone recorded 610 cáses of burning of women. They may still be an incomplete data. Presently, one is not aware of any standard practice in the police to record all domestic instances involving marital violence. The broad classification of complaints are:

(a) cognisable offences which are registered, and for which statistics are therefore available, and

(b) marital violence without injury, forming non-cognisable complaints, which remain untabulated.

Recently, we had an amendment in the Indian Penal Code making cruelty on a woman a cognisable offence. The impact of this new amendment will be known over a period from now. The thrust of the issue remains: Is the police, and should the police, be the only agency which could play an effective role in controlling marital violence in Indian conditions? Or should there not be also statutory institutions to play the necessary preventive roles?

Incidentally, it is interesting to point out that in the majority of cases where women report marital violence, they want "violence to end and not marriage to end." Women in distress look for help to accomplish peace, without a total upheaval and loss of security. It has been seen that such women in distress seek legal aid when they feel they have reached a breaking point and urgently need protection of separation from the man. In this state of mind they initiate legal proceedings and request institutional shelter. However, once the crisis is over, their needs and priorities undergo a change and the need to consolidate the family and return home, become upper-most. Solicitors in England taking up such cases have had women coming to them with requests for withdrawal of the cases, even when litigation was initiated in their case for the fourth time.

The ambivalence of the woman is understandable. In our society, going by police experience, we do get a large number of victims falling in the 'Moth and Candle' relationship; women who even when being badly battered want police help and protection to continue living in the house of the husband. For obvious reasons; she has no proper institutional shelter and no one to go to ! Parents do not want the married daughter back, for she now would be considered as a liability, and a stigma for the family.

If we are serious in tackling women's problems, as far as marital violence is concerned, the social system must provide for the woman in distress, healthy short stay homes, psychiatric help, free legal aid, with Citizen Advice Bureau. Till then women will continue using the police as the first and last resort, and in some exceptional cases as no resort.

A case can also be made out for the law enforcing agencies to be better trained with necessary aptitude towards handling of domestic violence, as a prevention of social crime, and in the larger service of social welfare.

Wife-Beating Still Rampant

Wife-beating appears to be as rampant as ever even after 40 years of Herculean efforts to better the lot of women. That the husband gets drunk and continues to take it out on the women is evident from a song which greeted the National Commission of Self-employed men and women in the informal sector during its visit to Rajasthani village.

Now Magazine, p. 52–53.

Demanding that liquor distillation be banned in their area the women said,

"This man of mine, Returns home drunk,

Sathin, he beats me every day, I toll the whole day

Sathin, I cannot bear the beating."

Observing that the song probably symbolised the plight of a majority of even after 40 years of independence, the Commission noted in its report that a similar refrain was heard by it from many a women entrenched in poverty that alcoholism brings upon their families. Women of Solan, in Himachal Pradesh, put in this way ! "When we ask the government for schools, it takes ten years, but the liquor shops appear instantaneously without even asking. "In fact liquor shops appear despite our vocal protests", they exclaimed. They were also very agitated about the Government's policy to open liquor shops for revenue. "No such shop should be opened in any areas without the resolution of a two-thirds majority of the village people to do so."

Women in Simla echoed their disgust by questioning the sincerity of the government in the welfare of women. "If the Government was really interested in our welfare, they would not open these "thekkas".

While the Government's income is increasing, "we become poorer day by day", asked a women activist. "If sugar, kerosene, foodgrains and other things of necessity are under ration, why liquor sale unlimited."

Liquor Poverty

The commission noted that liquor and poverty were a clearly linked equation for most of the women it came across. Noting that though the tribals in Orissa had licences which permit them to distill only a certain quantity of liquor for home consumption and festival times, it is not adhered to. Quoting a voluntary social worker the commission said "temperance is difficult to maintain because alcoholism is high amongst the tribals.

"Besides development work proceeds slowly if at all, in these areas, because of the negative effects of liquor on people's motivation.

"There is a belief among men that they cannot work hard without drinking", the worker said.

When the commission asked some fishermen why they drank so much, they replied, "we work in the water, on the sea, it is cold. To keep warm we have to drink hard." Asked, how come women worked harder and was still able to survive without drinking the response was "they are women after all".

Domestic workers in the Hyderabad slums said that most of them had been deserted or had become widows due to alcoholism among their men. Top priority for them was total prohibition of liquor in the town, according to the commission.

Women sweepers in Jammu also reported one of their major problems as alcoholism amongst the men of their community. Quoting the account of a sweeper the commission says, "they drink but it has such bad effects on us. Our hard earned income is snatched to support this habit."

Suicide Attempts

An increase in suicide attempts by women who cannot tolerate the strain has also been noticed. Women in Kanchipuram told the commission that though there were no liquor shops around "you will still find all men in our community drinking." Referring to illegal distillation they said, "you understand."

Uttarakhand

Women in Uttarakhand Kassauni also appeared to be quite frustrated when they told the commission that "we could not solve this problem even after organising. We had solved the problem to a great extent but the Government did not back us in follow up so the problem slowly seeped back in." Women in Punjab confessed that "90 per cent of our men drink as if they have to drink. The young drink more than the old. The son drinks more than the father and ruins his youth. Every village has at least one shop that drains our earnings." Bombay slum women had an unique solution up their sleeve when they demanded that "the drunkard's salary should go directly to his wife, and not given in his own hands."

The commission noted that in Assam the effects of the problem even filtered down to girls' education.

"Drinking is a serious problem on the plantations so mothers have generally stopped sending their daughters to school because they meet harassment coming home in the dark."[1]

Violence against Women Rising

Indian women's organisations in the United States and Canada are concerned by an increase in domestic violence against women from the sub-continent. As a result support hot-lines and shelters have sprung up in States like New Jersey, California, Chicago in the US and British Columbia and Toronto in Canada, all areas of concentrated Indian populations.

Violence against women has become a global phenonenon. As many as 15 million women the world over had been abused at one time or the other during their lives. Data collected on women in America show an estimated three to four million in the US are battered and assaulted, including rare, each year by their husbands or partners, Dr. C. Everett Koop, the US Surgeon General, said in a recent address before the Pan American Health Organisation. Beating by husbands is the single most significant cause of injury to women in this country, statistics showed. One out of every five women admitted to emergency

1. *Pioneer*, dated, 29–7, page–9.

had been abused by a spouse. Some 40 per cent of all women in the US experience sexual abuse, as children and as many as 44 per cent of adult women report completed or attempted rape, which includes rape by their husbands or other family members.

Reluctance to deal with the problem in the US and elsewhere had, Dr. Koop surmised, "trivialised a major problem of our times", and he called on international organisations to "demonstrate a clear recognition of the problems and provide the necessary leadership to us all".

Dr. Shelly Feldman of Cornell University, a specialist on Bangladesh, who also spoke on the issue of "Violence Against Women: The Global Perspective" said she was "pleased that finally it is being recognised as a problem here instead of always finger-pointing India or Pakistan."

Professor Florence McCarthy, also of Cornell University's Department of Rural Sociology, and an expert on South Asia, agreed that poverty exerts its own type of violence on people particularly women. "Even as social and economic conditions change in South Asia, there is no social legislation to provide for norms of behaviour that would protect women as they earn their living", she asserted adding, "very few of the government agencies at the local level speak on behalf of women and many of the non-government organisations reassert the patriarchal system."

In India too, women's organisations have been concerned by the problem of wife-beating. "For the past two years, Indian women's organisation have been looking at violence against women as a human rights issue", said Ms Shakun Mohini of the Bangalore based Vimochana. She is here to study the lobbying system of Non-Governmental Organisations (NGOs) in the US. It is a political issue, she maintained and unless human rights groups take it up it cannot become a priority. "We should challenge organisations like Amnesty International to include this violence in their definition", she asserted.

A representative of Amnesty in Washington told India Abroad News Service the organisation was not involved in defining the purview of human rights. "We don't deal with general violence against women", she said. However, Amnesty was about to start a round of discussions with other organisations on women and human rights issues because she said, it saw an "overlap" between Amnesty concerns and these of other NGOs.[1]

Commonwealth Confronts Violence against Women

A Book described as "a welcome tool" to curb violence against women a serious problem in both developed and developing countries has been published by the Commonwealth Secretariat in London. It contains advice for women's groups, lawyers, social workers, health and media professionals, police and the judiciary as well as individuals on how to tackle the problem. Subjects covered range from domestic violence to sexual assault. There is also a section on dowry-related violence against brides, Confronting Violence—A Manual for Commonwealth Action has been produced in response to a call by the first meeting of Commonwealth Ministers Responsible for Women's Affairs in Nairobi, Kenya, in 1985. The Ministers, meeting on the eve of the UN world conference marking the end of the UN Decade for Women, sought pan-Commonwealth action to confront the issue. They were particularly concerned to promote action against domestic violence, sexual abuse and sexual harassment. The manual has been divided into three sections : domestic violence, sexual assault and harassment and dowry-related violence.

Each section defines the various types of violence, examines current legal approaches in Commonwealth countries and explores mechanisms for providing support for victims or for bringing about a change in public attitudes.

"It is becoming increasingly evident that the problem of physical and mental abuse of women is of far greater magnitude

1. *The Hindustan Times*, New Delhi, Saturday, June, 3, 1989.

than has been imagined previously", notes the manual. "However, it is still common for people to take marital violence for granted and conclude that little can be done about it". Breaking the silence is the first stage in confronting violence, says, the manual which devotes a chapter to the subject. Gaining a victim's trust is important before she can feel safe in speaking about her experiences without feeling blamed or shamed.

The manual highlights methods of treating rape victims. It reproduces a guide, the Sexual Assault Examination Kit, for patients, police and doctors developed in Canada. Prepared by the Royal Canadian Mounted Police, the guide contains advice for rape victims concerning police, medical and court procedures. The manual notes that dowry-related violence continues to be a problem in several Commonwealth countries, particularly those in South Asia.

"Dowry demand have become associated with a rising number of suicides of young brides. In recent years, there has been a growing concern in South Asia at the explanation of a wife's death as suicide where the cause of death is more likely to be murder".

Further research and public education together with improved media coverage are essential if the problem is to be tackled, suggests the manual. The manual is based on the deliberations and recommendations of a multi-disciplinary group which met in 1985 to examine violence against women. The meeting was organised by the Women and Development Programme of the Commonwealth Secretariat and assisted by the Secretariat's Legal Division.

Members of the group, both men and women drawn from various Commonwealth regions, had long experience of dealing with issues arising from violence against women. They included lawyers, police officers, education, child care and health specialists and representatives of non-governmental organisations concerned with women's issues. Media professionals also served on the group. They were asked, among other things, to assist in defining a programme of action to promote initiatives at community and national levels, and in determining how best the Secretariat might act as an information clearing house.

Among the group's recommendations were public education campaigns, greater use of the media to create awareness of the problem, research into the incidence of domestic violence, training programmes for the police, social and medical workers and telephone hotlines which could be used by victims to report incidents in confidence.

The manual has been produced with assistance from Jane Connors of Australia, a consultant to the Women and Development Programme and a lecturer in law at the School of Oriental and African Studies of the University of London. Ms. Connors, who comes from Canberra and has made a special study of violence against women, says : "Women have to be made aware that they don't have to take beatings as part of life. "Reducing their economic dependence on men and raising the level of education could go a long way towards improving the situation."

Dorienne Wilson-millie, Jamaican-born Canadian director of the Programme, says in an introduction to the manual. "We hope that this pooling of our Commonwealth experience on confronting violence against women will help both governments and concerned individuals to move a stage further in the long process of social and legal change and contribute to direct and practical action." Copies of Confronting Violence – A Manual for Commonwealth Action are available from the Women and Development Programme, Human Resource Development Group, Commonwealth Secretariat, Marlborough House, Pall Mall, London Swity 5HX, Britain, Commonwealth Feature.

Rising Crimes Against Women

These days when one talks of crimes against women the first word that comes to mind is dowry. Then a sort of numbing of the senses occurs because the word has become so commonplace, dowry related atrocity stories so routine that if you've heard one you have almost heard a lot. Rising graphs of crimes against women induce almost the same feeling of ennui because all that the police stations are likely to come up with are generally inaccurate lists of dusty statistics relating to rape, molestation and 'eve-teasing' which is the best. The guardians of the law are able to do about the gamut of crimes against women.

Yet these 'officially recognised' crimes constitute only the manageable, visible tip of the problem. Few people, except a handful of radical women's groups, want to go any deeper into this disturbing social phenomenon because to do so is to risk looking into a mirror that reflects Indian society at its ugliest, its most barbaric. So occasionally, when a Roop Kanwar burns herself to death on her husband's funeral pyre and the horror of her act grips the imagination of the nation, the government's response is bafflement. It took the ministry of women's affairs two weeks to open its mouth not, as some people alleged, because of political, Rajput-vote considerations, but quite simply because it did not know how to deal with a *suttee*. There are laws on the statute books to prevent *suttee*. They were enacted by the British more than a century ago but everyone knew that a large segment of Indian society did not—and does not—regard *suttee* as a crime against women.

So what was the government to do? By the time it worked out a suitable reaction Roop Kanwar's death was already being celebrated as an expression of truth and beauty and the spot where she burned to death was attracting people in hundreds of thousands. At that time her family reportedly collected over Rs. 40 lakhs from pilgrims. And few leaders were prepared to stand up and state publicly that this was a sickening crime against women.

The same sort of confused incomprehension can be seen in the attitude towards female foeticide. Despite the mushrooming of amniocentesis clinics and the knowledge that almost no male child has ever been aborted, the general reaction to the issue is that such clinics are a necessary evil. Lately a senior minister in the union government, Vasant Sathe, publicly defended the right of amniocentesis clinics to exist. The argument: India has population problem severe enough to justify the existence of such clinics; so people should be allowed to choose the sex of the children that they want to have. It is alright for the West, the argument goes, to restrict amniocentesis to the detection of congenital diseases and birth defects, but in India things are different so we must try and see things from the usual uniquely Indian point of view.

This school of thought does mercifully draw the line at female infanticide but the quite unable to discern that amniocentesis clinics are merely a scientific evolution of an old and widely practised Indian tradition. The only difference is that in the old days the girl actually had to be born to be killed and of course the methods were cruder.

If a girl-child manages somehow to be born and to survive, the crimes against her begin in her own home and hearth at an early age. Ministry of Health statistics record that more girls die in the first five years of their life than male children and it is widely accepted that the reasons behind this are relatively inferior nutrition and lack of medical care. In villages the girl child starts working as an unpaid, domestic servant almost as soon as she can stand. By the time she is nine years old she is expected to virtually run the house and look after her younger siblings while male children of the same age go to school.

In urban India, particularly in middle-middle and upper-middle class families, attitudes towards the female child have certainly changed in the past few years, but again only marginally because a girl is still educated mainly in the hope of her landing a rich husband. Thus her chattel position remains substantially the same as that of her rural, less well-off sisters. It is against this social background that one needs to assess the phenomenon of rising 'officially recognised' crimes against women i.e. dowry related deaths, rape and *suttee.*

Madhu Kishwar, editor of the Delhi-based radical, feminist monthly magazine *Manushi* created quite a stir in liberal, intellectual, and feminist circles by stating quite clearly that the women's movement has an erroneous perspective of the dowry deaths problem. Kishwar argues that instead of agitating against dowry deaths, women's groups would do better to demand equal inheritance rights for women. According to her, dowry deaths are merely an extension of the phenomenon known as wife-battering in the West and that the main reason why Indian wives end up dead rather than battered is because they have fewer chances of getting out of a bad marriage.

In a recent feature article in the Indian Express (April 9), she pointed out that not only are Indian women rarely able to support themselves economically if they try breaking out of a bad marriage, but pressure from their own relatives generally keeps them in their husbands' homes until they end up dead. She writes : "Their parting words at the time of vidai indicate this : 'We are sending your doli today, may only your arthi (ashes) emerge from that house.' This pressure to keep the marriage going at all costs is the real killer of women, rather than dowry or the lack of it", says Kishwar.

The result inevitably is that the number of reported dowry cases has risen phenomenally in the past ten years or so because of which this social problem has perforce been noticed.

Dowry was first noticed as a proximate cause of death in the late seventies when women reporters became more common in the news rooms of major Delhi newspapers and began to investigate why the daily crime bulletin nearly always featured a one-paragraph item about a Manju, Shusheela or Geeta being burned to death. The Times of India was probably the first newspaper to investigate one of these news items and discovered women were being killed after months of demands for more dowry. Other newspapers followed this example and soon women's groups got into the act and dowry deaths became a cause *celebre*.

Statistics started to be compiled by government departments and it was calculated that around 300 women were being done to death every year in Delhi alone as a consequence of dowry related atrocities. In 1987, the union minister of state for home affairs told the Lok Sabha that 3,108 dowry related complaints had been registered in Delhi alone in 1985. Of these 382 cases were filed under the Dowry Prohibition Act and the Indian Penal Code.

But the statistics compiled by the government, if provided at all, tell a great deal less than the whole story. A recent study conducted by the Centre for Social Science Research has highlighted that although the Delhi police registered only 403 dowry crimes during the period 1982-86, in 1985–just one year–a woman's organisation in Delhi registered 360 cases of dowry victimisation. In the same year one Delhi hospital admitted 381 married women, between the ages of 16 and 30, with third degree burns.

According to women's groups, the number of dowry related deaths in Delhi alone could be well in the region of around nine hundred per year which means that they have trebled during the past decade. Asked whether this staggering statistic could be because people were less reluctant to register dowry death cases in the past, Prabeen Garewal of Saheli—a Delhi based women's group—says that this rising incidence of dowry related atrocities is rooted in contemporary social developments.

"Dowry related deaths have increased mainly because of the upward mobility aspirations of the newly emergent urban middle class. In the absence of an adequate system of obtaining loans for buying consumer goods, a wife is viewed almost as an investment to acquire high-priced consumer durables. The other problem is that women have now started working in a big way and in their work places they have a certain amount of independence. This makes it harder for them to come home and accept the subjugation that a woman is expected to suffer from her in-laws", says Garewal.

Independent views added to education appear to be a lethal combination for women. The study by the Centre for

Social Science Research (referred to earlier) reveals the horrifying statistics that 90% of the victims of dowry related crimes surveyed were educated, of which 30% were graduates. The reason why even an educated woman is unable to fight back is largely attributed to the shocking reality that a married woman's parents are nearly as reluctant to have her back as her husband's family is to keep her.

In the end, if the dowry deaths problem has worsened instead of getting better it could be because, as Madhu Kishwar rightly points out, women's groups have not assessed this phenomenon correctly. "For years we refused to attend weddings where dowry was being given without realising that if the girl gets something it is probably the only money or clothes that she is going to be given for a long, long time. Why should she be deprived of even that? What we should have been fighting for is absolutely equal inheritance rights and a law which would prevent fathers from willing everything they have to their sons", says Kishwar.

The other major 'officially recognised' crime against women is rape. On April 3, the union minister of state for home affairs told the Lok Sabha that the number of reported rape cases in the country had increased sharply from 7,308 in 1986 to 12,036 in 1988. The minister added that the largest number of cases were reported from the state of Madhya Pradesh (1,695) followed by 1,437 in Uttar Pradesh and 830 in Maharashtra. Even in Delhi which is blanketed by policemen guarding VIPs, the number of reported rape cases increased from 89 in 1986 to 111 in 1988.

Again, these statistics probably tell less than half the story because in rural India, where the largest number of rape cases occur, there are not many women who are prepared to report rape particularly if the rapist is a policeman, politician or bureaucrat.

In April, for instance, newspapers reported a spate of rape cases in Bihar of which Adivasi women from south Bihar, working in brick kilns were the victims. The incidents occurred in Pandui village, under the Parasbigha police district, in Kulhari village near Shakoorabad and in Dhakinbigha village near Makdumpur.

In all three incidents armed men appeared out of the darkness and dragged the women off despite there being a large police presence in the area to protect villagers from attacks by extremist groups. The Hindi newspaper Jansatta, reports that cases of this kind of armed rape are becoming increasingly frequent and the rapists generally escape. The most government could do for the victims in these cases was to pay out Rs. 2,000 and a sari each as *solatium*.

An even bigger problem is that policemen or government officials are increasingly emerging as rapists as indicated by the case of Guntabehn of Devidao village, near Rajpipla in Gujarat. This 25–year-old tribal woman was raped by six policemen on January 5, 1986 and decided with the help of a Christian legal aid agency to take the matter right up to the Supreme Court. The government responded by launching a massive cover-up operation and despite strictures from the Supreme Court, failed to take action against the policemen and officials involved in the cover-up. In the famous Maya Tyagi Case, where again policemen were involved, the death sentence was finally pronounced eight years after the rape and murder of the victim's relations.

Nevertheless despite the laws being made more stringent under pressure from women's groups, justice tends not just to be delayed but even denied. A couple of months ago, for instance the Supreme Court decided to reduce a mandatory jail sentence because a rape victim was pronounced as having "loose morals". Sadly rape has never become as much of a woman's issue as dowry because most rapes occur in the villages where women's groups are few and far between.

Officially, *suttee* was outlawed by Lord William Bentick in the nineteenth century. However when following Roop

Kanwar's suttee in 1986 the Indian Express conducted a survey to ascertain whether there had been other suttees in recent times, its reporters found that several suttee deaths had occurred in the eighties in Uttar Pradesh, Madhya Pradesh and Rajasthan. In one Uttar Pradesh village they found that Dasiya, a 55-year-old woman, had immolated herself in the presence of a large contingent of policemen. There were even photographs showing her chatting to policemen minutes before she stepped onto her husband's pyre.

As usual, the most horrifying stories came from Rajasthan where a nine-year-old girl and a fourteen-year-old were allowed to commit suttee. The paper wrote, "The Narayani Temple in Alwar district was built to hail the sacrifice of a nine-year-old barber caste (Nai) girl, Karmeti, who mounted the funeral pyre of her husband, Karnesh, after he died of a snakebite on his way back from his father's house. Karmeti gradually came to be known as 'Narayani' thus attaining the status of a goddess".

The union government has responded to these revivalist atrocities by tightening the law. But nothing whatsoever has been done to prevent worship at the country's 140 suttee temples and the Shankracharya of Puri continues his tirades against those who believe that encouraging suttee is tantamount to committing murder.

When to the list of these officially recognised crimes against women one adds child prostitution, casual sexual molestation (eve-teasing) and the inequities of the Devadasi system, it is easy to see why the government prefers not to expend too much energy compiling comprehensive lists of crimes against women.

Yet in the final analysis it is the society that is to be blamed and this could not have been expressed more poignantly than through the suicides of the three sets of sisters in Kanpur, Palghat and Chandigarh earlier this year. In all the three cases the girls were educated, good-looking and sensitive. But for them life was not worth living because their parents could not afford dowry money. The images of these girls hanging by their dupattas from ceiling fans are enough to make the celebration of International Women's Day seems a joke in poor taste.

Suicide

In our country 'Johar' was a well known phenomenon among Rajput women. When defeat and loss was imminent in the battle, women committed mass suicide. Until a couple of centuries ago, a widow was expected or forced to sacrifice her life when her husband's dead body was being cremated. Such a woman was regarded as 'Sati' or pious woman.

Suicide by Women

Indian society has particularly phenomenon of self burning 'Sati' or voluntary sacrifice 'Jauhar'. These forms of suicide in ancient and medieval times were the hallmark of the Brahmanic culture: Especially in upper caste-groups. Most of the women ended their lives by this non-volition but some were forced to do so by their relatives. Since polygamy was common, often many women would simultaneously immolate themselves during the cremation. This was in keeping with the belief that marriage is a spiritual relation between husband and wife that transcends the marital life. A form of group suicide, Jauhar, was committed by the women in the household of a vanquished chieftain or feudal lord. His wives, concubines and even maidservants would end their lives en masse by jumping from the castle or fort wall into the razing fire below. The motive behind the suicide was to safeguard possessed honour and dignity against subsequent humiliation by the victorious. This custom was widespread amongst Rajputs and gradually lost the popularity with the coming of Britishers. Another form of suicide–Sati, was prevalent due to intense and intrinsic relationships of Hindu husband and wife. This tradition moved the widow to jump over the pyre and become Sati in order to save herself from subsequent degradation and loneliness. But with the coming of Britishers this custom also gradually wanded, due to social reformations of Raja Ram Mohan Roy and legislation of Lord William Bentinck.

Debonair, May 1989- pp. 35–37.

Suicides have now taken a different course and now it is closely associated with dowry deaths and very often dowry deaths are pictured and projected as accidental deaths, suicide or homicide. Such type of a death is regarded as a dowry death of the victim is a married woman.

The incidence of accidental deaths and suicides in the country needs to be looked into. During 1967-1977, each year about 1,12,000 accidental deaths were reported to the police. In 1977 about 19 accidental deaths per 1,00,000 population occurred. In this, the population of women has been a little more than one–third. In 1967-1977 around 40,000 suicides were registered by the police each year. In 1977, the suicide population ratio was 6 for every 1,00,000. Among them women account for more than 41 per cent. What is remarkable is that the proportion of women is showing an upward trend.

Government has taken the case of dowry deaths and suspected suicides very seriously and it has issued instructions to the effect that such cases be investigated by Dy. Superintendent of Police and post-mortem conducted by two doctors.

She has to put up with ridicule or even downright denigration mostly at the hands of her mother-in-law and sister-in-law. In this sordid episode, the husband is surprisingly inert, he may even join others in castigating his wife and her parents. Though humiliated and miserable she has to continue to live in the household. In all likelihood, she may be a highly frustrated person–left with no choice but to end her life. The in-laws may provoke her suicidal urges or themselves decide to do away with her.

Many women, who are not able to stand on their own feet, cannot go back to their parents and become a "burden", leaving their husbands would be considered a blot on them and might also hamper the marital prospects, of their sisters. Even then who are economically independent may not be able to face the society attached to a divorced woman. Unfortunately, support for woman in distress is practically non-existent. Consequently many women see no escape except to take their own lives.

The police handling of dowry cases is still worse because inspite of the fact that Home Ministry has laid down clear guidelines for all cases of mysterious deaths and suicide case of newly married young woman, we still continue to ignore the instructions. The case should not be investigated by an officer below the rank of a Deputy Superintendent of Police.

Hansa Mehta and Amrit Kaur said that they wanted a uniform civil code because "one of the factors that has kept India back from advancing is nationalisation has been the existence of personal laws based on religion which keep the nation divided into watertight compartments in many aspects of life." In 1948 on the basis of the Committee's recommendations the Hindu Code Bill was introduced in Parliament and decided on the floor of the house. And suddenly on the eve of the first elections in 1957, the Bill was dropped because of the much opposition.

It was on this issue that women found great support from Baba Saheb Ambedkar, the then Law Minister who resigned on the issue. In 1956 and later in 1976 some changes were brought in Hindu Law but women still did not get equal rights. Even the idea that men and women should have equal rights within the family is not accepted by the law. According to a Senior Judge of Delhi High Court "Introductions of constitutional law in the house is not most inappropriate. It is like introducing a bull in a China shop. It will prove to be ruthless destroyer of marriage institution and all that it stands for is the privacy of the women.

Dying Declaration

Since the crime is committed within the four walls of the home, an important piece of evidence is the dying declaration of the girl. But often the investigating officer is bribed by the boy's family to manipulate it. Medival procedure clearly lays down that a dying declaration should not be recorded in the presence of a police officer but in the presence of a magistrate who should be summoned by the Medical Officer. Womens' organisations have also demanded that a lady doctor and a member of the girl's family should be present when the girl records her last statements.

Dowry deaths are increasing with sickening frequency.

The Dowry Prohibition Act 1968–lays down :

Section 4, Penalty for demanding dowry :

If any person demands directly or indirectly from the parents or other relatives or the guardian of a bride or bridegroom as the case may be, any dowry, he shall be punishable.

Suicide Case and Role of Law Enforcing Agencies

A view has also been taken that law enforcement agencies have been somewhat dragging their feet in processing such cases. The police should no doubt probe more thoroughly into the death of a recently married woman and the prosecution should be more vigorous and courts be more innovative in the interpretation of the law. However, the point should not be lost sight of that all these agencies function under a set of given rules and come into the picture well past the prevention stage.

38

Happy Endings Through Mediation

The 79-year-old woman and her neighbour had never been friends. And now a series of irritants were making things downright hostile Emotions peak and confrontation ensues. The woman brandishes a pitchfork in the face of the person she hates most in the world–a neighbour with whom she has probably exchanged less than a few dozen words. A true story, and one with a potentially sad ending. But the parties involved were referred by police to a mediation service, where, outside the legal system, their problems could be discussed and resolved to everyone's satisfaction.

Mediation programmes are springing up across the country. Their existence answers a growing need among Canadians for an alternative to the court system, one that is faster, cheaper, less stressful and in most cases more satisfying in its results.

The Delicate Art of Mediation

What is mediation all about ? The process is fairly standard across the country. People with disputes ranging from neighbourhood antagonisms to joint-custody problems come to a mediation service of their own volition or are referred, most often by the police, a lawyer, the court or a social agency. Mediation service personnel establish that all parties are present voluntarily and are committed to reaching an agreement. A mediation session follows, usually with two mediators in attendance who are best suited in their style and personal characteristics to the problem and disputants involved. Each session generally lasts two to three hours, and at its conclusion, a written memorandum of agreement is drawn up and signed to ensure that all participants understand what has been agreed to. Some services, usually those with better funding, follow up on successfully resolved cases at regular intervals.

It sounds simple enough, but the art of mediation is a delicate one, and its benefits can be numerous and far-reaching. The most important ingredient in the mediation recipe is the mediators themselves. They are usually volunteers, and can come from all walks of life. Melissa Miller, programme co-ordinator for Community Mediation Services in Kitchener, says that, when selecting volunteers, "we start from the view that all people are experts in conflict, that we all encounter it in our daily lives........ Most people know from experience what sorts of things increase and decrease conflict. "This knowledge is strengthened through twenty hours of training which helps feldging mediators to explore their own personal responses to conflict and teaches them how to listen, encourage agreement and defuse hostilities. Everything from neighbourhood disputes to custody problems can benefit from mediation.

The second ingredient in the mix is the disputants. Marge Burdine, a board member with the Westcoast Mediation Centre in Vancouver, reports that they can be members of a family, a volunteer board, even a co-op. housing association. "What has surprised me," says Burdine, "is how broad our range of clientele has been. It's really a matter of who hears about the service. That is the common denominator more than any other factor."

As mediation services are established, two types are emerging. The first is characterized by less serious disputes and early intervention, and is essentially a preventative model. The second deals with the cases that have been diverted from the court when a conciliatory, less adversarial approach is more appropriate. In many of these cases, charges have been laid, and successful mediation usually result in a stay of proceedings for the accused. Winnipeg Mediation Services is, at present, the largest mediation programme in Canada and the most successful of this type. The programme handles about 500 cases a year, and the majority are crime against the person or assault. It boasts a 91 per cent success rate among cases that reach mediation.

A Less Stressful, Less Costly Alternative

The benefits of mediation are various. To those involved in the dispute, it offers a solution that is certainly less costly and less time-consuming than going to court. Perhaps most important it is also less stressful and ultimately less traumatic than the adversarial legal system which usually demands that there be a winner and loser in every battle. Mediation avoids these polarities, encouraging a settlement where each participant has a say in the outcome. Burdine reports that such an approach has resulted in a 90 per cent success rate for those cases referred to her service that reached a mediation hearing. Miller reports similar figures. "People are more willing to live up to an agreement when they have had a say in shaping it," she adds.

The benefits of mediation services to the legal system can also be substantial. By diverting cases that are inappropriate away from the already congested court system, countless hours and dollars could be saved. Mediation can also provide a preventative service by resolving conflicts at an early stage before they escalate and ultimately require legal intervention.

Because of these important selling features, new research into conflict mediation is being initiated in several provinces, and interest appears to be increasing all the time. Dean Peachey was the first director of the Kitchener service, and is now coordinating the national Network for Community Justice and

---

Liaison – March 1989.

Conflict Resolution. Peachey confirms that mediation is inspiring "very broad interest that goes beyond criminal justice," reporting that, for example, some schools are exploring the benefits of conflict resolution training for staff.

The Network is attempting to build on this interest, providing links between existing groups and facilitating exchange of information. It has established a resource centre in Kitchener, and offers workshops and training to those who seek them. Last year, the Network also published a directory of dispute resolution programmes in Canada.

Good Mediation is Often Invisible

But despite these advances, mediation services are still struggling to establish themselves. This may in part be because mediation, simply by virtue of its nature, is a confidential process and successful resolutions, no matter how dramatic, usually cannot be publicized. As Peachey notes, "God mediation is often invisible."

The prevention component of successful mediation is also difficult to prove. How does one shows conclusively that early intervention in a conflict has prevented more explosive hostilities further down the line ? And like most social services, one of the biggest obstacles for mediation programmes to overcome is funding. Says Peachey, "The lack of formal support and public endorsement from the jurisdictions that are responsible for the administration of justice has served to keep the caseload; it's hard to argue for decent funding. If you have no funding, you can't promote yourself" Burdine adds, " It's very discouraging."

Peachey also believes that some of the problems mediation services are having in attracting clients may be because of poor public perception of what mediation is all about. "They think we advocate either kissing and making up or slugging it out," he says adding that there is little money of resources for public education to remedy the problem.

But Peachey says that the real difficulty facing mediation programmes seeking support may be a political one. He reports that there are two parallel movements within Canada's criminal justice system: one which advocates more punitive measures, more prosecution and more incarceration: and the other which proposes that, because these measures haven't worked effectively in the past, it's time for change and innovation in the form of such initiatives as mediation. "It's hard to say at this point which one is gaining ground," he says.

But the people involved in mediation remain committed. despite the obstacles "Mediation allows people to have control over their own lives," says Marge Burdine, "and to have respect for themselves and others. Everyone has a use for this at some time in their life .... We're not giving up."[1]

Mediation and Family Violence

Responding to the federal government's family violence initiative, Correctional Service Canada (CSC) held a national training seminar in Ottawa for correctional staff to help them better understand and work with offenders affectedly by this complex and disturbing problem. One in 10 women in Canada and about one per cent of men are abused by their married or common law partners. Wife assault is a major cause of homicide in Canada. Tens of thousands of Canadian children as well as elderly people are the victims of abuse and neglect in the family.

These are facts that cannot be and are not being ignored any longer. Over the past 10 years, social awareness and public concern about domestic violence has been growing. Once considered a strictly private family matter, the problems now being addressed on legal and social fronts, and is very much in the public domain. Much remains to be done, however, about this troublesome question which physically and psychologically scars family members, breaks up families and shatters dreams.

The study of family violence is relevant to correctional workers who will encounter offenders whose attitudes and

---

1. *Liaison* – January, 1987.

behaviours have been shaped by violent environments. A large proportion of federal offenders were abused as children. Others have been victims perpetrators, or both, or domestic violence. Given CSC's mission to protect the public and prepare offenders for reintegration into the community, it is apparent why understanding and responding to abusive and abused offenders, who will be reuniting or having some contact with their families, is of concern.

A pattern of fighting, repenting, fighting and repenting, creates a strong bond between partners. Dutton pointed out and one theory suggests there is a compulsion to repeat traumatic events. However, very few batterers believe they have the right to batter. Some offenders are timid or unable to express anger verbally. They feel powerless. Some have poor impulse control and problems with substance abuse. Others use the defence strategy and will not accept responsibility for their actions, externalizing the blame to factors beyond their control. The treatment for such cases, said Dutton, is to address the offender's defence system. Some men realize their problem when they are arrested but with time, their concern wear off. Some still do not see the problem after going through every stage of the criminal justice system. Many victims, too, do not consider such violence as a crime. Public education is essential, recommended Dutton, adding that treatment should channel anger, employ a buddy system for mutual support and change expectations in relation ships. Such treatment can achieve long-term results.

To treat perpetrators of family violence, said Greenland, the batterer's self esteem must be understood. Sexual frustrations must be considered as a cause of his violent behaviour. Discomfort with sexuality can also produce violent reactions. Greenland suggested that attitudes toward human sexuality must be addressed in solving the problem of family violence.

Power and Control

One of the most disturbing facts about the study of family violence is the perplexing gap between the prevalence and seriousness of the problem and the reluctance of society to tackle the issue. It is only in recent years that wife assault has been considered a crime with police more likely to lay assault changes in cases of domestic violence. Karla Digirolamo, Executive Director of Governor's Commission on Domestic Violence in New York State, said throughout history, violence against women and children was not only implied but codified in various laws and religious writings. For example, in the 18th century, an American law stated that a husband could not beat his wife with a stick thicker than the width of his thumb, thus the familiar saying, "rule of thumb". Today, there is still a tendency to talk about private versus public violence, said Digirolamo. Even today with the progress that has been made society continued to tolerate domestic violence in many ways, she stated. Most of the time, the problem is still not treated as criminal behaviour.

Tracing the evolution of the governor's commission, Digirolamo explained that it was not until the late '70s in the state of New York that the problem of wife abuse came onto public stage. It was during that time that aggressive advocacy from the grassroots level led to a series of public hearings during which, for the first time in the United States, battered women told state officials about the terror they endured as victims of conjugal violence. The hearings led to the creation of the first governor's task force which brought together the rare combination of academics, public officials, formerly battered women, feminists and community organizers, a membership which still exists today on the commission.

In 1977, New York became the first state to give public funds for a battered women' shelter. Much was needed in the late '70s regarding the development of policies, programmes and laws to make it clear that arrests could be made in cases involving family violence, recalled Digirolamo. Public hearings held in 1985 at the state maximum security prison for women were an eye-opening experience. Recalling painful accounts from two women incarcerated for killing their husbands, Digirolamo said these women tried to reach out but the system failed them. "There were women who had gone to emergency rooms and had been laughed at by doctors,"she said. "These were women who had called police officers and who had their batterers walked around the block. These were women who tried to reach out for help and the system could not and would not help them. They came to a point where they did not know how to save their lives and they ended up killing in order to do that."

Today, the commission works in the areas of policy and programme development for victims, offenders and family members, works with states agencies to ensure their mandates are meeting the needs of families who need help, and provides training and education to a variety of professionals including doctors, criminal justice personnel, district attorney and social workers. "The goal of family violence is not physical injury," explained Digirolamo. "It's to assert power and control. It's a pattern of controlling a family member or intimate partner using physical, psychological and sexual abuse as the tools for achieving and maintaining power and control. Violence is a pattern of behaviour that is learned over time, that is reinforced by social conditions and social beliefs that not only condone it but that equate violence and aggression and power."

Native Perspective

Maggie Hodgson enlightened listeners to the native situation, drawing on her professional experience which includes developing training programmes for addiction counsellors at the Nechi Training Centre in Alberta and personal background as a member of the Carrier Indian Community. Hodgson has co-authored several books, including *The Spirit Weeps*. Her philosophy concerns healing within the native community. For many years, native people experienced problems such as cultural disintegration, health epidemics, alcoholism and abuse in families and in residential schools, said Hodgson. "The Indian people are starting to come out of their midnight and into their daylight," she explained. She told correctional workers about Indian social structure, including the powerful extended family system, elders and various beliefs and customs that may be difficult for non-natives to understand. Being aware of how these systems operate will help service workers, she pointed out. She acknowledged that Indian individuals, families and communities have a responsibility to address problems such as family violence and alcoholism and to work from within to change them in order to become healthy once again.

Resource Handbook

A highlight of the conference was the presentation of CSC's new 76-page resource handbook, *Breaking the Cycle of Family Violence,* for correctional staff. It provides information to help recognize and respond to inmates and others under the jurisdiction of CSC who have been affected by abuse. It also provides an extensive resource directory, including a regional breakdown of group programmes and services, a listing of provincial contacts across Canada, national social service agencies, and training and resource materials.

Barbara Appleford of Appleford Associates conducted an indepth literature review on the subject of family violence and its relationship with correctional settings. The findings of this review comprise the major portion of the handbook. Appleford told conference participants that definitions of the problem vary, according to causal theories and different standards of tolerance. But many theorists maintain that family violence transcends all socio-economic, èducational and cultural boundaries. Wife abuse constitutes about 76 per cent of cases of family abuse. Both men and women are perpetrators of child and elder abuse. Among the most unfortunate effects of abuse in the family is that children from such families may penetrate that abuse in adolescence and adulthood. Studies have shown that children who witness violence can suffer similar academic, behavioural and emotional difficulties as children who are themselves abused.

Most programmes require the complete cessation of the violence and acceptance of responsibility for it. They also attempt to encourage greater assertiveness and communication skills, increased apathy, understanding of the destructive effects of violence, more flexible attitudes towards women and a broader, more flexible male identity.

Programmes which express a strong, pro-feminist orientation are gaining more widespread recognition, Appleford noted. These programmes de-emphasize anger control methods and place greater emphasis on men's abuse of power over women. Also underlying this approach are attempts to change beliefs and attitudes regarding the right to exert power and control.

Living Without Violence

"All family members have a right to a life free of violence and abuse of any nature." This statement is one tenet upon which a new CSC initiative Living. Without Violence has been built. CSC Senior Education Coordinator Elizabeth Fabino explained that the programme will be offered to inmates as part of the Living Skills Programme. Its aim is to change the attitudes of offenders towards violence and sexual aggression in the family.

The program and accompanying training handbook were developed by Michele Corbeil of James F. Hickling Management Consultants. Corbeil has worked with women's shelters, as a counsellor, organized public education programmes on family violence and developed programming for institutions. *Living Without Violence* will be available to identified and potential abusers. It takes a cognitive approach and consists of 10 two-hour sessions. A staff training course will be instituted for front line workers.

Some of the precepts upon which Living Without Violence is based include :

— victims are not to blame for family violence. The abuser must accept responsibility for the violence and for ending it;

— society has a responsibility to get involved and work towards ending violence in the family;

— education focussing on challenging and transforming attitudes and beliefs that perpetuate violence in the family is the first step towards permanent change.

Other underlying beliefs are that violence flourishes in a society that promotes and condones it through the mass media, and socialization of young men and boy to believe that force is acceptable in setting disputes and problems. The programmes and stresses that abusers have learned and have chosen to be abusive and can therefore unlearn and choose alternative non-abusive ways of resolving situations.

Treatment Programme Profiled

The roots of violence against women are imbedded in a society in which women are devalued and treated as inferior to men, he explained. It is patriarchal and traditional attitudes and values that permit wife assault. Finally, friends and family are part of this social milieu. They may make excuse for a men's abusive behaviour towards his wife or pressure a woman to stay in a relationship for the good of the family. Currie says abuse takes a variety of forms : physical, sexual, psychological and abuse of family property. Psychological factors taken into consideration in the programme's framework are the desire to control externalization of responsibility for behaviour, rigid thinking, low self-esteem and emotional isolation.

Although men often abrogate any personal responsibility for the violence, Currie said men entering the programmes are held fully responsible for stopping their violent behaviour. Over 80 per cent of the time men blame their wives for their actions. "It is something she said or did that he didn't like and felt justified in responding abusively towards her." He explained. Over 80 per cent of the men who come to the programme join, not because they think they have a problem, but because they are being threatened with separation from their partners. Services for abusive husbands should take a comprehensive approach, said Currie. There should be liaison with other community services, agencies and the police. Programmes should be part of an integrated community response to the problem, should provide professional training, public education and political action and take a clear stand opposing violence against women.

The programme is composed of two parts, the assessment programme and a 10-part treatment component. While opportunity is a treatment programme for men, it also provides a referral service for women to a variety of counselling and social helping agencies. Ongoing contact is maintained with the partner of the abuser throughout the programme and in the evaluation stages.

"It goes without saying that family violence is an important issue for Society and for the criminal justice system, certain aspects of family violence are of great interest to those of us who work in the correctional part of the system. Violence is an important factor in our criminal justice system. Family violence seems to hit us in a particularly hard way. We have all kinds of reasons to do whatever we can to make sure that those who have a potential for violence in the family or in the community are taken care of according to the best possible correctional principles and according to the best knowledge that exists in our society in combatting crimes of violence. I am confident, particularly after having received all kinds of positive reports from this conference, that the specialists, those who know something about family violence, those who have studied in that field and those who have experience in that field, have already shared with you the best of their knowledge.

39

Dowry : The Scourge

Dowry is not plain buying and selling. Neither it can be waived away in simplistic terms. It has no religious significance but only the sanction of a society that has reduced a woman to an un-productive position and has considered her a gift to a man to be sent to him in the most splendid packaging possible. Today the custom remains as a visible symptom of a deep malaise in society, inextricately knitted up with individual esteem, social pride and prejudice, a symbol of the position of women, the respective roles attributed to men and women and the institution of marriage itself. In a society which is highly divided into social stratification wiping out a custom which is being practised since ages, cannot easily be wiped out so easily. The fact remains that in Indian society, so much importance is placed on getting a girl married that parents of unmarried girls are willing to meet almost any demand in order to get their daughters married.

In fact, as long as men and marriage are over-rated in a woman's life, there will be a price to pay if not in dowry, than under other nomenclature. Till women are viewed as individuals worthy of respect in their own right, manifestations like dowry will not cease.

Bride is given gifts at the time of marriage, everywhere in the world but the gift settled as dowry before marriage and which equally strangely remains her personal property. Some consider a present to the in-laws, a gift to the bridegroom before, at the time and after the marriage. Some see it as pre-mortem inheritance from the bride's family, some as an insurance policy for the pride against any economic crimes. It has also been described as 'Stridhan'. According to Mura Sundaram, "Dowry is disguised, replete with hypocracy pickled in pretensions, hidden in a man of social and religious superstition and anarchanisms, thereby guised as a moral system."[1.]

Import of Dowry

Dowry system was not a part and parcel of Indian system. Dowry was introduced with the passage of time. The practice of dowry could be traced to hoary notions of giving valuable gifts to one's daughter at the time of marriage. Notions about the inequality between the sexes from the bed-rock of dowry through which a balance is sought to be brought about in matrimonial relations.

The milieu of newly married girl faced in the household of her husband has been outlined earlier. In case she has brought along sufficient dowry, she is treated well and with difference. On the other hand, if she has brought a meagre dowry, she is treated indifferently. Dowry is considered the just due to the man and complaints arise when the girl or her family are unable to afford what is demanded.

In Indian society, so much importance is placed on getting a girl married that parents of unmarried girls are willing to meet any demand in order to get their daughters married. For a woman, marriage is a passport to even such a basic thing as being acknowledged as worthy individual.

Ironically enough, women bring a productive member of society but is still accepted only as a bonus alongwith the more 'Valuable' material 'Assets'. She is not sold but buys for herself martyrdom and slavery. Dowry is variously seen as a gift to

1. *Imprint,* June 1981 p.–8.

the bride, strangely settled before marriage and which is equally and strangely does not remain her personal property. Some consider it as a present to the in-laws, some as a means to set up a new home. Some people try to identify it as 'Stridhan' which is not so.

Causes of Dowry

In recent years, the dowry system in India has spread both horizontally and vertically. Horizontally in the sense that it has spread to such regions and communities which, until recently, did not have it and which, in fact, had the bride price system. Vertically, in the sense that there has been a sharp increase in the amount of dowry demanded and given.

Age Old Practice

Some amount of wealth always changed hands in Indian marriages. This may be bride price in the form of cash or kind, or dowry known as 'Stridhan' among Hindus and as 'Mehar' amongst Muslims, in the form of cash, utensils, jewellery, etc. It was willingly given and accordingly accepted as part of Stridhan. It was not extorted or demanded as in case of dowry.

Educational Inequality

Educational inequality between males and females for a variety of reasons, a greater proportion of males than females in India are educated. Although literacy is not the same thing as education, the difference in the proportion of literacy among males and females has been increasing steadily. For example, in 1901, the production of literates was 9.8 per cent among females resulting in a difference of 9.7 per cent. But in 1981, the proportion of literates was 46.7 per cent among males and 24.9 per cent among females, resulting in a difference of 21.8 per cent. It is axiomatic that greater the difference between the educational attainment of prospective brides and grooms, the larger are the dowries demanded and given.

Economic Disparity

Although, it is difficult to produce hard data, it is common knowledge that there exists, economic inequality among marriageable males and females. Education being equal, males with moveable/immovable property, demand a larger dowry. Likewise, males with an education that is likely to enable them to earn more money, demand a larger dowry. Medical and engineering graduates fall in this category.

Dowry : Prestige and Prejudice

The status of women in many parts of the world must have been one of more bondage until the advent of modern ideas of freedom and equality. According to a recent issue of the 'Economist', "in most of the 19th century, a British husband had sole rights over his wife's property and their children. He could chastise her out without a penny. Not until the Married Women's Property Act of 1982 could see own, anything separately. Even then, she had no claims on his wealth."[1]

In our own country, our attitude to women has been ambivalent indeed. It has been full of contradictions. Hinduism has evolved over the centuries integrating the beliefs and attitudes of diverse racial and cultural groups. There is no single Hindu view of women valid for all time. The ancient law-giver 'Manu' proclaimed that, "where they are honoured, there the God rejoice, and that where they are not honoured, there all rites are fruitless." If the Hindu law-giver was harsh in some respects, they were liberal and far in advance of their times than in others.

The Dharmashastra nowhere mention the giving or taking of dowry and it is doubtful if there is sanction for burning or torture of widows. The Mahabharat says. "He, who sells his son or gives his daughter for a price, goes to hell." The idea of 'Dharmpatni' cannot obviously imply bondage or subservience for the wife. It means the pursuit together of a whole life. Manu said, "Let there be mutual fidelity ending in death alone.... This in a few words should be recognised as the highest law of duty for man and wife."

1. *The Times of India*, Sunday Review : From the bandop into Pyre- August 22, 1987.

Dowry has no religious sanction and it is not very old. In fact, it seems a recent phenomenon grown out of greed. It is also interesting to note that brides are often driven to suicide, not by the husband but by the mother-in-law, sister-in-law or other close relations.

Dowry

"Any youngman who makes dowry a condition for marriage discredits his education and his country and dishonours womanhood."
.... Gandhiji

Dowry is not of very ancient origin. It assumed abnormal proportion in later times only. Among the ancient Hindu, the custom of dowry did exist in simpler form though under different names. This custom of giving presents at the time of marriage is a universal phenomenon and continues to be so. Such type of custom prevails in India unheadedly. Parents of the girl give presents to the bride. The rational behind these presenting of gifts is the affection of the parents towards their children but in due course of time the said custom has grown rigid and became associated with social status and family prestige leading to great social evil.

Everyday we read in newspapers, many a cases of 'Bride burning' or 'dowry deaths' for bringing insufficient or no dowry. There is hardly a day when newspapers do not have several reports of murders by dowry seekers. This social evil has taken a worse turn.

Prohibition of Dowry Act

An act to prohibit the giving or taking dowry has been enacted by Parliament on 20th may 1961 viz. "The Dowry Prohibition Act, 1961" which makes giving, taking and abetting of dowry punishable u/s 3 of the said Act, which lays that any person after commencement of this Act gives or takes or abets the giving or taking of dowry, he shall be punishable with imprisonment for a term which shall not be less than six months but which may extend to ten thousand rupees or the amount of the value of such dowry, whichever is more.

Provided that the court may for adequate and special reasons to be recorded in the judgment, impose a sentence of imprisonment for a term of less than six months.

(2) Nothing Sub-section (i) shall apply to, or in relation to—

(a) presents which are given at the time of a marriage to the bride (without any demand having been made in that behalf),

Provided that such presents are entered in a list maintained in accordance with the rules made under this Act,

(b) presents which are given at the time of marriage of the bridegroom (without any demand having been made in that behalf),

Provided that such presents are entered in a list maintained in accordance with the rules made under this Act.

Provided further that where such presents are made by or on behalf of the bride or any person related to the bride, such presents are of a customary nature and the value thereof is not excessive having regard to the financial status of the person by whom or on whose behalf such presents are given.

Offences under this Act have been made cognizable and non-compoundable for certain purposes.

Some special provisions to supplement Dowry Prohibition Act 1961, to cope with cruelty to married women culminating in Dowry Deaths by suicide or murder to helpless married women have been introduced by Criminal Law Amendment Act 46 of 1983.

Amendment in I.P.C.

By introducing a new section 498A in I.P.C. cruelty to a woman by her husband or any relative of her husband has been made punishable with imprisonment for a term which may extend to three years and also with fine.

Amendment in C.P.C.

Provision has been made for inquiry by Executive Magistrate and for Post-mortem in all cases when a woman has within seven years of her marriage committed suicide or died in circumstances raising a reasonable suspicion that some other person has committed an offence.

Amendment in Indian Evidence Act

It has been drastically amended to provide that where women have committed suicide within a period of seven years from the date of her marriage and it is shown that her husband or any ralations of her husband had subjected her to cruelty the court may presume that such suicide has been abetted by her husband or by such relative of her husband under Act, 1983.

Dowry and Cruelty Against Women

Bride price was devised centuries ago and was thought to be demeaning to human dignity and the honour. A sure form of marriage that was characterised by the custom was considered unacceptable. In fact dowry seems to be just another manifestation of the age of opportunism that we live in with exploitation as the watchward. What better way of making easy money than to hold girls' future to ransom, conditioned and decidedly proportioned to the amount paid to add insult to injury today in accordance with the today's progressive norms of society, a girl must not only be well-educated, but also a 'worthy working girl' is preferred. And if parents are not exhausted enough by this, there is the request for 'decent' marriage. This is why, that the birth of a girl if treated with a 'calamity' in an average Indian family. The menance of dowry in all its insidious forms is essentially an urbanised evil originated from material greed.

Justice Krishna Iyer has pointed out that many a times women are sent to the lock up on charges to deprive them of property share or to get rid of them from the scene, when they become inconvenient.

Wife Beating Syndrome

Wife beating syndrome is quite common in India. It is clearly associated with social pattern of the society where family fued excessive alcoholism and frequent demands of subsequent dowry instalments are quite common. Any bye-passer can hear a wailing, a quiet wailing, moaning and groaning through the closed doors can be heard in most of the Indian homes. Wife-beating is in fact one of the most accepted crimes committed against women. It exists most in slums and amongst working class. In fact, now it is gradually creeping amongst middle class and rich families.

Violence in the family exists generally in a situation where the woman is totally in a situation where she is completely dependent on the person who physically assaults her. It is a strange situation in which women and often the children too, live in fear and terror, particularly when the woman is completely dependent on the person who physically assaults her. It is a strange situation to which the women and often the children too, live in fear and terror when the victims approach police and police in turn normally discourage them. The fact remains that after reporting the matter to the police, the women concerned knows that she has to go back to same house with a cruel husband obviously waiting for her and if the man knows that a complaint has been made, he may get even more violent. Then there are children who may become husbands' target if the mother protests too much. An Indian woman would rather accept cruelty against herself than see it perpetrated on her children.

The life of a beaten woman is isolated and under constant fear. So far as this has been an unspoken problem, hidden behind shame and embarassment. A problem, for which there is yet no solution, no place for the women to go, no understanding, no legal support.

The law dealing with wife beating has been defined in Sec. 498 A in these words, "whoever being the husband, or the relative of the husband of a woman, subjects such woman to cruelty, shall be punished with imprisonment for a term which may extend to three years and shall also be liable to fine. But the question arises is, who will bell the cat ? Nobody is going to volunteer to walk to a police station to lodge a complaint about a neighbour or a relation beating his wife and even if one goes to the Police Station, it is doubtful whether police will take the cudgles and investigate the matter with required promptness and dedication.

Violence Against Women

Violence in the family rarely arouses the social concern it deserves. Aggressive behaviour on the part of the husband towards his wife is largely overlooked and even tolerated owing to traditional notions arising from the patriarchal family structure. Violence against women can be sub-divided into two broad groups :

(a) They may fail victim to general crimes (theft, murder, cheating, etc.) or to crimes specific in relation to women (molestation, assault, rape, etc.), and

(b) they may be subjected to violence in the family which may or may not attract official notice.

Suddenly violence against women is on the rise in the land of Manu, 'where women are honoured, there the gods rejoice.' Today, the frequency of newly married woman being burnt to death in many urban areas is rapidly rising. This has caused an alarm and lower agencies have come in for heavy criticism for their failure to prevent this. Law is supposed to control and harmonise individual and group behaviour. Is it biased against women or does it have shortcomings inherent in it because of which those who commit crimes against them go unpunished ?

In order to protect the status of women, the Widow Remarriage Act, 1956, the Hindu Marriage Act, 1955 and the Hindu Succession Act, 1956 may be readily cited in this regard. The practice of dowry has also not escaped legislative attention in 1961, the Dowry Prohibition Act was included in the Statute book. Originally giving and taking dowry was a non-cognizable offence, but through a subsequent amendment the offence has been made cognizable.

A view has also been taken that law enforcement agencies have been somewhat dragging their feet in processing such cases. The police should no doubt probe more thoroughly into the death of a recently married woman and the prosecution should be more vigorous and courts more innovative in the interpretation of the law. However, the point should not be lost sight of that all these agencies function under a set of given rules and come into the picture well past the preventive stage. Whatever prevention influence they exert is mostly indirect. As such by streamlining them, we may be trying to remove the defect without paying due attention to the underlying cases, and hence a significant solution seems beyond sight.

The Dowry Prohibition Act has been variously described as a negative, limited penal and impractical Act, one which has not achieved its objective. According to Sec. 2 of the Act "any property or valuable security" given or agreed to be given at or before the marriage as 'Consideration for the marriage of the parties'. Any presents, given at the time of marriage, unless made as consideration for marriage will not be termed as dowry. The Act does not include any of the womens' objects like Sofa-sets, Television, Refrigerators, Cars, Jewellery and such items which accompany or even precede a bride into her home. The concept and definition of dowry itself is thus narrow and limited.

The Dowry Prohibition Act, 1968

Sec. 4 of the Dowry Prohibition Act lays down penalty for demanding dowry : "If any person demands directly or indirectly from the parents or other relations, or the guardians of a bride or bridegroom as the case may be, any dowry, he shall be punishable with imprisonment for a term which shall not be less than six months, but which may extend to two years and fines which may extend to Rs. 1,00,000/-.

Provided that the court may, for adequate and special reasons to be mentioned in the judgment, impose a sentence of imprisonment for a term less than six months."

Under Section 3 taking and giving dowry is similarly punishable.

Criminal Laws

Indian Penal Code, Section 498 deals with a husband of a woman subjecting her to cruelty.

Whoever being the husband or the relative of the husband of a woman subjects such woman to cruelty, shall be punished with imprisonment for a term which may extend to three years and shall be punished with imprisonment for a term which may extend to three years and shall also be liable to fine.

Explanation — For the purpose of this section 'cruelty' means :

(a) Any wilful conduct which is of such a nature as is likely to drive the woman to commit suicide or to cause grave injury or damage to life, limb or health (Whether mental or physical) of the woman, or

(b) Harassment of the woman where such harassment is with a view to coercing her or any persons related to her to meet any unlawful demand for any property or valuable is on account of failure to meet such demand.

Code of Criminal Procedure Sec. 174 - Sub-section (3) :

(i) when the case involved is a suicide by a woman within seven years of her marriage; or

(ii) the case relates to the death of a woman within seven years of her marriage in any circumstances raising a reasonable suspicion that some other person committed an offence in relation to such woman ; or

(iii) the case relates to the death of a woman within seven years of her marriage and any relative of the woman has made a request in this behalf; or

(iv) there is any doubt regarding the cause of death ; or

(v) the Police Officer for any other reason considers it expedient to do so.

He shall, subject to such rules as the State Government may prescribe in this behalf forward the body, with a view to its being examined, to the nearest Civil Surgeon or other qualified Medical-man appointed in this behalf by the State Government, if the state of the weather and the distance admit of its being so forwarded without risk of such purification as the road, as would render such examination useless.

40

Dowry — Divorce

Dowry is not plain buying and selling. Neither it can be waived away in simplistic terms. It has no religious significance. Only the sanction of the society that has reduced a woman to a un-productive position and has considered her as a gift to a man to be sent to him in the most splendid package. Today the custom remains as visible symptom of a deep malaise in society inextricably knitted up with individual esteem, social pride and prejudice, a symbol of the position of women, the respective roles attributed to men and women and the institution of marriage itself. In a society which is highly divided into social stratification, wiping out a custom which is being practised since ages, cannot easily be wiped out so easily. The fact remains that in Indian society, so much importance is placed on getting a girl married that parents of unmarried girls are willing to meet almost any demand in order to get their daughters married.

Bride is given gifts at the time of marriage everywhere in the world but the gift settled as dowry before marriage and which equally strangely remains her personal property. Some consider a present to the in-laws, a gift to the bridegroom at the time and after the marriage, some see it as pre-mortem inheritance from the bride's family, some as an insurance policy for the brides against any economic crimes. It has also been described as 'Stridhan'. According to Mura Sundaram, "Dowry is disguised, replete with hypocracy, pickled in pretensions, hidden in a man of social and religious superstition and anachronioms, thereby disguised as a moral system".[1]

Importance of Dowry

Dowry system was not part and parcel of Indian system. Dowry was introduced with the passage of time. The practice of dowry could be traced to hoory notions of giving valuable gifts to one's daughter at the time of marriage. Notions about inequality between the sexes form the bedrock of dowry through which a balance is sought to be brought about in matrimonial relations.

Dowry is variously seen as a gift to the bride strangely settled before marriage and which equally strangely does not remain her personal property. Some consider it as present to the in-laws—a gift to the bridegroom, some see it as pre-mortem inheritance from the bride's family, some as an insurance policy for the bride against any economic crisis, some as a means to set up a new house. Some people try to identify it as 'Stridhan' which it is not.

In recent years, the dowry system in India has spread both horizontally and vertically—horizontally in the sense that it has spread to such regions and communities which, until recently, did not have it and which in fact, had the brideprice system. Vertically in the sense that there has been a sharp increase in the amount of dowry demanded and given.

Dowry: Prestige and Prejudice

The status of women in many parts of the world must have been one of more bondage, until the advent of modern ideas of freedom and equality. According to a recent issue of

---

1. *Imprint*, June 1981, Page 8.

the 'Economist', in most of the 19th century, a British husband had sole rights over his wife's property and their children. He could chastise her without a penny. Not until the Married Womens' Property Act of 1982 could she own anything separately. Even then she had no claims on his wealth."[1]

In our own country our attitude to women has been ambivalent indeed. It has been full of contradictions. Hinduism has evolved over the centuries integrating the beliefs and attitudes of diverse racial and cultural groups. There is no single Hindu view of women valid for all time. The ancient law-giver Manu proclaimed that "Where they are......honoured, there the gods rejoice", and that "where they are not honoured, there all rites are fruitless." If the Gindy law-giver was harsh in some respects, those were liberal and far in advance of their times in others.

The dharmshastras, howsoever, mention the giving or taking of dowry and it is doubtful if there is sanction for burning or torture the widows. The Mahabharat says, "He who sells his son or gives his daughter for a price goes to hell." The idea of dharmpatni cannot obviously imply bondage or subvergence for the wife, it means the pursuit together of a whole life. Manu said, "Let there be mutual fidelity ending in death alone." This in a few words, should be recognised as the highest law of duty for man and wife.

Dowry has no religious sanction and it is not very old. In fact, it seems a recent phenomenon grown out of greed. It is also interesting to note that brides are often driven to suicide not by the husband but by the mother-in-law, sister-in-law or other close relations.

Dowry is of not very ancient origin. It assumed abnormal proportion in later times only. Among the ancient Hindus, the custom of dowry did exist in simpler form though under different names. This custom of giving presents at the time of marriage is a universal phenomenon and the same continues as

1. *The Times of India* - Sunday Review : From Mandap into Pyre-August 22, 1987.

such. Such type of custom prevails in India where parents of the girl give presents to the bride. The rational behind these presenting of gifts in the affection of the parents towards their children but in course of time, the said custom has grown rigid and became associated with social status and family prestige leading to great social evil.

An Act to prohibit the giving or taking dowry has been enacted by Parliament on 20th May 1961, viz. The Dowry Prohibition Act, 1961 which makes giving, taking and abetting of dowry punishable U/S 3 of the said Act. Section 3 of the Dowry Prohibition Act 1961 lays that any person, after the commencement of this Act, gives or takes or abets the giving or taking of dowry, he shall be punishable with imprisonment for a term which shall not be less than six months, but which may extend to ten thousand rupees or the amount of the value of such dowry, whichever is more,

(1) Provided that the court may, for adequate and special reasons to be recorded in the judgment, impose a sentence of imprisonment for a term of less than six months.

(2) Nothing in sub-section (i) shall apply to or in relation to—

(*a*) presents which are given at the time of a marriage to the bride (without any demand having been made in that behalf), provided that such presents are entered in a list maintained in accordance with the rules made under this Act.

(*b*) presents which are given at the time of a marriage of the bridegroom (without any demand having been made in that behalf), provided that such presents are entered in a list maintained in accordance with the rules made under this Act. Provided further that where such presents are made by or on behalf of the bride or any person related to the bride, such presents are of a customary nature and the value thereof is not excessive having regard to the financial status of the person by whom or on whose behalf such presents are given.

Offences under this Act have been made cognizable and non-compoundable for certain purposes.

Some special provisions to implement Dowry Prohibition Act 1961, to cope with cruelty to married women culminating in Dowry deaths by suicide or murder to helpless married women have been introduced by Criminal Law Amendment Act 46 of 1983.

1. Amendment in I.P.C.

By introducing a new section 498 A in the I.P.C. cruelty to a woman by her husband or any relative of her husband has been made punishable with imprisonment for a term which may extend to three years and also with fine.

2. Amendment in Cr. P.C.

Provision has been made for inquiry by executive magistrate and for post-mortem in all cases when a woman has, within seven years of her marriage, committed suicide or died in circumstances raising a reasonable suspicion that some other person has committed an offence.

3. Amendment in Indian Evidence Act

It has been drastically amended to provide that where woman has committed suicide within a period of seven years from the date of her marriage and it is shown that her husband or any relation of her husband had subjected her to cruelty, the court may presume that such suicide has been abetted by her husband or by such relative of her husband under Act 1983.

Dowry and Cruelty Against Women

Bride price was devised centuries ago and was thought to be demeaning to human dignity and a sure form of marriage that was characterised by the custom was considered unacceptable. In fact, dowry seems to be just another manifestation of the age of opportunism that we live in with exploitation as the watchward. What better way of making easy money than to hold girls' future to ransom, conditioned and decidedly proportioned to the amount paid to add insult to injury. Today in accordance with the today's progressive norms of society, a girl must not only be well-educated but also a "worthy working girl" is preferred. And if parents are not exhausted enough by this, there is the request for 'decent' marriage. This is why, that the birth of a girl is treated with a 'calamity' in an average Indian family. The menance of dowry in all its insidious forms, is essentially an urbanised evil having originated from material greed.

Justice Krishna Iyer has pointed out that many a times women are sent to the lock-up on trumped up charges to deprive them from property or to get rid of them from the scene when they become inconvenient.

Wife Beating Syndrome

Wife beating syndrome is quite common in India. It is clearly associated with social pattern of the society where family fueds, excessive alchoholism and frequently demands of subsequent dowry instalments are quite common. Any by-passer can hear a wailing, a quiet wailing, moaning and groaning though the closed door, in most of the Indian homes. Wife beating is in fact one of the most accepted crimes committed against women. It exists mostly in slums and amongst working class. In fact, now it is gradually creeping amongst middle-class and rich families as well.

Violence in the family exists generally in a situation where the woman is totally in a situation where she is completely dependent on the person who physically assaults her. It is a strange situation in which women and often the children too live in fear and terror, particularly when the women are completely dependent on the persons who physically assaulted them.

It is a strange situation to which the woman and often the children too live in fear and terror when the victims approach police and police in turn normally discourage them. The fact remains that after reporting the matter to the police, the woman concerned knows that she has to go back to the same house, with a cruel husband obviously waiting for her and if the man knows that a complaint has been made, he may get even more violent. Then there are children who may become father's target if the mother protests too much. An Indian woman would rather accept cruelty against herself than see it perpetrated on her children.

The law dealing with wife-beating has been defined in Sec. 498A in these words, "whosoever being the husband or the relative of the husband of a woman, subjects such woman to cruelty shall be punished with imprisonment for a term which may extend to three years and shall also be liable to fine.

But the question arises who will bell the cat ? Nobody is going to volunteer to walk to a police station to lodge a complaint about a neighbour or a relation beating of a wife and even if one goes to the police station, it is doubtful whether police will take the case and investigate the matter which required promptness and dedication.

Violence Against Women

Violence in the family rarely arouses the social concern it deserves. Aggressive behaviour on the part of the husband towards his wife is largely overlooked and even tolerated owing to the traditional notions arising from the patriarchal family structure-violence against women can be sub-divided into two broad groups :

(*a*) they may fall victim to general crimes-theft, murder, cheating, etc.—or to crimes specific in relation to women-molestation, assault, rape, etc., and

(*b*) they may be subjected to violence in the family which may or may not attract official notice.

Suddenly violence against women is on the rise in the land of Manu, 'where women are honoured, there the gods rejoice'. Today the frequency of newly married woman being burnt to death in many urban areas is rapidly rising. This has caused an alarm and lower agencies have come in for heavy criticism for their failure to prevent this. Law is supposed to control and harmonise individual and group behaviour. It is biased against women or does it have lawness inherent in it because of which those who commit crimes against them go unpunished.

In order to protect the status of women, the Widow Remarriage Act 1956, the Hindu Marriage Act 1955 and the Hindu Succession Act 1956 may be readily cited in this regard. The practice of dowry has also not escaped legislative alternation in 1961, the Dowry Prohibition Act was included in the Statute Book. Originally, giving and taking dowry was a non-cognizable offence but through a subsequent amendment the offence has been made cognizable.

A view has also been taken that law enforcement agencies have been somewhat dragging their feet in processing such cases. The police should not doubt prove more thoroughly the death of a recently married woman and the prosecution should be more vigorous and courts more innovative in the interpretation of law. However, the point should not be lost sight of that all these agencies function under a set of given rules and come into the picture well past the preventive stage. Whatever protective influence they exert is mostly indirect. As such by streamlining them, we may be trying to remove the defect without paying due attention to the underlying cases and hence a significant solution seems beyond sight.

The Dowry Prohibition Act has been variously described as a negative, limited penal and impractical Act, one which has not achieved its objective. According to Sec. 2 of the Act, "any property of valuable security given or agreed to be given at or before the marriage as 'consideration for the marriage of the parties', any presents given at the time of marriage unless made as consideration for marriage will not be termed as dowry. The

Act does not include any of the womens' things like Sofaset, television, refrigerator, car, jewellery and such items which accompany or even precede a bride into her home. The concept and definition of dowry itself is thus narrow and limited.

The Dowry Prohibition Act, 1968

Sec. 4 of the Dowry Prohibition Act, 1968 lays down penalty for demanding dowry. "If person demands directly or indirectly from the parents or other relations, or the guardian of a bride or bridegroom, as the case may be, any dowry, he shall be punishable with imprisonment for a term which shall not be less than six months but which may extend to two years and fines which may extend to Rs. 10,000,

> provided that the court may, for adequate or special reasons mentioned in the judgment, impose a sentence of imprisonment for a term less than six months.

(Under Section 3, taking and giving dowry is similarly punishable).

Criminal Laws

Indian Penal Code, Section 498 deals with a husband of a woman subjecting her to cruelty :

> "Whoever being the husband or the relative of the husband of a woman, subjects such woman to cruelty, shall be punished with imprisonment for a term which may extend to three years and shall be punished with imprisonment for a term which may extend to three years and shall also be liable to fine."

Explanation—For the purpose of this section 'cruelty' means :

(*a*) Any wilful conduct which is of such a nature as is likely to drive the woman 'to commit suicide or to cause grave injury or danger to life, limb or health (whether mental or physical) of the woman', or (*b*) Harassment of the woman where such harassment is with a view to coercing her or any person related to her to meet any unlawful demand for any property or valuable is on account of failure by her to meet such demand.

Code of Criminal Procedure, Sec. 174—sub-section (3)

(*i*) When the case involved is a suicide by a woman within seven years of her marriage, or

(*ii*) The case relates to the death of a woman within seven years of her marriage in any circumstances raising a reasonable suspicion that some other person committed an offence in relation to such woman, or

(*iii*) The case relates to the death of a woman within seven years of her marriage and any relative of the woman has made a request in this behalf, or

(*iv*) There is any doubt regarding the use of death, or

(*v*) The police officer, for any other reason, considers it expedient to do so, he shall, subject to such rules as the State Government may prescribe in this behalf, forward like body with a view to its being examined to the nearest Civil Surgeon or other qualified medical-man, appointed in this behalf by the State Government if the state of the weather and the distance admit of its being so forwarded without risk of such purification as the road as would render such examination useless.

Divorce

Marriage is no longer a sacred word and divorce no longer a taboo. Marriages are following apart at the families cause. With the passage of time, a large number of Indians are flooding the divorce courts to escape from unhappy marriages and assert their independence. In fact, divorce has become the way out and the Shah Bano case has high-lighted the rigidities of the society and drawn focus of media and intellectuals on this Vital problem of the society. As the divorce cases are increasing, the courts overflow with quorrecting couples. Many cities have had to create special matrimonial dispute courts. Delhi has five additional district and Session Judges. In Bombay there was only one Sub-judge, today there are three city courts and Ahmedabad has three courts.

In fact divorce has reached to such alarming proportion that the government has set up reconciliation bureaus in the major cities. Inspite of these bureaus, social organisations, psychiatrists, divorce cases are limelight tremendously with alarming pace. In Delhi nearly 25 divorce petition cases are filed every day. In Bombay cases have more than doubled during the last decade. Punjab and Haryana are not too far behind. Chandigarh courts witnessed 147 percent rise in divorce cases. The number of divorce petitions in Trivandrum Magistrates' Courts made a leap of 328 per cent during the last five years. The number of divorce applications increased more than four-fold in Bhopal district court in the last seven years. Calcutta has also witnessed marginal rise. Even in Madras, the bastion of tradition, there has been an annual increase of 10% in the number of divorces.

Causes of Divorce

Incompatibility in marriage causes, the instability between the husband and wife which ultimately results in fueds, dissensions and rising frictions lead to divorce. Jack Norman Sr., a lawyer, has listed following causes of divorce :

(*i*) *Money problem*—money worries trigger all the other problems of marriage.

(*ii*) *Sexual incompatibility*—Their husbands are physically unable to satisfy them or are too preoccupied with their jobs.

(*iii*) *Poor health*—The husband gets sidejob and can no longer hold on full time job. The wife has to go to work and for the care of the house she gets by the evening dead tired.

Rev. John L. Thomas, a Jesuist sociologist has analysed the causes of divorce in mid-west catholic families in America. His statistical analysis therein shows the following reasons for divorce :

Excessive drinking—	30 %
Adultery—	25 %
Irresponsibility—	12 %
Clash of temperaments—	12 %
In-laws—	7 %
Sexual incompatibility—	5 %
Miscellaneous—	10 %
Money problems—	1 %

Muslim Law

Divorce laws in India, particularly amongst the muslims were subjected to widespread debate when the famous Shah Bano Begum case was listed for hearing before Supreme Court. The Supreme Court observed that "this appeal does not involve any question of constitutional importance but that is not to say that it does not involve any question of importance. Same questions, which arise under the ordinary civil and criminal laws are of far-reaching significance to a large segment of society which have been traditionally subjected to unjust treatment. Women are one such segment. 'Nastres Swatantra Mastrati', said Manu the law giver and it is alleged that the fatal point in Islam is the degraded woman." The appeal before the Supreme Court came out of an application filed by a divorced Muslim for maintenance under section 125 of the Code of Criminal Procedure and raises a straight forward issue which is of common interest not only to Muslim women, not only to women generally, but to all those who aspirury try to create an equal society of man and woman, bore themselves into the belief that mankind has achieved a remarkable degree of progress in that direction.

The question of common code arose out of this whether Sec. 125 of the Code of Criminal Procedure applies to Muslims or not. Sections 125 (1) (2) clearly lays that a person, who having sufficient means neglects or refuses to maintain his wife who is unable to maintain herself, can be asked by the court to pay a monthly maintenance to her at the rate not exceeding five hundred rupees by Clause (b) of the explanation to Sec. 125 (1); wife includes a divorced woman who has not re-married. Thus provisions are explicit and admit no doubt. Religion has no place in these provisions. This is a Criminal Law Procedure in order to provide quick remedy to the aggrieved party, irrespective of the religion they belonged.

In Shah Bano case, the Supreme Court went into great details of Islami Law and provisions of Koran and came to the conclusion that "there Aiyats have no doubt say that the Quran imposes an obligation on the Muslim husband to make provision for or to provide maintenance to the divorced wife. The contrary argument does less than justice to the teachings of Quran. As observed by Mr. Hidayatullah in his introduction to Mullah's Mohammaden Law, the Quran is Al Furquars, that is one showing truth from falsehood and right from wrong".

Plight of Muslim Women

The furore over the Supreme Court's recent judgment on the Shariat has once again highlighted the grim plight of Muslim women. Though the judgment ostensibly ushers in a new era for Muslim womens' rights, the truth is something different. The message of Supreme Court's judgement is yet to percolate the masses. The Supreme Court's decision granting alimony to a divorced Muslim woman, Shah Bano Begum, celebrates the growing consciousness of womens' rights. There are large pockets where the land-mark judgement cannot beam its message of hope, where the much proclaimed legal aid service have yet to penetrate.

Today many Muslim women are unitedly common agency callously cast away by a Muslim male exercising his 'religious privileges' to divorce. Then women are critical of those aspects of the Shariat or Muslim personal Law, that tend themselves to abuse in the hands of men and which discriminates against women.

Perhaps more insiduous than the rigours of poverty is the lure of obscruantism among the hungry and desolate. There the Shariat becomes an instrument of repressive in the hands of callous men. Here the Shariat is involved to bolster fake motivations to butress the greed for quick money. Here Mohammaden Law turns into a legitimate means of female suppression. Here legal redress is fantasy. House after house harbours broken women who peer out like creatures of the dark, figures of male brutalisation, leaving back an ugly memory. Women can be pulled into marriage and adolescence discarded soon after or after years of mind-bogging domestic subjugation stranded penniless. Ever so often the man snaps of with his wife's jewels after setting up a small business with the dowry money she has paid him. These are men who turn the Shariat into an adventure in exploitation, going from one marriage to another or burning adolescent girls with the big gulf-dreams.[1]

The human dilemma that springs from the distortion of religious sanction has a diabolical dimension. Teenaged girls from poor Muslim favourites and young abandoned wives are particularly valuable to predators of the flesh who disguise their intension under the provisions of Muslim Personal Law. Foremost in this class of men are itinerant. Arabs sporting a fat purse and false promises of marital bliss.

Dowry Deaths

Almost every twelve hours a woman is burnt to death in Delhi. In 1983 alone 690 women had died by burn in the capital. How many of them are suicides or accidental deaths and how

1. *A Cry in Wilderness* - Venu Menon, The Illustrated Weekly of India, September 21, 1985.

many are murders, young women killed by in-laws for not bringing adequate dowry ? This question, raised by women activists fighting against dowry has been the central issue in judicial cases following such deaths. The increasing incidence of such deaths has also led to demands for change in the Dowry Prohibition Act of 1961 which is frequently violated and variously interpreted. No effective amendments have yet been made in the Act despite the appointment of a Lok Sabha Joint Select Committee in 1980. Meanwhile, the courts included bride-burning among the rarest of the rare cases deserving the death penalty. Most lower court convictions have been reversed by the higher courts. In fact, in the absence of well-defined code of punishment for bride-burning the fate of a case seems to depend upon the personal predilections of the judges concerned. In a separate place of circumstances leading to the death of a 21 years old are examined here to review the attitude of courts.

Dowry Deaths—An Analysis

Dowry deaths are caused due to ill-treatment at the hands of husband and in-laws leading to death of young women. Subjugated and suffering women are to be found in every socio-economic stratification. They are down trodden and humiliated alike by the oppressors and the oppressed among men and their female accomplices. Unfortunately, crimes against women are sought to be hushed up by a finely society that refuse to pry into the horrors perpetrated in the privacy of mental home? Very few cases are brought to the notice of the police. A microscopic minority of reports of bride-burning eventually find their way to the newspaper columns as true crime briefs which do not portray the physical and mental agony of women forced to live in pain and humiliation for rest of their lives. After all, for every woman forces to live in pain and humiliation for the rest of their lives, there are hundreds who reconcile themselves to living without any hope in a state of suspended animation where suffering is the only reality.

Dowry is only a part of the overall humiliation and subjugation of women that is sanctioned by our society. That something as pettey as dowry-the gold bangle, the T.V. set, a few thousand rupees, in case should be the cause of such depravity among young men from "Respectable" families, should boggle any imagination that is not warped by fables extolling the cult of 'Sutee' and Sita's ordeal by fire. But so culturally attuned we are to women sacrificing themselves and being sacrificed by their lords and masters that we cannot seem to work up a healthy indignation against bride-burning, dowry deaths as we choose to call them now.

Dowry deaths are now an accepted phenomenon in India. According to an official release, there were 2690 Dowry Deaths in 1976 and 2917 in 1977. Unfortunately in modern society everything is so commercialised that husbands demand dowries blatantly. Brides are burnt when demanded items are not received. Unfortunately, the attitude of the police is unsympathetic. The dowry prohibition law of 1961 too has its loopholes. To begin with, it does not define dowry and makes both giving and taking of a dowry an offence.

A look at police records reveals alarmingly high death rates among young women due to burning. The inadequacy of the investigation machinery is revealed by the fact that 690 women died in 1983 of whom 290 were between 18-25 years of age, out of this 23 were alleged dowry-burning in Delhi alone.

The Judicial View

Courts do not view with sympathy the dowry death cases. In this context, I may draw the attention of my readers towards an article written by Mr. J.P. Aray, D.I.G., C.I.D., Haryana in the column of the Times of India when he pointed out that in Haryana during 1977—1978, 106 cases were registered on account of dowry deaths out of which 59 were sent up and none was convicted. Even in those cases where there is evidence, the court choose not to believe the women, even her dying declaration is not believed. In one case of Shanni Kaur, mother of a one year old son died of burning in Delhi hospital. Before dying she gave her statement three times, once to the police and twice to two different doctors stating that her husband had poured kerosene oil on her and burnt her. The court disbelieved the dying declaration.

Sharda's extra-marital affairs were also overlooked. But the Supreme Court acquitted Sharda, released from custody and set at liberty. He flew away to America and got married again. Women all over Maharashtra organised protest demonstrations and public marches.

Suicide

The problem of bride-burning and dowry is closely linked with suicide by unconcerned and unmarried women. Suicide is prohibited under Sec. 309 I.P.C. According to a BPRSD Report in the year 1980, 41,697 persons committed suicide out of which 49% were men and consisted of 24,188 persons and 17475 were women which accounted for 419 per cent.

Women Favourite Victim of Fire

Saheli, a social organisation of Delhi has done a lot of field work for working out crime against women. This organisation investigated 109 cases of death by burning and came to the conclusion that out of 109 cases, 85 were married women and their average age was 26 in 80 cases and remaining 29 were 17 years. It is surprising that out of the 109 cases, 99 cases were closed because no foul play was suspected. Of the remaining 10 cases arrests were made in 7 cases and in one case bail was granted. Out of 99 cases, 34 cases were described as pure suicide in the presence of their husbands who allegedly tried to have them. Most of those women committed suicide because of serious domestic problems, such as wife-beating, drunken behaviour of husbands, harassment by in-laws, dowry and childlessness. A far higher number of death by burning were called 'accidents', 74 of the 109. According to the findings of the report, the police does not feel necessary to look into the domestic situation.

Equally disturbing are the post-mortem surveys. The study says that post-mortem were carried out in 83 of 109 cases. The police, however, assert that post-mortems were carried out in every single case of unnatural death. The report says that 20 of the post-mortems were waived on the request of the family but it also mentions that in some cases this was done on the request of the husband. Looking at the dying declaration, only 68 of 109 women made death-bed declaration, only in two cases were dying declaration recorded in the presence of a metropolitan magistrate. Only 3 of the 68 accused their husband or in-laws which led to the subsequent arrest of the accused.

Saheli has listed several irregularities in the police functioning, the quality or lack of it ? If their paper work is a clear indication of their lack of meticulousness and thoroughness it states. The victims history and background are not always recorded. There is great detail in some cases and none at all in others. When information of a post-mortem is given, no details of the results are maintained so there is no way of knowing what was found.

Delhi Police has opened an 'Anti-dowry Cell' with a Dy. Commissioner of Police as its incharge. In regard to bride-burning tragedies, the number of incidents rose progressively from 670 in 1975 to 1064 in 1979 and today it is much more in the whole country. Maharashtra and Andhra Pradesh were ahead of other states in the number of murder cases but the figures in respect of them includes suicidal and accidental deaths. In 1979 the states reported 362 and 249 cases respectively. Delhi reported 138 incidents and Rajasthan 98 cases.

The bias against women was most blatant in Sharda Birdhi case. Sharda, a chemical engineer was found guilty of both murdering his 20 year old wife Manjushree by suffocation and oral administration of Potassium Cynide. He was found guilty both by Sessions Court and the Bombay High Court. He appealed to the Supreme Court. The Supreme Court took note of the fact that the High Court had mentioned 17 circumstances which proved him guilty including—

(*a*) Written dying declaration by Manjushree in the form of letters written to his sister and her first oral statement made to her father, mother, sister and friend about her husband's ill-treatment.

(*b*) Sharda's extra-marital affair.

But the Supreme Court acquitted Sharda, released him from custody and set him at liberty. He flew away to America and got married again. All this infuriated public and there was widespread resentment and women all over Maharashtra organised protests and public meetings and submitted memorandum.

Sudha Goel's Case

On December 1, 1980, Sudha Goel, 21 sustained burn injuries in the courtyard of her in-law's house, a week before she was to deliver her first child. She died in hospital following morning. A case was registered with the police and challaned. Additional Sessions Judge, S.M. Agarwal, who heard the case in a lower court in Delhi, found the evidence strong enough to suggest murder and sentenced her mother-in-law, husband and brother-in-law to death in May 1983. Five months later, a Delhi High Court Bench acquitted them. Justice R.N. Agarwal and Justice Malik Sharifuddin of the Delhi High Court observed, "the learned Judges have found that the crime was calculated and pre-planned. We do not agree with the findings of the learned Sessions Judge. On an appreciation of the evidence we are of the view that there was no pre-plan and whatever happened, has happened between 8.45 and 9 p.m. Subhas, brother-in-law, is a married man alongwith two small children. We fail to see why he should be party to heinous crime."

The High Court judgement leaves many crucial questions unanswered when it chooses to subscribe to the accident theory. The judges also described the dowry theory pronounced by Mr. S.M. Agarwal in the Sessions as motive for murder. The High Court judgment also shows, how out of step, law is with the existing social realities.

Favourite Victim of Home-fires

Married women have been more severely burnt and maimed than men ten times more, so most women sustaining

80 to 100 per cent burns. They were in the 18–35 age group as 39 per cent of the men were from this group. Most of the women were Hindus. Married women were more victims than married men. Most of the women were from the middle–class and lower–middle class.

In regard to bride-burning tragedies the number of incidents rose progressively from 670 in 1975 to 1064 in 1979 in the whole country. Maharashtra and Andhra were ahead of other states in the number of cases but the figures in respect of them includes suicidal and accidental deaths. In 1979, the two states reported 362 and 249 cases respectively. Delhi reported 138 incidents and Rajasthan 98.

Police Role and Performance in Dowry Death Cases

Burning case is also a bone of contention between police, public and social organisations. The Maharashtra government has, however, set up six vigilance committees (VCs) on dowry matters for as many districts. District Magistrates of the district is the ex-officio Chairman of the District Vigilance Commission which consists of the district police chief, a gazetted officer from the social welfare department, the principal of a Women's College or School, a lawyer, a legal aid work, one or two social workers, concerned citizens and one or two representatives of womans' organisations.

Police Role in Dowry Burning Cases

Following lapses have been pointed out about police role and performance :

(1) Delay in reaching the scene and even after they reach the scene, they do not take relevant evidence in notice.

(2) Recording of Dying Declaration is often delegated.

(3) There is considerable apathy on the part of police in registering cases of bride-burning and making more ritual arrests. Police officers quite often say that this

problem is exaggerated and that with judges pondering to public opinion. 'Unscrupulus elements' will take advantage and already parents are stopping on the change of dowry indiscrimination even in the case of accidents.

Absence of a well-defined code of punishment for bride-burning, the fate of a case seems to depend on the personal predications of the judge concerned.

In a strict adherence to the rules of Anglo-Saxou jurisprudence in a milieu very different from the one in which were framed, leading to more law than justice? Anti-dowry activists whose shrill lobbying against the High Courts verdict in the Sudha Goel case has earned them a contempt notice, feel that the High Court is too conservative and too distinct from the sordid middle-class culture in the capital.

For the legal climate to change in favour of harassed brides, the police should be in time with the judiciary. They Manifestly are not according to a seasoned Police Officer. Most of the alleged bride burning case are suicides and in registering cases under Sec. 30 (abetment to suicide) is waste of time.

The Police functioning is hampered due to multiple factors, out of which one is that when the police arrives at the spot, the door, where the unfortunate bride has been burnt is already broken open and water thrown all over. Mrs. Kanwaljit Goel, the Dy. Commissioner of police operating the Dowry Cell says, "it is the duty of every citizen to give evidence, but neighbours do not want to be witnesses because they think answering Court Summons is too much trouble. Nor do they want to annoy the boy's family".

Judicial Views and Legislation on Bride-burning at Crossroads

Almost every twelve hours a woman is burnt to death in Delhi. In 1983 alone 690 women have died of burns. How many of these burning cases are suicides or accidental deaths and how many are murders ? Young women killed by in-laws for not bringing an adequate dowry. This question raised by women activists fighting against dowry has been the central issue in judicial cases following such deaths. The increasing incidence of such deaths has also led to demands for change in the Dowry prohibition Act of 1961 which is frequently violated and variously interpreted. No effective amendments have yet been made in the Act despite the appointment of a Lok Sabha Joint Select Committee in 1980. Meanwhile the courts, too have failed to evolve a consistent code of punishment for such norms. A division bench of the Supreme Court including bride-burning amongst the rarest of the rare cases deserves the death penalty. Most lower court's convictions have been reversed by the higher courts. Unfortunately, in the absence of a well-defined Code of punishment for bride-burning, the fate of a case seems to depend on the personal predilections of the judge concerned. Although the ends of this type of crime is at least half a century old, but judicial grapping with it is relatively recent phenomenon.

A deterrent death in cases of bride-burning or for dowry deaths has been in the offing for some years. In July 1980 Additional Sessions Judge S.C. Jain observed while awarding life imprisonment to Jagdish Lal Malhotra, a dowry seeking chartered accountant that "In most of these cases culprits escape the liability for want of evidence and such cases are given the label of a suicide or an accident. But whenever such a case is proved beyond doubt, the extreme penalty of death should be awarded to the culprits, who are enemies of society."

Can Amendment to Act Eradicate Dowry ?

The Dowry Prohibition Act has been variously described as a negative, limited, penal and impractical Act, one which has not achieved its objective. According to Section 2 of the Act, dowry is "any property or valuable security" given or agreed to be given at or before the marriage as "consideration for the marriage of the parties". Any presents given at the time of marriage can be made as consideration for marriage will not be termed as dowry.

Speedy Justice

Speedy justice in tackling such cases appears to be at hand. There are judges committed to widest possible interpretations of existing laws so that culprits can be brought to book.

Women Judges

It has been suggested that more and more women judges should be appointed and family courts established.

Dowry Consultation Committee

In some states the Dowry Consultation Committees have been appointed.

41

Dowry Deaths

Almost every 12 hours a woman is burnt to death in Delhi. In 1983 along, 690 women died by burns in the capital. How many of them are suicides, or accidental deaths–and how many are murders is a question which invites nation-wide attention of the people. Why are the young women killed by in-laws for not bringing adequate dowry? This question raised by the women activists fighting against dowry has been the central issue in Judicial cases following such deaths. The increasing incidence of such deaths has also led to demands for change in the Dowry Prohibition Act of 1961 which is frequently violated and variously interpreted. No effective amendments have yet been made in the Act despite the appointment of a lok Sabha joint select committee in 1980. Meanwhile, the courts included bride burning among the rarest of the cases deserving the death penalty. Most lower courts convictions have been reversed by the higher courts. In fact, in the absence of well-defined code of punishment for bride burning, the fate of a case seems to depend upon the personal predilections of the judges concerned. In separate place the circumstances leading to the death of a 21 year old woman are examined here to review the attitude of courts.

Dowry Deaths: An Analysis

Dowry deaths are caused due to ill-treatment, at the hands of husbands and in-laws and this act of theirs leads to death of young women. Subjugated and suffering women are to be found in every social economic stratim. They are down-trodden and humiliated alike by the oppressors and the oppressed among men and their female accomplices. Unfortunately, crimes against women are sought to be hushed up by a finely society that refuses to pry into the horrors perpetrated in the privacy of a mental home? Very few cases are brought to the notice of the police. A microscopic minority of reports of bride burning eventually find their way to newspaper columns as true crime briefs which do not portray the physical and mental agony of women forced to live in pain and humiliation for rest of their lives. After all, for every woman forced to live in pain and humiliation for the rest of life. There are hundreds who reconcile themselves to living without any hope–in a state of suspended animation where suffering is the only reality.

Dowry is only a part of the overall humiliation and subjugation of woman that is sanctioned by our society. That something as petty as dowry–the gold bangles, the T.V. set, a few thousand rupees in cash, should be the cause of such depravity among young men from "Respectable" families should boggle any imagination that is not warned by fables extolling the cult of 'Sutee' and Sita's ordeal by the fire. But so culturally attuned we are to women sacrificing themselves and being sacrificed by their lords and master–that we cannot seem to work up a healthy indignation against bride-burning, dowry deaths, as we choose to call them now.

Dowry deaths are now an accepted phenomenon. In India, according to an official release there were 2690 dowry deaths in 1976 and 2917 in 1977. Unfortunately in modern society everything is so commercialised that husbands demand dowries blatantly. Brides are burnt when demanded items are not received. Unfortunately, the attitude of the police is unsympathetic.

The dowry prohibition law of 1961 too has its loopholes. To begin with, it does not define dowry and makes both giving and taking of a dowry an offence.

A look at police records reveals alarmingly high death rates among young women due to burning. The inadequacy of the investigation machinery is revealed by the fact that 690 women died in 1983 of whom 290 were between 18–25 years of age: On this 23 were alleged dowry burning in Delhi alone.

The Judicial View

Courts, view with sympathy the dowry death cases. In this context, I may draw the attention of my readers towards an article written by Mr. J.P. Attray, DIG, DID, Haryana in the column of the Times of India, when he pointed out that in Haryana during 1977-1978, 106 cases were registered on account of dowry deaths out of which 59 were sent up and none was convicted. Even in those case where there is evidence, the court choose not to believe the women. Even her dying declaration is not believed. In one case of Shanni Kaur, mother of an one year old, son, died of burning in Delhi hospital. Before dying she gave her statement three times, once to the police and twice to two different doctors stating that her husband had poured kerosene oil on her and burnt her. The court disbelieved the dying declaration.

The bias against women was most blatantly revealed in Sharad Birdhi Chand Sardar's case. Sardar, a chemical engineer, was found guilty of murdering his 20 years old wife, Manjushree by suffocation and oral administration of poison pottasium cynide. He was found guilty by both the Sessions Court and the Bombay High Court. He appealed to the Supreme Court. The Supreme Court took note of the fact that the High Court had mentioned 17 circumstances which proved the guilt including-written dying declaration by Manjushree in the form of letters written to her sister and her friend. Her oral statements made to her father, mother, sister and friend about her husband's ill-treatment. Sardar's extra-marital affairs were also overlooked. But the Supreme Court acquitted Sardar. Sardar was acquitted, released from custody and set at liberty. He flew away to America and got married again. Women all over Maharashtra organised protests, demonstration and public marches.

Suicide

The problem of Bride-burning and dowry is closely linked with suicide by unconcerned and unmarried women. Suicide is prohibited under Sec. 309 IPC. According to a BPRSD Report in the year 1980, 41697 persons committed suicide, out of which 49.1 per cent were men and consisted of 24,188 persons and 17475 were women which accounted for 41.9 per cent.

Women Favourite Victim of Fire

Saheli, a social organisation of Delhi has done a lot of field work for working out crime against women. This organisation investigates 109 cases of death by burning and came to the conclusion that out of 109 cases 85 were married women and their average age was 26 in 80 cases and remaining 29 were 17 years of age. It is surprising that out of the 109 cases, 99 cases were closed because no foul play was suspected. Of the remaining 10 cases arrests were made in 7 cases and in one case bail was granted. Out of 99 cases, 34 cases were described as pure suicide in the presence of their husbands who allegedly tried to have them. Most of these women committed suicide because of serious domestic problems, such as wife beating, drunken misbehaviour by husband, harassment by in-laws, dowry and childlessness. A far higher number of death by burning were called 'accidents', 74 of the 109. According to the findings of the report, the police does not feel necessary to look into the domestic situation.

Equally disturbing are the post-mortem surveys. The study says that post-mortems were carried out in 83 of the 109 cases. The police, however, assert that post-mortem were carried out in every single case of unnatural death. The report says that 20 of the post-mortems were waived on the request of the family but it also mentions that in some cases this was done on the request of the husband. Linking at the dying declaration, only 68 of the 109, women made death-bed declaration. Only in two cases were dying declaration recorded in the presence of a Metropolitan Magistrate. Only 3 of the 68 accused their husbands or in-laws which led to the subsequent arrest of the accused.

'Saheli' has listed several irregularities in the police functioning, "the quality or lack of it?" If their paper work is a clear indication of their lack of meticulousness and thoroughness it states. The victim's history and background are not always recorded. There is great detail in some cases and none at all in others. When information of a post-mortem is given no details of the results are maintained so there is no way of knowing what was found. Delhi Police has opened an 'Anti-Dowry Cell' with a Dy. Commissioner of Police as its incharge.

In regard to bride-burning tragedies, the number of incidents rose progressively from 670 in 1975 to 1064 in 1979 and today it is much increased in the whole country. Maharashtra and Andhra Pradesh were ahead of other states in the number of murder cases but the figures in respect of them includes suicidal and accidental deaths. In 1979, the states reported 362 and 249 cases respectively. Delhi reported 138 incidents and Rajasthan 98 cases.

Sudha Goel's Case

On Dec.1, 1980, Sudha Goel, 21 sustained burn injuries in the courtyard of her in-laws house, a week before she was due to deliver her first child. She died in hospital following morning. A case was registered with the Police and challaned. Additional Sessions Judge, S.M. Aggarwal who heard the case in a lower court in Delhi found the evidence strong enough to suggest murder and sentenced her mother-in-law, husband and brother-in-law to death in May 1983. Five months later, a Delhi High Court Bench acquitted them. Justice R.N. Agarwal and Justice Malik Sharifuddin of the Delhi high Court observed, "The learned Judge has found that crime was calculated and preplanned. We do not agree with the finding of the learned

Sessions Judge. On an appreciation of the evidence we are of the view that there was no pre-plan and whatever happened has happened between 8.45 and 9 p.m. Subhas, Sudha's brother-in-law is a married man alongwith two small children. We fail to see why he should be party to a heinous crime."

The High Court judgement leaves many crucial questions unanswered when it chose to subscribe to the accident theory. The judges also described the dowry theory propounded by Mr. S.M. Agarwal in the Sessions Court as motive for murder. The High Court's judgment also shows how out of step, law is with the existing social realities.

Almost every 12 hours a woman is burnt to death in Delhi. In 1983, above 690 women have died of burns in the capital. The increasing incidence of such deaths has also led to demands for change in the Dowry Prohibition Act of 1961 which is frequently violated and variously interpreted. No effective amendments have been made in the Act. The courts have also failed to formulate a consistent code of conduct for such crimes. A Supreme Court judgment included bride-burning as 'rarest of the rare' cases deserving death penalty !

Married women have been more severely burnt and maimed than men ten times more so most women sustaining 80 to 100 per cent burns. They were in the 18–35 age group as 39 per cent of the men were from this group. Most of the women were Hindus. Married women, are more victims than married men. Most of the women were from middle and lower middle classes.

Police Role and Performance in Dowry Death Cases

Burning case is also a bone of contention between police, public and social organisations. The Maharashtra government, however, set up six vigilance committees (VCs) on dowry matters for as many districts. District Magistrate of the district is the ex-officio chairman of the District Vigilance Commission which consists of the district Police Chief, a gazetted officer from the Social Welfare Department, the principal of a Women's College or School, a lawyer, a legal aid work, one or two social workers/concerned citizens and one or two representatives of Womens Organisations.

Following lapses have been pointed out about police role and performance

(*a*) Delay in reaching the scene and even after they reach the scene, they do not take relevant evidence in notice.

(*b*) Recording of dying declaration is often delegated.

(*c*) There is considerable apathy on the part of police in registering cases of bride-burning and making more ritual arrests. Police officers quite often say that this problem is exaggerated and that with judges pondering to public opinion 'Unscrupulous elements' will take advantage and already parents are stopping on the change of dowry indiscrimination even in the case of accidents.

Absence of a well-defined code of punishment for bride-burning, the fate of a case seems to depend on the personal predications of the judge concerned. Is strict adherence to the rules of Anglo-Sexon jurisprudence in a milieu very different from the one in which they were framed-leading to more law-than justice ? Anti-dowry, activities whose shrill lobbying against the High Court's verdict in the Sudha Goel's case has earned them a contempt notice, feel that the High Court is too conservative and too distant from the sordid reality of the lower middle class culture in the Capital.

For the legal climate to change in favour of harassed brides, the police should be in turn with the judiciary. They manifestly are not. According to a seasoned Police Officer, 'most of the alleged bride-burning cases are suicides and in registering cases under sec. 306 (abetment to suicide) is waste of time.

The police functioning is hampered due to multiple factors out of which one is that when the police arrives at the spot, the door where the unfortunate bride has been burnt is already broken open and water thrown all over. Mrs. Kanwaljit Goel, the Deputy Commissioner of Police operating the Dowry Cell says, 'It is the duty of every citizen to give evidence but neighbours do not want to be witnessed because they think answering court summons is too much a trouble. Nor do they want to annoy the boy's family.'

Judicial Views and Legislation on Bride-burning at the Crossroads

Almost every 12 hours a woman is burnt to death in Delhi. In 1983 alone 690 women have died of burns. How many of these burning cases are suicides, or accidental deaths and how many are murders, young women killed by in-laws for not bringing an adequate dowry. This question raised by women activists fighting against dowry, has been the central issue in judicial cases following such deaths. The increasing incidence of such deaths has also led to demands for change in Dowry Prohibition Act of 1961, which is frequently violated and variously interpreted. No effective amendments have yet been made in the Act despite the appointment of a Lok Sabha Joint Select Committee in 1980. Meanwhile the courts, too have filed to evolve a consistent code of punishment for such norms. A division Bench of the Supreme Court including bride-burning amongst the rarest of the rare cases deserves the death penalty. Most lower courts' conviction have been reversed by the higher courts. Unfortunately, in the absence of a well-defined code of punishment for bride-burning, the fate of a case seems to depend on the personnel predilection of the judge concerned. Although the ends of this type of crime is at least half a century old, but judicial grapping with it is relatively a recent phenomenon.

A deterrent death in cases of bride-burning or for dowry deaths, has been in the offing for some years. In July 1980, Additional Sessions Judge S.C. Jain observed, while awarding like imprisonment to Jagdish Lal Malhotra, a seeking chartered accountant that "In most of these cases culprits escape the liability for want of evidence and such cases are given the label of a suicide or an accident. But whenever such a case is proved beyond doubt, the extreme penalty of death should be awarded to the culprits, who are enemies of society."

Can Amendment of Act Eradicate Dowry

The Dowry Prohibition Act has been variously described as a negative, limited penal and impracticable Act, one which has not achieved its objective. According to Section 2 of the Act, dowry is —"Any property or valuable security given or agree to be given at or before the marriage as 'consideration for the marriage of the parties'; any presents given at the time of marriage, can be made as consideration for marriage, will not be termed as dowry.

Speedy Justice

Speedy justice in tackling such cases appears to be at hand. There are judges committed to widest possible interpretations of existing laws so that culprits can be brought to book.

Women Judges

It has been suggested that more and more women judges should be appointed and family courts established.

Dowry Consultation Committee

In some states the Dowry Consultation Committees have been appointed.

42

Giving in to the Unceasing Demands does not Stop the Torture

"I never expected they would go to this extent although I knew she was being tortured, even deprived of proper food, says Narinder Singh, father of Arveen Kaur, who died of strangulation on November 23, 1988, in the New Friends Colony home of her husband, Paramjit Singh Rana in Delhi. The Rana says she committed suicide by hanging, but her father is certain she was murdered (see Weekly dated January 29, 1989). In numerous letters ever since marriage in 1984, Arveen wrote about the neglect and ill-treatment and pleaded pathetically to be taken back into her parental home.

Narinder Singh, a prosperous businessman of Bombay, reacted by trying to fulfil his son-in-law's demands as far as possible, and by taking care of Arveen's needs. In the four years of her marriage, all her clothes and most of her baby's clothes, were supplied by her parents.

But Arveen's pleas could not impel her parents to call her back. Narinder Singh says he felt if he recalled her, he would have to get her married once again and there was no guarantee she should be happier in the next marital home. But today he realises "I was hundred per cent wrong. All my assessments and decisions were wrong. I am guilty-I don't want to refuse my responsibility. I have lost my daughter. I couldn't save her life. But let people learn a lesson from my loss. If there were not many such foolish fathers like me, why would girls like Arveen die ? Every day they are dying, yet parents make the same mistake."

Suman Malik (a pseudonym), only by chance escaped becoming yet another Arveen, as her married life followed a very similar course, and her parents for a long time pursued, the same course of appeasement as Narinder Singh did. The only daughter of a prosperous businessman of Delhi, she was married at the age of 21 into another business family, in 1974. After marriage, her husband who was an alcoholic, began to beat her up regularly, even during her pregnancy. He used her as a hostage to extract money from her father.

The Maliks complied for eight years, giving large amounts of cash to the son-in-law and also paying for everything in Suman's house, from groceries to furnishings to clothing for herself and her two children. Every time she was thrown out by her husband she would return to her parents and then go back to her husband after negotiations. The last time she was thrown out her father decided not to send her back. Today, Suman and her children are living with her parents. Suman is running her own business set up with her father's help.

These two cases clearly illustrate that if fathers who express their love for their daughters by pouring money into the son-in-law's hands, were instead to use the money to equip the daughters for independence, they would not only ensure the daughter's survival but also a much more dignified life for them.

Some Form of Outside Support can Embolden a Woman to Fight Back

Sumitra, 39, resident of a resettlement colony in north Delhi, is a woman to whom other women of the neighbourhood go for aid and advice. Yet, it was only by chance that Sumitra escaped becoming just another anonymous murdered wife. Daughter of a poor weaver in a village in UP, Sumitra was married at the age of 13 into a poor family and no dowry was paid. She had studied up to the fifth standard but her husband was illiterate. On the first night of her marriage, her mother-in-law explained to her, "Look, you will have to live both with your husband and with your brother-in-law. That is how I lived, and so also your sister-in-law." Sumitra was reluctant to follow the practice. This angered his in-laws. In the day time, her mother-in-law would beat her and at night her husband would shower her with kicks and blows. Within a month of her marriage Sumitra returned to her parents' house and spent the next 10 months there. Yet, when she returned to Delhi, the treatment was even worse. She went to her parents home a second time and was again persuaded to go back to face the same beatings skilfully administered in the region between the waist and the knees so that no one could see the bruises. She finally decided who would leave for good. She stayed with her parents for five years until her father insisted she remarry. She refused and was told, "You can go wherever you like. There is no place for you in this house."

Sumitra was now in a desperate situation and had only one option. She returned to her in-laws house, fell at their feet and begged for forgiveness. But they beat her up and threw her out on the street. It was only when the panchayat met and insisted that they should take her in, that they did so, on the condition that she could never complain.

One day she collapsed on the road and began to haemorrhage. A passer-by took her to the hospital. When she returned home her mother-in-law caught her by the throat and began banging her head against a wall, accusing her of having been pregnant and aborting an illegitimate child. Inspite of witnessing such torture Sumitra's father started walking away, saying, "I won't take her back. You can finish her off if you want to." They would have done just that if Sumitra's sister had not intervened. She tried to mobilise some support within the community so that the biradari panchayat could be made to intervene in Sumitra's favour.

When the panchayat met, no one spoke in favour of the in-laws. Sumitra's relatives declared that no girl would have tolerated for eight days what she had tolerated for eight years. They said she would now stay only on condition that if anyone said a word to her, she would be entitled to say a dozen in reply. At this, Sumitra's husband began to ask forgiveness and it was decided that he and she would stay in a separate hut. After this, Sumitra's position slowly but surely improved.

Being the Breadwinners of the Family does not Protect Women Against Marital Violence

Jasmani is a tribal woman living in a village in south Bihar. She is in her late twenties. In her community, there is no custom of dowry. Instead, the groom pays a bride price to the bride's father. The women are the main workers on the land and the mainstay of the tribal economy. After her mother's death, Jasmani was compelled to leave her natal home because two of her brothers mortgaged the family land and went away to the city. Jasmani was not consulted and her usufructory right as an unmarried daughter was ignored. In anger and frustration she migrated to Rourkela and found work as a labourer in a steel plant. There she met Saluka Sundi, a co-worker. "One day he came to my hut and said to me : 'I have a lot of inconvenience cooking my food. I don't even have proper utensils. Let me live in your hut. That way, I won't have to pay Rs. 7 as rent for my hut.' "So they began to live together as husband and wife. After a year or two, he decided to return to his village and Jasmani accompanied him.

In the village, their relationship changed. Now she was living in his house, feeding off his land, and he spared no occasion to remind her of this. Jasmani had saved up Rs. 400 after four years of working. Saluka spent all this money on repairing his house and on buying seeds. Jasmani was now totally dependent on his land. He neglected her, beat her up.

Saluka also threatened to bring another wife. Once he brought home a woman from the fair. That morning he had snatched all the money Jasmani had-about Rs. 14 to spend at the fair. When she protested, he beat her severely. Jasmani does all the work on her husband's land. Saluka often refuses even to do the ploughing which traditionally is the man's job. Jasmani had to bring her 12-year-old nephew to live with her and do the ploughing. Saluka hates to work. Occasionally he may do an odd job and earn a few rupees, but most of the time he loafs around.

Jasmani feels very insecure because she has no foothold on Saluka's land. He can throw her out whenever he chooses to do so. He can also do what he likes with the land without consulting her. Jasmani always talked about wanting to leave Saluka, but she had nowhere to go. She said she would leave if he returned her Rs. 400. Her health has deteriorated after her marriage. She looks malnourished. She does not want any children because as she says. " I have no security myself, what will I do with a child?" But she admits that her position might have been relatively stronger had she produced a son. "Right now, he keeps saying 'the fields are mine'. Then I could say 'The fields are mine too.' I would acquire a right through my son."

Thus, despite being the breadwinner of the family and belonging to community where dowry is not practised, women are not protected against marital violence so long as resources and power remain in the hands of men.

Education and Earning Capacity does not Save a Woman from Humiliation and Cruelty

The cultural norm that a woman should place herself and all she possesses at the disposal of her husband leaves even women with high earning capacities at the complete mercy of their husbands, and near-destitute when abandoned.

Naiera, 31, married Derek Fulgado, 38, in 1981. At that time, she was an air hostess with Kuwait Airways and Derek, an architect. They met in Bombay. Naiera got Derek a work permit in Kuwait where she was posted. They lived there till 1987 when they returned to India. She gave up her job so as to devote herself to looking after her husband and their three-year-old son, Mark. Naiera had saved Rs. 550,000 during her years with Kuwait Airways. Derek made her deposit this money in a joint account in fixed deposit, with himself as co-signatory. Within a few months of the marriage, Derek started beating up Naiera on the slightest pretext, even when she was pregnant. But his cruelty increased after they returned to India. He was now actively encouraged and helped by his brother and cousins, the Ferreiras, prominent builders in Bombay, all of whom shared a house.

As often happens, the attempt to 'adjust' to humiliation and to 'win' the heart of the husband led to even more contempt for her : "But when I became pregnant my husband began battering and tormenting me. He said I had become fat and ugly because of my pregnancy. He wanted me to abort."

She now discovered that her husband had withdrawn all her money from the joint account as well as removed all her jewellery and valuables from her reach. Thus, within a few years of marriage, she was left penniless after having resigned her job to place herself at her husband's disposal. No wonder the cruelties and violence began escalating. "My husband locked me up in a room in the dark after removing the fuse. He beat me. I was not given food, almost starved to death and made to sleep on the cold floor without a blanket mattress or even sheets, even though I was pregnant. He, his brother and relatives dropped rats and insects in the room, after locking me in, so as to frighten me... Their idea was to force me to miscarry. In utter desperation I lodged a complaint with the Santa Cruz police station in suburban Bombay." This angered them even more. Repeated assaults by her husband with groups of his male relatives led to a premature delivery on September 20, 1988. After she left hospital Derek tried to strangle her and threatened to get her gangraped if she insisted on living in the house. On March 15, Derek was arrested after an attack on Naiera and the baby girl, but was in all likelihood released on bail.

Naiera, now with her mother, will probably spend years and years fighting a long-drawn-out legal battle for nothing more than a pitiful demand : that her money and jewellery be returned to her before she is deserted. Her husband, who is working in the firm of his prosperous relatives, will be in a much better position to fight the battle because of his influence.

Betty Rao, in her mid-forties, had been married 23 years and has two grown up sons. Hers was an intercommunity love marriage. Working in Grindlays Bank, Betty earned nearly twice as much as her husband. But throughout their married life, he neither told her how much he earned nor where his earnings went. It was always her salary that was used to run the house. Around 1983, Rao started having an affair with Betty's younger sister, Regini, who was staying with them. Anyone who remonstrated with him, including Betty, was beaten up. He stated that as a man, he had a right to do what he liked.

The house they had built in Janakpuri now became the bone of contention. It had been paid for by Betty but was in Rao's name. Rao claimed the house was his and refused to move out. He and Regini began living on the first floor where Regini opened a nursery school. Betty, her two sons and Rao's mother lived on the ground floor. Rao filed a suit for divorce, accusing Betty of being crazy, and of subjecting him to mental cruelty. Betty is uncertain whether she will be allowed to live in the house she has paid for and equipped because Rao says he has the legal right to throw her out, once they are divorced.

Walking out of a Violent Marriage can be the Difference between Life and Death

It is often assumed that women who are well educated and earning should be better equipped to walk out of violent marriages than uneducated and unemployed women. However, numerous cases testify that the most important determinant in saving a woman's life is whether or not she has the support of her natal family in breaking out of a bad marriage. The cases of Radha and Shakuntala Arora illustrate this clearly.

Radha was married to Krishnaswami in 1974 at the age of 24. She topped to university in B.A Hons. (music) and got a scholarship to continue with an M.A. degree but had to give up her studies and her music because her in-laws were opposed to her being better qualified than her husband. The marriage was arranged on the insistence of Krishnaswami's family who said he had fallen in love with her and would marry no one but her. They said they were not keen on a dowry. Radha's father, who had just spent Rs. 50,000 on this eldest daughter's wedding, spent Rs. 25,000 on Radha's.

Radha says that after marriage, she did everything to please her in-laws. She would get up at 4 a.m. to start work. There were 10 members in the family. She had to prepare breakfast and even packed lunch for the men by 9 a.m. She got no time to eat breakfast because when the men left she had to start cooking for the women. She would eat her first meal at 1.30 p.m. and sometimes felt too tired to eat at all. Immediately after lunch, she would start grinding rice for the men's evening tiffin. The in-laws had a mixer but would not let her use it.

After her father-in-laws retirement, Radha and Krishnaswami were asked to move into a separate place, a tiny hovel of a room with a cupboard-sized kitchen. Here, matters deteriorated rapidly. Krishnaswami began to give most of his salary to his parents. He also began drinking heavily, bringing his friends home, embarrassing Radha who would have to stay in the varandah till late at night. She was also expected to cook for his friends. She again took up a job and ran the house on her salary. Any money she managed to save would be spent by her husband.

Radha had till then tolerated everything quietly because she was afraid that if she walked out it would adversely affect the marriage chances of her two younger sisters. But by 1980 both her sisters were married. After this, she started questioning Krishnaswami and resisting his behaviour. She thought that whatever happened now, the consequences would be faced by her alone. She demanded to know how much he earned, what he did with the money and also objected to his drinking. Krishnaswami would get very angry and beat her up. Temporary peace was brought about only when she apologised. Often, a quarrel saw her being beaten out of the house and she ended up spending the night in the varandah or in her sister's house. She now also got to know of his affairs with other women.

The breaking point came when Krishnaswami (who had refused to let her continue singing because he said his house was not a prostitutes' den) began suggesting that she 'go out' with his friends late at night. Radha protested forcefully. As she said, "I was ready to adjust over everything. For years I danced to his tune. I always said yes to him. When they didn't give me proper clothes or food I didn't complain. But I feel more for my virtue than for money." One day, a major quarrel broke out when Krishnaswami brought home a woman and sat drinking with her leaving their son standing outside hungry, till Radha returned from office. When she protested, he beat her badly and issued an ultimatum : "If you want to stay here, you have to adjust with me. You have to go out with anyone I tell you to, otherwise, get out." So Radha left and went to her parent's place.

When she first came to Manushi Radha was visibly depressed and her father did most of the talking on her behalf. But within the year she was a changed person, glowing and confident. She had resumed her one passion in life-her music. "Now I don't care what people say. My father understands me very well. He says 'Radha, it is your life. You have full right to live for yourself.'

In stark contrast to Radha's story is that of Dr. Shakuntala Arora, lecturer in Hindi at the S.P. Mukherjee College. She died of burns on June 5, 1982. Her colleagues described her 10-year marriage to Subhash Arora, lecturer in Hansraj College, as a "hellish nightmare." At the time of the wedding, Subhash insisted on a scooter as an item in the dowry. When Shakuntala entered her in-laws house, she was asked to pay Rs. 25,000 the amount her in-laws had incurred for the wedding. Though earning a good salary, all she got to keep was a meagre Rs.100. She suffered the brutal neglect and beatings even during her two pregnancies. Just before going to hospital for her second delivery, her husband kicked her in the stomach.

Two days before her death, Shakuntala was beaten up severely and dragged out of the house in front of the neighbours, all because Subhash did not want her to attend a function related to her brother's impending wedding.

It would be simplistic to interpret the violence as resulting from excessive greed. The beatings were part of a larger design to humiliate her, destory her sense of self. The deadly power he could exercise over her life arose not from her economic dependence on him but because her family and social circle could not provide her the assurance that a dignified life without marriage was possible.

Though she was far more educated than Radha and had a much better job, she could no translate her earning capacity into independence, because she got no social support to build an independent life. Even her colleagues woke up to her plight only after she died.

In a Violent Environment, even a Violent Husband is Protection

Jaya works as a domestic servant in a middle class colony in south Delhi. She and her husband came as migrants from a village in Tamil Nadu. She was married at the age of 15 and in the 16 years of her marriage has produced five children. She works in six houses, cleaning floors, utensils, washing clothes and earns about Rs. 450. Her husband earns Rs. 600 as an unskilled labourer with the railway. He spends about Rs.15 a day on himself including bus fare, bidis, tea, snacks and liquor. Jaya spends practically all she earns on providing for the family. She has never bought herself a cup of tea or any snacks in the six years she has been in Delhi. Her earnings are not enough to provide even food for the family of six (her eldest daughter got married recently). She also has to pay off a large debt.

Her husband contributes very erratically to household expenses. Sometimes, he gives Rs.150 or 200, sometimes, nothing; often he takes her money to buy liquor. Like most women in the slum where she lives, Jaya gets beaten regularly. He generally beats her when drunk. Quarrels erupt when she questions him about his earnings and insists that he contribute more to the household. She says she now tries not to question him. If there is no rice in the house, she borrows money on interest. Her husband has destroyed his health by drinking, and now has a liver complaint.

Yet, Jaya is grateful that unlike some other men, her husband doesn't keep another woman, and has not abandoned her. Apparently, the process of adjustment is made easier by the thought that the husband could be far worse. To live alone, without a husband, in a slum is unsafe and unviable. So women like Jaya seem to have little choice but to continue under the 'protection' of a violent husband.

CLEAR BIAS (The law enforcing agencies, too, share society's prejudices in dealing with cases related to battered wives.

Several cases dealt with by us reveal that when maltreated wives approach law enforcing agencies such as the police and the courts, they are confronted with the same societal assumptions regarding a wife's duties and a man's rights, which are built into the present-day family structure. Take the case of Karuna Sharma, in her mid-forties with two teenaged sons. Throughout her 19-year-long marriage she has been violently maltreated by her husband, who is a drunkard and drug addict and constantly loses jobs due to his drinking habit. He often disappears from home, but insists on returning to harass her, and to sell off whatever he can lay his hands on in the house, to buy his drinks. He has sold all her jewellery and at times even sells off the family's clothes. Karuna bore all this for the family honour, but now that her sons are old enough to support her, has decided to resist.

She had taken a job as a school teacher and one of her school-going sons too began to earn while studying. Karuna has not received any protection from the police though she has often sought it. Her son recounted how he was rebuffed when he went to the police station to complain that his father was trying to kill his mother by strangling her. On one occasion, the police said contemptuously: "Catching her by the throat is not a crime. We'll come if and when he actually strangles her." On another occasion, they abused and scolded the son, saying, "Don't you feel ashamed to report your father to the police? Go and look after him, serve him, and get him treated. We'll beat you up if you dare bring him here." They even called Karuna's brother who was helping her, and scolded him, saying, "Don't you feel ashamed to treat your brother-in-law like this? Go and get him treated." In other words, the police saw the man as a victim of his drinking habit, deserving of care, but did not perceive the wife as a victim deserving of redress. To be beaten was seen as a routine part of married life.

At the Crimes Against Women Cell, the police officers were often relieved when a man agreed to "take" his wife back and would put much effort into trying to persuade the wife to go back, no matter how severe the violence to which she had been subjected. One complainant was told, "You should come to a compromise, A man does beat his wife from time to time. It happens." The most telling case was that of Kesro (name changed). Aged 46, mother of four, wife of a jat farmer who owns 11 acres of land on the outskirts of Delhi and according to her, earns several thousand rupees from several sources, she decided to fight back after 30 years of savage maltreatment. Now she has a grown up son to support her. She approached the cell, asking that her husband give her maintenance money or a share in the land on which she has toiled throughout their married life. He has beaten her brutally and never given her any money.

When summoned to the cell, Kesro's husband stated that he was willing to take her back but she would have to live "as all wives and mothers live". The officer saw this as an offer of reconciliation and repeatedly asked her, "Your husband is ready for a settlement. What do you say?" Even though the cell was set up to deal with crimes against women, the officers running it spent far more energy, as per their mandate, on persuading wives to go back to violent husbands, than on protecting women from maltreatment.

Court judgments too, even in cases of wife murder, often betray a similar bias. For example, in a case where a man, Madhavan, had axed his wife Madhavi to death, the court sentenced him to only five years' imprisonment because she was said to have offered "grave provocation" by taking off her mangalsutra in the course of a quarrel, which action the judges considered sufficient to "upset any reasonable man". In another case, 17-year-old girl Teja was forced to marry Chet Ram, who was having illicit relations with her mother. This continued even after their marriage. When Teja angrily refused to have sexual relations with Chet Ram and abused him, saying that he should have sex with his mother sister, the judges considered this "grave and sudden provocation" enough for his having hurled a grindstone at her, killing her instantly.

In 1984, the husband and in-laws of Shani Kaur, whom she had accused in three separate dying declarations (to the chief medical officer, Lohia hospital, to a sub-inspector and to the SDM) of having burnt her to death, were acquitted by additional sessions judge K.B. Andley of Delhi, on the speculative grounds that since Shani was unhappy in her marriage she may have committed suicide and falsely accused her husband and in-laws. Shani's 'unhappiness', in fact, was due to the fact that ever since her marriage two years earlier, she had been mercilessly harassed by her husband and in-laws. On the night of her death, neighbours saw her being dragged into the house by her hair. In her dying statements Shani said that she was not given food that night, was beaten with cooking implements and was prevented from running out of the house. Her husband, mother-in-law and sister-in-law had poured kerosene on her and burnt her.

Giving reasons for his belief that Shani "could not have been murdered", the judge said that since she was fair and the husband Udham Singh was dark he would not "normally" have wanted to kill her but would have "felt Lucky" to have such a wife. Since there was no written evidence of dowry demands having been made, the judge also stated that there was no motive for Udham Singh to kill Shani. The history of violence in the marriage was not seen as linked to the murder. On the contrary, the judge suggested that Shani had a motive for committing suicide since she had wanted to move away from her in-laws, and stay separately with her husband, but her wish was not granted.

The logic of the judgment is that women are silly, easily misled (the judge suggests that the dying Shani may have been influenced by her relatives to falsely implicate her in-laws) and capable of killing themselves on impulse for no particular reason, but men do not kill their wives except perhaps for dowry, so if dowry demands are not proved in writing, murder could not have taken place.

Thanks to anti-dowry campaigns and media publicity given to this issue. The police and the judiciary now consider marital violence legitimate only if dowry demands can be established, if not, they are not prepared to take the woman's allegation of violence seriously.

The Illustrated Weekly of India – September 24, 1989 – p. 11–19

43

Divorce

Marriage is no longer a sacred word and divorce no longer a taboo. Marriages are falling apart at the tiniest cause. With the passage of time a large number of Indians are flooding the Divorce Courts to escape from unhappy marriages and assert their independences. In fact divorce has become the way out and the Shah Bano case has highlighted the rigidities of the society and drawn focus of media and intellectuals on this vital problem of society. As the divorce cases are increasing, the court overflow with quarreling couples. Many cities have had to create special matrimonial dispute courts. Delhi has five additional district and sessions Judges. In Bombay, there was only one sub-judge but today there are three city courts and Ahmedabad has three courts.

In fact divorce has reached to such alarming proportion that the government has set up reconciliation bureaus in the major cities. Inspite of these bureaus, social organisations, psychiatrists; divorce cases are increasing tremendously with alarming pace. In Delhi nearly 25 divorce petition cases are filed everyday. In Bombay cases have more than doubled during the last decade. Punjab and Haryana are not too far behind.

Chandigarh Courts witnessed 147 per cent rise in divorce cases. The number of divorce petition in Trivandrum Magistrates Court made a quantum leap of 328 per cent during the last five years. The number of divorce applications increased more than fourfold in Bhopal district court in the last seven years. Calcutta has also witnessed marginal rise. Even in Madras, the bastion of tradition, there has been an annual increase of 10% in the number of divorces.

Causes of Divorce

Incompatibility in marriage cases, instability between the husband and wife which ultimately results in feuds, dispensions and rising frictions lead to Divorce.

Jack Norman Sr., a lawyer, has listed following causes of divorce:

(1) *Money problem*—money worries trigger all the other problems of marriage.

(2) *Sexual incompatibility*—the husbands are physically unable to satisfy them or are too preoccupied with their jobs.

(3) *Poor health*—The husband gets side jobs and can no longer hold on full time job. The wife has to go to work and for the care of the house. She gets by the evening dead tired.

Rev. John L. Thomas, a Jesuit sociologist has analysed the cases of divorce in mid-west catholic families in America. His statistical analysis therein shows the following reasons for divorce :

Excessive drinking—	30%
Adultery—	25%
Irresponsibility—	12%
Clash of temperaments—	12%

In-laws—	7%
Sexual incompatibility—	5%
Money problems—	1%
Miscellaneous—	1%

Muslim Law

Divorce laws in India, particularly amongst the Muslims are subjected to widespread debate when the famous Shah Bano Begum case was listed for hearing before the Supreme Court. The Supreme Court observed that "This appeal does not involve any question of constitutional importance but that it is not to say that it does not involve any question of importance. Same questions which arise under the ordinary civil and criminal law are of far-reaching significance to a large segment of society which have been traditionally subjected to unjust treatment. Women are one such segment. 'Na stree swatantra mastrati', said Manu the law giver, and it is alleged that the fatal point in Islam is the disregarded women. The appeal before the Supreme Court came out of an application filed by a divorced Muslim for maintenance under Section 125 of the Code of Criminal Procedure and raises a straight forward issue which is of common interest not only to Muslim women but to all those who aspiring to create an equal society of man and woman, bore themselves into the belief that mankind has achieved a remarkable degree of progress in that direction.

The question of common Code arose out of this whether Sec.125 of the Code of Criminal Procedure applies to Muslims or not. Sections 125 (i) (2) clearly lays that a person, who having sufficient means neglects or refrains to maintain his wife who is unable to maintain herself, can be asked by the court to pay a monthly maintenance to her at the rate not exceeding five hundred rupees by Clause (b) of the explanation to Sec.125 (1). Wife includes, a divorced woman who was not re-married. Thus provisions are explicit and admit no doubt. Religion has no place in these provisions. This is a criminal law procedure in order to provide quick remedy to the aggrieved party, irrespective of the religion they belonged.

In Shah Bano case, the Supreme Court went into great details of Islamic Law and provisions of Koran and came to the conclusion that "Their Aiyats have doubt that the Quran imposes an obligation on the Muslim husband to make provision for or to provide maintenance to the divorced wife. The contrary argument does less than justice to the teachings of the Quran. As observed by Mr. Hidayatullah in his introduction to Mullah's Mohammaden law, the Quran is 'Al Furqusars' that is one showing truth from falsehood and right from wrong.

Plight of Muslim Women

The furore over the Supreme Court's recent judgment on the Shariat has once again highlighted the grim plight of Muslim women. Though the judgment ostensibly ushers in a new era for muslim womens' rights, the truth is something different. The message of Supreme Court's judgment is yet to percolate to the messes.

Today many muslim women are unitedly facing the common agony callously cast away by a muslim male exercising his 'religious' privileges to divorce. The women are critical of those aspects of the Shariat or Muslim Personal Law that tend themselves to abuse in the hands of men and which discriminates against women.

The Supreme Court's decision granting alimony to a divorced muslim woman, Shah Bano Begum, celeberates the growing consciousness of womens' rights. There are large pockets where the landmark judgment cannot beam its message of hope, where the much proclaimed legal aid services have yet to penetrate.

Perhaps more insiduous than the rigours of poverty is the lure of obscurantism among the hungry and desolate. There the Shariat becomes an instrument of whim in the hands of callous men. Here the Shariat is involved to bolster fake motivations to buttress the greed for quick money. Here Mohammedan law turns into a legitimate means of female suppression. Here legal redress is a fantasy. House after house harbours broken women who peer out like creatures of the dark, figuscus of male brutalisation, leaving back on ugly memories. Women can be pulled into marriage and adolescence discarded soon after or after years of mind bogging domestic subjugation, stranded penniless. Ever so often the man scamps off with his wife's jewels after setting up a small business with the dowry money she has paid him. These are men who turn the Shariat into an adventure in exploitation, going from one marriage to another or burning adolescent girls with big gulf dreams.[1]

The human dilemma that springs from the distortion of religious sanction has a diabolical dimension. Teenaged girls from poor muslim families and young abandoned wives are particularly vulnerable to predators to the flesh who disguise their intention under the provisions of Muslim Personal Law. Foremost in this class of men are itinerant Arabs sporting fat purses and false promises of marital bliss.

The Elusive Laws and Protracted Legal Proceedings

The first class Magistrate's Court in Calicut is littered with maintenance laws (....) and in most days of the weak women crowd the corridors of the courtroom where their petitions for maintenance are heard. Most of the women are Muslim dressed in their distinctly rural attire are almost all of them belong to the poorer sections of society. Many hold wailing babies on their arms. The scene is atonce tragic and hopeful. Tragic because many of these women have been divorced by their husbands on whims; hopeful because the crowded corridors of the court bear testimony to the burgeoning spirit of emancipation among oppressed muslim women. Indeed awareness has grown to militancy.

The procedural hurdle of securing alimony to itself is a horrowing experience for a muslim divorced. From the moment she files a petition before the Ist Class Judicial Magistrate, the woman faces the perspect of having her quest for justice scuttled at various stages by the husband. Apart from the delays that cripple swift dispension of justice, the award of maintenance by

1. A cry in wilderness – Venu Menon – The Illustrated Weekly of India – September 21, 1985.

the Ist Class Judicial Magistrate can be challenged by the husband at the Sessions Court. The Sessions Court is empowered to stay the earlier verdict. Many cases go up to Supreme Court.

After running his legal marathon from the Ist Class Magistrate's court to the Supreme Court, which takes several years, the women armed with favourable verdict has to approach the Magistrate's court again for the execution of the order.

44

Today's Family

Sooner or later it happens in the best of marriages. Conflict. It may be over money. Lack of conversation. About, which television programme to watch. A Mother-in-law. Sex. Who feeds the dog. Or who can't read the map. Most of our conflicts are minor-something to be laughed at after the initial sharply spoken words.

Our First "Conflict"

According to an American couple : My wife and I now often chuckle at our first conflict. We laugh because what caused it still happens from time to time. It all started just a few weeks after we were married. We were assigned to pastor a growing church in the San Francisco area. We hoped to visit each family during the early months of our ministry. Each day we had visit appointments. We had to use a city map to get around town. My wife was navigator. I was the pilot.

However, my wife was not able to read maps very well, whizzing down a freeway or in rush hour traffic coming off the Bay Bridge. She had to have the map turned exactly the direction we were going. Sometimes she was unable to tell me which exit to take until we had already passed it.

My patience wore thin. "Who taught you to read a map?" I snapped.

She began to cry. "I'm doing the best I can. I just can't read this tiny print. And it's getting dark. If you want to know which exit to take, you need to let me know sooner."

At the time the conflict wasn't very funny. However, we did begin to learn a very valuable lesson–to resolve our conflicts.

Our Successful Outcome

My wife had been hurt. I had not spoken that sharply before. She had to talk it over light then and there. You see, she understood the scripture, "Let not the sun go down upon your wrath" (Eph. 4:26) Or to paraphrase : "Solve your conflict before you go to bed."

Don't let them build over weeks, months or years. If you do, conflict will dominate your marriage-possibly destroy it.

When I realized how I had reacted, I apologized. I was wrong and I admitted it. Fortunately, that set the tone for our marriage. Conflicts would come from time to time. But we have always been able to talk them out. And for the most part, we have each been able to see our faults and go to work on them.

Every once in a while, while we are travelling, we miss a turn on the freeway. My initial reaction still might be to groan but then we both break out laughing. Twenty-eight years and many maps later, we have a very happy marriage.

But in some marriages, conflicts are not minor. They build up over time. Then, like a powder keg, they explode. Often the marriage deteriorates. Unhappiness results. Divorce occurs. Those things shouldn't be. How can you solve the not-so-big and even the giant conflicts that may occur in your life? Here are some helpful pointers.

Discuss It Now

First, try to solve your problems day by day. "Let not the sun go down upon your wrath." That means solve the problem while it is a little one. All relationships are subject to some conflict. Jesus said, "For offenses must come, but woe to that man by whom the offense comes!"[1]

He then showed how to go about solving the problems of offenses. The same principle applies to husbands and wives.

Jesus said, "If your brother sins against you, go and tell him his fault between you and him alone. If he hears you, you have gained your brother (verse 15).

If you practice that principle, you will find almost all your problems will be solved before they really are conflicts.

Be Willing To Forgive

Then Jesus showed one of the most vital Christian principle which is our second point—It's called forgiveness. We all make mistakes. In marriage each partner will make hundreds of mistakes during the years you live together. How often you must forgive each other? "I do not say to you, up to seven times, but upto seventy times seven, "Jesus said (Verse 22).

Please don't start a chart when you first marry. You might find you reach the magic 490 times only after a few years. Then What? Jesus meant there is no end to forgiveness.

The Important Time and Place

Third, it's important you choose the proper time and place to resolve difficulties. We already showed, you should solve your problems quickly-even before you got to bed at night. But choosing the exact time and place to discuss your problems is also important.

---

1. (Matt. 18:7, New King James).

If you have children at home, you should be careful not to have arguments in front of the children. If you wait till too late in the evening, one or both of you will be sleepy. Perhaps in the early evening before dinner would be a good time to take a walk and talk over the present problem.

Some may prefer to wait until after the evening meal. You can then retire privately to the study or bedroom where, away from the children, you can freely discuss what is bothering you. Still others may find a drive in the country or to a nearby park a better way to be able to freely discuss What's on their minds. The point is, agree how, in your relationship, you can best deal with open discussion.

See Your Part In The Problem

Be willing to admit when you are wrong. Most marital conflict is generated by two people. One seldom is all wrong and the other all right. As a marriage counsellor, I could not count the times a troubled person has come to me with, "Why can't my husband see how wrong he is ? "Or," Why can't she do anything right?" I have heard many times, "I did not." "You did, too." "No, I didn't." "Yes you did." "Did." "Didn't too." "Did not."

Conflict resolution begins with each of us personally understanding our individual parts in the conflict. To admit wrong or guilt is one of the hardest things we humans do.

But if you want to have a happy marriage, if you want to solve the problems while they are small ones, you will have to see what part you played in the problem. Why should it be so hard to say, "I'm sorry, honey. I was wrong ?"

Listen To Your Mate

That brings is to the fifth and most important point: Solving problems requires listening to your mate. And I mean LISTEN! Sound easy? It's not. When a couple comes in to counsel, one of the hardest things is to get each of them to listen to the other. Each is anxious to be heard. But to listen? That's the Key.

Until you are willing to listen, you will not be able to define exactly what the problem is. Only when you know what the trouble is will you be able to talk about the solution. If you each listen to the other, more than 90 per cent of the time you'll find the problems will be solved before they are major conflicts.

Learning From The Queen

I read a story that illustrates how to start solving problems. It was about Victoria, Britain's Queen from 1837 to 1901. Victoria and Albert had a happy marriage. But even the Queen had to learn how to solve the everyday problems that arise in any marriage. As the story goes, shortly after they were married, Victoria and Albert had a quarrel. Albert went to his private room and locked the door. The angry Queen followed him, banging the door.

"Who's there?" Albert asked.

"The Queen of England demands to be admitted," Victoria responded. Another banging on the door.

"Who's there?" Albert asked again.

"I said the Queen of England," Victoria snapped.

This continued a time or two more. And still the door remained locked. Finally, a light tapping on the door.

"Who's there?" Albert once again asked.

"Your loving wife, Albert." the Queen responded.

Albert opened the door and they resolved their conflict.

You see, even a queen had to practice the art of conflict resolution. Perhaps she then understood the wisdom of Solomon who observed, "A soft answer turns away wrath, but a harsh word stirs up anger" (Prov. 151, NKJ).

All conflicts can be solved

All conflicts can be resolved in your marriage. Big ones, small ones. What it takes is a little patience. The ability to admit it when you are wrong. A lot of love. Be willing to listen. Be able to forgive. You'll find solving problems is a skillful art you can master. It's just a matter of knowing what to do and how to do it.

Ronald D. Kelly – The Plain Truth.

45

Women and Crime

Women do two third of the world's working hours, receive a tenth of the world's income and own less than a hundredth of the world's property. Men take the decisions and women face the consequences. Thus how unfair has been the world to the fair sex.

With the current spotlight on sex crimes, women honoured in legend and history seem to be passing through traumatic times. During the period of puranas and smritis the woman was much respected and it was considered absurd to condemn a woman if she was over-powered and ravished. The Agni Purana also asserted that a woman was not polluted by forcible assault and conception. Such case was considered as an accidential circumstance and the victim would be readmitted to her previous position after the birth of the child. Atru also holds that unavoidable misfortune ought not to ruin the whole life of a woman.

Contemporary Scene

The prevailing permissiveness eating into the vitals of the Indian Society and, until some immediate and drastic measures and taken, the consequences of sexual crimes against women, particularly rape and abduction, are exceedingly grave and lasting because, for no fault of her, the fate of the victim is doomed for ever. The unfortunate girls remains for the rest of her life a social outcast. Therefore, amongst the flotsam of modern society, sexual offenders require firm handling and harsh punishment. In fact the crux of sexual offences impinges upon social normality and religious beliefs, and the ordinary citizen is tempted to appraise sexual misconduct in accordance with the manner in which is personality confronts him rather than by the measure of its social importance. The old man occasionally ignores the tenets proclaimed by religion and science and establishes his own standard of sexual behaviour.

It is necessary to remind ourselves from time to time that marriage protects women from themselves as well as from men, and raises the status of both sexes in their intimate relationship with one another. Unfortunately most of the sex crimes go unreported. Police finds it difficult to obtain respectable witnesses to accompany them in raids for detecting cases under 'The Immoral Traffic (Prevention) Act, 1956 (New name of Act is the Immoral Traffic (Prevention) Act, 1956 (Act No. 104 of 1956).

Prostitution

In our own times prostitution in mostly a result of economic necessity but environment, intimidation, seduction, enticement, bad company and a desire for an easy life are other factors. Then there are other reasons like early marriage immaturity or marriage with an older person for consideration. Prostitution has now deeply permeated into society from where its eradication is very difficult. In fact, closely linked with this sordid profession are the pimps, brothel keepers and even petty shop owners who may be directly or indirectly involved.

Inspite of the fact, that 'The immoral Traffic (Prevention) Act, 1956' has been in operation for quite some time. The results achieved are negligible. The provisions of the present legislation are no doubt, impractical from the point of view of enforcement, particularly in respect of those hardened anti-social elements who exploit the trading in flesh in innumerable and insidious ways taking advantage of the helplessness and waywardness of the immature girls.

Procurement is instrumental for prostitution because it consists of living on the earnings of prostitution and detaining women in brothels. Any person above the age of fourteen years who permits himself or herself to be so carnally known is a principal perpetrator of the offence. Attempt to commit unnatural offences, including assaults with intend to commit unnatural offences, indecent assaults upon male persons and soliciting for immoral purpose is punishable. Homosecuality is also described as unnatural offence but now it is regarded as a normal method of sexual expression in the west.

Eve-Teasing

Defilement of girls under sixteen years of age also comes under this category. In fact rape is worse than murder because it is a crime against society. This was consensus at a seminar which held that "The definition of rape should be reconsidered in order to afford real protection to the harassed and oppressed women." The law needs to be amended on this score because it treats women as second class citizens.

The other forms of crime against women are adultery, dowry, indecent behaviour, criminal assault and eve-teasing.

Adultery and eve-teasing have become the curse of contemporary society. The menace of eve-teasing is increasing and the Police is becoming increasingly concerned about unmannerly and rude behaviour of young men towards young women. These fuffians hover near girl's schools, colleges, bus stops, cinema houses, bazaars of fairs and festivals. These broadwide romeos make provocative remarks, stare brazenly and jostle against women. The offenders being mostly riffraffs and desperate characters, prudence dictates that even respectable persons who happen to hear or see the ugly incident much to their mental enguish much pretend not to have heard or noticed it and to pass off the place quickly in their own safety. The result is that the offenders indulge in the crime freely and with impunity without any fear of consequence to themselves. Public apathy is also largely responsible for eve-teasing. The specific factors which are responsible for eve-teasing be summed up as turbulence of youth and adolescence, impact of cheap films on impressionable mind, banal influence of romantic novels and sexy pictorial books, lack of parental control and guidance, social biological, physical and psychological.

Preventive Measures

It is proper to protect women from the sexual depredation of misguided adults and sexual pervers. There has lately been an increased Police awareness and concern about the problem of rape. Rape is the only crime which involves a role reversal between the accused and accuser, thereby placing the victim on trial. The victim must prove traumatic forms of victimization in which the subject survives after gruesome ordeal of producting an imperishable amount of evidence. Such preventive measures can be thus formulated like effective legal enforcement, making personal security system, social fight against sexual offenders and role of the press.

The task of making people law abiding is that of the police through strict enforcement of the laws. The Police should make it clear to the young adventurer that culting of indecent jokes or indirect remarks on passing girls, whether it is jostling or getting hold of the girls by their arms, whether it is whistling and humming of cheap song at the sight of girls and whether it is snatching of their exercises books or their dupattas or pinching of the bottoms, all these offences can be dealt with suitably within the ambit of the present laws. In such cases, Police must make it known that arrest can be made promptly u/s 151 I.P.C. Some of the other provisions of the law which deal with indecency in public behaviour are :

(*i*) **Sec. 294 IPC** : However to the annoyance of other does any obscene act in any public place or sings recites or utters any obscene song, balled or words in or near any public place, shall be punished with imprisonment of either description for a term which any extend to three months or with fine or both.

(*ii*) **Sec. 354 IPC** : Whoever assaults or uses criminal forces to any woman, intending to outrage or knowing to be likely that he will thereby outrage her modesty shall be punished with imprisonment or either description for a term which may extend to two years, or with fine or with both.

(*iii*) **Sec. 509 IPC** : This section can be effectively enforced. Whoever intending to insult the modesty of any woman, utters any words, makes any sound or gesture, or exhibits object intending that such gesture or subject, shall be seen by such woman, or intrudes upon the privacy of such shall be punished with simple imprisonment for a term which any extend to one year, or with fine or with both.

As regards some other steps that Police can take are summed up below :

Active Vigilance : The vigilance by the police both in uniform and civilain dress will keep the offenders at boy. Police should protect girls to their impressionable age from being kidnapped, abducted and exploited by taking action u/s 317 IPC.

Prompt Registration : Police must readily register sex offences and promptly investigate so that clues in the form of medical evidence, broken bangles, with clothes ect., may not be lost with the passage of time.

Women Police : In order to make police role more effective women Police has to be developed, the Police women carries out with devotion her duty in the prevention of crime by bringing the criminal to justice and in this, her Police duties merge with welfare work.

Active Law Enforcement : If deterrent punishment is awarded by the course and accused are not acquitted on minor legal flaws, sex offenders will be discouraged. Defence lawyers may be barred from putting awkward and objectionable questions to the victim who out of shame may give contradictory statements.

Adultery

The existing provision u/s 497 of the Indian Penal Code which deals with adultery is outdated and unjust. The law commission in its 42nd report suggested that, besides a man who has an adulterous relationship with the wife of another man without the later's constant or connivance, can be failed for five years, the wife is not punishable. The commission observed that the reasons which weighed with the law commissions in the last century in exempting the wife from punishment were no longer valid and there was hardly any justification for not treating the guilty pair alike. Yet there is another school of thought which believes sexual relationship of two individuals is a private affair between them and it is none of the State's business to poke its nose into it. Individuals can have divorce when a marriage breaks down. The question of guilt and punishment does not simply arise. The concept of punishment for adultery arose from the feudal notion that the wife was a chattel bought by men. But this notion has changed and, therefore Sec. 497 of the Indian Penal Code must be done away with altogether.

"यत्र नार्या पूजयन्ते, तत्र रमयन्ते देवता"।

"Where women are worshipped, Gods take refuge" so say the scriptures. If the measures suggested are persued vigorously with the active, cooperation of the people, then there is no reason that the dignity, honour and modesty of the Indian women will be restored. Time has come when one must act, and act effectively to curb crime against women and give fair sex a far deal.

46

Crime by Women

Women have always been known as perpetrators of crime but unfortunately the number of women arrested in murder cases in India is higher than other countries, while 4.4 per cent of the total arrests of women were for murder and murderous assault as compared to countries like U.S.A., West Germany, Japan, Ireland and Thailand. It was less than one per cent. In fact, the number of women criminals is rapidly increasing in the country-during a four year period the number of women arrested for IPC crimes has gone up by almost 50 per cent and the rate of increase in female criminality is keeping pace with the increase in the male criminality. This has been revealed by a study on. "Criminality of women in India", done by the Bureau of Police Research and Development. The report explains the common assumption that women play a negligible role in crime in the country. The Bureau has called for an urgent need to re-orient policies which have so far been designed largely to deal with the male criminals. The study has been based on comparative figures of arrests from 1971 to 1975 and sample survey of 641 females.

The field in which women criminals operate is not confined to petty crime alone. While more and more persons are being arrested for crimes like dowry and burglary. It is theft which engages the attention of the largest members. More than 20 percent arrests are for the crime which includes shop-lifting, petty pilferages and even pick-pocketting. In this report the women criminals of India show the same trend as in other countries where most women are arrested for thieving, normally attributed to the fact that they have more opportunities than men to come into contact with shopping areas and such other places where thefts are easy to commit. Women are arrested even for rioting, kidnapping, abduction and beggary. Now their involvement in smuggling, white-collar crimes and even terrorism has come to stay as a big poser.

Women in Terrorist Activities

In recent years, in the non-communist countries, female involved in terrorism have shifted from support functions (intelligence couriers or collectors, nurses, doctors, document forgers and safe house-keepers) to active operational roles in murder, arson, robbery, kidnapping, maiming and bombing. According to an study carried out in 1970 by the Sisters International, Alexandria, it came to light that female participation in assassination, kidnapping, hijacking and some of the serious attacks on authority accounted for nearly 12 percent by female offenders. European and Latin American females have highest per centage of women participation. The strangest reason for their participation has been given due to following factors:

(*i*) Involvement of friends or family members.

(*ii*) Desire for revenge resulting from arrest or death of a loved one.

(*iii*) Radical political beliefs.

(*iv*) Desire to dominate others, especially men.

Role of Women in Terrorism

A study of female terrorists, a growing phenomenon was studied by RISKS International Inc., Alexandria. The study revealed that the growing phenomenon of female terrorists in active rather than support roles throughout the world, particularly in non-communist countries. It has come to light that in recent years females involved in terrorism have shifted from supported functions (intelligence couriers or collectors, nurses, doctors, document forgers and safe house-keepers) to active operational roles in murder, arson, robbery, kidnapping, maiming and burglarŷ.

In the year 1970, female participation in assassination, kidnapping, and hijacking was under 12% in 1978, 21%. Europe and Latin America has the highest rates of female participation. Use of women terrorists reflects leaders recognition that women terrorist teams can reduce police suspicion and access to the target and increase the operation chances of success. Data on 204 female terrorists indicates that they are usually young (mean age 25 years), single or divorced, from middle or upper class homes and frequently university trained. The temptation for taking the terrorism has been worked out as :

(*i*) Involvement of friends or family members.

(*ii*) Desire for revenge resulting from arrest or death of a loved one.

(*iii*) Radial political beliefs, and

(*iv*) Desire to dominate others especially men.

Women and Sexism in Drug Abuse

Mr. D.L. Adi Borok, conducted research about women and heroin abuse under the auspicies of R and E. Research Associates, Inc., California. The heroin abuse attitude survey was mailed to 72% subjects, including the Governor and all drug abuse administrator Directors. The result of this study revealed some glaring disparities and social complications.

Studies of female criminality were carried in USSR (former Union of Soviet Socialist Republics) and it came to light as per the researches of the Soviet criminologists that criminality was not simply an abnormal form of behaviour, but rather as a distinct manifestation of an individual's social behaviour. An analysis of some unpublished and some secretly published statistical data about the state of criminality has not been reduced but has increased continually over time. The number of criminals sentenced to prisons and correction labour camps in 1972 alone came to 900,000 persons. The entire population of inmates had reached nearly 3 million in the Mid 1970's. The long term records of crime statistics confirms the existence of historical regularity in the proportion of males to females. Male criminals have always outnumbered their female counterparts but the share of females among all criminals has increased continually alongwith the growing complexity of social life.

Sample survey has revealed that 80% of those serving sentences were housewives and 96% were illiterate. Most of the crimes hover round sex crimes. The study also revealed that 4 out of 10 women convicts were in the age group of 21 to 39 and those held for murder were between the age groups of 36-39.

The involvement of women in crime has also increased. The reasons for this would have to be separately discussed. There was a 92.2% increase in the total number of women apprehended in cognizable (Indian Penal Code) cases from 1966 to 1976. The rise in the number of juvenile girl offenders increased by 77.4% from 1960 to 1970. For the same period there has been a 61.4% rise in the number of women offenders apprehended under the SITA. The number of women convicts rose from 11,000 to 13,471 and that of women undertrial prisoners from 12,158 to 22,220. According to a survey done by a team of doctors from five of the largest hospitals, one woman out of 20 in Bombay in the 13—40 age group is a prostitute.

Sex Roles and Criminality

In the west detailed studies have been carried out to determine female criminality, to determine if any unsupported beliefs and assumptions have influenced the theorizing and research process. Report studies have now shown that female delinquency is not different basically from male delinquency. Statistics on arrests, convictions and incarceration rates for male offenders into United States are summarised. As one self report data from surveys of juveniles and data indicative of the characteristics of female offenders. Those data suggest the following conclusions:

(*i*) Female crime is increasing especially in the larceny/theft category.

(*ii*) The menance is greatest among young females, especially for the most serious crimes.

(*iii*) Despite the increase in number of crimes committed by females, the vast majority of crimes are still committed by males.

(*iv*) Females present on even smaller proportion of the incarcerated, population than their proportion among arrests would suggest.

(*v*) Female juvenile offenders have a greater tendency than males to come from unstable situations and to be described as having emotional problems.

Whom is She Offending?

A study carried out by the Ontario Ministry of the Solicitor General of Canada revealed that the increase in female arrests has been particularly marked for young women under 18 years of age between 1960 and 1975. Arrests of this group increased 253.9 per cent. The reason cannot be solely attributed to challenges to the traditional female role. Even today, juvenile roles can be taken into custody for a wide range of behaviour that are not criminal but rather custody for a wide range violation of parental authority.

The outdated notion of faminity and weaker sex is no more valid, particularly in the West where wide range of crimes are being committed by women and there has been phenomenal increase in female crime.

Criminality Amongst Criminal Tribes Women

Women of Baori and Mangaredi tribes of Madhya Pradesh prefer to give birth to babies in jail. These tribes which traditionally have a criminal record, have a firm belief that a child born in jail becomes a perfect criminal. Before the due delivery date, the women of these tribes commit crimes with the sole intention of being caught and sent to jail. In their bid to stay behind bars for reason of proper food, care and medical coverage they refuse to get themselves bailed out.

Female Criminality

A study of female criminality carried out in French jails in the year 1977 revealed that the overall prison population in France was 851 out of a total prison population of 54,000; 49.01 per cent of the female inmates were serving sentences for offences against property; 32.11 per cent for simple theft; 7.32 per cent for qualified theft; 563 per cent for swindle and confidence trick; 13.8 per cent for sexual offences; 2.8 per cent for pimpering; 13.52 per cent for crimes against children and 13.09 per cent for writing bad cheques.

Enquiries at correctional establishments have revealed that offences on increase are theft, voluntary bodily harm, homicide, forgery and use of forged documents and drug abuse. There are apparently fewer incidents of infantile child beating, corruption of minors and abortion. A total number of 10 percent of the female inmates were illiterate, 81.9 percent had primary education and 8.69 percent had secondary education. Dress makers, cleaners, hospital workers, barmaids and typists were the occupations most representatives of the female inmates. Few trends also points to the incarceration of younger women, with 21 out of 190 prisoners being less than 21 years and 50 between the ages of 21 and 25. It was revealed after thorough investigation that the controlling factors for female criminality appear to be a preposition toward impatience, emotional behaviour and unstable house life, low intellectual level, lack of trade, alchoholism and lack of roots in surroundings.

The enquiry committee recommended that first offenders and drug addicts should be separated from the general prison population and rehabilitation of female offenders should be provided with employment.

According to a study conducted by Ontario Ministry of Solicitor General of Canada, young women suffer from a double standard set by the role of parents patience. The solicitous father figure—which makes certain action illegal for girls and laudable for boys.

The increase in female arrests has been particularly marked for young women under 18 between 1960 and 1975. Arrests for this group increased to 253.9 per cent. Even today, juvenile indulges in violation of parental authority. This is because families have very different expectations of their male and female children.

The Portrait of a Woman Offender

The profile of a woman offender has been described as black, disformed body, black approximately 20 years old, unskilled, under-educated, uninitiated, lonely subject to excessive drug or alchohol abuse, and having a low income. Her most frequent terms are for prostitution and occasionally forgery or burglary. Female offenders are often for disorderly conduct, drunkenness, vagrancy, larceny, drug-abuse, prostitution. Many a times they are in the most fraudulent business, retail thefts and very often homicide usually involving an abusive husband or paramour.

A study of the Bureau of Police Research and development has revealed that the percentage of women arrested for murder is higher in India than in other countries while 4.4 percent of the total arrests of women are for murder and murderous assaults, in countries like West Germany, Japan, Ireland and Thailand, it was less than one percent in India.

In fact the number of women criminals is rapidly increasing in the country-during a four year period the number of women arrested for IPC crimes has gone up by almost 50 per cent and the rate of increase in female criminality is keeping pace with the increase in male criminality. The report has exploded the myth that women play a negligible role in crime in this country has called for an urgent need to orient policies which have so far been designed to deal largely with male criminals. The study has been based on comparative figures of arrests from 1971 to 1975 and a sample survey of 641 female convicts.

The field in which women criminals operate is not confined to petty crimes alone. While more persons are being arrested for crimes like dacoity and burglary, it is theft that engages the attention of the largest numbers. More than 20 per cent arrests are for this crime which includes shop-lifting, petty pilferage and even pick-pocketing. In this respect Indian women criminals show the same trend as in other countries, where most women are arrested for thieving, usually attributed to the fact that they have more opportunities than men and came in contact with shopping areas and other such places where thefts are easy to commit. Rioting, kidnapping, abduction and beggary are other crimes for which they have been arrested. Their involvement in whitecollar crimes and smuggling is increasing.

While Maharashtra reported the highest number of arrests under IPC crimes in the country, the other states lag far behind, most probably because crime by women is still not seriously taken.

The study has further revealed that crime among older women is increasing at a more rapid rate. While the number of female involvement (those below 21) went up by less than 35 per cent, the rise in the above 21 was about 50 per cent. Four out of every 10 women convicts are in the age group of 21 to 39 but it is a much less group of 21 to 39. Those held for murder are mostly in the middle age group of 30—39, but it is a much older group which is responsible for thefts and house-breaking those between 40 and 49.

Marital Crimes

A study of women criminals either convicted or yet not convicted, either serving terms of imprisonment inside the jail has revealed that the crimes committed by women criminals range from petty thefts and shop-lifting to kidnapping and murder. Infanticide, attempted suicide and murder are the three most common offences and then there is prostitution. Most serious crimes committed by women involve men. Rarely their actions are pre-meditated and in most of the cases victims are husbands, next are mother-in-laws. In fact, most of the murders are the result of marital conflict, usually after the women were ill-treated for by their victims.

Most murders occurred in families where there were more than one woman living in the same house, where the husbands and parents were traditionally and uncompromising or in small families where there were relatives to turn to for help. Murder appeared the last resort to women to end an intolerable person, women who knew of no other way to escape their torture.

Acts of infanticide are also acts of desperation, one woman tortured and treated by family members of her husband for not being capable of bearing a child, became so desperate that she killed a child in desperation. Other cases of infanticide which have come to light concern of killing baby girls due to fear of dowry and there are instances where childless women murdered infants for fertility rites.

Most of the women criminals were illiterate and poor, till they left their husbands' houses. In their parents' homes also they had spent a shattered, eventless lives, most even going to school, just growing up, existing obeying their parents' orders without any experience of life's complexities.

Why Women are Driven to Kill?

Women convicted of crime, serving terms from a year to life, having done so we push them out of our minds. Why ? Because they have done wrong they must be punished. Convicted women prisoners' crimes vary form petty thefts and shop-lifting to kidnapping and murder. Infanticide, attempted suicide and murder are the three most common offences. And then there is prostitution. Most serious crimes committed by women involve men. Rarely their actions are pre-meditated, the consequences of much plotting and planning. Most of the women are married. Widows make the next largest group. Almost all the women are uneducated. They are aged between 20 and 40 and belong to rural poor. The victims of murder were almost always the husbands. Next in line of danger were the mother-in-law. Most murders were the result of marital conflict, usually after the women were ill-treated for long by their victims. Violent quarrels in which the women were severely beaten up generally preceded the crime - often in the morning on the day of the crime.

Some murders wear the consequence of the discovery of the illicit relations of the women with other men; the men with whom women had their affairs were usually within the husbands' families—brothers, sons, sisters, husbands. Murder appeared the last resort to women to end an intolerable present, and those secured no other way to escape the torture. A detailed study of these cases was made by Shanaz Anklesoria who has enumerated some remarkable cases listed below:[1]

1. *Statesman*, July 4, 1983

(1) A 13 year old girl married a 31 year old man. She was his third wife and she went to live with him, when she was 14. At her trial for murder, she said that her husband had been cruel and aggressive; her body bore marks of his brutality. One day he had beaten her before leaving for the fields, she killed him with his axe when he was asleep.

(2) Another women was married when she was four years old to a boy of six. She went to his house when she was eight. From childhood to youth was one long process of adjustment as wife and daughter-in-law. Her husband had little time for her, he was busy studying, later she had an affair with a young village patwari who visited her husband frequently and appeared to be the only one to have time to spare for her. He assured her that if she killed her husband he had enough influence to take her away and they would live together. She did. He fled and she received a life sentence.

Why Infanticide?

Quite often, acts of infanticide are also acts of desperation. One woman tortured and teased by members of her husband's family because she could not have a child, murdered one of the children of the family. Another woman, who left her home with her three children after her husband brought another woman to the house and both began maltreating her, in desperation, she pushed the child into a well and jumped herself.

Then there are cases of young widows, victims of constant attack by their husband's families who have tried to kill their children and commit suicide. Other cases of infanticide concern baby girls killed because of the parents fear of having to provide dowry, when they grow up and of childless wives killing children in fertility rites.

Most of these women criminals were illiterate and poor, till they left for their husbands' houses they had spent shattered, eventless lives, not even going to school, just growing up, existing, obeying their parents' orders, without any experience of life's complexities, they found themselves adrift in a strange world, amid strangers with none to protect them. Their criminal actions were the direct consequence of their having been born women and poor.

Trends in Female Criminality

Early theorics of female criminality were examined by J. Pollock, which revealed that the first stage of research on female criminality was the pre-scientific stage, which continued up until the 20th century. The few things written about female criminality during this period concentrated on environmental cases but women were not then seriously taken as criminals. They did not get proper attention from the researchers. The next stage, in the early 20th century, consisted of studies concerned with psychological determinants of crimes and studies done by a group called" The American Statisticians. In the 1930s the third stage considered constitutional and environmental cases and in 1940s. Research tuned to 'number and offences' Statistical studies of crimes and criminals. The fifth stage focussed as women in prison. It has been suggested that research on females taken on the basis of following three theories:

(*a*) Caesane Lombroso whereas exemplified the extreme of pseudosance in studies of woman;

(*b*) W.I. Thomas, who applied a psychological model of crime consistent with the emerging features of the 1920s and 1930s; and

(*c*) Otto Pollock whose study on female criminals in 1950 is probably the most ambitious work was completed on the subject.

The American statisticians were another major influence. The studies of those predominantly female statisticians preceded any serious statistical investigation of male criminality. The reasons for lesser criminality amongst women have been attributed to the factor that women have greater morality and a natural biological and psychological trait. But now feminist criminologists are blasting old myth with new found theories.

New Trends in Criminality

Interaction between womens' emancipation and female criminality—a cross cultural perspective by Frede Adler and Rita James Simon is relevant. In this brilliant creation moments towards socio-politic-economic opportunities for women in the United States and other countries have been noted and co-related with increasing female crime rates in different nations of the world.

Movements for equality for women in countries or widely divergent culture have been characterised by women clamouring for an attaining opportunities in legitimate vocational fields formerly dominent by men having representation is in legitimate fields has also been matched by progressive female involvement in major crime categories which traditionally have been for 'men only'. Between 1960 and 1975, the number of women arrested rose for robbery in the United States by 380 per cent compared to 214 per cent rise for men. Similar differences are found in fraud (up by 465 per cent for women, 11 per cent for men). There has not yet been a comparatively accelerated increase in female arrests for murders and aggravated assaults. Data collected from other nations like Japan, England, Wales, Federal Republic of Germany, Canada, Norway, Brazil and Poland are quoted to show similar trends in female crime. In many cultures undergoing change, adolescence has become a span of psychological lombo fraught with attempts to use role models who themselves are in attention position with technological advances reducing the number of unskilled jobs and cultural changes referring to the female role.

The arrest statistics examined for Americans women indicate that the proportion of women arrested in 1974 was greater than the proportion arrested one or two decades earlier and that the increase has been covered almost entirely by womens' greater participation in larceny, embezzlement and fraud will be commensurate with womens' representations in society in a matter of years. Comparisons of female arrest statistics in the United States has been moved from 12th place in 1963 to 9th place in 1968 and fifth place in 1972. The data collected by internal police organisation for the 25 countries in 1963, 1968, 1970 and 1972 shows that the percentage of women involved in crimes of Asia, Africa and the Carribeans. In fact all over the world United States is the only country which has experienced movement for women' liberation which has experienced women participation in the areas traditionally dominated by men.

Attention is given to the arrest statistics for women in the United States in many respects and Japan because they provide interesting comparison due to social, economic, cultural and other aspects. The fact that during this period there have been both a significant increase by women in the labour force and an increase in property and economic crimes by women seems consistent and participation. The fact that such increase have not occurred in Israel and Japan seems consistent and logical, since women's participation in the labour force has not increased there has not been much support for woman liberation movement.

Women Murderers in India

Most serious crimes are committed by women involve may rarely are their actions premeditated, the consequences of much plotting and planning. Most women are married and widows make the largest. The victims of murder were almost always the husbands, next in line were the mother-in-laws. Most murders were the result of marital conflict, usually after women were ill-treated for long by their victims. Violent quarrels in which the women were seriously beaten up generally preceded the crime - often in the morning on the day of the crime.

A study by the 'Bureau of Police Research and Development' has revealed that the percentage of women arrested for murder is higher in India than in other countries.

While 4.4 per cent of the total arrests of women were for murder and murderous assaults in countries like U.S.A., West Germany, Japan, Ireland and Thailand, it has been less than one per cent. In fact, the number of women criminals is rapidly increasing in the country during a four year period the members of women arrested for IPC crimes has gone up by about 50 per cent and the state of increase in female criminality is keeping pace with the increase in male criminality. The report has exploded the myth that women play a negligible role in crime in this country, has called for an urgent need to orient policies which have so far been designed to deal largely with male criminals. The study from 1971 to 1975 and a sample survey of 641 female convicts.

The field in which women criminals operate is not confined to petty crime alone while more persons are being arrested for crimes like dacoity and burglary; it is theft which engages the attention of the largest numbers. More than 20 per cent of arrests are for this crime, which includes shop lifting, petty pilferage and even pick-pocketing. In this respect, Indian women criminals show the same kind as in other countries where most women are arrested for thieving— usually attribute to the fact that they have more opportunities, than men to come into contact with shopping areas and other such places where thefts are easy to commit. Rioting, kidnapping, abduction and beggery or other crimes for which they have been arrested. Their involvement in white collar crime and smuggling is increasing.

While Maharashtra reported the highest numbers of arrests under IPC crimes in the country, the other states lay far behind, not probably because crime by women is not still seriously taken. The study has further revealed that crime among older women is increasing at a more rapid rate. While the number of female criminality (those below 21) went up by less than 35 percent, the rise in the above, 21 was about 50 percent. Four out of every 10 women convicts are in the age groups of 21 to 39. Those held for murder are mostly in the middle age group of 30–39 but it is a much older group which is responsible for thefts and house-breaking—those between 40 and 49.

Women criminals either convicted or yet not convicted, either serving term of imprisonment inside the jail. The crimes committed by women criminals range from petty theft and shop-lifting to kidnapping and murder, infanticide, attempted suicide and murder are the three most common offences and then there is prostitution.

Most serious crimes committed by women involve men. Rarely their actions are pre-meditated and in the most of the cases victims are husbands, next are mother-in-laws. In fact, most of the murders are the result of marital conflict, usually after the women were ill-treated for long by their victims.

Most murders occurred in families where there were more than one woman living in the same house, where the husbands, parents, were traditional and unimpromising or in such families where there were relations to him/her for help. Murder is the last resort to women to end an intolerable person, women who knew of no other way to escape their torture.

Acts of infanticide are also acts of desperation. One woman tortured and teased by members of her husbands family because she could not have a child, murdered one of the children of the family. Other case of infanticide concern baby girls killed because of the parents fear of having to provide the dowry when grown up and of childless issues killing children, in fertility rites.

Although most of the women criminals were illiterate and poor, till they left for their husbands' homes, they had spent shattered, eventless lives, not even going to school, just growing up, existing obeying their parents orders, without any experience of life complexities.

Women and Prostitution

Prostitution is an age old profession the custom of devadasi is well known in Sanskrit literature and as harlot or prostitute in European literature.

Prostitution as practiced and profession was banned through SITA - Suppression of Illegal Traffic in Women Act. Although prostitution has been banned legally but clandestine prostitution has spread manifold. Prostitutes continue to function under the cover of music, dance and entertainment houses are run by gharvalis, pimps, dadas and quite often corrupt policemen who receive haftas.

Surprisingly, today new voices are being raised to regularise and recognise prostitution as a professional trade in flesh.

Prostitution as Profession

The law upholds the double standard of sexual morality the most dramatic example is the law on prostitution. This is contained in the Suppression of Immoral Traffic in Women and Girls Act, 1956 (SITA). The Act does not seek to have prostitution as such. It forbids trafficking in girls and women. Living off the earning of a prostitute and disown prostitution near public places. The Act also makes provision for setting of protective houses for women rescued from brothels. Such girls are locked away in government run Nari Niketans all over the country. These girls are mostly victims of rape, or were sold into prostitution by family members and some runaway from the houses and poverty of their homes. In the Nari Niketans, they are herded together and are abused and humiliated.

Unfortunately, the law invariably regards the women victims the guilty party and punishes her. There is no provision for punishing the male partner. However, the Sixty Fourth Law Commission report deals with this vital question. But the burning question yet to be examined remains:

(*i*) What happens to the men who raped the women?

(*ii*) Or, the person who sold her?

(*iii*) The person who seduced her with false promises and used-abused her.

Adultery

Another crime closely linked with female immorality is adultery which is today regarded as a private affair by mutual arrangement on voluntary consent basis and it is nobody's business to poke its nose into it. Individuals can naturally arrange for extra-marital relationship or in the matter or disengagement can have divorce when a marriage breaks down, as in England. The question of guilt and punishment does not simply arise. The concept of punishment for adultery arose from the feudal notion that the wife was a chattel brought by men. But this notion has changed and, therefore, Sec. 497 of the Indian Penal Code be done away altogether.

Child Abuse

The cases of child abuse by women are normally due to family discord, insufficient income, lack of tolerance, continuous child care duties, lack of control and self-discipline, inadequate housing, mental health problem, alchoholism, social isolation, physical abuse of spouse, history of being a subject of abuse in childhood and a subject of authoritarian discipline.

Whom is She Offending?

A study carried by the Ontario Ministry of Solicitor-General of Canada revealed that the increase in female arrests has been particularly marked for young women under 18 between 1960 and 1975. Arrests in this group increased 253.9 per cent. The reason cannot be solely attributed to the traditional female role. Even today, juvenile roles can be taken into custody for a wide range of behaviour that are not criminal but rather custody for a wide range of behaviour that are not criminal but rather violation of parental authority.

The outdated notion of feminity are no more valid, particularly in the west where there has been phenomenal increase in the rate of crime by women. In this respect varied stands have been made in the United States of America.

Future Perspectives of Crime and Women

A study carried out by Maxwell House, New York has forecasted future trends in female crime, "Women will likely continue to marry, raise children and work outside the home. The distinctions between men's and women's spaces will disappear as women are employed in previously male-dominated occupations and men take more responsibility for home maintenance. The opportunities for women to engage in certain type of crime should increase and more women will be arrested for the category of crimes generally labelled confining, domestic circumstances for females that tend to foster aggression and hostility. In addition child abuse by women will gradually decline with the wide dissemination of birth control information and the increase in supportive services. The number of women arrested for prostitution and related offences will gradually decline as women are able to obtain better paying and more socially acceptable jobs and the number of female juveniles adjudicated delinquents will decrease as more young women have economic and status opportunities opened to them."

Demystification of Law for Women-by Nandita Haksar, Lancer Press-Post Box No. 3802, New Delhi-110049.

47

Women Crime and Punishment

Statistics show that proportion of women in crimes in 1974 was greater than at any time since World War II, however, the increase has been in certain type of offences, including forgery, fraud, and embezzlement. Crimes of violence and traditional female crime of prostitution and child abuse have not increased. If this trend continues, in 20 years, women will be involved in white collar crimes in proportion with their representatives in society *vis-a-vis* women. The fact that female arrests have increased for the aforementioned offences in consistent with the opportunity theory of crime pattern, which has the increased employment of women in the market place as an expanded opportunity for female crime in that area. In a joint study carried out by Freda Adler and Rita James Simore-interviews were conducted recently with 30 agencies in four large cities in the midcrest, asking them to describe their experience with female offenders in terms of types of offences, offender characteristics and any variation between the conviction and sentencing men and women.

Explanation of murders committed by women generally have been simplistic reflections of stereotypes views. The women who murder is portrayed as fascinating and mysterious in the sexist accounts that faces almost entirely, on sexuality as the root of all female behaviour. Sexist explanations also over emphasize the deviant character of murder by women convict, substantially fewer murders than man is understandable in cultural terms. Females are socialized to be less aggressive, are more closely surprised, and more strictly taught to conform to rigid standards. Women traditionally have spent a great deal of time at home and other interactions have been confined to family members. Another 'fact' about women who murder-that they are more disturbed than their male counterparts-is open to question. One useful approach to understanding murder by women is an exploration of psycodynamic pattern such as that undertaken in a California study identified six personality styles-masochists, overtly hostile, covertly hostile, psychotic, ansoral and inadequate -in women who murder. The rise of feminism is bringing greater depth to the study of women murder.

Treatment of Women Convicts in the Courts

Treatment of women by the courts appear to be less lenient than early studies indicated. If the activity is violent, the court seems likely to respond harshly, particularly if the women cannot provide other evidence of confirmation to the standards of womanhood.

A review of the judicial responses to female misbehaviour suggests that while police may be arresting more young women for criminal misconduct, these women tend not to remain in the system unless their misbehaviour is defined by parents or court officials as part of a larger pattern of defying parental authority. Women who violate the adolescent sex role requiring obedience to their authority are seen by court officials as more serious offenders than their counterparts who have actively committed crimes, consequently while some young women are accorded chivalrous treatment in the juvenile system, the evidence indicates that it is the young women charged with crimes who are beneficiaries of the positive side of paternalism. The evidence also shows that young women who present the possibility of becoming sexual delinquents receive harsher treatment than young women suspected of crimes. Young women accused of violating parental authority and sexual norms also are harshly censured than young males charged with these offences.

However, it has been observed by the Womens' Liberation Organisation that the courts' role in enforcing parental authority and adolescent morality results in a process of differential perception that constitutes sex determination in two ways—

(1) The court is clearly applying the law in an unequal manner; and

(2) The court is punishing the non-criminal behaviour of females as harshly as criminal behaviours of males.

Crime and Punishment of Women Criminals

We deal with women criminals in the same way as with any other criminals, anywhere in the world. Most of these women are not of criminal inclination we must remember that they do have personality aberration which need to be examined and treated. Instead, we put them in jail. And jail is where again, by virtue of this sex, they are exploited and tortured. Most women are kept in separate wards in mens' jails, the keys of which are held by the jail staff. Consequently they are exposed and damned.

The Mulla committee made in depth study of the jail conditions and the law on punishment. According to Justice Mulla, Section 302 of the Indian Penal Code and the recent insertion of Section 433 A of the Code of Criminal Procedure need reform. By fixing a minimum period of imprisonment for 14 years for crimes committed under Section 302 of the IPC, the legislation is locking and sealing the door of rehabilitation' for every person sentenced to life imprisonment. After spending all these years within a brutal jail atmosphere the women who did not enter the jail as a criminal but as a simple villager, emerges dehumanised. 'Under the present law, a lesser sentence cannot be imposed, says Mr. Justice Mulla, although there may be any number of extenuating circumstances to have provoked the crime. The reason for murder, points out Mr. Justice Mulla, range from the most atrocious to the most excusable. He has extensively given examples and quoted from the legal systems of different countries where, if a judge can find extenuating circumstances, he can reduce the term of imprisonment. Speaking about Indian judiciary, Mr. Justice Mulla says, "It is not able to leave the rut of tradition."

It still believes in vengeance, retribution and deterrance as the main purpose of punishment. Whereas, under Sec. 235 (2) of the C.P.C. indication that the legislation clearly wants the judiciary, while awarding punishment, to first assess the gravity of the crime before determining the punishment. This is of particular significance in case of women offenders.

Punishment of Women Criminals

Mr. R. Short in his book 'Case of long term Prisoners' has suggested out that punitive treatment is counter-productive to rehabilitate and also does not present prison violence. The book deals at length with the conditions of women in American prisons where due to frustration of sexual deprivation and the resulting pervasiveness of prison homo-sexuality and the alternative of conjugal visits.

Problem of Keeping Women in Jail

And jail is where again, by visitors of their sex, they are exploited and tortured. Most women are kept in separate wards in mens' jails, the key of which are held by the jail staff. The A.N. Mulla Committee on Jail Reform that examined Indian Jails from 1930 to 1982 regretted that in the entire country there were only six institutions for the treatment and rehabilitation of convicted women prisoners, in each state a recommendation that was ignored. The Mulla Commission found the living conditions worn. The women themselves felt too dejected to write even their own petitions. Nobody wanted them back.

According to the report of the Commission, strangely, none of the women knew of the existence of jails or that crimes like theirs were punishable under the law. Such was the extent of their ignorance. Social workers state that they have said that they would have acted the way they did if they had any idea of the punishment in store for them.

The Mulla Commission has gone beyond recommending jail reforms. In a little known preface to the report, Mr. Justice Mulla has raised fundamental question about what Indian Society means by the term "Punishment". According to Justice Mulla, Sec. 302 of the Indian Penal Code and the recent Section 433-A of the Code of criminal procedure need reform by fixing a minimum period of imprisonment for 14 years under Section 432-A of the C.P.C. for crimes committed - under Section 302 of the IPC, the legislation is 'locking and sealing the door of rehabilitation'. For every person sentenced to life imprisonment, after spending all these years within a brutal jail atmosphere the man, who did not enter the jail as a criminal but as a simple villager emerges as a determined criminal. Under the present laws a lesser sentence cannot be imposed', says Justice Mulla, although there may be any number of extenuating circumstances to have provoked the crime. The reasons for this, warns Justice Mulla, range from the most excusable. If a judge can find extenuating circumstances, he can reduce the terms of imprisonment.

The judiciary, Mr. Mulla says, still believes in the old norms of punishment. If not able to learn the rut of tradition. It still believes in vengeance. Retribution and deterrance is the main purpose of punishment. Section 235 (2) of the C.P.C. indicates that the legislation clearly wants the judiciary, while awarding punishment, to first assess gravity of crime before determining the punishment. In the case of women offenders, this is of a particular importance. In his crudite 'Prefacc' of the recommendations of the Commission he questions the whole line of thinking which holds that brutality and terror are deterrants to crime. Those who believe in deterrent sentences forget, he says, that punishment can only be of some effect. On premeditated crime not on impulsive acts. And brutality and terror make reformation impossible.

Today, there is an increasing demand for the appointment of women judges.

Women Convicts

The sample survey of women convicts carried out in jails in Delhi, Mathura, Kanpur, Fatehgarh, Allahabad revealed that more than 55 per cent of them came from urban areas and interestingly more than 86 per cent were housewives. In fact, the study concluded that married women commit more crimes than unmarried ones and more than 96 per cent of those serving sentences are illiterate. Twenty six case studies of those who were serving life sentences showed that women who commit murder or largely from joint families, uneducated and were often there for killing a member of their family, sometimes their own children.

The treatment inside jails and the facilities thereof seem to emphasize perceived sex roles with such common procedure or forced internal examination of all girls at the time of entry.

Steps towards Reformation of Female Offenders

Female offenders have traditionally been forgotton and their problems have remained subject to neglect by the criminologists, lawyers, penologists and social scientists. The female offender has more disadvantageous economic standing than women in general. Their average educational level (10th grade) is lower. In fact, women offenders are economically dependent on men economic, moral and public support and whoever crimes are done by the woman, are done for or with those men.

Vocational programmes are taken in America and other European countries for the benefit of female offenders but in India we still lag far behind. In America good work is being done by womens' community centres which is a private, non-profit, community cased residential programme designed as an alternative to incarceration for adult female felony offenders for offences committed by them.

Steps towards reformation have been taken by Womens' Community Centre (WCC) of Seattle, Washington. A community-based alternative to incarceration for adult female felous. The WCC began operation in 1975 with a grant from National Institute of Law Enforcement and Criminal Justice, Washington and the State Department of Social and Health Services. The goal of the WCC is to provide residents with the tools for making the changed they could effect with themselves by self-therapy positive self-images and by acquiring social and marketable skills for the purpose of functioning productivity in the community. The programme is premiered on the assumption that community-based corrections are more humane, less costly and more effective in decreasing recidivious than in traditional incarceration.

Behavioural Pattern of Women Prisoners Released on Bail

In the last few years, the National Counsel on crime and delinquency centre at Davis, California has published an annual newsletter in which parole out comes for the country as a whole are reported. Parole outcomes for men and women are shown by the type of offence for which they were committed, their history of dry and alchohol use and their prior prison sentences. Preferential treatment for women does not appear to be a significant factor at the parole hearing stage. Men who were convicted of homicide, forgery and fraud and violation of narcotic drug laws were less likely to be paroled than were women connected of these offences. The percentage of parolees who maintained a successful parole for one year, by type of offence for which they were originally committed is shown within most offence categories, except for violations of dry law. A higher proportion of the women are continued on parole after one year than are the men. In forgery and fraud convictions paroled women were more successful in staying out of prison than men and in doing violations they were less successful.

Juvenile Delinquents — Self Mutilation in Adolescent Female Offenders

Canadian Journal for criminology has reported a study carried out by the Canadian Association for the Prevention of Crime in which Adolescent residents, ages 12 to 17 of a training school for female offenders were studied to document the extent of and motivation for self-mutilation in the form of coverings on the face, arms, legs, breasts and stomach. At the time of study there were 136 girls in the institution 117 of the (86 per cent) had carved themselves at breast, arm during their stay. Although one third of the girls reported having heard of carving before admission, hence had carved prior to their institution closed. The subjects classified their initial feelings towards carving as good, neutral or stupid. Over 80 per cent reported that when first hearing of carving they thought it a stupid thing to do but subsequently changed their minds due to group motivation and frustration. Quite often they resorted to tattooing also.

In order to improve the condition of juvenile female delinquents voluntary organisations have been motivated to develop one to one relationship between adult volunteers and young delinquent girls. The programme arises to serve the female juveniles who have already had contact with the criminal justice system and delivers supportive services directed at rehabilitation and social adjustment. The programme seeks to increase resources available for dealing with female juveniles, since rehabilitation resources are largely concentrated on the needs of males. Group activities including counselling, intensive tutoring, recreation, house-making cultural programmes and conversation sessions aid at improving self-awareness and life styles. Supportive family services are provided and planned house type activities are offered.

48

Handling of Women Criminals

The piquant situation in which the police finds itself has been best described by Shri N.S. Saksena in these words, "Few things arouse so much anger against the police as illtreatment of women and the news, true or false, that the modesty of women has been outraged. It is rarely treated as the misconduct of individual policeman. Anti-social elements and political forces opposed to the government find a readymade issue to launch an agitation. All the good work done patiently over a long period of time by a police unit is wiped out in one single day."

The unfortunate part of the story is that criminal elements know how vulnerable the police are on this score and often make elaborate plans and subsequent arrangements to carry on their anti-social activities by using alleged police atrocities on women as a pretext. Often heavy weather is made of the little bit of horse play. This fact can best be illustrated from the incident of November 2, 1959 of Kanpur which is better known as "Shantia Kand" where it was alleged that a village woman was raped by a Head Constable Soon wild rumours spread round Clutterbuckganj police station and in the chain of events the police opened fire and the toll was 17 dead and 50 injured. This was the price which police had to pay !

In order to safeguard the dignity and honour of women, the Central Government has issued guidelines to the State Government and Union Territories on steps to be taken to prevent the police from misbehaving with women or subjecting them to indignity. The State and Union Territory governments have been directed to abstain from arresting women and if arrest is warranted, no women should be arrested between sunset and sunrise. And in case the arrest is warranted late at night, reasons must be recorded in writing and permission of the next senior officer must be obtained. The State governments have also been asked to enforce safeguards promised in the Criminal Procedure Code and in the State Police Manuals.

In some states only police officers above the rank of assistant Sub-inspector or above are empowered to arrest women and also to report all such arrests to the sub-additional police officers or district Superintendent of Police. Moreover in bailable cases bail should be granted 'without delay.' If the offence is non-bailable, the arrested woman should be released on bail or remanded to judicial custody with utmost expedient. While being escorted to the jail a male relative should be permitted to accompany the escort party and where a woman has to be detained in police custody she should be kept in female lock-up. Where there is no separate lock-up for women, she should be kept in a separate room.

The cases where a woman is to be examined as a witness, she should not be ordinarily summoned to a police-station and in such cases women police should be utilised, whenever available and in cases of complaint enquiry by a magistrate be made.

In cases involving female criminals, the police must keep in mind the following guidelines :

(*i*) Women police should be employed as far as possible and the concerned women should be sent to Nari-Niketan or orphanage, whatever is available.

(*ii*) Only police officers of the rank of Asstt. Sub-Inspectors or above, preferably women police officers should arrest female offenders.

(*iii*) While being escorted to jail, a male relative should be permitted to accompany the escort party.

(*iv*) If women police was not available some male or female relative of the arrested woman should be permitted to stay in the police station.

(*v*) Whenever a woman witness is to be examined, she should not be summoned to the police station, instead the investigating officer should go to her house.

A review of research on the treatment of young women by police suggests that police traditionally have ignored much of the criminal conduct of young women, particularly if the young women behaved in a stereotypically female manner (e.g. crying) when apprehended.

Handling of Women Criminals

Mr. R. Short in his book "Care of long term prisoners has pointed out that punitive treatment is counter productive to rehabilitation and does not permit prison violence. The book deals at length with the condition of women in American prisons where due to frustration of sexual deprivation and the resulting pervasiveness of prison homosexuality and the alternative of conjugal visits.

Central government and State Governments have issued guidelines to the police personnel for dealing with crimes concerning women and holding of women criminals, some of which are as follow:

(*i*) Only police officers of the rank of Asstt. Sub-Inspectors or above, preferably women police officers should arrest offenders.

(*ii*) While having escorted to jail, a male relative should be permitted to accompany the escort party.

(*iii*) Where a woman has to be detained in police custody she should be kept in the female lock up.

(*iv*) If woman police was not available some male or female relative of the arrested woman should be permitted to stay in the police station.

(*v*) Whenever a woman witness is to be examined.

Woman Police to Handle Woman Convicts

In an attempt to further protect women from being exploited the law requires that women be exorted, recorded and otherwise handled by women police. If she has to be taken to a police station for questioning, she must be accompanied by a policewoman. If she must be kept in police custody for a night, there must be women police on guard duty.

Woman make up 0.4 % of the police force in the country, a total of 3,000 in the entire country. In Delhi there are 179 women in force of 17,709 people; West Bengal has 117 women in a force of 39,289 and Tamilnadu has 814 in a force of 41,000.

Police Women being a touch of honesty to a service that is labelled as "Corrupt" Women would hesitate to bribe a police woman.

49

Women in Jails

India's Constitution is a value-loaded document. It guarantees equality of sexes, but somewhere on the way to implementation, the guarantees get lost. The IPC, which is the most important penal legislation in the country, says that "no woman shall be summoned to police station". Only in the rarest of rare cases should a woman be remanded to police custody. And in that rare case, too, the reason for remand should be recorded by the judicial magistrate.

Yet women are taken into custody, summoned to the police station and detained in the most flimsy grounds. Sometimes they are kept in informal custody, which is still worse because all sorts of illegal things happen when she is in the information custody. Sometimes such cases are not correctly entered or the entries are tampered with. And when friends and relatives seek redress through habeas corpus petitions, their efforts are foiled by institutional conspiracy and cleverness.

The system, however, is heavily balanced against the woman in custoday, whether under the police or in prison. The long history of prison reform has failed to alleviate their sufferings. In 1836, Loard Macaulay first set up a committee to go into prison reforms. The resultant commission of enquiry into jail management and discipline of 1864 recommended that women prisoners should be kept separate from men prisoners.

The Indian jails committee of 1919 again laid stress on segregation of woman prisoners from men. It stated categorically that the object of imprisonment is not to isolate the offender from society, but to make efforts to reform and rehabilitate the offender so that he or she can be absorbed into society on release. Unfortunately, when it comes to the rights of women even the most progressive legislation encounters lukewarm support or non-implementation.

The situation of women in custody has been a matter of great concern to the women's department of the human resource development ministry. It set up in 1986, a national expert committee on women prisoners under the chairmanship of Justice V. Krishna Iyer, retired judge of the Supreme Court. The committee was asked to study the handling of women detenus and to review conditions of their treatment, to examine the efficacy of services for the rehabilitation of women, and to suggest measures to ensure fair and proper care of women offenders.

According to the committee's report women in custody are a tragic testimony to judicial futility. Women languish in asylums because there is no one to take them back even when they are cured. Wards are overcrowded and filthy. There are no beds, not even pillows. No medical care is provided to restore them to normalcy.

Garibi Hatao

The life of begger women is worse. When the government fights and wins election on the slogan of *Garibi hatao* (remove poverty) it appears ironical that punishment is given for being poor and vagrant. Women who are beaten up in their homes and thrown out take to begging on the streets. It is convenient for the government to push them out of sight and lock them up in asylums because of its own failure.

The anti-beggary law is a convenient tool, especially when dignitories come visiting and a clean look is to be given to the city. The poor women cannot defend themselves because they do not have the means or the knowledge and are, therefore, kept in custody indefinitely. Loopholes in the law give the police the freedom to detain women, allegedly for interrogation. Hundreds of girls are kept in lock-ups to languish for years. And nobody knows what happens to them ultimately.

The need for separate prison accommodation for women inmates has been stressed repeatedly, yet indifference is evident in implementation. There are approximately 4,000 women prisoners in India. The approximately 1,195 prisoners are just about enough to accommodate 180,521 inmates. As against this, there are only six institutions for women prisoners with a santioned capacity of 975. It is evident that besides the few who can be housed in separate prisons, the others continue to be housed in wings where male prisoners are kept. Apart from this, the existing institutions are old and shabby. Many of them were built nearly a 100 years ago.

About 44,000 women are arrested every year under the IPC. This does not include arrests under local and special laws. India has a total of 9,870 police stations though only a few are for women. There is no woman IG of prisons anywhere in India and in most jails, women superintendents report to and are supervised by men.

The national expert committee on women prisoners in its report has recommended that a major project 'Destination deliverance of womanhood from indignity' has to be initiated to induct more women into the system to bring about better gender sensitive training for the staff, to have new building in the form of cottages of hostels, give more freedom and introduce useful crafts so that on release they become self-reliance persons.

Under Article 51, India is bound to respect international laws as we are signitories to the Universal Declaration of Human Rights and its consequent covenants which bind us to the elimination of discrimination against women and maintain international standards of prisoners' rights. It is binding for us to provide a custodial fair deal to women. Para-legal aid should be made accessible to women prisoners and separate police stations with well-trained women police officers empowered to investigate, should be set up immediately. Men in uniform should not be allowed inside women's lock-ups.

The committee, in making its recommendations, has relied on information obtained through visits by its members. It was observed that there was no segregation of different categories of prisoners. Therefore, it recommended that "custodial facilities should be set up separately for convicted and undertrial women". Just because women prisoners are less in number, it cannot to justified as a limiting factor for providing suitable custodial conditions for women. As it is, the existing malpractices in various forms of custody tend to be prejudicial to women.

The national expert committee has made its recommendations fully realising that the subject of prison reform is a state subject and the different states may react differently. However, gender justice cannot be sacrificed to individual whims. Therefore, there is a strong need for a national policy on custodial justice to women.

Since no policy is effective unless it has an enforcing mechanism, the committee has recommended the creation of a statutory autonomous body to be designated as the national authority on custodial justice to women. This authority should have representatives of the criminal judicial system, voluntary agencies, media, medicine and so on to be presided over by a "distinguished personality" who will be selected solely on merit and commitment.

The key function of this body will be to assist in maintaining a high standard of professional competence. This boby will also be responsible for the compilation of an annual state report which will be in the nature of a critical assessment of the quantitative and qualitative parameters of the status of women and girls in custody.

The committee has also made similar recommendations on the legislative side, particularly the setting up of mobile judicial camps as an immediate modality for rendering speedy justice to women in custody. The list of recommendations is long and impressive but so is the history of the long reform movement which started by Lord Macaulay's first attempt in 1836. But it remains to be seen whether the committee's eye-opening observations and landmark recommendations will succeed in shaking the government out of its lethargy.[1]

Women just Locked Away

In Indian jails women prisoners need not be offenders. A love-sick-runaway, a female witness, a neurotic housewife, a homeless teenager or a victim of atrocity-all these women are being locked away in prisons because under our custodial system the line between a female victim and offender is often blurred.

These findings are just one of the many startling facts revealed in the Report of National Expert Committee on Women Prisoners. The first Government document which has in exhaustive detail investigated the state of female prisoners. Mooted by the Ministry of Human Resources Development, in 1986, the study was entrusted to a committee under Justice Krishna Iyer. Within one year the group of eight produced a keenly researched document on custodial and state reform institutions making a fundamental statement—hunderds of women in custody languish in total deprivation of their basic human rights.

1. AGENDA, *The Times of India*, New Delhi — May 1, 1988 P-3.

Lock-ups Worst Equipped

The cases mentioned are few but stark. Police lock-ups (PLUs) were found to be the worst equipped to safeguard inmate and very rarely had the mandatory segregated cells for women. The report notes : "In many cases it was only after a female inmate had been raped in custody that the police station decided to send women to separate stations staffed fully by women".

One-sixth of the unconvicted prisoners are non-criminal lunatics (NICs) who under the Indian Lunacy Act 1912 can be held in jail "for their own protection". A committee member who visited Calcutta Presidency Jail found that out of the 35 women prisoners 170 were NLCs. "But most of these women were just depressed or nervous and needed medical care. Instead locked away by their families who do not want them back, they are languishing among prisoners," she said.

In the eastern states NLCs were found to be very high and are the most vulnerable group since their release depends on the whim of their families and state authorities rather than the judicial process. In homes for the 'retarded' even when girls were proven to be normal, the researchers found that the visiting psychiatrist through callousness, apathy or obligation to the authorities continued to diagnose them as "retarded."

Corrupt System

Women who were aware of their rights found their access limited by a brutal and corrupt system. A female convict said that she did not attend her young son's funeral because when she had applied for parole to visit him in hospital the warden had demanded money.

The Calcutta jail is a bizarre collection of female inmates whose imprisonment has no legal definition. "Love cases" is the word coined to incarcerate young teenage girls whose fathers have complained that they "want to run away with boys". Held as minors the detention itself violates the Indian Penal Code but freedom for these girls too depends on the will of the authorities and the parents. The members noted that boys were never arrested under "love cases".

Juvenile girls are routinely arrested, usually for theft. The report notes that 8,700 girls are imprisoned for cognizable crimes. But in most states the requisite reform homes do not exist so that young girls are locked away with criminals, other destitute and homeless girls.

Illegal Custody Extension

Their custody is unlawfully extended often because the state cannot provide a simple escort service. "Hundreds of children and women languish in jails because the state does not have a proper service and will not recruit a voluntary agency for the job. Imagine that girls are in prison because their safe journey home connot be ensures, "says Ms C.P. Sojaya, joint secretary and committee member.

And then there are those that are simply held in custody as "hostages to compel the men in their families to confess or submit to the authorities." The report also cites a High Court Judgement which notes, "Quite a few women were held in jails without ever being accused of any offence merely because they happened to be victims of an offence or were required to give evidence".

Very Low Wages

It was also revealed the preponderance of female undertrials. Almost 70 per cent of the prisoners were undertrials in 1986. The undertrials suffer a greater attack on their human rights and medical facilities and wages for their labour are arranged on an ad-hoc basis by the jails. Wages for female prisoners are in any case very low and while in a men's prison skilled work pays them Rs. 5.50 per day, women get only Rs. 2.50 for the same work. Semi-skilled work can pay as low as 50 paise to women prisoners. Underpaid and unpaid work by women prisoners is the commonest finding, says the report.

Interestingly the patriarchical traditions dog the women right into prisons where they find themselves cooking and cleaning for male prisoners but the reverse is not true.

Poor-civic Amenities

Basic amenities are in short supply and toilet and sleeping facilities are substandard. The per-capita expense on a prisoner's diet in one of the southern states was found to range between Rs. 1.80 is state-aided private institutions and Rs. 4.80 in a vigilance home. Beating with straps and bamboo sticks and specified tortures have been widely reported by the prisoners and report concedes that indignities inflicted on the female prisoners are far worse than males. Rape continued to pose the greatest danger.

Therefore, the committee found that the key flaw in the system was that lack of separate prison for women. Despite repeated recommendation by police commissions and funds sanctioned to the state Government of the 9,869 prisons existing in India only a handful are solely for women.

Some 44,000 women are arrested annually under the IPC and account for only 2-3 per cent of total arrests. They constitute only 2-6 per cent of the total prison population and 79 per cent of these are unconvicted. The report then evolve an unusual code for reform which strikes at basic legal tenets for arrest and custody to reframe the system for protection of women from custodial abuse and neglect[1].

Crime and Punishment

"Had I known, I would never have done it, but I had heard of a number of husbands murdering their wives in broad daylight and nothing had happened to them. So why should

1. *Indian Express*, New Delhi — Wednesday, September 6, 1989 P-3.

anything happen to me ?" said Manjula who has murdered her husband. Revati was married in 1982. She was jailed in 1983, eight months later for murder. She murdered her husband and confessed it without hesitation. "If a person has entered into your life and you always feel that he is more dangerous than death, what would you do ?" she demands. Born into a middle-class family, Revati was married when still in her teens, to a man in his forties. She disliked her husband. But she found her young brother-in-law good company. Generous, liberal and of like temperament she could relax with him. Her husband on the other hand treaded her cruelly. When the situation became intolerable, she killed her husband with a stone while he was sleeping. She told her brother-in-law what she had done.

For six years she was waited for her brother-in-law to come and take her away: She is firm in her belief that he would come one day and she will go with him and they will enjoy the rest of their lives together. She has written a number of letters to her brother-in-law. Did she get any reply from him ? Tears roll her cheeks but she does not say "no". She does no want to face the cruel truth that he will never come. She says "Every now and then he appears in my dreams and assures me he will come." She passes her days with this dream which will be never translated into reality. After coming out of jail she doen't know what will be her lot. She does not know that she has committed a heinous crime and that she should have a guilty conscience. "There was no way out except murder," she murmurs.

The story of Badi is a tragic one. She gave birth to a female child, thereby, in the lexicon of her culture, bringing a curse upon the family. Her husband taunted her with "it is better to have a chhora (male child). A chhori is always troublesome but you, my lady, were incapable of having a boy. "The words wounded her to the heart. After all, the girl was her first creation. She was often unable to bear her husbands's sarcastic comments in silence and argue back. That enraged him. For a woman, a mother of a female child, to dare to answer back to her husband was intolerable. He took to beating her up and burning her with hot iron rods. Badi says she was happy with her little daughter but she was terribly worried about the child's future. Her husband wouldn't touch the baby, reasoning that it would be better for the child to die than to suffer all her life. She put a wooden plank over the Infant's face and allowed it to suffocate to death.

As she tells her tragic story, 26 year-old-Badi cries bitterly," I was really unaware of the turmoil after the murder of my own baby. I thought it would be better to end her life since nobody wanted her. I didn't think it was wrong," she pleads pitiously. Sometimes there is anger in her voice, directed at her husband who lives peacefully—may be he has even married again.

Although Badi comes from a well-to-do-Rajput family, no one came forward to defend her in court. Badi doesn't complain against any one; no one could save her from the justice that had to be done. But she is terribly hurt that no one of her relatives has come to see her : neither from her in-law's house nor from her parent's house. Not in a court of law alone but in the eyes of her world she is solely responsible for the crime. But, she asks," Is it not true that the entire family of my husband, the villagers too, are responsible for the murder of my baby ? I lost my baby. It is the most severe punishment for me but what punishment has been awarded to them? " That anguished cry is destined to remain unanswered.

Tippu's Story

"I was running as fast as I could, my two-month old baby clasped to my heart, the other two children following me screaming 'where are you going ma '..............' My husband, mother-in-law and brother-in-law armed with axes, spears and lathis were chasing us. Their intention was to kill us all. "Tippu recalls the terror of that day vividly. " I saw a well and seeing no other way of escaping certain death, I jumped into it with my youngest child Pappu and the other two who were clutching at my sari. When I came to my senses, I found all the children were dead, the children who were my own creation." Tippu paused for a moment, then continued : " I was brought out of the well alive, but only to face grief and humiliation and at the cost of losing my own flesh and blood, my dear children. And to suffer the sentence of life imprisonment." Tippu's eyes were dry and vacant. The grief was too deep for tears.

Tippu is lodged in the Jaipur Central Jail. When she comes out, after serving a sentence she did nothing to merit, she will be homeless. Tippu is one of the many women in prisons everywhere in the country who are behind bars not because they are die-hard criminals, but because nobody can be bothered to go into the circumstances of their so-called crimes.

Constant Threat

Married when still a child, Tippu who is now 38 years old, never spent a single happy day in her-in-law' house. She lived through 17 years of married life being threatened daily and fearing that she could be murdered at any moment. There was no one to care for her, no one she could tell of the mental torture and physical assaults which were a daily routine. She was kept hungry. Even her children were not spared. One day her husband and mother-in-law hatched a plan to murder her. The reason was not complex : they simply did not like her, and so little is the worth of a woman in such a society that they would kill her casually as they would a fly. Tippu got to know of the plan and panicked. Her instinct was to just flee the house with the three children. When she was rescued alive from the well into which she had blindly plunged, she was charge-sheeted for the murder of her three children. There was no one to plead in her defence. The law of the land went by her confession only. Jurisprudence demands that at least the details of the circumstances which compelled the crime be examined. Was she really a murderer ? Did she really want to kill her own children ? What were the factors that compelled her to flee from her home ? No one volunteered any information on the kind of ill-treatment she had been subjected to and no one bothered to enquire into her past history and circumstance. Tippu has been behind bars for the last 11 years. She has three more years to go. After that she has no idea what will happen to her, where she will go or how she will live. She will be that most unenviable creature on earth : a woman with no education, no money, no training and no family.

Not with a Criminal History

Many of the women in the Jaipur Central Jail have histories like Tippu's. In June 1989, there were 41 women in Jaipur Central Jail, six of them undertrials. They were there on charges of killing their husbands or children, for burning their daughter-in-laws, for dacoity and attempted suicide. They are almost all from the interior villages, all are married, illiterate, and from the lower strata of society. Not a single one has a criminal history.

Forty-two per cent of the women have been charged with killing their husbands and more than 21 percent with murdering children in their own families, less than 10 percent for attempted suicide. Their crimes are thus limited to the family sphere as are their lives. The crimes are mostly the result of the suffocating, frustrating and exploitative family structure of a closed society. This is true not for Rajasthan alone, but for the entire country. According to one all-India survey, more than 40 percent of the crimes committed by women are the result of tense family and social relations.

50

Police and Crime against Women

The task of the police is strict enforcement of laws. The police should make it very clear on the young people that making of indecent jokes or indecent remarks on passing girls, whether it is jostling or getting hold of the girls by their arms, whether it is whistling and humming of lowed songs at the sight of girls and whether it is snatching of their exercise books, or their dupattas all these offences can be dealt with suitably within the ambit of laws. In such cases, police must make it known that arrest can be made promptly U/S 151 IPC. The other provisions of the law which deal with indecency in public behaviour have been discussed and explained in subsequent paras.

The police should take following steps in order to safeguard the modesty of woman :

Active Vigilance—The vigilance by the police both in uniform and civilian dress will keep sex offenders away. Police should protect girls in their impressionable age from being kinnapped, abducted and exploited by taking action U/S -319 IPC.

Prompt Registration—Police must freely register sex offences and promptly investigate so that clues in the form of medical evidence, broken bangles, with clothes, etc. may not be lost with the passage of time.

Active Law Enforcement—Police should make use of following legal provisions of Indian Penal Code.

Sec -294 IPC—Whoever to the annoyance of other does any obscene act in any public place or sings, recites or utters any obscene song ballad or words in or near public place, shall be punished with imprisonment of either description for a term which may extend to three months or with fine or with both.

Sec - 354 IPC—Whoever assaults or uses criminal force to any woman, intending to outrage or knowing to be likely that he will thereby outrage her modesty shall be punished with imprisonment of either description for a term which may extend to two years or with fine or with both.

Sec - 497 IPC—The existing provision under Sec. 497 of the Indian Penal Code which deals with adultry is outdated and unjust. The Law Commission in its 42nd Report suggested that besides a man who has an adulterous relationship with the wife of another man without later's consent or connivance can be jailed for five years, the wife is not punishable. The commission observed that the reasons which weighed with the Law Commissions in the last century in exmpting the wife from punishment were no longer valid and there was hardly any justification for not treating the guilty pair alike. The exemption provided to the wife is not valid.

Sec - 509 IPC—Whoever intruding to insult the modesty of any woman, utters any words, makes any sexual or gesture or exhibits object, including that such gesture or object shall be seen by such women, or intrudes upon the privacy of such shall be punished with simple imprisonment for a term which may extend to one year, or with fine or with both.

Social Security Scheme

An ideal Social Security Scheme was launched by Mr. E.S. Modak when he was Inspector General of Police, Maharashtra Police in 1976. He went into details of causes of women leaving their homes unceremoniously and falling in the hands of undesirable persons. The following factors came to light—

(*i*) In some cases husbands had abandoned them, either because they had found other women or because they found the dowry insufficient.

(*ii*) Occasionally they left their homes because their in-laws ill-treated them.

(*iii*) Quarrel with parents.

(*iv*) Did not get enough to eat.

(*v*) The glamour of Silver Screen also attracted few good looking girls from good families.

(*vi*) Women from Nepal and Bangladesh were often sold by the parents to the brothel-keepers.

Measures

Mr. Modak drew up a scheme in consultation with his associates and decided that police women, would be kept in 'plain' clothes at all the big railway stations and bus stands in Bombay as well as in Pune, Nagpur, Sholapur, Akola, Aurangabad and some other cities. Their duty would be to maintain a sharp vigil for young women and girls who seemed to be unescorted and unprotected. They would be taken to the Government Reception Centres or Remand Homes. The police would try to trace their relatives and in case they were willing police would escort them back to their homes, all the way. Police enlisted support of social organisations like Senior Police Officer Wives Association, the Social Responsibility Group of the Y.W.C.A., The Maharashtra Women Council and the

Association for Social Health in India. The scheme was a great success.

The Growing Need for Women Police

The National Police Commission in its report presented to Parliament in 1983 pointed out that the total number of women in police force all over the country was 3000 - hardly 4 per cent of the entire police force. The percentage of women in police is much higher in other countries. According to figures published by the International Criminal Police Organisation in 1978, this percentage is 2.5 in Bangladesh, 1 in Sri Lanka, 3 in Malaysia, 5 in Phillipines, 12 in Singapore, 11 in Argentina 4.3 in South Australia, 1.65 in Canada, 4.26 in Chile, 3.11 in France and 1.94 in Japan, 7 in England and Wales and about 5 in America.

Third National

The Police Commission 1978 recommended enlistment of more women in the police force in the ranks of Sub-inspectors and Asstt. Sub-inspectors rather than in the ranks of constables. The S.Is and A.S.Is should be graduates with Diploma in Social Sciences. The commission has suggested that provision should be made for the recruitment of widows as police-women, provided they are fit and qualified for appropriate grade.

The commission does not favour the present practice in some states of constituting a separate women police wing or branch of confining recruitment and promotion in it to the women in that branch only. In order to have greater involvement of women police in police administration as well as to provide equal opportunities to them. The commission recommended that they should be recruited increasingly in view of growing urban problems of sophisticated policing.

The police commission noted that the crime by women had more than doubled than that in the case of men as in 1977. The percentage increase of delinquency in girls over the year 1964 was 286.2 whereas in case of boys it was 118.3. In order to stall this rising trend of crime, the commission felt that women police can play a useful role in checking crimes against children, and immoral traffic among women, investigations in cases of kidnappings, abduction, rape and can also undertake patroling in slums, labour colonies, supervise traffic operations near schools, market places, fairs and festivals. One of the difficult problems facing the police these days is handling of women and children demonstrations in situations arising from unrest in industrial and peasant labour and students in colleges and universities.

Women Police

Police Women have now been accepted as part of the police force. Unshaken, the police woman carries out her duty in the prevention of crime or the bringing to justice of the criminal and in this her police duties forge upon welfare work—in the protection and rescue of the young, the exploited and the inexperienced. Within a few hours of dealing with some appealling case, the police woman may be back on her beat, trim, alert and ready for whatever is to be next job of work. Which may as follow:

(*i*) Uniform stitching and storage

(*ii*) Aptitude or attitude

(*iii*) Tackling of suspects

(*iv*) Technical jobs

(*v*) Wireless and communication jobs

(*vi*) Types of investigations-

(*a*) Domestic troubles, (*b*) Cases of runaway children.

(*vii*) Tackling women prisoners

(*viii*) Welfare affairs in the lines.

Reaction of a Women Police

Police officer Dina Acha, Badge 5090, of the same percinct, is also young, blond and attractive and like Sharon Cataldo, did some modelling before she joined the force. She holds, ~Policemen usually keep their wives out of their professional lives," she said, "Wives are using the situation to get more involved. They want to limit us. The divorce rate amongst cops has always been high. It was high before we came into the force—we had nothing to do with it. "She further points out, "Men in offices have affairs, but cops are supposed to be more lecherous than other men. And we are supposed to be better than other women."

The women police can be more fruitful in plainclothes work, decoy work, narcotics and vice.

Police and Women : Norms of Conduct

Strict measures to deal with the delinquent policemen will take the edge off public agitation, but the image of the police will still be soiled. It is wiser to take permanent measures to minimise the possibility of such incidents taking place. Experience shows that several disastrous incidents were caused by policemen whose early misbehaviour was styled as 'Minor'. We should not retain in the police force those who have been proved, on careful enquiry, to have been guilty of such offences. Early dismissals in service may appear harsh but are essential in the public interest. Many such policemen owe their survival to political patronage.

Again, in order to minimise the chances of complaint, it is necessary to employ women police for a number of operations which involve direct contact with women. Unfortunately, all district police forces in India do not have women police. Also in several states where this wing exists, the number of women police personnel is so small that they are generally available in big cities only. The recruitment of women should be stepped up because section 160 (1) of the Criminal Procedure Code lays down that the woman must be interrogated at her residence.

It would be better if this interrogation were done by or at least in the presence of police women.

At present we have to consider situations in which women police may not be available, which will almost always be the case in rural police stations.

The Procedure

Whenever females are arrested, they should immediately be sent, with the permission of the magistrate, to the nearby orphanage, women's home, Nari Niketan or, in the absence of all these, to the house of some respectable citizen. In no case should they be allowed to remain at the police station or at any police outpost.

When policemen have to contact women as witnesses, they should be contacted in the presence of the husband or other male members of the family. If this is not possible, the officers should request some woman—even his own wife—to remain present while the woman is being interrogated. Unless the weather is too rough, the woman should preferably be interrogated in the open. If a room is essential, it should be an open office where people have free access. The police officer's own room is the most unsuitable place.

Most state secretaries get busy issuing circulars after shocking exposures. Such directions should be incorporated permanently in the police manuals. In spite of all precautions, it is not always possible to avoid false allegations which are a good way to demoralise the police. Women of easy virtue have often been employed to make false allegations against honest and upright policemen. The motives may range from a desire for personal revenge against a particular police officer to the desire to make political capital. The fantastic lengths to which those making such false allegations can go, cannot always be visualised. One such instance may be quoted.

Juicy Story

In September 1968, it was alleged by two political parties that atrocities had taken place at the Bakewar police station in Etawah district (Uttar Pradesh). A Harijan boy and his mother had been beaten at the station and the boy was forced by the station staff to commit incest with his mother. In protest, a mob collected under the leadership of a well-known local leader, attacked the station and the police had to fire several rounds in self-defence as a result of which a few persons were killed.

It was a juicy story and made sensational news for several days. The Uttar Pradesh Government ordered a judicial enquiry. According to the judge, the story of the officers' conduct was a pure lie to provide a pretext for the Samyukta Socialist Party and the Communist Party to stage the demonstration the object of which was to gain support, especially that of Harijans in the forthcoming general elections in the state. The judge not only exonerated the police and the district administration of all blame but held the two political parties responsible for the unfortunate happenings. This judgement of the commission still deserves to be read.

It should not be assumed that all allegations of this nature are either true or false. There is a third category, partly true and partly false. For example, the allegation may be that a police officer has misbehaved with a woman but it may turn out to be an affair in which the woman is a consenting party. Such cases are of numerous types but a few examples may be cited. A police officer may develop illicit relations with a female relative of the accused. The accused may permit this under duress as he knows that he is guilty of a crime which may lead to a stiff sentence. The woman may be a consenting party but this does not minimise the misconduct of the police officer.

A woman may complain that a police officer has established illicit relations with her and she has submitted under duress. Inquiry may reveal that, in fact, the woman comes from a family of criminals. She takes the initiative and the police officer falls into her trap. The woman may keep this up as a safe insurance for the criminals in her family. Many colleagues will have sympathy for the police officer, yet there is no doubt that his utility and effectiveness to the police department are finished.

A police officer goes to the house of a witness not an accused. He does not neglect his official duty in this manner but develops illicit relations with a female. Here also the consent of the female does not absolve the police officer from blame. Such examples can be multiple. It has to be remembered that a good deal of emphasis is placed on physical fitness, height, build, looks and personality in recruiting policemen. No officer can be permitted to take advantage of his official contacts or to exploit the glamour of his uniform and personality in a way in which the service may be brought into disrepute.

The restoration of the public confidence depends a good deal on the choice of the agency making a thorough inquiry.

CID's Role

If a cognizable criminal offence has been registered, it is always desirable to entrust the inquiry to the state CID. If it is a departmental inquiry, it should be done by an officer in whom the local people have confidence. The officer conducting the inquiry should be at least two ranks higher. When the people are very agitated or where political leaders are involved in the controversy, there must be a judicial inquiry.

In a few cases the administration tries to buy immediate peace by agreeing to all that the agitated public demands without any real intention of fulfilling the spirit of the assurances. This is a dangerous game as it creates a creditability gap between the people and the administration. When the next crisis comes, the people will insist on punishment being metted out on the spot. It is this spirit of vengeance which is often the root cause of ugly incidents like gheraoing police stations, stoning the houses of police officers, publicly humiliating them by blackening their faces and even fatally assaulting them.

On the other hand, the accused officer should not be made to feel that he is going to be publicly lynched. The truth should be uncovered in an atmosphere free from passion and prejudice.

Sexual misbehaviour is mostly done in private and it is difficult to get evidence. However, there is a misconception that the nature of proof required in departmental inquiries is the same as in judicial trials. The main point, the disciplinary authority has to determine is whether the conduct of the delinquent official was such as was unbecoming of a police officer and whether that conduct renders the officer unsuitable for retention in the force. The surest safeguard against police misbehaviour with women is the general improvement in the quality of the police force. Very few seem to be interested in this as it implies a non-political force in which everything-recruitment, appointment, promotion, demotion is done on an objective basis.

The Times of Indis, dated April 11, 1980 – N.S. Saxena.

51

Law Enforcement and Women Police

Women Police have a great potential to cool, defuse and de- escalate many situations. In non-combative roles requiring restraint, patience and endurance, they can be employed with advantage.

Why Women in Policing ?

The deployment of women in law enforcement has been a controversial issue. Even in a country like United Kingdom, which was pioneer in this area, in 1820 policewomen were described as 'extravagant eccentricity'. But by 1885 much awareness had grown about women police, as is evident from the writing of Miss Louisa Twining, guardian of the poor who wrote in Evening Standard "although women in custody may not be numerous there is no one of their sex in the building.Though female searchers are provided by day in the police station, women frequently pass the night in the lock ups and are then under the care of male policemen alone"[1].

1. Women in Policing by S.K. Ghosh.

The idea that women should enter male dominated areas seemed quite impossible to some but with the turn of the century, the movement of policewomen was sponsored by the National League of Women Voters and other Womens' Social groups in the United States of America and International Council of Women.

Multifarious Jobs

India's policewoman can wield a shield and a batten as competently as her male counterpart. Today women police are being increasingly used to search houses with women inmates, to assist in the watch over brothels and in the rescue of minor from there. Women have been jail ideal for dealing with juvenile and delinquents. At Airports they frisk women passengers. They assist in the collection of intelligence and interrogate women offenders and undertrials. Recently the newly raised women CRPF battalion was inducted in Meerut at the time of riots and it acquitted well. Mild jobs like receiving phone calls, reception work, registering complaints, operating wireless system and controlling traffic is being entrusted to them. Kiran Bedi was the first to break the taboos and underwent the rigorous training for IPS officers.

Till 1968, only married women were admitted in the police but after the Commission's report women began to be admitted even before marriage. Thus since 1969 the women constables, ASIs and SIs have continued to join the police service.

Rape and Need for Women Police Officers

For successful investigation, the officers investigating rape cases must try to establish proper rapport with the rape victims and help the latter to overcome their feelings of shame, nervousness and reluctance in sexual assault cases. The female victims feel shy and embarassed to answer properly the delicate question posed by the male investigating officers. These probing questions, though delicate, are relevant to the case. And this failure of the male investigating officer to get detailed information from the reluctant victims ultimately weakens the case at the investigation stage and subsequently is losing effect at the trial stage. It will be useful, if statements of rape victims are recorded by the women police. But, unfortunately, the number of women police available is scanty in this country. In U.S.A. and other western countries there are 'Rape crisis assistance Centres' to help rape victims. Some of the centres maintain 'Sexual Assault Evidence Kits.'

All offences against women be treated as 'Special Report Cases' and under no circumstances such cases should hangover beyond 90 days. There should be speedy disposal at the level of courts as well.

Women and Police

Government of India has issued instructions from time to time regarding search and arrest of women. In this respect, Ministry of Home Affairs has drawn the attention of policemen towards following basic principles :

(*i*) Section 51 (2) and 100 (3) of C.P.C. make it obligatory that a women should be searched by another women and with strict regard to decency.

(*ii*) According to Section 46 (1) C.P.C. a police officer making arrest required to actually tough or confine the body of the person to be arrested but in case of a woman their submission to the custody should be prevented unless proved otherwise and there should be no occasion for a police officer making arrest of a woman to tough her person. In bailable cases bail should be granted without delay.

(*iii*) Females should be specifically locked in female lock ups and a female guard be kept besides permitting a male or female relative of the arrested woman.

(*iv*) Female witnesses should not be called in the police station, instead, they should be called in courts.

Women Police and Protection of the Rights of People

In order to make police role more effective, woman police has to be developed. Unshaken, the police woman carries out her duty in the prevention of crime or the bringing of justice of the criminal and in this the police duties merge in welfare work such as the protection and rescue of the young women, the exploited and the experienced, within a few hours of dealing with some appalling case. The police women may be back on her beat, trim out, serene and ready for whatever is to be next job on the beat.

Traditionally, law enforcement has been viewed as a field exercise involving substantial use of physical prowess and, therefore, has tended to remain mostly a masculine job. The possibility of women functioning as full members of a police force and playing a role for achieving its objective was not well percieved in the early years of evolution of police system. However, changes in the social situation, with increased association of women in the performance of field duties in several branches of administration, and the problems arising from increased juvenile delinquency and involvement of women in crimes, either as victims or accused, progressively necessiated the employment of women police officers as such in a variety of police tasks. Women police have now become an integral part of the police forces in almost all countries of the world[1].

Duties of Women Police

The police is now being increasingly used for various functions which were formerly stronghold of men.

(*i*) **Investigational Work.** The National Police Commission has recommended more active and direct involvement of women police in the investigational work in specific crimes. They can be and should be entrusted with investigation of crimes relating to women and children and can also be employed on intelligence work connected with such crimes. "We recom-

1. Page 56—Chapter XLII—Women Police—Fifth Report of the National Police Commission 1988.

mend that women police should be an integral part of the police force with a special role in juvenile crime squads, specially in urban areas, as recommended in paragraph 28.39 of the Fourth Report. Women Police should be trained and employed to handle investigational work in a much greater measure than at present."

The number of girls involved in crime has always been and still is much smaller than the number of boys but in recent years the rate of increase of crime in the case of girls is more than double than that in the case of the boys. Delinquency among girls is a more serious problem than delinquency among boys, since girls are potential mothers and a mother plays vital role in bringing up the children. Though delinquent girls and boys get same protection under the Immoral Traffic Act, 1956 and Children Act but this protection cannot be forced till women police is specifically deployed for the purpose.

(*ii*) **Patrolling and Survillance**. Women police effectively undertake day time patrolling in slums, labour colonies, railway stations, bus stands, hospitals and other places.

(*iii*) **Women Police and Law and Order Duties.** Women Police can also be successfully employed in law and order duties doing V.I.P. duties, Fairs and Festivals, Demonstrations, University demonstration and other labour strikes. Of late, the demonstrators place women and children demonstrations in the forefront and as a cover for more aggressive agitations to follow. In fact, now women themselves are coming to the forefront in staging agitations, demonstrations and dharnas on issues like price rise, dowry, eve-teasing, black-marketing, hoarding of essential commodities, etc. For dealing with such rallies and demonstrations by women, a sizeable contingent of women police would need to be deployed. They women police require to be fully trained and well-equipped to deal with such agitations.

(*iv*) **Work at the Police Station**. Women police have a greater potential to cool down and de-escalate many situation and, therefore, greater use should be made of them. In non-combating roles requiring restraint, patience and endurance, they can be employed with advantage. Many women victims of crime are usually deterred from going to police stations to make a complaint because of lack of confidence in having a sympathetic and patient hearing at the police station.

Policing by Women

A police station "manned" entirely by women has been handling cases of peculiar women with a high rate of success since it opened in August, 1985. The first such police station was inaugurated by the late Mrs. Indira Gandhi at Calicut in 1973. It was set up on an experimental basis as it was felt that women were often reluctant to approach policemen with their problems. The women police mainly handle cases like wife-beating, desertions, family quarrels and eve-teasing. The experiment proved a success. As the Cochin Police Commissioner Mr. Sily Mathews put it, "Women prefer to discuss their problems with their own sex."

Police and Women

It is prime duty of the police to protect the honour and dignity of women but when police fails to perform it sincerely, the public reaction is adverse which has been described by Shri N.S. Saxena, "Few things arouse so much anger against the police as ill-treatment of women and the news, true or false, that the modesty of women has been outraged. It is rarely treated as the misconduct of individual policeman. Anti-social elements and political forces appeal to the government find a ready-made issue to launch an agitation. All the good work done patiently over a long period of time by a police unit is wined out in one single day."[1] The unfortunate part of the story is that criminal elements know how vulnerable the police are on this score and often make elaborate plans and subsequent arrangements to carry on their anti-social activities by using alleged police atrocities on women as a pretext. Quite often

1. Police and Women—Norms of Conduct—The Times of India—April 11, 1980.

heavy weather is made of the little bit of horse play. This is best illustrated from the incident of November 2, 1959 of Kanpur, which is known as 'Shantia Kand' where it was alleged that a village woman was raped by a Head Constable. Soon wild rumours spread round Collectorganj police station. And in the chain of events the police opened fire and the toll was 17 dead and 50 injured.

In order to ward off such an embarassing situation Shri N.S. Saxena, has suggested to take certain precautionary measures which can be thus summarised:

(*i*) If a police officer has committed a cognizable offence involving the modesty of a woman and the case is *prima facie* established, the police personnel should be immediately arrested and sent to jail.

(*ii*) Secondly, in the case of non-cognizable offences, permission to investigate the cases should be immediately obtained from the local magistrate.

(*iii*) The press, public and local politicians, where necessary should immediately be informed of the action taken against the alleged offenders so that the public may come to know the facts before anyone circulates incorrect version.

(*iv*) It is also wrong to let cognizable offences be dealt with a mere departmental misconduct, for this is always suspected as meshing up strict measures to deal with the delinquent policeman, the edge of public agitation.

(*v*) Women police should be employed as far as possible and the concerned women be sent to Nari Niketan or Orphanage, whatsoever is available.

(*vi*) If a cognizable offence is registered, it is always advisable to entrust the enquiry to the C.I.D. so that local police is not blamed for bias.

(*vii*) Moral improvement of the force is also one of the methods to improve the functioning of the force.

Guidelines

In order to safeguard the dignity and honour of woman, the central government has issued guidelines to the state government and union territories on steps to prevent the police from misbehaving with women or subjecting them to indignity. The state and union territory governments have been directed to abstain from arresting women and if arrest is warranted, no woman should be arrested between sunset and sunrise. And in case the arrest was warranted late at night, the reasons must be recorded in writing and permission of the next senior officer must be obtained. The State governments have also been asked to enforce safeguards provided in the Criminal Procedure Code and in the State Police Manuals.

In some states only police officers above the rank of assistant sub-inspector or above are empowered to arrest women and also to report all such arrests to the sub-divisional police officers or district Superintendent of Police. Moreover, in bailable cases, bail should be granted 'without delay'. If the offence is non-bailable, the arrested woman should be remanded to the judicial custody with utmost expedition. While being escorted to the jail a male relative should be permitted to accompany the escort party and where a woman has to be detained in police custody, she should be kept in the female lock up. Where there is no separate lock up for women, she should be kept in a separate room.

In cases where a woman is to be examined as a witness, she should not preferably be summoned to the police station and in such cases, women police should be utilised wherever, available and in cases of complaint, enquiry by a Magistrate be made.

How Fair is the Law to the Fair Sex

The condition of both married and unmarried women is as bad as a person in quarantine. At her home she is under the protective wings of her parents and after marriage under the control of husband and mother-in-law. She cannot flop her wings and fly on her own.

In the year 1988 was passed Family Courts Act 1984, which laid "Provide for the establishment of family courts with a view to promote convictions in and secure speedy settlement of disputes relating to marriage and family affairs." The act envisages that there judges shall be responsible for bringing about conciliation who are 'committed to the need to protect and preserve the institution of marriage and to promote the welfare of children...' and lawyers will not be ordinarily allowed and the proceedings shall be in camera and once an agreement is reached between the parties, there will be no appeal. Unfortunately, today women are taught to bear up with any humiliation, beatings, molestation and even be burnt but not speak out because the honour of the family will be put in jeopardy. And thus the woman becomes very vulnerable to violence within the four walls of her house-away from public gaze.

The most unfortunate part is that when a woman goes to the police station to lodge a complaint she is most often told not to bring family matters to the police or the police themselves try to recommend the husband and wife and by that time all evidence is destroyed.

The Condition of Muslim Women

Shah Bano Begum filed her case under Sec.125 of the Criminal Procedure Code for maintenance in April 1978, in the local court of Indore, Shah Bano's husband, an advocate said, he had no obligation, under his personal law to maintain his wife. Shah Bano did not give up her contest and she argued that she had the right to maintenance under the common Criminal Code, Section 125 of the Code of Criminal Procedure, 1973, the husband has an obilgation to maintain his wife which includes a divorced wife, children and parents. Shah Bano fought her case for more than seven years but she finally won.

Her contention was upheld by the Supreme Court in 1985. The court held, "It is a matter of regret that Article 44 of our Constitution has remained a dead letter ...." A common civil code will help the cause of national integration by removing desperate loyalties to laws which have conflicting ideologies. Shah Bano won the case not only for herself but thousands of other ill-fated muslim women like her.

Women's Right to Carry on their Work Independently

If a woman decides to work and stand on her feet, Article 19(1)-(g) guarantees every citizen the right to carry out their occupation. Whenever, a woman has decided to look at it, it has meant that she has to live away from her husband. The courts have held that she does not have the right to work or an equal right with her husband to decide where they will live after marriage Art.19(1). The courts do this by granting the husband a decree for restoration of conjugal rights. The marriage laws of all religious communities provide for this.... it means that the husband has a right to sexual cohabitation and the courts can force the wife to cohabit with him.......

52

Women Police

"Traditionally, law enforcement has been preserved as a field exercised involving substantial physical prowess and therefore has tended to remain mostly a masculine job. The possibility of women functioning as full members of a police force and playing a role for achieving its objective was not well perceived, in the early years of evolution of police system. However, changes in the social situation with increased association of woman in the performance of field duties in several branches of administration and the problems arising from increased juvenile delinquency and involvement of women in crimes, either as victims of accused progressively necessiated the employment of women police officers as such, in a variety of police tasks. Women police have now become an integral part of the police force in almost all countries of the world."[1]

Though Women Police deployment has been recent phenomena in the modern world, but the earliest introduction of women police in Europe was in 1820. In ancient India during Ashoka period they were being used as 'Prativedikas' for assisting women, poor, destitutes and people of low origin to

1. National Police Commission (Fifth Report) Nov. 1980.

be escorted before 'Ashoka the Great' even if he was in the interiors of court.

Early Beginnings

In India early history of policing by women is available in Ramayana, Mahabharata 'Arthasastra' of Kautilya and Ashokan edicts. Ramayana gives vivid description how Sita was put under the surveilance of Police women who carried all round vigil. Likewise Ashoka edicts frequently speak about Prativedikas who protected the Royal Chambers from intruders and kept the being informed about day to day happenings and often escorted important cellers.

The idea that women should enter male dominated areas seemed quite impossible to some but with the turn of the century, the movement of policewomen sponsored by the National Council of Women of Great Britain. The league of women voters and other womens social groups in the United States of America and International Council of Women strengthened the idea of policing by women.

Policing by Women Police in Foreign Countries

The employment of police women in foreign countries progressed in slow stages. It started with the tentative employment of a few women. Then followed the general acceptance of women as full members of the police organisation, in recongnition of their value in dealing with women and children. Thereafter, police women were listed duly trained and clothed with necessary powers for the performance of their tasks. In most countries of the world, policemen do not constitute a seprate female unit of police but are mixed with the general police units. In France and Finland there are special units exclusively made up of policewomen for handling exclusively investigation pertaining to women and children.

The physical standards for women are slightly relaxed in U.K. The basic training given to female members of police is practically identified with that given to the male personnel, except for the training given to women for searches and dealing with the cases of women prisoners. In Japan, the training is different for both. There is more emphasis on cultural training in respect of women. In Italy, both male and female police recruits attend the senior police training courses for different periods.

The men are given training that is focussed more on law and order, while the women are given more detailed courses on psychology and allied subjects. In Australia Northern territory Police, and the Metropolitan Toronte police, physical training for women is less extensive than it is for men.

Woman police officers, are generally employed to carry out all police duties, but in a few countries some restrictions, have been imposed on the police jobs that are assignable to women police. In Australia (Tasmania) Japan, Malaoi and Siychalles, the restrictions have been imposed on the employment of police women at night. It is also seen that only male police officers perform Motor-Cycle patrol duties and search and resume duty,. Police-women in Italy have very limited police powers in connection with crime investigation, in comparison with male officers, and the women police do not perform law and order duties. In France and Brazile also, women police officers are never called upon to participate in operation conducted for the purpose of maintaining order. However the broad level duties which women police perform in different countries of the world can be thus enumerated.

(*i*) Searching of women.

(*ii*) Guarding women prisoners.

(*iii*) Participating in the investigation of sex offences against women, or minor females.

(*iv*) Law and order duties against female agitators.

The two first women police were appointed by the American female society as early as 1845. In 1880 the movement for women police was promulgated by various national ladies and in 1906 a regular women police force was established. At present America has 5,617 women police. In U.K. the women police force was formed in 1919. Today there are 4,300 policemen in Britain, Japan has also sufficient number of women police.

Women Police in Great Britain

The role of women in the Metropolitan Police dates from the First World War. Early in the war womans voluntary organisation formed patrols to tackle the interests of women and girls and in 1919 some of these were absorbed into the Force as the force as the first world metropolitan Police officers. Initially their appointments were temporary and they were not allowed to work in as constables indeed, in 1922 economy measures included the disbandment of the patrols but there was such a storm of protest that the Home Secretary agreed that a small number be retained under their own superintendent. They were given full support from constables. Women officers received training with their male counterparts and patrolled. But much of their time was spent in dealing with womens and children who were victimes of offences or in moral danger.

In 1933 a children and young persons Act was passed which increased the rope of their duties and they because specialists in juvenile problems. The Second World war gave the women police the chance to show that they were capable of performing every type of duty. The numbers of women police was strictly contracted, each stations having its allocation, and promotion was only possible within their own rule structure. They were administered by a separate Branch at New Scotland Yard under a women Superintendent.

In 1973, the Commissioner, Sir Robert Marls introduced a policy of integration under which the separate women's wing was abolished and a unified Counsell created. Now regardless of sex, all officers are free to compete equally for promotion and may hold any post in the Force. The fixed upper limit on the numbers of women has been withdrawn and now women officers hold senior roles in a variety of uniforms and C.I.D. posts in both operational and administrative roles. In September 1955 this policy of equal opportunity was taken a step further with the introduction of girl cadets. These girls undergo the same training as the boys had never the same academic and sporting opportunities. Both leave the cadets to join the force, men and women.

Training

All recruits of the force, men and women, receive the same 15 week training course at the training Centre. There they are posted to a Police Station to learn the practical side of police work and complete their two years probationary period. Of course, women receive the same pay as men. Towards the end of this period, officers take a final examination and then an officer may, if he or she washes, apply for specialist duty. This could include duty in the Mounted Branch, C.I.D. the Dog Sections the Traffic Division on the special Patrol Groups. As a general rule officers may sit for promotion to Seargent after two years. There is, if lower, no need to special patrolling and the majority of officers prefer to remain at a Police Station dealing with the enormous variety of work which makes up the lip of any police officer.

United States of America

New York was the first city in the United States to adopts female police, as far back as 1840 when first female matron was appointed. In 1888 it was made mandatory to appoint female matrons in New York and Massachusfits. In 1893, the city of Chicago appointed women "patrol women, who served for 30 years. In 1910 Los Angeles Police Department appointed the first police woman with full police persons and by 1916 police women were appointed in 25 cities, and since then women police has not looked back. President Jamsan appointed 'Presidents Commission on few Experiment and Administration of justice. Qualified women should be utilised in such important staff service units as planning and research, training, intelligence, inspection, public information, community relations, and as legal advisor. They should also serve regularly in patrol, vice and investigating division more and more qualified women enter the service, they could assure administrative responsibilities."

Canada

Females had always been part and parcel of the force. Females were employed during the Gold rush in 1896. In October 1973 it was observed that "It is true that police women are particularly effective in dealing with certain specialised areas of law enforcement work. It is recognised that they have a significant role to play in those areas. The principle that there is room for female police officers, we have yet to define the specific role to be played and the particular career path that might be offered, becoming mind that not all police functions may be handled by women."

Some of the basic functions of condidates of women police have been thus enumerated:

1. Search of female suspects.
2. Escort female prisoners, local and out of town.
3. Escort of female mental patients to institutions.
4. Investigation of crimes committed by juveniles, delinquency control, inspection and supervision of premises which may tend to contribute to the delinquency of females, e.g. dance halls, restaurants, pools, plazas, breaches, hotels, laterns, bar, rooming houses.
5. Location of missing persons.

6. Investigation of complaints involving women and children who are ill, injured, destitute, alrounded neglected or sexually assaulted.

7. Liaison work with juvenile and family courts and social agencies.

8. Investigation of certain crimes committed by or against women, that is thefts, abortions, fraud, and sexual assaults.

9. Execution of outstanding warrants, and service of summons for females.

10. Undercons work in offences which liquor, gaming, betting, varcities, prostitution, and other offence of immoral nature.

11. Surveilance of known criminals and their movements and "decoy" assignments in certain criminal investigations.

12. Public relations and crime prevention programmes, *e.g.* in schools, service, herivers, cultural organisations and participation in community projects and traffic safety measures.

13. Traffic direction, enforcement of traffic laws and by laws, beat patrol and car patrol.

Japan

Women Police was introduced in Japan on March18,1946 when 63 women officers donned this uniform for the first time. This new introductions was widely acclaimed. On May 1,1947, "Regulation for women police officers uniform" were officially adopted and enforced throughout the country by imperial Ordinance No. 183. By October 1947, total strength of women police officers in active service in Japan was 1,173 spread over 31 Prefectured including Metropolitan Police Department Tokyo.

In March, 1948 certain reforms were made to the Japan Police System, when police forces were divided into the "National Rural Police" (N.R.P.) and Municipal Police on a national basis. But in 1954 the Japan Police was again reorganised as "National Police Agency".

Rise of Women Police and International Criminal Police Organisation Interpol

The question of "Women Police" was discussed at the international level as early as in 1976. The III session of the General Assembly of the International Criminal Police Commission (I.C.P.C) held at Britain from 27th to 30th September, 1976 recommended, this question needs to be brought to the attention of all government and police administration as it considers to collaboration of women in different activities west appropriate for public welfare". At its IVth Session of the General Assembly of the I.C.P.C. held at Amesterdom, Netherlands, passed following resolution.

The I.C.P.C. is of the opinion that women are of great use in the practical care of children, girls and young womens in moral danger and that women have for same considerable time worked with the police in this way with good results.

Role of Women in Policing

At its XXVIth Session of the General Assembly held in Lisbon, Portugal from 17-22 June,1957, I.C.P.C. General Assembly presented a report on "Junnil" police— the care of women police. The report said, "whether in the criminal or general police forces, whether it be *'de facto'* there is tendency for the women police for some reason or another, to reserve for itself certain duties however, there are certain areas where the women police can be effective. The report classified the duties which can be performed by the women police therefore.

1. Preventive Duties

(*a*) The discovery of children and winners or physical danger to children who are neglected abandoned, may ward, etc.

(*b*) Family investigation.

(*c*) Discovery of juveniles without occupation or with a tendency to become prostitutes.

(*d*) Teaching and helping school children to deal with traffic.

2. Administrative Duties

(*a*) Searching for children who have run away and absconded.

(*b*) Transport for children.

(*c*) Establishment of card index system for minors and feordes.

(*d*) Liaison with social, medical and school services, etc.

3. Supervise Duties

(*a*) Investigation concerning juvenile delinquent of both sexes and also young women offenders.

(*b*) Interrogation of children and adolescents (the interrogation of male adults to be done by male police officers.

(*c*) Investigation into cases when a child of either sex is the victim of a sexual offence.

(*d*) Interrogation of adult women who are particularly sensitive or emotional.

(*e*) Detection of clandestine prostitute.

(*f*) Searching arrested women.

Women Police Role in Juvenile Deliquency Cases

The International Association of childrens judges has suggested that women police can be in increasingly used for following purpose :

(*a*) in each case where effective surveillance and detection is required women police indicated;

(*b*) in the fight against juvenile deliquency "duty" in the police some of the term should be of secondary consideration, the ideal being to concentrate more on social work as such with the purpose of preventing crime;

(*c*) police women, however, should have nothing but social welfare workers;

(*d*) police women should retain their supreme function, especially in matter concerning sexual offences where women and children are responsible for the victims or witnesses of such acts; and

(*e*) women police, are particularly useful in the interrogation of juvenile victims of sexual offences.

53

Women Cops

Sometimes back the U.P. Government's proposal to open police stations to be manned exclusively by women was welcomed by all but like all political crimes of various types against women have gone up at an alarming pace. And the most shocking part of this dismal story is that very often policemen, instead of helping a woman in distress, have exploited her helplessness in ways that are now well known. It may be true that only a handful of cops indulge in condemnable behaviour. But even a few deplorable incidents involving cops are sufficient to give a bad name to the entire police force. That is why many aggrieved women prefer not to go to the police with their problems for they knew not whether their plea would be heard. The added fear is that instead of getting justice they might be shabbily treated. The Government's proposal in a way is, therefore, an indirect indictment of the male police force.

Incidentally, a senior police official, who made the announcement at Allahabad the other day, said that women managed police stations had been a great success in developed countries because women approached these stations without any hesitation. If this fact was well known, why wasn't the proposal put forward earlier ? The police official concerned also quoted a study to say that women are more tolerant than men and that their knowledge of their own sex helps them work out cases concerning women with greater care and efficiency. But a certain school of thought may not agree with this. Just among men, all cops are not bad, and the number of blacksheep is very small, likewise this school of thought might say that it would be unrealistic to assure that among women all cops would be perfection personified. This school of thought would also say that women cops might at times show greater cruelty then their male counterparts.

Some would allege that women by nature are jealous of one another, that behind almost every dowry death there is a hand of a woman and that brothel-keepers, where tender girls are sold and exploited, also happen to be women in most cases. Hence their conclusion would be, that the mere existence of women's police station may not necessarily ensure justice to the female accused. Even if they are spared the barbaric treatment meted out to them at some male police stations. The debate can go on. But when all is said and done, it would not be unrealistic to conclude that women police stations manned by properly selected candidates, would definitely tend to create a greater sense of safety and security among the aggrieved female citizens of the State than otherwise[1].

Women Police not Getting Equal Share

Despite having proved useful in performing specialised tasks, women police have not been given an equal share in various other areas of police work. This is the finding of the Police Commission in its report presented to Parliament recently. The total number of women in police force all over the country is now 7000 which is hardly 0.4 percent of the entire police force. The percentage of women police in several other countries is much higher. According to the figures published by the International Criminal Police Organisation in 1978, this percentage

1. Northern India Patrika, October 1, 1983.

was 2.5 in Bangladesh, 1 in Sri Lanka, 3 in Malaysia, 5 in Philippines, 12 in Singapore, 11 in Argentina, 4.3 in South Australia,1.65 in Canada, 4.20 in Chile, 3.11 in France, 1.94 in Japan, 7 in England and Wales and about 5 in the U.S.A.

The Police Commission recommended enlistment more and more women in the police force in the ranks of sub-inspectors or assistant sub-inspectors rather than in the rank of constables. The ASIs and SIs should be graduates with diploma in social work. The commission had suggested that provisions should be made for recruiting widows of policemen killed in action provided they are otherwise fit and qualified for the appropriate grade. Residential accommodation and rest and retiring rooms for them should as far as possible be located near the place of their work. The commission does not favour the present practice in some states of constituting a separate women police wing or branch or confining recruitment and promotion in it to the women in that branch only. Apart from being an exclusive branch scheduled from general police stream, promotion prospects in a small branch will remain limited and restricted. In one state, the Police commission came across women Assistant Sub-inspectors who had rendered 25 years of service, had not been able to earn a single promotion although most of their male counterparts had in the meantime been promoted as Inspectors and above.

In order to have greater involvement of women police in police administration as well as to provide equal opportunities to them, the commission recommended that they should be recruited in vacancies in general duty posts after careful estimation of the requirement of women police on the basis of analysis of factors such as population, incidence of crimes by women and juveniles, etc. The commission visualised that in the years to come women police would form an important integral part of the police force specially in the cities, towns and other thickly populated areas of the country.

The Police Commission noted that crime by women had more than doubled than that in the case of boys in 1977, the percentage increase of delinquency in girls over the year 1964 was 286.2 whereas in the case of boys, it was 118.3. The commission feels that women police can play a useful role in checking crimes against childern and immoral traffic among women, investigations in cases of kidnapping, abduction, rape and can also undertake patrolling in slums, labour colonies and can also be successfully utilised in traffic control operations near schools, market places, fairs and festivals.

Since one of the difficult problems facing the police these days is handling of women and childern demonstrators in situations arising from unrest in industrial and peasant labour and students in colleges and universities. The Police Commission has stressed the need for deployment for a sizeable contingent of women police[1].

First Women Police

The two first women police were appointed by the American Female Society as early as 1845. In 1880 the movement for police women promulgated by various national bodies and in 1906 a regular women police force was established. At present America has 5617 women police. In U.K. the women police force was formed in 1919. Promotions are best in U.K. police force. Today there are 4300 policewomen in Britain. Women do patrolling on motorcycles and Fraud Squad duties. Japan too, has women police. They are given traffic duties and act as consultants for parents of problem children.

More Varied Duties for Policewomen in Bombay

She was only 22 when she was first used as a decoy by the police. A gang of abductors was reported to be operating from a well- known city restaurant. Laden with jewellery, she waited to be approached. But it seemed the plain clothes men hovering around were not unobtrusive enough and no one was nabbed that night. Other such exploits have turned out more favourably for the law, and Shanti Parwane has been involved in several exciting cases in her long career with the Women's

---

1. *Indian Express*, April 15, 1983.

Police Wing, Bombay. Now an inspector with the Vigilance Branch, she feels that the main attraction of this profession is the adventure it offers, though she grants that she has never been in any real danger, and many women in the lower ranks (those who are constables) look upon this job as just one way of making a living.

Yet women police in Bombay (which was the first city to have women on the force) have more extensive duties than their counterparts in other cities. Though, like women police every-where else, they too advise way ward girls, rescue them from brothels, firsk women at airports and trace relatives of lost childern, they also aid male police in Bombay with detection work gathering political intelligence and *bandobasts* for strikes and political meetings. They also help enforce the prohibition act and accompany male police on raids conducted under food control order. Few policewomen are being trained to direct traffic and will join the traffic department.

While much of the work is limited to instances where women are involved, policewomen are trained in the use of force, both for defence and offence, they learn to use rifles and a few are learning karate, which may soon become part of regular training.

The First Indian Police Station Staffed by Women

The Prime Minister Indira Gandhi opened at Calicut the first police station for women in India. She expressed satisfaction that women, who were playing a very important part in the economic liberation of the country, were taking increased interest in the modernisation and uplift of society. She pointed out that after Independence, the nature of the function of the police had changed considerably and today they were not only apprehending those who committed anti-social acts, but also helping those who needed assistance. The inaugural function of the police station was noteworthy on several other counts as well.

Perhaps for the first time in the history of the police, a woman police constable, Rosakutti, had the unique privilege of welcoming the Prime Minister. The vote of thanks made by another police constable, Kuttimalu, was also a surprise, especially since it was in Hindi.

A posse of 18 women constables in khaki uniforms and caps presented a guard of honour on her arrival. The Prime Minister inaugurated the police station by lighting a brass lamp. The Chief Minister, C. Achyuta Menon, the Home Minister, K. Karunakaran and the Inspector General of Police, M. Singaravelu were present. The novel idea of a police station for women came from Mr. Singaravelu and had the sanction of the Kerala Government. Kerala has always been in the forefront in departing from static policies. For instance, it was the first to lift prohibition throughout the State. Similarly, the idea of a State conducting lotteries first emerged from Kerala.

The police station was to be a full-fledged one with a Sub-inspector, Padmini, who was a graduate, three head constables and 12 constables. It is situated in the heart of Calicut city at the site of the D.S.P's office. All the duties that are usually carried out by policemen are now being conducted by women. But the difference is that they not only handle cases directly concerned with their sex but complaints have arisen about the indecent advances on women in police lock-ups by some policemen and a couple of months ago, the suicide by two women in Kerala was allegedly attributed to molestation while in police lock-up. These violations are still under investigation by higher authorities. In the meantime, the home minister of Kerala has issued directions to the police not to retain any woman in police lock-up, no matter what the charges are against her. In the wake of these happenings, the idea of an all-woman police station was implemented in State.

Tamil Nadu Report

The Tamil Nadu Government has sanctioned the recruitment of one woman Sub-inspector, three Head Constables and

20 Constables, who, after their training, will be stationed in Madras. If this scheme proves to be a success, Madurai, Tiruchi and Coimbatore will also follow suit. The first batch of women police was trained at Vellore in January 1974. Mr. F.V. Arul, then I.G. of Police, said that women police could prove very useful in controlling traffic, accompanying women prisoners to court and in conducting investigation in immoral traffic.

Policewomen of Delhi : Less Brawn, Equal Skill, More Grace

India's policewomen can wield a sheild and a batton as competently as her male counterpart. To prove that she is in no way inferior to men, a woman Deputy Superintendent of Police (DSP) has run seven times around the parade ground holding aloft a rifle. She has even stood second in the district shooting competition. But 21 years after the formation of the women police force its role is limited. The intrinsic feminity of the women, even in as rough and rugged a service as the police force, comes in the way of their getting challenging assignments. Only 70 per cent of the Indian States have women police and in all these States, their work is limited to investigation of offences involving women and children. Women police are asked to search houses with women inmates, to assist in the watch over brothels and in the rescue of minor girls from them. Women have been found ideal for dealing with juveniles and delinquents. At airports they frisk women passengers. They assist in collection of intelligence and interrogate women offenders and undertrials.

Even mild jobs like controlling traffic, receiving phone calls and registering complaints as duty officers at police stations are not given to them. A duty house officers's work is simple enough and requires no brawn. But senior police officials do not give them this job because they are afraid that even on duty the women will while away the hours in gossip and take their time in answering phone calls. In a place like Delhi it would be also a problem to staff 47 police stations on all three shifts. The total strength of the women police force in the capital is just 140.

Research has shown that police-women are keen to participate in all spheres of police work. Senior police officials also agree that policewomen would bring a streak of honesty to a service that is labelled "highly corrupt". Men would hesitate to bribe a policewoman. If policewomen were allowed to do traffic duty, for example, there would be less racketeering. It is no secret that many policemen work in collusion with truck operators and other heavy transport drivers.

As in a number of services where women are wrapped in cotton-wool and 'spared' the tough work, in the police service, the women are considered incapable of certain duties. You cannot expect a woman to go out on an investigation at midnight, a police official pointed out. She would have to be escorted to work by two male constables. Does not the police officer, out at midnight, have his subordinates assisting him ? Policewomen have been pleading for proper uniforms. They wear khaki saries and blouses and in Delhi the subordinate ranks wear the salwar-kameez. At parade the women are expected to march briskly and efficiently with six yards of cloth wrapped around them. The plea that they be allowed to wear trousers has been turned down by officials who maintain Indian women cannot discard their culture and the sari. Policewomen are not to ride horses or jeeps or to fire tear gas shells.

Women Police in Gujarat

In all there are about 2,000 policewomen in India, the largest number being in Gujarat-600-and Maharashtra-400. Tamil Nadu had no women policewomen. It is probably too conservative a State to even consider having policewomen. However, the Tamil Nadu Government has sanctioned the appointment of policewomen.

Though the male force in Delhi numbers 18,000, there are just 140 women. There are just two women DSP'S in India, both posted in India, both Delhi. Mrs. Mayadevi Batta, the plump grandmother DSP, joined the police service in 1949. The other DSP, Mrs. Shakuntala Vashist joined the railway police force, Punjab cadre. She is now in Delhi in the general police. Only

Haryana, Maharashtra and Delhi have women police inspectors. In all, there are about 100 Sub-inspectors in India.

Women in police force have done some excellent work in the Missing Persons Squad and detecting juvenile delinquents. Raids are conducted in thickly populated areas and children who have run away because of poverty or broken homes are picked up. The policewomen's eyes get accustomed to protecting and picking up such children. For example, Mrs. Sushma Arora, inspector, detected a boy going from one well-dressed person to another. She immediately summoned a constable and asked the child to be brought to her. A search revealed that the boy had one-fourth of a blade in his pocket. Examination of his hands revealed umpteen cuts between the fingers of his hand.

Police Inspector Jaikumari, has done some excellent work at Delhi railway station. There were a number of complaints of theft from the Deluxe train at Delhi. Jaikumari was asked to investigate and went to the station in plain clothes. On three occasions, she noticed a slim, smart girls of about 22 years at the station at the time the train left. On the third occasion, she tailed the girl. Just as the train was about to leave, passengers flocked the windows and there was a scurry of people trying to get off. The slim girl would take this opportunity to open purses left on the seats, and to grab money and sun-glasses. Sometimes the purse was also snatched. As the train speeded she would jump off. The girl was arrested. A search of her house revealed 81 purses and 90 sunglasses. One small velvet purse contained jewellery. This girl pointed out that zip purses were the most difficult to steal from. Stealing from a buckled purse was an easy job.

In another equally interesting case, she caught a young, pretty girl who would ask for lifts from the stations saying her people had not come to fetch her and she did not know Delhi. Her victims were invariably men on two-wheel scooters. On reaching a dark spot she would ask the man to give her all he had or she would scream he was molesting her. The men usually paid up.

Difficult Task

A good police officer, man or woman, must experience all duties, even those involving mob control. The experience of police-women has been that demonstrators can get violent. Once while trying to control demonstrating prostitutes, a woman Sub-inspector was literally picket up and hurled back by the madam of the prostitutes. The slim ASI returned with a handful of women constables. A number of policewomen's dupattas were torn in the unsuing melee. Mrs. Batta had her finger bitten while controlling some political demonstrators.

There is no denying that the police service has a certain glamour. Even a woman constable wields power. But probably the biggest attraction is the accommodation that is given to women in the police service. Upto the Inspector's rank accommodation is free. They also get free uniforms, a washing allowance and can travel free on buses. Till the Khosla Commission report of 1968, women aspiring to the police service had to be married. The Commission also recommended more appointments in the higher ranks. Since 1969, five ASI's and five SI's have recruited every year. Their recruitment is through advertisements and the employment exchange.

Elaborate Training

The ASI's and SI's have to undergo an elaborate training programme of two years. In the first year, they are trained in the Delhi School of Social Work. They study juvenile delinquency, child psychology, general social problems and correctional services. In the second year, six months are spent in P.T., Parade, revolver firing and judo. The next six months are devoted to learning law. For practical training, the girls are sent to various police stations. During training, the policewomen are expected to run atleast half a mile but they are not taught to ride jeeps or horses. Instead taking to crime in a particular field of smuggling will have to depend on our women police. Seven months ago, a Delhi ASI caught a foreigner smuggling cocaine in a tube tied around her waist.

Prostitution has also become the game of the educated and well-dressed. Only a woman can unearth and smash such rackets. For this, the standard of policewomen has to be raised. The constable is only an eighth class pass getting a pittance. Entrance to the gazetted posts has been almost nil. You cannot expect intelligent, young women to join the police till conditions improve, and the glamour of the police force becomes a reality.

54

'Women Police Face A Tremendous Bias'

It was some 16 years ago that India got her first woman IPS officer Mrs. Kiran Bedi. Her appointment raised several eyebrows. The question uppermost in people's minds was: can a woman fit into a police officer's boots? Mrs. Bedi did fit in and after her, more than 30 women have joined the IPS. However, police-women in India still have to establish their identity. Mrs. Bedi spoke to Sunil Saxena on why policewomen in India have such a low profile and what can be done to improve their status. Excerpts.

Q. Why is it that the woman police has such a low profile in India ?

A. Firstly, they form a very small percentage of the force. And secondly, the majority of them are not in a decision-making level. They are assigned jobs that are non-challenging in nature.

Q. Do you think that if more women are inducted at the decision-making level a change will come about ?

A. Absolutely. Overnight, it will make a difference.

Q. What are the non-challenging jobs that the women police are asked to do ?

A. For instance, searching a woman. The majority of Delhi Policewomen are assigned duties at the airport to search and frisk passengers. Now, that is not much of a challenge. They feel totally lost in that job. All that they are doing there is "Uthak and Baithak" (standing up and sitting down while frisking). Then, frustration sets in.

Q. Are there are many requests to move them out of such jobs?

A. Yes, There are many.

Q. Why is it that no effort has been made to increase the number of policewomen ?

A. I remember when in headquarters there was a stage when they were saying that we will give you 50 women Sub-inspectors if you surrender 50 male sub-inspectors. To which we replied that we cannot reduce the number of men Sub-inspectors. We need women Sub-inspectors for a purpose which urgently needs attending to.

Q. What was that purpose ?

A. Well, here was a situation where the needs of the community were not being attended to, because there were not enough policewomen. We shouldn't forget that women make up almost half the country's population.

Q. Who are the complainants who are not coming to the police station ? Are they only women, or men too ?

A. It is also the men. There are certain problems, like the family problems, that you cannot separate by saying that this should be handled by a woman and this by a man. There are certain problems that need to be handled by a team approach. Probably the man may be better handled by a woman officer and the woman by a male officer.

Q. At what level do you think the induction should take place in the force ?

A. At all levels. You need women constables, you need women Sub-inspectors and you need gazetted women police officers. In Delhi Police, just a few years ago, women constables were not being recruited at all. As a result, Sub-inspectors were performing certain tasks which should have been done by the women constables, like escorting women prisoners. So there was resentment. We were downgrading them.

Q. Do you think that the strength of Delhi policewomen is adequate today?

A. No it is inadequate. The bulk of the force has gone into two duties : one, airport security, and two the VIP security. So, we really don't have women police working for women on the streets.

Q. What should be the adequate staff position ?

A. I suggest that to begin with every police station in the metropolitan cities should have at least one women duty officer, sitting from 9 a.m. to 6 p.m. alongwith the male duty officer. She should at least be of the rank of Assistant Sub-inspector, if not a Sub-inspector. Then I would recommend at least one women Sub-inspector to be an investigation officer in each police station.

Q. Why do you advocate a higher representation for women in police stations ?

A. Fifty percent of problems coming to the police station are family problems, social problems. Some of them may not be offences in the statute book. But they do have the potential of becoming dangerous later. The presence of women police officers can help considerably in defusing such situations.

Q. What are the main problems that the Indian policewomen face ?

A. Most important is the tremendous bias both from within the force and from outside. I have come across women constabulary who have been harassed by their own male colleagues. Especially, if they happen to be unmarried. Also, the public does not expect a woman constable to be as tough as the male constable.

Secondly, they often feel left out. Invariably, the male officer starts with a complex. Well, here is a woman police constable, who better be kept in reserve. For example, if there are two women constables in a police station and 80 men constables when it comes to selection of beat constables the women constables will never be put on the beat. Instead, they will be put on the desk where they will sit twiddling their thumbs, and getting used to doing nothing.

Policewomen Sore at Promotion Policy

Policewomen, by and large, are emphatic that there is no sexual harassment in the force. "Our relations are of an exceptionally high order," says Mrs Meera Verma, Ahmedabad's S.P. adds Pratibha Kumari, "We have till now been treated as members of the force and not as women." But Mrs. Bedi says that "in the constabulary, a girl, especially if she is unmarried, faces peculiar problems."

And in Madras, Mr K.N. George, Director of the Madras School of Social Work, quantifies "the cases of misbehaviour by superiors as two per cent." Says George, "These instances may be because of a single woman seeking emotional support, or because of a fear complex or because of the pressure that the male officer might interfere with her promotion. There could be 'weakness' from the woman's side. A woman seeking favours, could on the other hand, be a willing victim."

But one area where the women feel that they have the upper hand is in their dealings with politicians. Unlike the policemen, they find themselves less exposed to unwanted pressure. "People don't approach a woman with impunity," says Ms. Prabha Rao, Bangalore's Superintendent of Police. And Bihar's Pratibha Kumari, adds "they avoid me because if they want a favour done it is more difficult to bribe a woman than a man."

However, there is general dissatisfaction about promotions, especially among the lower ranks. It is only in Karnataka and Delhi, where there are separate lists for the constabulary, that promotions are in tune with the policewomen's hopes. Says Delhi's Mrs Bedi, "The promotion avenues are good in Delhi Police, because it is still a growing department. Women police form a separate cadre till the level of Sub-inspectors. It is only after that the women's promotions are clubbed with that of women." However, as the spokesman for U.P.'s police chief, explains, "One doesn't see many women being promoted as recruitment began only in 1974."

Different Training

Surprisingly, different states have set up different training standards.The most rigorous are being adopted in Delhi, where the training is at par with that of men. Besides basic physical training is at par with that a men, women are trained in the use of stenguns, light machineguns, fire-fighting, rescue work and mob dispersal.

However, in West Bengal they are trained in a separate school, where riding and driving facilities are not available. In Maharashtra while male constables undergo training for nine months, prior to assuming their duties, women constables have only a three-month stint. Similarly, while the male Sub-inspectors are sent to the Nasik Police Training College for two years the women Sub-inspectors are trained for just six months.

Happily, examples of individual bravery and courage set by high-profile women police officials as Mrs. Kiran Bedi and Mrs. Anurag Mathur have motivated more educated women to join the force recently. Thus, the Mahila Battalion in Delhi has seven post-graduates and 40 graduates, though the basic qualifying mark is just Class VIII. In Tamil Nadu, two women constables manning an all-woman police station are post-graduates, while another one is a graduate; one head constable too is a graduate. In other states too, the number of women graduates joining the police force is going up.

Significantly, policewomen have softened common man's perceptions of the law and order force. Mrs Bedi, recounting her experience, says, "Initially, there was resistance. People thought it is too tough a job for women. However, the public at large is now accepting policewomen with confidence. We are now at an advantage for the public expects us to be more amenable, fair and honest." And lawyers in Bangalore feel that women constables and Sub-inspectors are competent in the jobs given to them, are relatively honest in comparison to men and more gentle in their approach to work. Mr. M. Shambulingappa, first Additional Chief Metropolitan Magistrate in Bangalore goes even one step further. He feels that women have "humanised the police force."

Opinion in the force is, however, divided about their future role. While Maharashtra's Director-General of Police, Mr. D.S. Soman said flatly that he "does not envisage a larger role for policewomen in the near future," Karnataka's Director-General of Police, Mr. A.R. Nizamuddin, says a proposal to have a company of armed policewomen is being worked out in his state. The Uttar Pradesh Government last year announced the decision to raise a full battalion of women, and in Hyderabad a proposal to set up two model police stations fully manned by policewomen in under consideration. In Delhi, Mrs Bedi points out, "Fifty per cent of our population is women. To meet their needs the women's police must be given a larger role."[1]

But only a radical change in perception, both within and without the force, can give India's policewomen a spanking new image.

1. *The Times of India*, New Delhi, May 17, 1988, Page-1.

55

Battle for Prestige

Bedi is transferred but nobody is happy. She was the eye of the tempest. For an unprecedented period of two-and-a-half months striking Delhi lawyers demanding her suspension had stopped courts from functioning-not just in the capital but in most of the northern states. Now the battle moved into the lawyers' den, the Delhi High Court, where a specially constituted two-judge committee of inquiry had begun its hearings. In the bright yellow court hall 17, the opposing counsel, a battery of some of the best lawyers, had produced damning police wireless messages. The committee, consisting of Justice N.N. Goswamy and Justice Wadhwa, asked her for clarifications. In her hour of reckoning, Kiran Bedi, the country's first woman IPS officer, decided to do what she knew best.

Come out Fighting

She stood up boldly and the packed-largely male and hostile audience fell silent. She flicked her closed-cropped hair into place and adjusted her epaulette. Glancing down at her notes she began : " I joined the police force not out of a sadistic attitude but because of my love for justice. For 16 years I have slogged. I have not earned a bad name as is being made out."

"What I am facing today is a public trial," she continued." Not me alone but my family too. If an adverse interim report is tabled I'm finished - for the rest of my life all I would be doing is explaining." With that she launched into a systematic defence of her case, concluding: "I am not a battle-loving officer. I would like the law to protect me. And I would like this committee to come out with suggestions on how to bridge the gap between the lawyers and the police. I'm willing to extend my hand first to them."

At the end, K.K. Venugopal, the redoubtable lawyers' counsel, told the committee : "Listening to her I was almost convinced until checked facts from the records and found she wasn't right."[1]

Reading out from police wireless messages, he showed that on February 17 every police station in the zone was aware that a 2,000-strong mob was heading towards the Tis Hazari Courts, where the striking lawyers were on a hunger strike. Yet hardly any police force was deputed to protect lawyers against the attack that led to 20 cars being damaged, glass-panes of their offices being smashed and one lawyer being injured. This evidence looked convincing enough for the committee to haul up to police in its interim report. But even as P.K. Jain, the committee's secretary, was handing over the report to Delhi's Lt. Governor H.L. Kapoor, news that Bedi had been transferred leaked out. She had been shifted from her controversial post of Deputy Commissioner of Police in Delhi's north district to Deputy Director (operations) in the Narcotics Control Bureau.

The Union Government's move was clearly pre-planned. In an attempt to get the lawyers back to work, it tried to make Bedi's transfer coincide with the committee's interim report. Later, a senior Home Ministry official confirmed : " The decision to transfer her had been pending for several days. Already the waters had been muddled and we were trying to bail her out".

---

1. *India Today* April 30, 1988.

Instead, it pushed the situation into even murkier waters. "It's absurd," said Vijay Shankerdass, the police counsel. " They could have transferred her two months ago without subjecting her to the traumatic hearings." The striking lawyers were, however, even more upset. They accused the Government of deliberately withholding the report because (or so they believed) the committee had recommended sterner action against Bedi. The lawyers had wanted nothing less than her suspension.

Two days later, the Delhi Bar Association decided that it would continue the strike till such time as the report was made public. Rajiv Khosla, Secretary of the Delhi Bar Association's Action Committee, said : "We would accept any recommendations that the interim report makes but the Government must release the report first". If the lawyers were agitated, so too were many in the police force. Not all her colleagues had approved of Bedi's handling of the fracas with the lawyers. But her sudden transfer was demoralising. As one officer said : "The message is loud and clear: if the going gets tough, let the tough people go."

Ironically, the committee's interim report was, according to well-formed sources, not as harsh as the lawyers would have liked. Formed last month, the committee was to enquire into three crucial events : the arrest and handcuffing of Rajesh Agnihotri, a district court lawyer, that had sparked off the protest of January 15 this year; the alleged lathi-charge on lawyers-in the Tis Hazari complex on January 21–protesting Agnihotri's arrest in front of Bedi's office; and the mob attack on the striking lawyers at Tis Hazari Court on February 17 which they allege Bedi had instigated. The committee was also to go into the question of whether the police officers-including Bedi-involved in these incidents should be suspended.

The interim report is said to reflect a middle-of-the-road stance. It reportedly expresses concern over certain lapses of the police in both the incidents. But the judges also wanted to investigate the matter further before pinning the blame. The report's most important recommendation was the transfer of five police officers - including Bedi- serving in the north district, to facilitate a fair inquiry. (The four others indicated in the interim report were transferred two days later).

Caught on the wrong foot, the battery of lawyers quickly dismissed it as inconsequential to the hearings. Instead they concentrated on the February 17 incident. In her defence, Bedi claimed that she was informed that the 2,000-strong gathering was heading towards the Lt. Governor's house and not Tis Hazari. To disprove her contention, Venugopal read out a series of messages. One of them to all the police stations read: "There is a gathering of 2-3 thousand from N 26 (meaning: sent by the station house officer, Shalimar Bagh). First to demonstrate at Tis Hazari, then to go to L.G. House." Significantly, the Shalimar Bagh officer who sent the initial message was in fact proceeding for a weekly crime review meeting of all officers with Bedi.

Under mounting sarcasm from the judges, Bedi stuck to her guns. At one point an irritated Justice Wadhwa asked :" "Do you mean to say you allow over 2000 people to walk on the streets without making any traffic arrangements or providing a police escort to see that they don't get violent?" Bedi's fight-back was certainly spirited. But as the Goswamy- Wadhwa hearing continue, she will have to come up with hard evidence, especially of the mob attack, to support her claims. While she seems confident of doing that, the lawyers already smell victory. As Khosla says sarcastically : "She can join our profession after the committee delivers its final verdict."

"I'M A comeback girl, " Kiran Bedi

She likes her hair short because she doesn't like to spend too much time in front of the mirror. She listens to Jim Reeves but says she's not sentimental. Not anymore at least. She doesn't believe in crying. For her control of emotion enables you to take positive action. She knows how to cook - just a little, a good omlette, may be.

And for her life is a constant fight, "It's a fight for survival, a fight for your convictions, a fight for the truth." The words come like machine-gun bullets. Her eyes never lose their sparkle. Kiran Bedi is the kind of person who evokes extreme emotions. You either like her or hate her. But you can't be indifferent to her.

For the striking lawyers she is *'Danda Bedi'*, a female Ravana. For her juniors she is tough, honest and an inspiring leader. To her detractors she is hrash, over-zealous and publicity hound.

Ved Marwah Defends Kiran Bedi

The Police Commissioner, Mr. Ved Marwah defended the action of the Deputy Commissioner of Police (North), Mrs. Kiran Bedi, and said that the Delhi Bar Association's prayer for her suspension was not maintainable because the judicial committee enquiry was not directed against any individual. Mr. Marwah said this in his reply before the two-member judicial committee comprising Justice N.N. Goswami and Justice D.P. Wadhwa regarding certain events between January 15 and February 17 which led to the lawyers' strike. The committee on March 30 had directed the Delhi Police to file a reply on a petition of the Delhi Bar Association seeking suspension of Mrs. Bedi.

Discounting the case presented by Delhi Bar Association, Mr. Marwah said it was entirely "ill conceived, false, devoid of any merit and frivilous," and could form the basis of finding against Mrs. Bedi by way of interim report. The 10 page reply filed before the secretary of the committee, Mr. P.K. Jain, said unless all evidence recorded and validity of various events as alleged were fully established no order could be passed by the committee.

Regarding the lathi-charge on advocates on January 21 and the mob violence in Tis Hazari Court premises on February 17, the reply said that the DCP, Mrs, Bedi, had discharged her duty with ability and utmost care along with other police officials. Therefore, there was no dereliction of duty on the part of Mrs. Bedi as well as the other officers.

Attack Engineered

As if this was not enough, a mob attack on the lawyers was engineered. A 1,000-strong mob armed, according to a report, with brickbats, hockey sticks and small rods" and led by a congress municipal corporation member Rajesh Yadav, arrived in about 40 vans at Tis Hazari, and raising slogans in support of Mrs. Kiran Bedi and Mr. Rajiv Gandhi, stoned and ransacked the lawyers' chambers and smashed the windscreens of their cars. The police which was earlier so anxious to beat down the peacefully assembled lawyers was, on this occasion, by all accounts a mute spectator. (In fairness, it must be said that there were some cases of individual policemen who showed devotion to duty and tried to control the mob).

The legal correspondent of the Times of India "was witness to the refusal by the duty officer of the Tis Hazari police post to register the lawyers' complaints". For over half-an-hour the duty officer procastinated before agreeing to lodge a complaint. Again, Mrs. Kiran Bedi, DCP (North) denied police connivance in the incident, said that a (single) teargas shell had been fired, and, true to type refuted that the police had refused to register the FIR by the lawyers.

Connivance

Even the most unbashed of ruling supporters was hard put to deny that the mob attack could not have taken place without the connivance of the police, implicit, if not open. Surely a new chapter in the criminal-politician-police nexus, that too, in the heart of the capital.

Yet such is the predicament of those who have eyes, but do not see, and ears, but do not hear, that three "eminent citizens" issued an appeal to the lawyers to call of their strike as the demand for "suspension of dismissal of a police officer is certainly not defensible". Not a word was said against the handcuffing, the lathicharge or the mob attack on lawyers. By a strange twist of logic, the suspension of a police officer had, to these distinguished senior citizens, become more important than all of these issues.

Not that there is no precedent for suspension of a police officer pending enquiry, one can site any number of instances (The Sub-inspector of Roshanara police station was suspended in this very case for the handcuffing). And, as for IPS officers, Mr. Gautam Kaul Additional Commissioner of Police (Security) was placed under suspension pending enquiry, following the Rajghat assassination attempt on the Prime Minister on October 2, 1986. Under the All India Service Rules, suspension is not a punishment, according to a reliable report. Mr. Kaul, who also heads the IPS Officers' Association, told a reporter that "a suspension is meant to help in any enquiry that the administration may contemplate."

So much for the brouhaha over the suspension demand. The government can surely find a way to suspend Mrs. Kiran Bedi if it wants to. It is, however, a different matter whether it will agree to do so.

What many people do not realise is that if the police are attacking the lawyers, who are described as officers of the court, today, tomorrow they may well turn their wrath on judges. And that will be the end of an independent judiciary and of democracy.

That this is not an idle fear, is proved by a recent report that the Calcutta High Court has sent one of its judges to Raigunj in West Dinapur in North Bengal, to enquire into the rioting and ransack by police in the court and residence of a sub-divisional judicial magistrate. The incident caused resentment among lawyers of the district who have struck work since then (early February). And the state chief secretary said that two policemen had been suspended following the incident.

Fearless

The senior advocate, Mr. F.S. Nariman, who is opposing the strike, writes : "Lawyers have been and are, feared. And it is because of their fearlessness that lawyers are harassed and persecuted in many parts of the world today-often by the minions of their own government. Fearlessness is their badge of fame." Another noted anti-striker, Mr. Soli F. Sorabjee, admits that an attack on lawyers is "a violent blow to the administration of justice and the rule of law."

If lawyers are on strike today, if not for better economic conditions for themselves. As a matter of fact, many of them are hard-hit by strike. They are fighting for an adherence to and respect for norms, which is, after all, the cornerstone of democracy; they are fighting to teach a lesson to the excutive that official arrogance ends where the citizens' rights begin. If democracy is to continue in this country and lawyers have as much of a stake in its survival as anyone else, the least that they can expect is support from the press and the public.

In passing one may add that the attempt by some women's organisations to convert the issue into a "gender war" is unfortunate. This sort of approach will only help to sully, rather than serve, the women's movement. It is surely not their contention that a police officer is above the law merely because she is a woman.

56

All Woman Police Force

All woman police force would be raised in all the 45 districts in Madhya Pradesh, the state's Home Minister, Mr. Bharat Singh, announced, inaugurating a new police station and a housing complex for policemen, Mr Singh said a total of 185 women police up to the rank of DSP would be recruited soon, to deal with cases relating to atrocities on women-PTI.[1]

Women Man Police Control Room

Dial '100' and a female voice says 'Hello, Delhi police". Many, used to hearing a guttural male voice have been known to put down the phone, thinking they must have got a wrong number. But it is true. For the past month the police control room is being "manned" in part by police-woman. "We did it because we had several complaints of rudeness on the part of our control room staff," said Mr. Prakash Singh, additional CP, here on Monday. "This apart, there were complaints that many complaints were not being recorded at all." And so, the police took two steps to improve the PCR. They began taping every call that was make to the control room to ensure that all com-

1. *The Times of India*, New Delhi, Page 8, 23-7-88.

plaints were, in fact, being recorded. Secondly, to get rid of their 'rude' image, they decided to get police women to attend phones. "It began as an experiment a month back, "said Mr. Prakash Singh. "We were afraid that some men would start being to our police-women or begun making lewd calls. May be because we can trace every call or may be because of the way the girls are conducting themselves, we haven't even received one such call."

To start with, 20 girls in two shifts have begun receiving calls at the police control room, said Mr. Pradeep Shrivastava, DCP police control room. Since it is the first time that so many new recruits have been inducted into the control room in a single batch, there are some minor teething problems, one official said. For example, the girls were finding it difficult to trace numbers of senior police officials, as many of them have changed recently. A computer giving all such information has now been installed in the cabin where the girls sit and an experienced officer has been deputed to guide them.

"Soon we will have girls in the third shift too, Mr. Shrivastava said.[1]

Police-women are as Good as Men

Heels click smartly to attention. They salute as they enter the room, heads erect, eyes bright and alert. Confident and articulate, the young women in the Indian police force, like most Indian career women, can hold their own with their professional counterparts anywhere in the world. During my long career, I have met them in the police stations, in their homes and rapidly the stereotype image of a police-women as a hefty, loud-voiced matron has vanished. These women, brisk in speech and action, green saris neatly pinned, epaulettes stating their rank, are thorough-going in their work. This is reassuring. For the Indian policewoman is being called upon to perform tasks the police force had not envisaged even ten years ago.

---

1. *The Indian Express*, New Delhi August 30, 1988, page-1.

Painful Awakening

As the Indian woman is slowly and painfully awakening from her slumber she has become aware of her potential-and started asserting herself. Whether it is sporadically through demonstrations, sitins, protest marches or through direct involvement in causes which affect her and society, women are colliding with the established order. In the process, every vulnerable aspect of her sex has been attacked, occasionally with brutality exposing the authorities in the process. Women police have a special role to play in the transition.

The involvement of women in crime has also increased. The reasons for this would have to be separately discussed. There was a 99.2% increase in the total number of women apprehended in cognizable (Indian Penal Code) cases from 1966 to 1976. The rise in the number of juvenile girl offenders increased by 77.4% from 1960 to 1970. For the same period there has been a 61.4% rise in the number of women offenders apprehended under the Suppression of Immoral Traffic Act. The number of women convicts rose from 11,000 to 13,471 and that of women undertrial prisoners from 12,158 to 20,220. According to a survey done by a team of doctors from one of the largest hospitals one woman out of 20 in Bombay in the 15-40 age group is a prostitute.

In an attempt to prevent women from being further exploited, the law requires that women be searched, escorted and otherwise handled by women police. If she has to be taken to a police station for questioning, she must be accompanied by a police-woman. If she must be kept in police custody for a night, there must be women police on guard duty. How equipped are the women police to meet the requirements of the law ? Their number is quite inadequate. While their work has increased, their numbers have remined static.

Women make up 0.4% of the police force in the country, a total of 3,000 in the entire country. In Delhi there are 179 women in a force of 17,709 people. In 1979 the number was 171-an edition of eight in three years. West Bengal, excluding

Calcutta, has 117 women in a force of 39,289. Tamil Nadu perhaps has the largest number-814 in a force of 41,030. Why is this so? The answer is that it is still a men's world. Somewhere along the line, it was decided that policing was a man's job. It required, as they say, "toughness, strength (brute force) and a thick skin. Women are too sensitive for all this." In the exclusive preserve of this trigger-happy and baton-wielding profession where third degree methods have to be used, the place for women is outside it.

Consequently, recruitment of women into the force has been on an ad hoc basis. Until 1972, the Indian Police Service was closed to women. Then came Mrs Kiran Bedi and the police force has never been the same since. Among the other ranks, women were admitted on "compassionate" grounds—they were appointed as constables if their husbands or fathers had died in the force while in service. I was told that in Delhi every year, just five women Sub-inspectors and five Assistant Sub-inspectors were recruited. And the scheme was given up after five years.

Women police are given what a police report described as "milder" jobs. They are expected to "assist" in tracing lost women and children, "help" in investigating offences in these categories, keeping a watch over places of ill repute, rescuing women from brothels and escorting them to shelter homes and so on. They are also given duties which require tactful handling of the public-at airports and escorting VIP.

Women Physically and Emotionally ill-equipped for the Job

"We haven't just joined the police force by chance, you know. We are here, and fully aware of the demands made on us. Of course, not every woman can be a police-woman just as every man or woman is not cut to be a surgeon or an artist. That women cannot be as physically fit as a man is merely a "bahanna" (excuse). During our training, one of the first things we had to do was run seven miles. Many of us, men and women had never run that much. But two of us women made it while several boys huffed and puffed and fell out. You cannot generalize about the endurance of either sex. Training makes you as fit as your colleague."

"Give us one single instance from the record where a woman has taken leave in excess of her due or has been dismissed because of irregular attendance. You get 15 days leave and that's it. There is no question of asking to be exempted from duty. You are marked absent if you stay away and action is taken. Ask them to check statistics."

Domestic Discord and Consequent Work Inefficiency

"Please, again, let's talk on the basis of facts. Give us one instance of a woman resigning her job because of such a problem or of a woman's marriage breaking up because of her job. We take to the profession, knowing full well its limitations, after we have discussed things clearly at home. If we enter the profession when we are single and if we intend to continue after marriage, our future husbands are clearly informed about the nature of our job-accept us or move on. And what is all this about tension-we all know when a male colleague has quarrelled with his wife. Peace of mind has the same value for men and women and normal people take life in their stride."

Women Police need Protection by a Male while on the Job

"It is normal policy to send two police people together-on a beat or on investigation; almost nothing is done single-handed. So why not send one man and one woman. And do not go by all this talk-brute force is almost never used in a one-to-one encounter. Either you use arms or techniques-like judo or karate. And please add that it is a woman police officer who won the President's Medal in U.P. for capturing dacoits.

"We have often come to duty alone at night. Remember, our uniform protects us. Our work environment, our training and our experiences have put an end to any fuss or fear. When we were in college, of course we would look over our shoulders in fear to see who was behind us. Now, if we sense anything we give hard look and ask what's the matter. Those days of fear are part of the past."

In fact, they laughingly say that what is now happening is that they are placed in the front line of attack when the force goes out to stop a procession. "They know we will not rough people up and the people coming will not attack us easily." Even in communal riots, they say, women are sent first into the mosques for instance, to reassure the people there and to ask them to send the women and children away from the scene, if the police have to enter for investigation. None of the women police of respectability have ever failed-in fact they have won acclaim for their excellent work. Yet, according to Mr. S.K. Ghosh, Inspector-General of Police, Orissa, in his book "Women in Policing": Women police are treated as a novel joke." The attitude of the rest of the force towards them is one of tolerance, amusement or indulgence. They are given mundance jobs and kept as a reserve at Range Headquarters or in the districts. Older women constables whom I talked to said they were not even trained in the use of firearms. The women police I talked to, would, if pushed into routine odd jobs, where they cannot make use of the best of them, would be drained of self-confidence and self-respect.

Today's young policewomen are in the force because they have decided that it is a career. The myth about their being there out of economic necessity is outdated. A survey done in Delhi showed that of the 69 women interviewed, only 19 gave "economic necessity" as one of the reasons for joining the force. Being career women, their approach to the job is a professional one. However, the Delhi policewomen had no complaints of harassment by their male colleagues. What they found annoying was the public conception of their role-as women forced to do such "dirty" jobs because they had no other choice. Aware that they are dealing with professionals, the National Police Commission, in its fifth report has castigated the police force for treating women police the way they do. Stating that they must be allowed to fully share all the duties performed by their male counterparts, it has listed 25 additional areas of work where women police have a special role to play. Women police, it stated, have a great potential to cool, defuse and de-escalate many situations. In non-combative roles requiring restraint, patience and endurance they can be employed with advantage. The presence of women police in police stations will greatly help in creating confidence and trust in the police. They should handle all investigational work in a much greater measure than they do at present. It is easier for them to get leads about offenders, particularly in cases of sexual assault. In just one instance, the posting of women police in the University of Delhi resulted in scores of young men harassing women being caught [1]

Not Corrupt

Senior police officers from Bombay said that there was a great problem in dealing with bootlegging and vice in Bombay because a few police officers overcame the temptation of being won by the business magnates operating in the area. Women could not be tempted with either alcohol or sex-yet. Anti-corruption squads of women police could perhaps be created to deal with corruption where the men had failed.

Ultimately, more women in the police, particularly more women in positions of authority, could project a more human face for the entire force. Women are already indispensible to the force. "Whether it is protecting the Prime Minister or dealing with demolitions, they cannot do without us," they say. Recruiting them in greater numbers to meet the present crises would modernize the Indian police force.

Effective Policing by Women, for Women

A police station "manned" entirely by women has been handling cases peculiar to women with a high rate of success since it opened here in August, 1985. (In Cochin.) The first such police station was inaugurated by the late Mrs Indira Gandhi at Calicut in 1973. It was set up on an experimental basis as it

---

1. *The Statesman*, 18-7-83.

was felt that women were often reluctant to approach policemen with their problems. The women police mainly handle cases like wife-beating, desertions, family quarrels and eve-teasing. The experiment proved a success. As the Cochin police commissioner, Mr Siby Mathews put it," Women prefer to deal with policewomen rather than men." Another such police station was opened at Trivandrum in 1983, followed by the one here.

A women's police station is "manned" by a sub-inspector, five head constables, two lance naiks and 18 constables. It functions from 7 a.m. to 6 or 8 p.m. Women constables have also benefited from the experiment. Previously, their work was confined to arresting women law-breakers and guarding women prisoners. The new stations have given them experience in all fields of police activity.

Dressed in white saris with green borders and matching green blouses, the staff usually play the role of good smaritans but do not hesitate to use strong-arm tactics when necessary. They use khaki uniforms when on watch, traffic of law and order duties. Sub-inspector Eliamma of the women's police station here says it handled more than 160 cases during its first year. Most of these were eveteasing and pick-pocketing, but the police-women have also helped reunite estranged couples. Curiously, many complaints of assault on women proved false on inquiry.

To catch eve-teasers women constables in Mufti are posted at bus stops, railway stations and other crowded places. After spotting an eve-teaser they follow him to his residence and then call in policemen to nab him. There has been a considerable decline in the number of such cases here during the past year. But the women police are happiest about their success in reuniting estranged couples. In one case, a woman who had been formally divorced and granted custody of two of her children lodged a complaint that her former husband's family did not allow her to see the eldest child who was in their custody. The women police took up the case and through persuasion the reunited couple.

In another case, a middle-aged Muslim divorced his young wife because he suspected her of infidelity. He sent Rs. 100 by money order as "meher" though they had been married 11 years ago. The women refused to accept the money order and took her case to the women's police station. After four visits to the police station, the couple were convinced they could live together happily. The divorce lasted just three months.

The only men in whom the policewomen have found it necessary to instill fear are some errant husband.[1]

A Police Women in a Man's World

After 13 years of service as a police officer, Ms. Kanchan Chowdhury, at present Inspecter-General of Police in CID, U.P., Lucknow looks more like a housewife, but talks and works like a professional that she is.

One associates an MA in English literature with an academic aura, where Shakespeare is the theme and Milton, Shelly and Keats the postscript, but that is how synthesis takes place in life, when professions diametrically opposite on the surface blend in one human being. At first glance, she looks like a trendy, well-groomed young mother, who has learnt her mannerisms from a finishing college in Delhi. The air about her is distinctly urbane, but when one speaks to her, she is hesitant, almost shy. However, once she gets going, she is all professional.

Kanchan Chowdhury had set her heart on becoming a police-woman, from the very beginning. Having finished her schooling from Amritsar, she joined the Indra Prastha College in Delhi. Belonging to a middle class family, her father being an agriculturist in Punjab she give due credit to her parents,

1. *The Times of India*, 15.10.86.

who she says gave up social life to ensure a better future for their children.

Being a woman and working in a male-dominated profession, did she feel a sense of isolation in the beginning ? Yes, but she was too thrilled and happy to be in the job to notice it at first, and as time passed, her colleagues accepted her as they would any other male collegue. She did prove her worth as a professional. Now that she is a senior officer, the question arises, whether given the chance, she would again choose the same career ? Yes, she would. "At work, I feel I am exploiting my potential to the fullest extent and growing to the best of my ability. It has given me inner strength and a lot of love from the people. Interacting with people from all walks of life, trying to set right things that have gone wrong, is a tremendous satisfaction to me", she said.

Earlier, when she was posted to Malihabad as an Asstt. SP, she had a wonderful experience of dealing with people and many cases where the male touch would have been unsuccessful, she was able to get result. Later, when she left the district and has now been sent on deputation to Bombay, people from the district still come to her when she is in Lucknow, asking when she would come to Malihabad.

And what of the problem of adjusting her family life with the demands of her job. At first there were difficulties, but soon they were ironed out. "Teething troubles are there everywhere, but though I spent in terms of quantity lesser time with my children, whatever time, I did spend was qualitatively more effective. This has also made my children more independent, compared to kids of the same age." About work, she says, a policeman's lot is not a rosy one, and a policewoman is no exception either. Whether it is an encounter with dacoits (she has quite a few to her credit), or it is investigation of crimes, the drill is the same. Handling firearms training in them, legal procedures administrative work, is all part of the duties that such a uniform entails on the person who wears it.

"An old woman, whose son had been killed by the decoits, told me her story, My insides churned at the callous inhuman behaviour of man towards man. Subsequently, in an encounter, the dacoit in question was caught and I felt that justice would eventually catch up with him."

57

Role of Women in Army

Gen. S.F. Rodrigues, the Chief of the Army Staff, had announced that there is a proposal to induct women in selected branches of the army. This proposal has received mixed reactions. While advocates of the equality of sexes have hailed this proposal as 'historic' and 'momentous', others have raised their eyebrows. Since this proposal had varied ramifications, it needed closer scrutiny. There can be no two opinions that women should get equal status in our society for they have been discriminated against for long. Women have been treated as the 'weaker sex.'

The emancipation of women is handicapped by a number of causes like their passive role, social ills, domestic compulsions, illiteracy, wrong perception, ignorance and superstition. The women's uplift depends on two pre-requisites: Self-reliance and economic independence. Education and employment go hand in hand. Now more and more women are emerging from their cocoons and entering the male bastions. There are women employed in education, health, banks, industry, social services; and even aviation. One of the major openings for women lies in recruitment of uniformed services. The formation of Mahila Battalions in CRPF has brought laurels to the force, including their role with IPKF in Sri Lanka. Army offers wider horizon for women due to size, variety of jobs, opportunity for promotion, organisation and discipline. Recruitment in the army is governed by an Act of Parliament as enshrined in the Army Act 1950.

Why are women considered ineligible for enrolment in the regular Army? The prime reason is physical standards. The army is for fighting war where not only physical fitness but physical toughness is required. Every army jawan and officer, depending of his age group, has to undergo periodical PPTs (Physical Proficiency Tests) and BPETs (Better Physical Efficiency Tests).

Unfortunately, nature has not bestowed the 'manly' qualities of a soldier on women and it is unfair to push the women in front of the enemy. Requirements of maternity including leave, furlough, AWOL (Absence Without Leave) not only upset the smooth functioning of an army unit but adversely affect morale and discipline. Soldiering and woman normally do not go together. One of the primary functions of a Commanding Officers is to keep women 'out of bounds' for soldiers. Entry of women in units is strictly taboo. The DSR (Defence Services Regulations) para 1399 specifically prohibits entry of females in barracks or areas under the command of the OC Unit with certain exceptions like Officers' families and visitors thereto; private servants; sweepers on conservancy duties.

A uniform does not necessarily mean a combat role. The Army is broadly divided on a five-tier basis. In the front are the Combat arms like Infantry and Armour; along with the Supporting Arms like Artillery, Engineers and Signals; looked after by Administrative Services like Army Supply Corps (ASC), Army Ordnance Corps (AOC), Army Medical Corps (AMC); rear services like Base Hospitals, EME Workshops, FODs (Forward Ordnance Depots), FADs (Forward Ammunition Depots) and Static Units/Formations/Depots like CODs (Central

Ordnance Depots), Record Offices, Training Institutions, NCC, Area/Sub-area HQ. Women should be kept off the Combat Arms and also the Supporting Arms.

Women can be gainfully employed in ASC as Clerks and Drivers; as SKTs (Store-keeper Technical), Ammunition Examiners in AOC. The AMC provides maximum opportunities for recruitment. Besides LMOs (Lady Medical Officers) and Nursing Officers, they will do well as Radiographers, Laboratory Technicians, Blood Transfusion Orderlies, Dispensers, Mental Nursing Orderlies, Operation Room Assistant, Sanitary Assistant, X-ray Orderly while in ADC (Army Dental Corps), suitable jobs are Dental Hygienists and Nursing Orderlies. In rear areas, women should be employed in force in Base/Army Hospitals e.g. Delhi Cantt. Base Workshops e.g. Meerut; CODs e.g. Shakurbasti.[1]

Women in the Armed Forces

Interest in the announcement by Gen. S.F. Rodrigues, Chief of the Army Staff, some time back, that women will soon be inducted into the Army, has been revived following the participation of women soldiers in the Gulf War. Women have been part of the Armed Forces of most countries for many decades. In our own country, the Military Nursing Service (MNS) has always been composed of women alone. Similarly women have been serving as medical officers in the three services for some decades. Perhaps the announcement by the Army Chief has led to raised eye-brows because some people have hurriedly conjured up visions of gun-troting women soldiers, or of women fighter pilots, or of women submarine commanders! Such day is still far off.

Section 12 of the Army Act, 1950, provides that no female shall be eligible for enrolment or employment in the regular army except as the Central Government may by official notification specify. By a proviso to this section the then existing employment of women in the MNS as well as in the Army

1. *The Hindustan Times*, February 13, 1991.

Medical Corps (AMC) was allowed to continue. Corresponding provisions in the Air Force Act, 1950, and the Navy Act, 1957, are to similar effect. The present legal position is that unless the Central Government issues a fresh notification, women are not eligible for enrolment or employment in any of the branches in the three services, except the medical branch and the MNS, the latter being only an auxiliary service. There has been understandable resentment amongst young women to this seemingly discriminatory ban on their entry into more branches of the Armed Forces. In fact a lady challenged the constitutionality of Section 12 of the Army Act. The Delhi High Court upheld the provision and held it to be not violative of Articles 14-16 of the Constitution.

Liberal Thinking

Women are employed in the regular armed forces of some countries, notably the United States and Israel. Nothing adverse about their experience is known. During the last decade or so, there has been considerable interest in our country on this issue. The effective presence of women in the All India Services including the IPS, in the fields of engineering, medicine, management and so on, has given impetus to the view that no vocation or profession could be termed unsuitable for women. The waves of liberal thinking started lashing the shores of South Block.

Officers of the Army/Navy/Air Force belong to one branch/corps or the other, depending on the duties. Normally an officer remains in the same branch/corps all through his service. Those below officer rank, are grouped as technical and non-technical, with further sub-division under both categories. The structure of our Armed Forces and the duties of its "officers and men—sing a known expression till a unisex term is coined are such that there are a number of distinct areas where women could be employed with advantage. Provide adequate privacy and security for women ORs. The Officers' messes would allow for provision of separate rooms for women officers.

The feeling in some quarters that the incidence of sexual offences in the Armed Forced is high compared to the civil society is wrong. In spite of an easier opportunity, instances of homosexuality or adulterous conduct are relatively fewer in the Armed Forces, and for two reasons. First, service personnel live in cantonments-stations which are insulated from civil areas. News of sexual misdemeanour spreads quickly and harms the reputation not merely of the individuals concerned but also of the unit/formation. The erring individuals find life miserable thereafter. Secondly, there is a constant interaction between superior and subordinate personnel and even their families—at all levels. Such social contact enables the superior to get scent of anything undesirable brewing. Every ICO and senior officer is always alert to nip in the bud any erring tendency. Where matters gets out of hand the erring person is either tried by court-martial and generally-imprisoned on conviction, or administratively dismissed/removed from service. In no case the offender allowed to go scot-free.

In the civil services, on the other hand, sexual misconduct is seldom dealt with through departmental action. The complainant is left to proceed under the civil laws and the outcome is imaginable. Be that as it may, with the induction of women in the regular Armed Forced greater vigil will be necessary. One can rest assured that the commanders at all levels will do everything possible and permissible to prevent anything untoward happening. A sprinkling of women in uniform is least likely to upset the fine web of service life. If the pessimist are to be appeased, the Armed Forced laws may be amended.

Women are good as teachers and in acquiring visual and communication skills. On a rough reckoning, it would be possible to employ women in such branches/corps as Education, Supply (ASC), Air Traffic Control, Security Intelligence, Legal (Judge Advocate-General's department), Personnel Administration Welfare and so on, in the officer category and in trade corresponding to these duties in positions below. The Naval Headquarters had reportedly formulated plans for the induction of women in the Navy almost two years ago but the Central

Government deferred the decision with a view to evolving a uniform policy. The IAF too favoured gradual and limited induction of women in some of the ground duty branches. Now that the Army too has supported the proposal, a final decision may not take very long.

The actual implementation may require a lead time of at least two years. Initially the induction will have to be limited to about 10 per cent in the selected branches in case of officers and to perhaps five per cent in the case of non-officers. Based on experience gained, the percentage could be gradually increased. Necessary selection/recruitment will have to be followed by the normal period of training before women are inducted into units and formations. Undoubtedly there can be no dilution in the selection or training standards.

Privacy and Security

The proposed step will not be without problems. The saree may have to yield place to pant-jacket combination. Accommodation for single woman may pose problems. Jawans and their equivalent are housed in billets/barracks. It is a hall type accommodation for 20 or 30 persons with toilet facilities at one end. In the initial years the number of women posted to a formation is likely to be far less than a billet strength. Hence segregated accommodation will have to be created so as to providing a minimum punishment for sexual offences.

Family Life

The family life of women joining the Armed Forces, however, may be affected in some degree. In civil vocations, women can live with their husbands and children in most cases. Even in transferable jobs, the frequency of transfer is low and separation is minimal. Further they are housed in towns with good schooling facilities. But military service entails frequent transfer. The unit/camp is located far away from the nearest city. Except for the few women who are fortunate to get married to another member of the same service, frequent separation from family is inevitable in the long run. The attendant emotional problems are not insurmountable, but they cannot be merely wished away. Family life is not easy even for serving officers. Experience reveals that it is wellnigh impossible for the Service Headquarters to arrange successive postings of couples together.

The solution would be to grant women only a short tenure of 10 years. Assuming an entry age of 21 for officers and 17 for ORs, it will be possible for most to complete their service tenure before marriage. Even from the operational point of view a short tenure is advisable. In course of time, if the scheme works well, provision could be made for grant of Permanent Commission or extension of service.

Inducting women on a short tenure has a financial advantage and this perhaps is hidden reason why the Finance Ministry has not let the issue drag on for a decade before concurring! No precise figures are available, but the ex-servicemen outnumber the combined strength of our Army, Navy and Air Force. The minimum qualifying service for pension is 20 years in case of officers and 15 years for ORs. Due to restricted career prospects in recent years, a large number of servicemen are seeking release on completion of minimum qualifying service for pension. And a good many are being retired every year with pensionary benefits. Most of them are in their late thirties or early forties and will be drawing pension for over 25 years. Thus the annual pension pay-out for the ex-servicemen will soon be larger than the provision in the annual budget for pay and allowances of those in service! The practical way to correct this imbalance is to have reduced initial service tenure whereby at least 20 per cent of the Force is released without pensionary entitlement. Of course reasonable terminal gratuity should continue to be paid to them.

Good via Media

A truncated tenure of 10 years is, however, not cost-effective. The first three years will be spent in training courses and during the last two years the individual will be preoccupied with his resettlement plans. This will leave an effective utility period of only five years, which is too short a return for the heavy expenses to be incurred on selection and training. Further, for at least 50 years or more, the main stay of the Armed Forces will continue to be males. Bright youngmen will not to be attracted by a tenure of 10 years. Nor do we want to have second- rate Armed Forces. To draw the best youngmen, the existing tenure will have to be continued so that their entitlement to pension is not disturbed. Induction of women on short tenure will be a good via media, serving three goals. It will help elevate women to equal status with men; it will not disturb the social structure radically as family life will not be affected; it will also arrest the increase in the pension liability.

We, however, should not drift too far under an exaggerated concern for equality between sexes. The branches/corps in which women are to be employed has to be selected with care so that the operational capability of the service is not jeopardised. Grant of Permanent Commission or extended tenure will have far reaching consequences. Prolonged absence on maternity leave of compelling young mothers to make a hard choice between service requirements and home commitments, are not conducive to military discipline or efficiency. The Armed Forces have an arduous task and the Government should not burden them with avoidable peripheral irritants. One hopes that South Block will do its homework well before formulating the final scheme.[1]

1. *The Indian Express*, March 13, 1991.

58

Regiments of Women

On a remote hillside in north-east Alabama, a cluster of wooden cabins sits innocuously among the dense pines. A group of teenagers pullgas masks over their heads, adjust them nervously and file hesitatingly into one of the cabins. A tall man in his early thirties steps casually out of a jeep, pocketing his sun-glasses. He throws a canister into the cabin. The room immediately fills with tear-gas. The teenager breathe deeply through their masks, counting upto 30. Then they rip the mask off, shout out their name, rank and number and rush outside. Some panic and leave the cabin before they have finished; they are rounded up and sent back to do it again.

Outside the teenagers collapse under the pine trees, gas masks dropped casually on the grass. A quarter of them are women with 'crafted' hair-dos, the rest crew-cut males. All are soldiers in the American Army, undergoing their first six weeks of basic training.

Women on Man's Jobs

This scene is enacted every week at Fort McClellan Army training base in Alabama. The base adjoins one of the most popular and best known of the national parks; it is also in the middle of some of the poorest and most depressed towns in America. It covers an area equal to that of Birmingham and has all the facilities of a small town-three churches, a hospital, bank and shops. Through its gates have passed many of the 45,000 women who have enlisted in the American Army in the last seven years to receive equal military training with men. In the last five years, 189,000 women have enlisted in the four military services as a whole (army, navy air force and marine corps).

The integration and acceptance of women soldiers is a recent innovation, provoked by 'chronic shortfalls in recruitment.' Policies that previously barred women from direct involvement in combat have been whittled down. Prompted by the Department of Defence, the military are drastically recasting their rules to prepare massive and increasing numbers of women for roles on or near the front lines. Until 1972, only two percent of the army were women, 16,300 in all. By 1980, the figure has risen to 61,000, or eight per cent. By 1984 it was 12 per cent, 97,000 women, roughly the population of a city like Exeter.

All Are Combatants

In 1977, the then Secretary of the Army, Clifford L. Alexander, under direction from Jimmy Carter, ordered a review of all military occupations. Traditionally those that related to combat were barred to women. The review changed all that. It made a fine distinction: 'All units which aim weapons by line of sight at the enemy are combat units. All others are not.' This meant that only the infantry and a small part of the artillery forces would remain barred to women; every other branch of the military would now accept women for equal training. The change in policy left only 24 out of 305 military specialities still closed to women. Other changes, no less revolutionary, followed as the 1970s drew to a close. These included admitting women to West Point Military Academy, ending 170 years of male exclusively; and the disbandment of the Womens Army Corps.

New female recruits to the army also take advantage of 'revised', entry requirements, such as lower minimum height standards, and, is since 1980, the dropping of the rule that women must have finished high school before enlisting-a rule that never applied to men at any time.

A quarter of the new recruits who now arrive by chartered bus at Fort McClellan's 'reception centre' are women. Both male and female recruits who have had a long journey relax here for a day or two among sports facilities, games room and sweet and drink dispensers.

Pregnancy Tests

Those few days also allow time for the female recruits to be pregnancy tested. In the words of the Fort's reception centre director, Major Douglas Nichols; 'If they are found to be pregnant we wrap them up and send them home. Simple as that.' Simple or not, the army has recently altered its rules on pregnancy. Previously 'grounds for immediate discharge', pregnancy is now defined as 'a temporary medical disability' with an entitlement to six weeks' paid maternity leave.

By the time they are back from their run, the sun is rising fast, pushing the temperature into the low seventies Fahrenheit. It is six O'clock. There are 45 minutes in which the new recruits can catch their breath, swap hard luck sorties, eat breakfast and collect their rifles before starting the day's combat training. As they queue in the breakfast 'chow' line, a female drill sergeant singles out a male recruit. He woke up late and omitted to shave before starting his physical exercise at five a.m. The drill sergeant, male and female, are distinctive in Aussie-style bushhats; and they all have the strut of lower echelon command. The unshaven recruits stands immobile, perfectly erect with an unflinching stare as the drill sergeant rips through him verbally, then sends him back to quarters with orders to dry- shave before trying to re-join the breakfast queue. All around the incident, other new soldiers carefully look away or shift slightly aside, trying for a little immunity through distance.

At breakfast, the new recruits sit in small groups and talk quietly among themselves. Many told that the army was their first job, and almost as many that it was their first time away from home. Those in their first week of basic training had a wary apprehension of what lay ahead, in little more than a month, they will have become soldiers as to the manner born, effortless and unselfconscious in everything that soldiers do. On graduation day many will march past parents who at first will not recognise them.

Whatever the reasons for the temporary halt in female recruitment, there have been many practical problems. Female recruits at Fort McClellan could be seen hobbling on crutches or more frequently, wearing tennis shoes. Until recently the only boots available for them were those designed for nurses in World War II. Women doing road marches or heavy training in boots designed for the average male foot had often ended up with hairline fractures of the feet; now, a remodelled boot is just one sign of change.

A 'unisex' gas mask has been designed, so it is said, to 'safely fit women's tighter faces'. And a new kit pack has been issued with straps that do not cross the breast area.

The army pays basic training recruits $ 501.30 a month, but very few of the recruits mention money. The privates from Delta company had spent a morning climbing in and out of foxholes in temperatures that reached the low nineties and at lunch time, spread out under the trees, generally men and women apart. Within earshot of their drill sergeants, the female recruits give fairly traditional reasons for enlisting: the chance to learn a skill or travel, security, or in a few cases, pay.

Why Women Join Force

Out of earshot of their superiors, their reasons appear more realistic: many of them come from towns in neighbouring states, and nearly all complain of the intolerable dullness of civilian lives in small towns in the mid-west and south. These towns are virtually map references with population barely into four figures. Television had dangled the 'American dream' continually in front of them; whether the army could realise that dream was not the point. The army was a way to get out; often the only way.

"All I wanted, 'said one recruit", was to get out. Out of home, out of my parents' grasp, and out of the 7-Eleven (a supermarket chain). You don't really think I wanted to work in the 7-Eleven all my life, now do you?"

Another says she left home (Ioretto, Tennessee) for the first time in her life when she joined the army. She had worked as a cook in the Waffle House and says, 'the most exciting thing that happened to me in 18 years was a hurricane that missed the town by three miles.'

A drill sergeant said that when she enlisted in 1981, 'Mother cried, my family said, "Jeez, you can do better than that", and my friends freaked out. Now when I go home, I'm sort of a home- town hero, although my mother always asks if they can't move me somewhere a little nearer home.' One recruit says she quit high school to enlist; the reactions of her friends almost made her change her mind. The man in her school class said she must be a lesbian, so the army was the best place for her; her girl friends just formed into a huddle every time she walked past.

Strict Discipline

A female recruit is pulled out of the lunch queue, ordered into a clearing in front of the mess tent, and made to do 10 push-ups, an instant punishment for a word out of turn. The other recruits studiously ignore her; there are no cat-calls, no cries of derision as there would have been if it happened a few weeks ago before at school or on the shop floor. Here, punishment for new recruits is a contagious disease; to show involvement in some else's punishment is to court personal disaster. There are no clowns in the unit I was with, no court jesters living dangerously on a certain licence from their drill sergeants.

The limelight is systematically and largely successfully, shunned.

Public and private opinions on women in the army vary. In a recent widely quoted statement, former US Commander in Vietnam, General William C. Westmoreland stated that 'no man with *gumption* wants a woman to fight his battle.' A staff sergeant at Fort McClellan said he has 'blown his chances' of promotion through continually speaking out against 'female interference' in the 'camaraderie' of his male soldiers.

At Fort McClellan, male soldiers tell me, unprompted, of something in the army, some strenuous activity, some hazardous duty, that they just *know* women won't be able to handle. They have seen women match them at every stage of training, they have often seen them get higher scores on the rifle ranges; they have seen women pick up more merit awards at graduation than men; but they just know there is somewhere a vital duty that women won't be able to handle. But the only specific thing they can cite is infantry training-which is still exclusively male; they are sure women cannot handle the 12-mile road march carrying a 70 lb. kit. This constant consciousness of competing with the opposite sex is, however, an exclusively male obession. No women at Fort McClellan ever made a serious reference to be about competing with men in daily training. Obsessional fear of being shown up was a singularly male preoccupation. Female recruits derided the whole idea; they had joined the army for their own reasons, for their own ambitions, and not to prove themselves better than anyone else; to better themselves was all they wanted to do.

On the rifle range in a flat and barren corner of Fort McClellan a class from Delta company is making slow progress. Toting Armalite rifles that reach literally from their heads to their knees, the new, smaller recruits of the 1980s spend all morning climbing in and out of foxholes that come up to the armpits. The silhouetted rifle targets, always a long way, are now even harder to sharply through the heat haze. Drill Sergeants strut backward forwards before the group of recruits in their command. Only the drill sergeants raise their arms can the action begin. There are interminable delays. When driven to total exasperation, the drill sergeants speak directly to a recruit sweating in a foothole; at all other times, commands, insults and groading issue from the corner of the mouth, while Polaroid-covered eyes stare moodily into the distance. 'What you do in' Private? I have seen nobody sight a target like that since John Wayne.'

The Trainers Experience

The drill sergeants are the world weariest of soldiers; and now, goddamit, they have to teach 'girls', no bigger than their kid sisters. 'Soldier, the enemy gonna die laughing you shoot him with the safety on.' In public they play their roles like big stars; in private, many of them say they prefer teaching women, saying that female recruits listen more carefully, ask more questions and retain more information. On the rifle range, one drill sergeant says all the male recruits have handled a gun at some time in their civilian lives, without proper instruction; all arrive thinking they can shoot 'like Dirty Harry' and he imitated the classic film pose; arms outstretched, hand together on a pistol butt. The women, he says, have generally never handled a gun before and so listen to every word they are told. It is one of the first steps in what is, ultimately, the whole point of basic training; the skill of firing weapons, planting claymore mines or throwing hand grenades. Combat skills.

The privates from Delta company are finishing rifle practice, but their day's work is only half over. After dinner they will be out practising night manoeuvres, being strafed by helicopters in forest clearings.

Before they left I asked them how they felt about going into combat. One women said, 'For myself, I couldn't handle it. I know it sounds bad to want to come in and work next to a guy, then when it comes down to fighting to chicken out, but I know I couldn't handle it. My mind wouldn't allow it.' Her friend standing close asserted that she has 'no doubts about my mental ability.' But she is not in favour of anyone, male or female, being sent into combat.

The drill sergeant in charge of this unit had a different view; she formed the privates into formation, and marched them back towards the barracks. She watched them go and remarked, 'If a woman is capable of doing a job, she should be allowed to do it. If I was in charge of a unit deployed in war, I would take these women with me. They chose to come in, and by God they're going to do their job. But I just don't think that society, with all its morals, prejudices and discriminations, is ready to make a woman and infantryman. I just don't believe they're ready for that.[1]

1. The Geographical Magazine—March 1988—p. 7-10, Keith Bernstein.

59

A Feminine Touch

In Khaki caps and uniforms, some are wielding lathis with great elan, some are undergoing foot drill while others are being taught how to handle pistols and stenguns. Does that sound like a National Cadets Corps (NCC) training camp? From a distance, they could be mistaken for male cadets. But no, they are the women recruits of the Central Reserve Police Force (CRPF), undergoing intensive training. The women's battalion that has been recently added to this force is the very first of its kind since the inception of the paramilitary forces in the country. And while women have made their mark earlier in the civil police and the NCC, this daring venture is unparalleled.

The CRPF, over the years, has come to be known as the "crowning glory" of the paramilitary forces. Having performed, the sensitive tasks of combating terrorism and large-scale violence in Punjab and Assam, containing insurgency in Tripura, Nagaland, Manipur and Mizoram and countering sectarian and communal riots in Meerut and Moradabad, the force has acquired an imperative dimension in the contemporary context of simmering unrest. Today, the CRPF-formed in 1939 is one of the largest and most experienced of the country's armed police forces, with as many as 83 battalions and 18 group centres spread across the nation.

It was only a matter of time before women were recruited into the force. Smart and alert in their attractive uniforms, clocking their heels and smartly saluting the commandant, these women soldiers have succeeded in shattering the myth of the so-called weaker sex. What led to this remarkable development (unthought of till 38 years after Independence)? The idea, apparently was floated after the police found itself discomfited while confronting the massive participation of women in the agitations in Gujarat and Assam. And at the behest of the Prime Minister, this concept saw the light of day.

Determined Recruits

The response was overwhelming. There were 3,000 applicants even after the initial screening and physical fitness tests, while the actual number of those recruited at the Delhi Group Centre at Jharoda Kalan, near the Haryana border, was only 186. Other recruits of the battalion are scattered in various centres at Rampur, Jammu, Durgapur, Trivandrum and Gauhati. Of the women recruits in Delhi, 61 are graduates, seven post-graduates, some are about to graduate and only one third are matriculates or below, although the minimum educational requirement for recruits is only the eight standard. Among those who scored in this stiff competition are national athletic champions, a Karate black-belt holder, six gold medallists and one silver medallist in Judo.

What prompted these young, enterprising women to opt for such an unconventional and tough career, which will probably involve living away from their families? Some have even defied parental pressure. Is it a sense of adventure? Or something more? Their grit and determination to rough it out is remarkable. "People doubt the ability of women, so I thought its time to disprove this. Physical strain is part of the job", states a recruit from Ghaziabad who is a graduate. Another, from Rajasthan, had always been fascinated by the uniform. Still another recruit, a post-graduate in sociology from Delhi, says: "I always had this inclination because my maternal grandfather was in the police. It is a very conscious choice." They claim, unanimously, that they will pursue their careers in all earnestness, notwithstanding the fact that it is bound to hamper their personal lives.

The commandant of the battalion, Sultan A. Khan, comments: "Their (the recruits') since of commitment is far more because of their interest and enthusiasm. They are in no way inferior to the male cadets and are doing exceptionally well. Much better than we had expected. We had our fears initially, but they are tough and proving their mettle. We never expected this kind of response from the girls of Gujarat and Orissa. It has been very educative for us also". Interestingly, at the Trivandrum Group Centre, the women's battalion defeated the men's team in volleyball, after which the latter refused to compete with them.

Toughening

After the preliminary foot and lathi drills, the women are being trained in the use of arms-pistols, stenguns, rifles and light machine guns. And of course, handling of riots, which is the crucial aspect of their job. After this basic training, a separate course in infantry is likely. Khan, elaborates on their specific functions: "In other forces, women are there in very small numbers. Here, we will have a large number of trained, armed women, who will work as a group of soldiers in the field, with emphasis on better training in weapons and tactics. Whereas the civil police is a law-enforcing agency, we are called in when the situation is already explosive or is getting out of hand. We are called for tougher jobs, so, these women have to be tough."

When their rations come from the Food Corporation of India, the women pick up sacks-weighing a quintal each, and take them to the barracks. "They have never given us a chance to say 'You can't do it," says Khan. We will be training them in signals, teleprinters and they will also be handling light vehicles. Some will be promoted as naik radio operators. This will be followed by special courses in internal security and VIP security, and gradually, they will be taught to combat terrorism and urban "insurgency, since today, women are infiltrating such groups."

Good Prospects

Another notable fact is that the chances of these women making it to the officers' ranks are much higher than those of the male constabulary because of their better educational backgrounds. On being asked whether the Mahila constabulary was a source of distraction for the male force, Commandant Khan says; "distraction is too strong a word. Earlier, the men were curious and would come to the grounds on one pretext or another. And these girls were shy. But in our traditional Indian families, we are brought up to be restrained, and I don't foresee any clash. And what is more, the men have even become conscious of the language they use. In terms of discipline, we are the best among the Central forces."

Is the possibility of dropouts, 5-10 years later, being kept in mind, or for that matter, of these girls deciding to settle for family life? "This has already been looked into. We will plan their leave and arrange their deployment accordingly", "says Khan. "Because of their education and training, they will be able to space and plan their careers and personal lives. We have a few married women here also, and till date, we have not had a single dropout, unlike in the case of the male constabulary. Even if it happens in the coming years, the number will, at no point, be insurmountable." He adds: "Initially, we posted them region-wise, and they do not mind being transferred. But we will be changing the rules soon. Fifty per cent of the family quarters will be given to women, and this percentage can later be enhanced. We will also consider other facilities for them."[1]

With their successful entry into the CRPF it seems possible that a decade or two hence, women will be able to invade the all-male domains of the three armed forces as well. Women will finally have come to the force.

---

1. Probe India—September 1986—p. 44-45.

60

Policing by Women Police in Foreign Countries

The employment of police women in foreign countries progressed in slow stages. It started with the tentative employment of a few women often untrained and without police powers, to perform selected duties. Then came the general acceptance of women as full members of the police organisation, in recognition of their value in dealing with women and children. Thereafter, police women were listed duly trained and clothed with necessary powers for the performance of their tasks. In most countries of the world, policewomen not constitute a separate female unit of police but are mixed with the general police units. In France and Finland there are special units exclusively made up of policewomen for handling exclusively investigations pertaining to women and children.

The physical standards for women are slightly relaxed. In U.K. the basic training given to female members of police is practically identified to that given to the male personnel, except for the training given to women for searched and care of women prisoners. In Japan, the training is different for both. There is more emphasis on cultural training in respect of women. In Italy, both male and female police recruits attend the senior police training courses for different periods.

The men are given training that is focussed more on law and order, while the women are given more detailed courses on psychology and allied subjects. In Australia's Northern Territory Police, and the Metropolitan Torente Police, physical training for women is less extensive than it is for men.

Early Beginnings

The first two women police, were appointed by the American Female Society as early as 1845. In 1880 the movement for women police was promulgated by various national bodies and in 1906 a regular women police force was established. At present America has 5,617 women police. In U.K. the women police force was formed in 1919. Today there are 4,300 police women in Britain. Japan has also sufficient number of women police.

Women Police in Great Britain

The role of women in the Metropolitan Police dates from the First World War. Early in the war Women's voluntary organisation joined patrols to watch the interests of women and girls and in 1919 some of these were absorbed into the Force as the First Women Metropolitan Police Officers.

Initially the appointments were temporary and they were not sworn in as constables. In England in 1922 economy measures included the disbandment of the patrols but there was such a storm of protest that the Home Secretary agreed that a small number be retained under their own Superintendent. They were given the full powers of constables. Thus from those early days women officers received training with their male counterparts and patrolled the streets in uniform. But much of their time was spent in dealing with women and children who were victims of offences or in moral danger.

In 1933 a children and young persons Act was passed which increased the scope of their duties and they became specialists in juvenile problems. The second World War gave the Women Police the chance to show that they were capable of performing every type of duty. The number of women police was strictly controlled, each station having its allocation, and promotion, was only possible within their own rank structure. They were administered by a separate branch at New Scotland Yard under a woman Commander.

In 1973, the Commissioner, Sir Robert Mob introduced a policy of integration under with the separate womens' rank structure was abolished and a unified rank created. Now, regardless of sex, all officers are free to compete equally for promotion and may hold any post in the Force. The Fixed upper limited on the number of women has been withdrawn and now women officers hold senior ranks in a variety of uniform and CID posts in both operational and administrative roles. In September 1975 this policy of equal opportunity was taken a step further with the introduction of girl cadets. These girls undergo the same training as the boys and have the same academic and sporting opportunities. Both leave the cadets to join the force, men and women.

Training

All recruits of the Force, men and women, receive the same 15 week training course at the Centre Training School at London. Then they are posted to a police station to learn the practical side of police work and complete their two years probationary period. Of course, women receive the same pay as men.

Towards the end of this period, officers take a final examination and then an officer may, if he or she wishes, apply for specialised duty. This could include duty in the Mounted Branch, C.I.D., the Dog Section, the Traffic Division or the Special Patrol Group. As a general rule officers may sit for promotion to Sergeant after two years.

There is, of course, no need to specialisation and the majority of officers choose to remain at a police station dealing with the enormous variety of work which makes up the life of any police officer.

United States of America

New York was the first city of the United States to adopt female police as far back as 1845 when first female Matron was appointed. In 1888, it was made mandatory to appoint female matrons in New York and Massachusetts. In 1893, the city of Chicago appointed women patrol who served for 30 years. In 1910, the Laos Angeles Police Department appointed the first Police Woman with full police powers and by 1916 policewomen were appointed in 25 cities of U.S.A. and eversince the recruitment and expansion of women police has not looked back.

The President of the United States of America appointed "President's Commission on Law Enforcement and Administration of Justice" to undertake a most comprehensive view of the crime problem and of women police. The commission recommended :

"Qualified women should be utilised in such important staff service units as planning and research, training, intelligence, inspection, public information, community relations, and as legal advisors ... (and) communications... (and) should also serve regulary in patrol, and investigating divisions ... (and) more and more qualified women enter the service, they could assume administrative responsibilities."[1]

Women Police in Canada

Female had always been part and parcel of the Force. Matrons were employed during the Gold Rush in 1896.

In October 1973, it was observed that "It is true that police women are particularly effective in dealing with certain

1. Women in Policing—Page 22.

specialised areas of law enforcement work. It is recognised that they have a significant role to play in those areas. While we have recognised the principle that there is room for female police officers, we have yet to define the specific role to be played and the particulars of career path that might be offered, bearing on mind that not all police functions may be handled by women."

Some of the basic functions of Canadian women police have been examined :

(1) Search of female suspects.

(2) Escort of female prisoners, local and out of town.

(3) Escort of female mental patients of Institutions.

(4) Investigations of crimes committed by juveniles, juvenile delinquency control, inspection and supervision of premises which may tend to contribute to the delinquency of juveniles, e.g., dance halls, restaurants, pool balls, bowling alleys, plazas, bus and train depots, parks, breaches, hotels, taverns, bars, rooming houses.

(5) Location of persons.

(6) Investigation of complaints involving women and children who are ill, injured, destitutes, abandoned, neglected or sexually assaulted.

(7) Liaison with juvenile and family courts and social agencies.

(8) Investigation of certain crimes committed by or against women, that is shoplifting, thefts, abortions, fraud, bigamus sexual assaults.

(9) Execution of outstanding warrants and service of summons for females.

(10) Undercover work in offences which involve liquor, gaming, betting, narcotics, prostitution, and other offences of moral nature.

(11) Surveillance of women criminals and their movements and "decoy" assignments in certain criminal investigations.

(12) Public relations and crime prevention programmes, e.g. lectures in schools, service, cultural organisations and participating in community projects and traffic safety measures.

(13) Traffic direction, enforcement of traffic laws and by-laws, beat patrol and car patrol.

Japan

Women Police was introduced in Japan on March 18, 1946 when 63 women officers donned their uniform for the first time. This new introduction was widely acclaimed. On May 1, 1947, "Regulation for Women Police Officers Uniform " were officially adopted and enforced throughout the country by Imperial Ordnance No. 183. By October 1947, total strength of women police officers in active service in Japan was 1,173 spread over 31 prefectural including Metropolitan Police Department, Tokyo.

In March 1948 certain reforms were made in the Japan Police System, when police forces were divided into the "National Rural Police" (N.R.P.) and "Municipal Police" on a nationwide basis. But in 1954, the Japan police was again reorganised as "National Police Agency."

International Criminal Police Organisation, Interpol and Women Police

The question of "Women Police" was discussed at the international level as early as in 1976. The IIIrd session of the General Assembly of the International Criminal Police Commission (I.C.P.C.) held at Berlin from 27 to 30th September, 1926 recommended, 'this question needs to be brought to the attention of all governments and police administration as it considers to collaboration of women in different activities cost appropriate for public welfare. At its IVth session of the General Assembly of the I.C.P.C. held at Amsterdam, Netherlands, passed following resolution: "The I.C.P.C. is unanimously of the opinion that women are of great use in the practical care of children, girls and young women in moral danger and that women have for some considerable time worked with the police in this way with good results ..."

Role of Women in Policing

Women police officers, are generally employed to carry out all police duties, but in a few countries some restrictions, have been imposed in the police jobs that are assignable to women police. In Australia (Tasmania), Japan, Malawi and Sychalles, the restrictions pertain to the employment of police women at night. It is also seen that only male police officers perform motor-cycle patrol duties and search and rescue duty. Police women in Italy have very limited police powers in connection with crime investigation in comparison with male officers, and the women police do not perform law and order duties. In France and Brazile also, women police officers are never called upon to participate in operations conducted for the purpose of maintaining order. However, the broad based duties which women police perform in different countries of the world can be enumerated:

(*i*) Searching of Women.

(*ii*) Guarding women Prisoners.

(*iii*) Participating in the investigations of sex offences against women or minor females.

(*iv*) Law and order duties against female agitators.

At its XXVIth session of the General Assembly held in Lisbon, Portugal from 17-22 June, 1957, I.C.P.C. General Assembly presented a report on "Juveniles" police—the use of women police. The report said "whether in the criminal or general police forces, whether it be *'de facto'* or *'de juro,'* everywhere there is tendency for the women police for some reason or another, to reserve for itself certain duties. However, there are certain areas where the women police can be effective." The report classified the duties which can't be performed by the women police.

They are :

1. **Preventive Duties :**

(*a*) the discovery of children and minors or physical danger to children who are neglected, abandoned, wayward, etc.,

(*b*) family investigations,

(*c*) discovery of juveniles without occupation or with a tendency to become prostitutes,

(*d*) teaching and helping school children to deal with traffic.

2. **Administrative Duties :**

(*a*) searching for children who have run away and abandoned,

(*b*) transport for children,

(c) establishment of card index system for minors and females,

(d) liaison with social, medical and school services, etc.

3. **Suppressive Duties :**

(a) investigations concerning juvenile delinquents of both sexes and also young women offenders,

(b) investigation of children and adolescents (the interrogation of male adults to be done by male police officers),

(c) investigation into cases when a child of either sex is the victim of a sexual offence,

(d) interrogation of adult women who are particularly sensitive and emotional,

(e) detection of clandestine prostitutes,

(f) searching arrested women.

Women Police Role in Juvenile Delinquency Cases

The International Association of children judges has suggested that women police can increasingly used for following purposes :

(a) in each case where effective surveillance and detection is required women police are indicated,

(b) in the fight against juvenile delinquency, "duty" in the police in the sense of the term should be secondary consideration, this ideal being to concentrate more on social work such with the purposes of preventing crime;

(*c*) police women, however, should have nothing but social welfare workers,

(*d*) police women should retain their suppressive function especially in matters concerning sexual offences where women and children are responsible for or the victim or witnesses of such acts, and

(*e*) women police, are particularly useful in the interrogation, if possible, victims of sexual offences.

61

The Changing Pattern of Women in Indian Society

The status of women in many parts of the world must have been one of mere bondage until the advent of modern ideas of freedom and equality. According to a recent issue of the Economist "In most of the 19th century a British husband had sole rights over his wife's property and their children. He could chastise her, have her forcibly return home or turn her out without a penny. Not until the Married Women's Property Act of 1982 could she own anything separately. Even then she had no claims on his wealth."

Our attitude towards women has been ambivalent and full of contradiction. Because, Hinduism is not a monolithic religion and it has evolved overt the countries integrating the beliefs and attitudes of diverse racial and cultural groups, Manu summed up the ancient ideas about women in these words "where women are honoured there all rituals are fruitful. "Manu has laid the rule that "the daughter is equal to the son". But inspite of this dictum, the women of India have always been relegated to a secondary role vis-a-vis men. The practice of child marriage, suttee, infanticide of new born girl to avoid payment of bride money, prohibition of female education and widow re-marriage, polygamous marriage, slavery, purdah system and the dowry system--all these prescribed by society left the women weak and fragile and dependent on men from the time of their birth to death.

By the turn of the century, many of these malpractices were abolished for which the credit goes to social and intellectual reformers such as Raja Ram Mohan Ray and Ishwar Chand Vidyasagar. In recent years, the Indian constitution abolished discrimination against any citizen of India on grounds of religion, race, caste, sex or place of birth and guaranteed equality of opportunity to all citizens in matters of public employment. The old laws of divorce and marriage have been amended by the Hindu Marriage Act 1955 and the Special Marriage Act 1954. A single act of adultery has been made a ground for divorce. Simple cruelty is added as a new ground for seeking divorce. As a matter of fact today, women have no doubt emerged from their traditional role as housewife and mother, entering the political business and professional fields previously dominated by males and in fact the two sexes legally have become equal in almost all areas of interaction. The oft quoted observation of Tulsidas the drum to the village fool, the shudras, animals and women all those are fit to be beaten' is often misinterpreted to support perverse arguments.

Vouchsafingof Women's Rights

Social reformers like Ishwar Chand Vidyasagar--the champion of widow re-marriage expounded the hypocracy of this so called religious leader through their pamphlets and their campaign for reformation.

Under pressure of the social reformers, a bill was introduced in July 1956 to make widow remarriage permissible under the law. There was a hue and cry from the orthodox society. One petition against the bill was signed by 37,000 persons led by Raja Radhakant Dev and the Pandits of Nadia, Bansbare and another petition enumerated the following reasons for the practice of enforced widowhood.

It would be difficult for a woman to contract a second marriage, because her husband will never consent to it. She has no chance of having any personal acquaintance or interview with those to whom she might be married.

Women also organise themselves and join the debate. They had expressed their dissatisfaction against hypocracy of the pundits. Ramadevi Saraswati (1858-1922) the great saint, scholar and social reformer expressed her views in these words "but there are two things on which all the books, the Dharm Shastras, the sacred epics, the puranas and modern poets, the popular preachers of the present day and orthodox high caste men were agreed, that women of high or low caste as a class were bad, very bad, worse than demons, as untruth, and that they could not get Moksha as men. The only hope of their getting this much desired liberation from Kama and its results, that is countless method of births and deaths and untold sufferings, was the worship of their husband."[1]

Despite all the opposition this bill was passed. In 1876, widows were legally allowed to re-marry. On Dec. 9, 1850, the first ever widow re-marriage was solemnised in Calcutta.

Under the presence of social reformer, the British rulers were forced to pass series of laws making various inhuman practices illegal, these landmarks of legislation can be briefly thus enumerated.

1825	Sati outlawed.
1856	Widow remarriage made legal.

1. Demystification of law of women, Nandita Haksar, p. 48.

1870	Special Marriages Act passed to allow inter-community marriages.
1891	Age of consent revised to 12 years.
1921	Women got the right to vote in Madras Province.
1937	Women got limited right to property.

Women in Post-Independence Era

And then came independence and a body of men and women sat in the Constituent Assembly to write the Constitution of Independent India. This was an opporunity to do away with discrimination between men and women based on religion and give our country a new civil code - a secular law which would incorporate the spirit of New India. After all millions of women had taken part in the long struggle for independence from colonial rules, Raj Kumari Amrit Kaur observed 'the way Article 25 was made, it would make future legislation impossible'. In a minute of dissent Mrs. Hans Mehta and Amrit Kaur said that they needed a uniform civil code because "One of the factors that has kept India back from advancing the nationhood has been the existence of personal laws based on religion which keeps the nation divided into water-tight compartments in many aspects of life".

In 1948, on the basis of the committee's recommendations, the Hindu code Bill was introduced in Parliament and decided on the floor of the house. And suddenly on the eve of the first election in 1957, the bill was dropped because of the weak opposition. It was on this issue that women found great support from Baba Saheb Ambedkar, the then law minister, who resigned on this vital issue.

In 1956 and later in 1976 some changes were brought in Hindu law but women still did not get equal rights. Even the idea that men and women should have equal rights within the family is not accepted by the law. According to a senior judge of a Delhi High Court "Introduction of constitutional law in the house is most inappropriate. It is like introducing a bull in a china shop. It will prove to be ruthless destroyer of marriage institution and all that it stands for in the privacy of the home, and the married life, neither ariticle 21 nor article 14 has any place. In a sensitive sphere which is at once not intimate and delicate, the introduction of the old principles of constitutional law will have the effect."

Media and Women

Most of the Indian advertisers are guilty of sexism in their advertising, propagating negative images of women as a household display with or without half dressed banners on of dashing men. Normally, Indian women never took seriously to these advertisements, but some energetic women formed a committee on the portrayal of women as a seductive Gopi, clustered around contemporary Krishna, who is holding up a razor of displaying his underwear of a new range of suiting. Always, a decorative, often half dressed appendage to the male image.

Confronting advertisers with their numerous sins, the committee found that many of the copywriters won women, and a lot of them did not think that they were being sexist at all. Some advertisers protested that their depictions were drawn from Kamasutra--Khajuraho, Konark and exploits of Krishna, the projection of ancient romanticism.

62

Rise of Woman Power

This is based on the papers presented at the national seminar on "Women's movement in India - a review of achievements and issues." organised by the Research Centre for Women's Studies to evaluate the role and impact of the new women's struggle in India. Contributions by several activists and researchers makes the book a comprehensive and valuable work. It covers a wide spectrum of activities, issues and ideological debates faced by the women's groups in different parts of India - Assam to Gujarat, the Himalayas to Tamil Nadu.

The section on mainstream organisations highlights the role of established organisations - a case study of All India Women's Conference in Surat, policies and programmes and structure and methods of functioning adopted by women's groups in Gujarat. It delineates the activities and issues taken up by the National Federation of Indian Women during 1975-1985.

Growing awareness on women's issues was reflected in the changes in the social, economic and political fabric as well as the legislative reforms vis-a-vis women. A series of legal provisions such as Equal Remuneration Act (ERA), 1976; Marriage Laws Amended Bill, 1978, that recommended "irretrievable breakdown of marriage" as a ground for divorce; Dowry Prohibition (Amendment) Act, 1984; Family Courts Acts 1984 and some landmark judgements given by the Indian judiciary, which were the outcome of the pressure built up by new women's rights movement and individual women contesting discriminatory aspect of the law.

In 1984, some tibal women from Dhulia and Singhbhum filed petitions in the Supreme Court demanding land rights for women, as the land reforms of the post-independence period had taken away their customary land rights. Around the same time a divorced muslim woman Shehnaz Sheikh challenged in the Supreme Court the Shariat law that does not allow maintenance by divorced wife, provides for unilateral pronouncement of *talaq*, ploygamy and unequal share of the daughter on succession.

Several Supreme Court judgements have been represented by the women's groups due to the sexist bias. The shabbily written and summarily passed judgement in case of film actress Sarita contesting the restitution of conjugal rights filed by her husband angered women's groups a great deal. In Manjushree Sarda's murder case, the Supreme Court acquitted her husband.

Says advocate Indira Jaisingh in her paper, "the zig-zag of judicial intervention in women's issues makes it impossible to come to any firm conclusion on the role of the judiciary in furthering the rights of women"(p.58).

Contradictions of the mainstream media vis-a-vis the women's question are succinctly brought out by Pamela Philipose in her paper "media response to the decade". The section

"Organising the grassroots" has significant contributions by women activists such as Gail Omvedt, Nagmani Rao, Lalita Krishnaswamy, Jaya Arunachalam and Manushi Mitra.

In this connection, Imention a recently released book which also provides holistic perspective on the process of social transformation in Maharashtra. The Marathi publication edited by Prof. Ramesh Panse has been able to get comprehensive and analytically powerful articles such as "Movement for social change" by Prof. Nalini Pandit "Dalit Movement" by Bhaskar Bhole, "Peasant and agricultural labourers movement" by Ramesh Padhya, "Women's liberation movement" by Sujata Gotoskar and Vijay Kanhere, "People's science movement for people-oriented modernisation" by Dr. Anant Phadke, "Wandering tribes' struggles" by Motiraj Rathod, "Muslim satyashodhak movement" by Hussain Jamadar, "Consumers movement" by Leela Jog, "Voluntaryorganisationsand economic change" by S.H. Deshpande, "Science education" by V.G. Kulkarni, "Laboratory of rural child education" by Ramesh Panse, "Maher - An experiment in rural female education" by V.V. Chiplunkar, and so on.

Coming back to the book under review, I must comment on Chandi Prasad Bhatt's perceptive article "Women protect forests". After giving a vivid account of women's role in maintaining the ecological balance, he says"... it is very natural to conclude that it is most unfortunate that women are not taken in respect of preservation, extension and administration of forests. No set-up can be either effective or permanent without women's co-operation" (p. 113).

The last but very important section provides an analysis of the phenomenon of emergence and proliferation of autonomous women's organisations that take up their rights issues from a militant transformatory and participatory perspective. Case studies of Assam, Bihar, Maharashtra, West Bengal and Madhya Pradesh distinctly bring out the fact that it is only due-to these organisations' activities that women's rights issues such as rape, domestic violence, sexism in media, ecological degeneration, drought developmental issues, health, employment and education of women, prostitution, political participation and Panchayatiraj, women's issues that figure in the agenda of planners and policy makers, politicians and people at large.

In spite of regional differences, these new women's groups have been able to establish links with the mass organisations in rural and urban areas, to influence democratic rights movements and the academic institutions.

The editor rightly states in her preface that this volume is a symbol of the "happy alliance between the university and the women's movement. This is an example of constructive politics. By providing an environment for women to discuss, debate and evaluate issues and their outcomes, we can strengthen the link between knowledge and action".

This book provides valuable guidance to established women's organisations, development planners, NGOs and mass organisations, women's studies academicians and activists involved in campaigns and grassroot movement[1].

No more a Man's World

With the recent appointment as judge to the Supreme Court, M. Fathima Beebi has created history: she is the first Muslim woman in the world to be thus appointed and the first woman in India to bag the exalted position. In what turned out to be a rather reluctant interview to *Kumkum Chaddha* Fathima Beebi spoke guardedly about her professional and personal life as under -

Q. - From the shackles of a community advocates purdah and coming out on your own, what problems and difficulties did you combat ?

A. - Not many, because my parents were very co-operative and particular that their children should

1. *The Economic Times*, New Delhi, Sunday November 12, 1989, p. 6.

be educated. The community however, was very conservative and believed that the girls should not and need not be educated beyond a certain level. They felt that it is not the job of a woman to go out of the house and that principally she is meant for the house - to work within the house. But that was in the thirties. I am not speaking for the present.

Q. - Did you agree with that concept at the time or the role society had designed for a women ?

A. - I was too young to be decisive about such things or to have a firm opinion.

Q. - Did society oppose your plans at any point of time or were you unacceptable to it simply because you were different ?

A. - There were a few murmurs when I decided to enroll myself in law, and later when I started practising, I was above the accepted marriageable age and society then thought that why would a woman - particularly an unmarried one go out on her own for the sake of a career instead of staying indoors. In the early forties, a legal profession was not considered very suitable for women, because it meant intermingling with all sorts of people - mostly men.

Q. - What were the accepted - rather safe if you will allow me to use that term - professions for women?

A. - Teaching or medical profession....or an office job...you knew the traditional areas of working women.

Q. - What are the demands of a legal profession which make it an untraditional area for women as it were ?

A. - A lawyer's profession is one which requires hard work and a substantial degree of self confidence and above all the ability to handle people, to tackle them and deal with them. As a lawyer you are expected to deal with all kinds of men and women and sometimes one may find it difficult to handle certain types of people.

Q. - Did you have any such difficulties to combat ?

A. - I practised for a short while - barely eight years. The first few days I was a bit nervous, but later I could stand on my own - rather fight on my own. Having opted for this profession I liked it and knew that I had come to stay.

Q. - What were your most taxing and trying moments within and outside courts as a practicing lawyer?

A. - As a sitting judge, I would not like to comment on this. I have my own reservations.

Q. - Did you, in your profession, have a problem of acceptability simply because you were a woman?

A. - Not really...There was not much against me except perhaps petty jealousies...

Q. - Which may have magnified now that after you have 'made it' as it were to the Supreme Court?

A. - I don't know...

Q. - You have created history by being the first Muslim woman in the world to be appointed to the Supreme Court. What message would you like to send to the women of the world in general and to those of your community in particular ?

A. - A would like them to be inspired and I would be happy if I can set an example for them and make them realise that their role is not only limited to the house and that they can be useful to the society and an inspiration to others which would result in the overall advancement and development of women. If women waste their talent then they would be doing disservice to both the society and the world.

Q. - Have you been able to inspire some women to follow your footsteps ?

A. - Certainly. Many parents have, following my example, enrolled their daughters in law or encouraged them to take up other careers.

Q. - Do you observe purdah or is yours a family which did or does ?

A. - Not in the real sense but out of modesty we cover our heads, whenever we go out of the house. Some of our women keep their head covered even when they are inside the house and they are not free with men.

Q. - From a set up where to quote you "women were not free with men" to a world where you had to work with men, for men and relate to men, what problems did you face particularly in communicating with them ?

A. - I was very ca-eful. All my dealings were with a degree of modesty which would neither raise eyebrows or give rise to protests from any quarter.....For any lawyer man or woman the first few months is very trying period. You need the initial confidence to be able to deal with matters.

Q. - Men and matters ?

A. - Of course!

Q. - What has been your source of inspiration ?

A. - My own parents. I was very interested in pursuing my studies and my parents encouraged me.[1]

Focus is on Women Artists

To mark the International Women's Day on Mark 8, a number of rallies and seminars were held in Chandigarh.

The Chandigarh Museum Art Gallery put up an impressive show of about 75 works of art from its permanent collection, executed by women artists.

The star attraction of the whole show is Amrita Shergil's painting done in 1937. This small rare painting, Amrita's only piece in this museum's collection exhibits her complete liberation from the western influences that she had imbibed during her training in art in Europe. But sadly, the painting has not been maintained well. The museum's accession number, marked behind the canvas, is clearly visible on its chipping front in relief.

Though majority of the exhibits, that include graphics, scuptures and drawings, has been displayed earlier, the show with the addition of some recent acquistions, has a fresh look. In the old lot, paintings by Jaya Appaswamy, Anjolie Ela Menon and Damyanti Chawla; drawings by Anupam Sud and Arpita

---

1. *The Hindustan Times Magazine*, Sunday, October 29, 1989, p.9.

Singh; sculptures by Harbhajan Sandhu, Surya Panwar and Sudha still maintain their charm, because of their innate lyrical and expressive qualities.

Kanchal Malhotra's two fine etchings, Kavita Nayar's skilful litho-print portraying a simple stoic woman's figure in black, and Mirnalini Mukherjee's small grey-print are the highlights of the graphic section with their sensitive, serious rendition.

Arpana Caur's new addition to this museum attracts one not only because of its large format, but also by its confident execution in simple style. Her use of contrast, both between the colours and forms, represents a certain kind of tension that the subject, 'Ritual' required.

There are also on display a few antiquated, but engrossing embroidery pieces that present the artistic perfection of the craft of the past.

Perceptive

Susheela Thakur, another woman artist from Himachal Pradesh (at present stationed at Patiala, Punjab), exhibited her 70 paintings at the Punjab Kala Bhawan's exhibition gallery. Done on paper with oil-pastes, currently a not so popular medium, the mini-sized paintings clearly demonstrated her full control over the medium. Some of her works extremely perceptive and poignant. But she should have been more prudent in the selection of the exhibits, for, majority of them appeared to be mere academic exercises.

Crafts on Show

The Punjab Women and Children Development and Welfare Corporation (PUNWAC), a State Government undertaking, organised a craft exhibition, at a local hotel.

The State run organisation manages a number of training-cum-production centres of various handicrafts in Punjab. By taking up the responsibility of marketing their products, at a mere 10 per cent additonal charges, the organisation is trying to eliminate the middleman completely.

After the warm public response, PUNWAC received here and at a previous show at Madras, it is planning to put up similar shows at Calcutta, Lucknow andBangalore soon.

At the Chandigarh Museum's new exhibition gallexy Ajmer, an enthusiastic art student, held his maiden exhibition of pencil drawings. His meticulously executed drawing, in black and white spoke high of his skill. Though he appeared to be on the right path he certainly has a long road ahead of him[1].

How The Other Half Lives

She is a post-graduate from the London School of Economics and holds a PhD from Bombay University. Her articles appear regularly in leading national and international financial newspapers. She has authored a book on Indian industrialists and is a visiting professor at the Indian Institute of Management at Ahemedabad. In between all this, she never misses her game of badminton, the evening swim and the "one book a week" regime. Meet Gita Piramal: author, business journalist, teacher, and, by the way , a CEO's wife she is married to Dilip Piramal of VIP Industries.

Gita belongs to an exclusive set--the first ladies of the Indians corporate sector. All these years, with the spotlight firmly focused on their husbands, the CEO's wife lived in quiet anonymity, holding sway in an empire that rarely extended outside her home.

But all that is changing. These days the CEO's wife is likely to be a hard driven achiever, determined to prove her worth. Take Jyotsna Poddar, for instance. Impeccable lineage-she is the daughter of industrialist, K.K. Birla and the wife of

---

1. *The Hindu*, 22.3.91.

Saroj Poddar, co-promoter of Indian Shaving Products. Jyotsna is busy planning her second book on cricket. Her first book, also on cricket, has already won two awards from the Sports Authority of India.

But writing is hardly more than a part-time hobby for Jyotsna. If anything, in fact, it is the topping to a widely diversified career that ranges from tourism and advertising to real estate, publishing and cricket.

Jyotsna started out fairly modestly. She look over travel agency Lionel Edwards, one of the smallest companies in her father's group. Today, she claims to have turned it into a money-spinner, the second largest travel agency in Calcutta.

Buoyed by her success, Jyotsna is now spreading her wings. She plans to start an advertising agency LEAS but has delayed the launch. "I can't find the right people" she complains. At the same time she is moving in other directions, playing an active role in her husband, Saroj Poddar's real estate business. Says Jyotsna: "The Birla daughters have always played an active role mostly in the form of social services--looking after the family-run trusts and hospitals. But like my sister Shobhana--who helps to manage The Hindustan Times-I wated to be in active business."

One of the most highly-rated ways of staying ahead of the CEO's wife next door is to set up one's own business separate from the husband's. By this yardstick, Anita Lal, the wife of Eicher Goodearth CEO, Vikram Lal, made it a long time ago. Ten years back husband Vikram put in the money to help her start shop, Tulsi, in New Delhi, which sells lacquered pots designed by Anita.

Today the investment has been more than paid back and Tulsi has a daily turnover of around Rs. 2,000. It has already bagged a sizeable number of orders from overseas and from large Indian companies. And, no. For the record - Eicher doen's buy the pots.

The fact is that being the boss's wife does not help to ward off boredom. And in these days of working wives and two-income families, even the CEO's wife needs to be able tosay that she has her own achievements to her credit. For some the opportunity comes late in life. Asha Modi, the wife of industrialist Yogendra Kumar Modi, never got the chance to really get out of the house until the last few years when her children grew up. When she was young she studied economics at Loreto College, Calcutta, and always wanted to do her PhD. Now, with the children in their mid-teens, she is putting her nose to the grindstone once again. A few years ago she might have been thought of going back to economics. Instead, she is getting involved in numerous different ways, in contemporary economic issues: she writes articles for newspapers, attends day-long seminars and devours magazines like Fortune and Businessweek. Her first article on housing was carried by a financial paper and she is now getting down to writing her second.

If Asha Modi is trying to make her mark, Panna Bharat Ram, wife of Vinay Bharat Ram of DCM, is a veteran who has established a secure niche for herself over last few years. In her time Panna has notched up an impressive string of achievements to her credit. She comes from the Lalbhai family and helped to run a textile mill in her youth. Since then, she has organised melas for the Festival of India, and set up a puppet repertory to promote contemporary puppet theatre. But the main activity into which she has thrown her heart and soul is managing the Shri Ram Centre for Arts in the capital. "There are days when I am at the Centre till 9 p.m., and there is still so much to be done," she says, and adds, "But I am too much of an autocrat. Everything is built around me."

Kofta, and even Asha now finds little time to cook.

Now that they have careers of their own to look after, what role do the wives in their husband's business ? Almost all claim that they play none whatsoever. says Gita Piramal : "I am in no way involved in my husband's business. Of course, we do discuss our respective careers and hence I am aware of his work. But that's about it." Adds Gita Sapur : "I don't advise him at all, but I certainly help him unburden the tensions, if any."

The message is clear. In the past, the CEOs wife was a wife first and last. Today, they still play a dominant role in the family, but they are no longer appendages to their husbands; they are individuals in their own right.

63

Women's Lib in Asia

In the western world, even the casual observer will hardly see any market gap between men and women, whether socially or in matters involving tradition, culture or behaviour. In other words, the male doesn't look at the females as inferior - or superior - to him and vice versa one needs some sort of special consideration just because one is a he or a she. That kind of social equality, alas, cannot be said of Asian women.

As so many of us have found out, Asian women are not anywhere as liberated as their Western counterparts, nor as aggressive and independent. In fact, our women are divided and disorganised not only by reason of geography but also in religion, culture, politics and customs and traditions.

Some countries like the Philippines have liberal democratic societies where others like Malaysia and Singapore are under autocratic male patriarchal rules. One example of this divisiveness are the Chinese women who, although found in almost all over Asia, are still unintegrated within those countries.

Xenophobia, racial, class and sex discrimination still exist in the Orient. Most women suffer from various other problems specific to their gender, like abandonment by husbands, poor income, sex harassment, poor education and frequent pregnancies.

In almost all countries of Asia, bettering of women is not uncommon. Wives undergo brutality from their husbands gone drunk after a day's night out, or even after work during a drinking spree.

Still other women in other countries continue to be plagued with problems specific to them. Indian women are still suffering from certain traditional practices like bride-burning and dowry requirements. I was told by an Indian friend that last year there were 85 cases of bride-burning in one State alone. The killing of female foetuses and babies was also rampant in India. But what revolted me was when widows who do not have any other sources of livelihood choose to join their dead husbands as their bodies are cremated. This is called sati.

In the Philippines, on the other hand, women resort to working abroad no matter how dare the working conditions are. Some opt to be mail-order brides.

In Japan, wives suffer in silence the consequences of having husbands who seek other pleasures in the arms of other women rather than lose, their financial security. The highly industrialised Japan had bred men who must enjoy their nights out after a gruelling day at office. This they do by visiting nightclubs where forcing nude entertainers can be found. Wives sometimes experience incest because of being frequently left alone, with their older sons. This is especially true in rural areas where the husbands go to the city for lengthy employment.

There is, however, a glimmer of hope among them. Likethe Western sisters, Asian women are beginning to assert themselves. In India, for example, women lug ladders in front of billboards or advertising posters to pain or wipe out ads for films which portray women simply as sex objects, just like what the women do in London.

In the Philippines, women's groups resort to writing letters to editors denouncing sexist ads and cartoons, or going out in the streets and demonstrate or hold conferences.

In Papua New Guinea, women talk to their political officials when they think they are being excessively discriminated against.

In Malaysia, a women's group has set up a battered women's house giving shelter to wives and their children suffering in the hands of their violent husbands. Also, Malaysian women are slowly discarding traditional customs, like in the wearing of clothes to show menfolk that they too know what is good for them.

Thus, in the face of society's lack of awareness of solutions to alleviate, if not totally obliterate, women's problems groups of female activists have devised new methods that run counter to their traditional image in society of being meek, quiet, unassuming and unmindful of what is done to them.

But I believe, as many others do that it is too much to assume that Asian women are already carrying out a movement all over far from that : in fact, in all my trips in this part of the world I have yet to witness a countrywide campaign against, for example, abortion or divorce.

On the contrary, if ever some opposition on their part gets a warning, one can be sure only scattered groups of females will actively show anger or approval, as the case may be. This is part of the Asian psyche. I presume that they be unassuming, unobstrusive and simply hardworking. Sometimes they could be positive but most of the time, they are simply a negative factor.

What then is in store for them ? I really don't know, but from what I have observed among western women, the women of Asia owe it to themselves to rise up from their submissive and patient image and try to overcome their own tradition-bound state of helpessness and subservience. As one macho told me: "I love a fight, especially if my opponent is a woman."[1]

1. *Arjuna, The Pioneer,* Lucknow, September 12, 1989, p. 10

64

Extensive Benefits to Women

More than ten years ago, MGR set a trend that has become irreversible - woo the "Thai Kulam" (womenfolk). And it was not surprising at all that when MGR died, the contenders for the Chief Ministership made several promises to woo this section of the electorate. The DMK, too, did so, but the promises have not remained promises.

Since coming to power in January, Chief Minister M. Karunanidhi has set in motion the process for fulfilment of many of his election promises and high on the list are those relating to women and their welfare. The Karunanidhi government began with a 30 per cent reservation of women in jobs in government offices, state government undertakings and local bodies. This, along with a decision to recruit only as teachers for standards one and two in elementary schools, was taken at the very first meeting of the new Cabinet.

Other schemes and employment generation programmes followed in quick succession. In order to tackle the low literacy rate as well as the high drop-out rate among women Mr. Karunanidhi has introduced two schemes to promote women's education. One is a school to provide free education to women belonging to poor families upto graduate level which comes into force from the 1989-90 academic year. A scheme for granting Rs. 5,000 as marriage assistance to girls from poor families who have studied at least upto eighth standard is also being set in motion.

On the general welfare side, a scheme for grant of Rs. 50 a month from the eight month of pregnancy to two months after childbirth is being introduced for women labourers.

A Rs. 46 crore scheme for the economic uplift of women with assistance from the International Fund for Agricultural Development will be implemented by the TN Corporation for Development of Women from July in three districts - Salem, Dharmapuri and South Arcot. The project will benefit 40,000 women over a seven-year period.

The most progressive and wide-ranging among the measures adopted by the DMK government is the recent one conferring equal property rights on Hindu women. This measure, brought about by an amendment of the Hindu Succession Act in its application to the State, will check the dowry system, the Government feels. It is also seen as a fruition of a resolution, passed in February 1929 at the first provincial conference of Periyar EVR's Self-respect Movement, calling for equal rights in property and inheritance for women.

An earlier attempt in this direction had been made by MGR, who in April 1983, had announced that the Government would introduce a comprehensive bill providing for inheritance rights to women and training, employment and security to women who left their homes protesting against dowry. But the bill never came. The bill now passed by the Tamil Nadu Assembly confers equal inheritance rights on Hindu women with respect to coparcenary property in joint Hindu families governed by the Mitakshara law. The rights are conferred on the survivors of the daughter, if she pre-deceases the coparcenary partitioning of the property. The law is also applicable to daughters married after March 25, from which date the law will be made effective after the bill gets the Presidential assent.

The law has its own weaknesses, in so far as it makes a distinction between daughters married before and after March 25, and fears were expressed in the Assembly that this might be a ground for the law being struck down by courts. But Law Minister Sadiq Pasha expressed the Government's hope that the courts would take a liberal view, if the law was challenged. Moreover, there is also the question of the applicability of this Tamil Nadu law to coparcenary properties held in other states.

Apart from these measures, Mr. Karunanidhi has set into motion a scheme to help destitutes, widows and families headed by women by helping them acquire autorickshaws. Assistance will be provided to 200 women from the current year with an allocation of Rs. 13 lakh towards the subsidy.

The representation for women in Madras Corporation has been increased from eight to ten. But the representation that women have in the 17 member ministry is restricted to one - Mrs. Subbulakshmi Jagadeesan - and including her the DMK has only five women in the Assembly.

Mr. Karaunanidhi has fulfilled his election promises for women and gone beyond the party manifesto also. It remains to be seen whether this will give him the kind of stranglehold that MGR had on the "Thai Kulam"[1].

Call to Help Women's Self-Employment

The need to enhance contribution of small and medium-sized enterprises set up by women entrepreneurs to the overall trade in Asian regions was emphasized by Mr. C.K. Modi, development commissioner (Small Scale Industry), in a 12-day

---

1. *Indian Express*, May 23, 1989.

seminar on effective business management for export marketing for women entrepreneurs organised jointly by the World Assembly of Small and Medium Enterprises (WASME) and PRODEC (Programme for Development) of Helsinki School of Economics, at New Delhi. Twenty-two women business leaders from 10 Asian countries participated in the seminar[1].

Mr. Modi said to increase exports from the small and medium enterprise (SME) sector, its production bases needed to be expanded. India, Philippines, Thailand and quite a few other Asian countries have built small and medium units on import substituion policy. He also pleaded for motivating the banking system to back up potential good exporter and putting into place specific institutional arrangements to provide collective strength to the sector. It was important that intermediate agencies taking on the responsibility to export products of small enterprises to be fair and share equitably the profit margins.

He conceded that one of the weak areas of SMEs is their access to new technologies and their ability to meet the changing needs of the international market. He also emphasised the need for efficient international trade information networking. Mr. Modi said that a special cell has been created in the Small Industries Development Organisation (SIDO) to actively promote self-employment and entrepreneurs of developing countries will foster trade.

Mr. Chakradhari Agarwal secretary general, WASME said that special programmes for women entrepreneurs in least developed countries of Asia and Africa will be organised by WASME to enhance their ability to claim larger share in world market.

WASME was also actively engaged in creating and strengthening associations of women entrepreneurs and ensuring that they get a better deal from their governments and financial institutions.

---

1. *Observer* - January 15, 1991.

Mr. Hele Granfeldt, training manager of PRODEC, explained the objectives of the seminar and aims and goals of PRODEC of Helsinki School of Economics which was financed by the government of Finland.

A Better Deal for Rural Women

With her small piece of land located in an undulating and inhospitable terrain in K. Kundalam hamlet. Thulasibai, a tribal women, had not ever dreamt of a harvest worth the name. To her surprise and of her neighbours, a transformation has taken place, as if a magic wand has been waved. The 1.96 hectare holding, which used to secure her an annual income of about Rs. 2,500, recently fetched Rs. 2,000 from the first crop of green peas and there is the prospect of getting another Rs. 15,000 from the second crop of flowers and groundnut. An open well sunk on her land and smoothening and shaping of the land for irrigation through a pipeline all executed at a cost of Rs. 19,500 have triggered the miracle.

There was some kind of an unwritten taboo in the sleepy hamlet of Chinnabaleguli in the interior of Soolagirl block against women going out of jobs. Children were not sent to school. The practice was given a go by recently;thanks to the formation of the Ellamma Mahila Sangh (women's group). According to Mrs. Lakshmi, representative of the Sangh, there is a growing realisation by the women in the hamlet that they can usher in a new era of development. The lifestyle has changed, with some women taking up sericulture and dairy farming for supplementing the family income.

"We have contributed our labour for erecting a community hall and have pooled our resources for improving some local roads and also for putting up a water tub for cattle," said the members of the women's groups in Korattagiri hamlet, about 20 km from Hosur. The group also donated Rs. 200 from its savings to a woman in the neighbouring Kamanapalyam village when the bread-winner of the family was killed in police firing at Denkanikottah.

There are a few success stories in silent revolution sweeping the most backward pockets in Dharamapuri district in Tamil Nadu, thanks to the implementation of the Women's Development project assisted by the International Fund for Agricultural Development Exculsively evolved for the benefit of disadvantaged rural women, its primary objectives are in the tune with the Central and State Government policies for improving their status, welfare and standard of living. This is being partly achieved through increasing their income earning potential by integrating them into the regular system for credit, technical support and services.

The target group has been identified as those in the age group of 18 - 55 whose annual family income is less than Rs. 4,800. Preference is given to those whose income is below Rs. 3,500. The bulk of the assistance is expected to be changed to this group.

Tamil Nadu has the fourth highest percentage of female-headed households in the country: women head 20 - 25 per cent of the households *dé jure* because of widowhood, desertion and the like of *de facto* by virtue of migration, unemployment or abnormal behaviour of their husbands. Also, only 25 per cent of rural women are literate as against 51 per cent of the men. Nearly 90 per cent of women workers are in the informal unorganised sector, 80 per cent of them in agriculture.

Initial project developments are centered in Dharmapuri district with provision for extension to Salem and South Arcot in 1991-92 (A proposal for covering some pockets in Madurai and Pasumpon Thevar Thirumagan districts is also there). The three districts are among the least developed in the state and have been selected on the basis of State-wide indicators of the status of women. These included women's representation in the workforce, the types of work they are engaged in, their dependency on agriculture for employment, the percentage of Scheduled Castes and Tribe women in the female population, literacy, health and mortality rate. Analysis of the date has shown Dharmapuri as a pocket where women are most disadvantaged, followed by South Arcot and Salem.

The indices also reflect the general poverty levels. In Dharmapuri 82 per cent of the households have an annual income of less than Rs. 5,000 and 56 per cent less than Rs. 35,000. Although Dharmapuri district was born out of the bifurcation of Salem district as far women even now. Female literacy there is said to be the lowest in the State.

Some major innovations have been introduced in the project approach for plugging the loopholes usually noticed in most poverty alleviation programmes. These are identification and selection of beneficiaries by a non-government, use of trained animators at the village level for encouraging women to form themselves into viable groups, total freedom for the groups in decision making even in the selection of beneficiaries and identification of activities, and above all, promotion of thrift habit and self-reliance through self-managed group savings fund and credit. Significance is attached to the condition that the patta (title deed for the land) should be in the name of the beneficiary either individually or jointly. It is believed that the ultimate goal of economic independence for women can be achieved, even if to a limited extent, only through this process.

The Rs. 46-crore seven-year old project to benefit 40,320 women in the three districts has covered some blocks in Dharmapuri district. In 1989-90, 1,135 women were formed into 53 groups. Of them, 540 were assisted with credit totalling Rs. 27.56 lakhs for income generating activities. In 1990-91, 6,013 women have so far been formed into 259 groups and of them 1,124 have received assistance of Rs. 80.36 lakhs. The groups have made a savings of Rs. 10.35 lakhs under the common group fund.

Before becoming eligible for a loan, the members are required to make contributions to the savings fund for at least three months. This stipulation, introduced to inculcate the thrift habit in the members, is a novel component of the project. The fund will be managed by the group itself for providing loans to the members to meet their consumption and emergency needs. A rate of interest slightly higher than the bank's is collected.

The major economic activities are on farm development, horticulture, sericulture, animal husbandry and cottage industries. The project funding is almost similar to that under the Intergrated Rural Development Programme (IRDP) and other such programmes. The credit is channeled through the Indian Bank, the lead bank of the district, which is entitled to refinancing facilities.

MYRADA, a Bangalore-based voluntary agency engaged in agriculture and rural development, operates in Dharmapuri and Periyar districts. Its aim is building up self-reliance among the poorest rural sections with group interaction. It has been entrusted with the task of screening the beneficiaries, training animators for creating awareness among the members of the groups and training the beneficiaries themselves for managing the assets created. The animators, who constitute the most important base level motivation force, shoulder the task of educating women in family welfare, including child care, nutrition, health, environmental sanitation and safe motherhood in addition to the assigned work of monitoring and supervising the activities for which credit is given.

A visit to some of the villages covered by the project indicates a major breakthrough in the first two years of operation itself. The inital resistance of men to women joining the groups and hesitation to transfer the patta in the name of women have been largely overcome. A women's group in Denkanikottah engaged in making bamboo articles spoke about the men realising that their income has been supplemented by the earnings of their wives.

The other positive signal is that even mostilliterate among the rural women, who had till now an attitude of resignation, have become aware of their right for a share in the services extended to the rural parts.

Mr. K. Allauddin, Collector of Dharmapuri, who is in overall charge of the monitoring the project in the district, said that in view of the progress noticed, he has mooted the idea of enrolling some representatives of the groups in village vigilance committees so that they can have a say in all matters concerning their place of living.

Mr. S. Adiseshiah, Managing Director of the Tamil Nadu Corporation for Development of women, said a review by a UNP mission, which visited the project area recently, found that barring a few minor shortfalls because of adverse climatic conditions, the progress has been quite satisfactory. In certain areas such as agriculture, sericulture and cottage industries, the achievement has even exceeded the target.[1]

Women in Banking

Though more women are taking up jobs, their number is still far too little to make an effective dent in the male-dominated organised sector. The maximum number of women is in the banking sector where they for a mere 12 per cent of the work force. In the civil services they are even less than 10 per cent. Not only are women in the organised sector treated as any other minority group, but their behaviour pattern is also affected at their workplace. In fact, most of the time they are being observed as 'token specimens', thus creating a two-way disfunctioning.

These observations were made by Ms C.P. Sujaya, former member of the Commission for Scheduled Castes and Scheduled Tribes and now with the Indian Institute of public Administration, on the concluding day of the seminar on 'women in public sector'. She referred to the poor self-perception of women and said this made them imitate other successful men in their style of working and contribute very little of their own to the organisation.

'Marketing' for Women : Women form a mere six per cent of the work forces in the organised sector. This number should increase to at least 40 per cent. She stressed on the need for 'marketing' for women by those women who were in the managerial position in public sector. This would mean giving

1. *The Hindustan*, Sunday, January 6, 1991, p. 23.

enough opportunity of management training to women and producing the sort of manpower required by the market.

In the traditional sector, women had been relegated to work with lower level of skill development, that which involved long hours and drudgery. But stereotyping of women is obvious even in relatively modern sectors where most of the time they were pushed to jobs "they are capable of doing better", Ms. Sujaya said.

It is a systematic bias and can be solved only through a systemic solution. Telephone operators, stenographers, teachers, nurses were a few jobs where women were unproportionately in a large number. Even in the civil services, women were naturally pushed towards education, health and social welfare and it was only exceptional when they were in the 'money sector' or the hard sectors. Likewise in medical sciences, women were found mostly in the non-clinical departments.

" It is the time the women realised that they are as much a factor of development in their organisation as the men", she said. Most of the time the women looked upon the more successful men in their organisation and tried to imbibe their style. Why should not the women try to impress their own style of working and management and in the process offer something to the organisational style and management?

Holistic approach is needed. Ms. Sujaya and some other participants said women and men were equals yet not similar and therefore it was necessary to adopt a holistic approach by blending the male and female styles of functioning. Women were *ipso facto* mere considerate, less aggressive and emotional and there has been no reason why they should imitate men and become different. They felt that it was time men got used to the women's way of working.

The participants highlighted the need for proper support services for working women. Ms Anjali Hazarika, member of the forum for women in public sector said their northern chapter was planning to approach all public sector undertakings to ensure that facilities of creches were made available. It was ironic that while the government had ensured that laws had been made with respect to industrial houses for providing creches facilities, the government itself, which was the largest employer of women saw this facility as a 'welfare measure'. Thus in government offices, child-care services like creches were provided if only funds were available, it was pointed out. Ms Sujaya said government, public as well as the private sectors should recognise that composition of work force was changing and therefore they should bring in the necessary changes suited for their working conditions.

Importance of providing counselling services at workplaces was highlighted at the seminar. The participants felt that since in the Indian context counselling was a fairly alien concept and response to such a service, though the need was felt, would not be satisfactory, the forum would hold discussions and seminar on the issues of mutual interest such as stress management and job-related problems.[1]

Mode of Sustenance

Among the poor, most women work and, therefore, their need for credit, though very small, is very genuine.

Poor women need credit for sustaining their existing employment and for the generation of further employment and to create assets for them. Perhaps, asset-building is the single most important intervention towards both thier empowerment and economic well-being. The government is aware of this to some extent and, therefore, has reserved 30 per cent of the IRDP loans for women so far.

However, in the present system, women do not have easy access to credit even if the amount is very small. In spite of the Reserve Bank's instructions that no security is required for loans upto Rs. 10,000, collateral is generally asked for,

1. *The Hindu*, January 20, 1991.

particularly in the case of women. An analysis of the existing mainline credit schemes for the poor shows that the poor women are marginalised because of illiteracy, lack of information and asset ownership. Therefore, money lenders are a very real part of their lives. The banks, for various reasons, are still distant for them, in spite of the fact that banks are aware that there is a much higher repayment rate among women than men.

The banks, however, have been successful in providing credit to poor women through voluntary organisations like Sewa Bank Ahmedabad Maryada Karnataka, WWF Madras, Annapurna Bombay, Samakhya Hydrabad and others. These organisations have, over time and through experience, found appropriate ways to enable the credit to reach poor women and help them to make productive use of it. These experience of these organisations have shown that the credit requirements of these women are very small, their repayment rate is small and frequent and their need to save urgent.

As chairman of the National Commission on Self Employed Women and Women in the informal sector, I had the opportunity to observe the loan performance of poor women all over the country. And on that basis , I can state with confidence that what these women need is not loans on soft terms. It is just that they require *a suitable mechanism* which accommodates their needs.

Therefore, there is a strong case for an exclusive credit body at the national level for rural poor and urban women in recognition of their socio-economic realities. It will be an additional effort in support of existing institutionalised credit system like banks system.

The proposed exclusive credit body, called say Mahila Kosh, for instance. Since the voluntary sector has unequivocally proved its effectivenss in delivering credit to the target sector i.e. poor women, the Mahila Kosh should be given the necessary funds for the purpose. This will also be instrumental in initiating many more voluntary efforts all over the country especially in the so-called backward regions. The loans could also be channelised through Mahila mandals, women's groups and so on. The ownership and management of this body should represent the voluntary sectors.[1]

Need for Special Fund

CLARA of a Bangalore slum makes toy sun-glasses at home and sells them to a shopkeeper. She needs Rs. 35 to double her income. Govindamma, an idli vendor requests for Rs. 150 to be able to store her supplies. The interest that slum women pay is simply unthinkable from 2 per cent to 20 per cent a day. In Vellore, the price of a loan in emergency is pawning a child's labour. Most of the rural poor do not know that no guarantee is needed for them to acquire a small loan. Unmarried daughters are usually not granted loans by banks. In general, banks hesitate to lend to women, despite the evidence that in most cases women have proved themselves good re-payers.

While recording the above observations, the National Commission on Self-employed Women in the Informal Sector, in its report 'Shamshakti' recommends to the government the need for setting up an exclusive credit body for poor women in recognition of their socio-economic realities. Following up the recommendation, the government seems to have been, for quite sometime, seriously deliberating on the subject. However, it is now hightime that the subject took the concrete shape of a definite proposal detailing its role, activities, structure, etc.

To begin with, the basic objective of the proposed National Credit Fund for women is to improve poor women's access to credit for sustenance of their existing employment, generation of further employment for asset creation, asset redemption

---

1. *The Times of India* New Delhi, Thursday October 19, 1989, p.9.

and for tiding over consumption, social and contingent needs. The availability of credit is one of the necessary conditions for the economic advancement of the poor through self-employment. Amongst the poor, all women work. They are workers and producers, and therefore, they need credit for fixed and working capital, though usually in small quantities.

In the present system, women do not have easy access to credit even when the amount required is very small. This is in spite of specification of women's share in several credit based development programmes such as IRDP. In fact, an analysis of the existing mechanism of institutional credit shows that poor women are marginalised because of handicaps, such as illiteracy, lack of information, low self-confidence, and lack of asset ownership. The money lender continues to be a very real part of their lives as a source for both consumption and production credit, as banks, generally, do not still consider women as economic contributors in their own right.

Programmes such as the IRDP, have adopted the 'household approach' and only the 'head' of the household is considered eligible for the loan. Where women are considered eligible, collateral is generally asked for, in spite of the Reserve Bank of India's instruction that no security be demanded for loans up to Rs. 5,000 (now raised to Rs. 10,.000). Women do not own assetsto be able to provide that collateral.

It is also being realised that credit is only a necessary but not a sufficient condition for self-employment. To be successfully self-employed, it is also necessary, *inter alia*, to have a marketable skill, entrepreneurial ability, access to raw material inputs and productive infrastructure and markets. Banks traditonally, do not provide these usually, nor do most of the government agencies engaged in promoting women's development. As a result, women either have to fend for themselves or get assistance from voluntary organisations, which are few in number compared to the need.

The instances where banks have been successfully tapped for poor women is when voluntary organisations such as SEWA,

Ahmedabad; MYRADE Karnataka; Working Women's Forum, Madras; Annapurna. Bombay; ASSEFA, Tamil Nadu; Samakhya, Hyderabad and the like have acted as intermediaries. These voluntary organisations do not stop at credit, they also assist the loanees is using the credit productivity, and to save. The organisations have over time, through experience, designed appropriate credit programmes for rural and urban poor women and have learnt some important lessons while reaching credit to them. Some of these are; the credit needs of poor women are small and often lower than the minimum loan levels that the banks would find viable; repayment of loans must be frequent and in small amounts; the propensity to save high amongst women in this sector, and, they can save small amounts for frequent repayments. Making credit available for purchase of capital assets is not enough because poor women need credit for working capital as well as for pressing consumption needs. If they have to turn to money-lender for the latter needs, his claim on their savings takes precedence over institutional borrowings. As the money-lender may charge upto 120 per cent interest, there is little left over to service the institutional debt.

One of the most important lessons learnt from the voluntary sector's experience is that these poor women are not asking for soft loans. They can borrow at the normal official bank rate, that is, 12 to 18 per cent. But what they require is a suitable delivery mechanism which accommodates their needs.

It has been proved by these women, from experience of the voluntary sector, that women are honest and disciplined where repayment of credit is concerned. Most of the industrial organisations mentioned above have a 80 to 85 per cent rate of repayment. The experience with the banking system indicates, however, that a number of voluntary agencies have had to waste precious efforts in assessing bank credits for their members. In many cases, they have given up, and in others they have to set up their own parallel saving and credit infrastructure. However, a parallel banking system is not feasible. Banking is a specialised activity requiring skills usually not available with voluntary organisations and it also involves a lot of time consuming compliance with procedures which are likely to make heavy demands on the voluntary sector's already stretched organisational capability.

In this context, it suggested that there is an urgent need for a national agency to promote women's access to credit within the mainstream banking system, as well as, to ensure the availability of comprehensive micro-enterprise development support, to be provided by voluntary as well as government's development agencies. Such an agency viz., National Credit Fund for Women. I would prefer to call it by a name to be easily understood by all women, that is, Mahila Khosh-would work at the national level policy and bank management level to promote appreciation of women's credit needs and design of suitable delivery mechanisms in response thereto. The Mahila Kosh work with women's groups to increase their capability for accessing the commercial and co-operative banks for their credit needs.

It would also refinance the lending operations of women's savings and loans groups so as to enhance the resources available with them. In recognition of the fact that credit is but one ingredient in fastening self-employment, the Mahila Kosh would also involve national and state development agencies in improving marketable skills and entrepreneurial capabilities of poor women and in strengthening input-output linkages for their self-employment activities.

The Kosh would need a fairly broad mandate and objects and would need to vary its activities to suit the requirements of the situation considerably. It would engage in promotional activities in the area of policy and institutional re-orientation, It would also provide support to NGOs by way of design an delivery of training programme aimed at strengthening of the capacity of women's groups to access and effectively utilise credit.The Kosh would assist NGOs in evolving working relationships with local banks and sectoral development agencies. It can also help network among the NGOs to promote wider sharing of lessons and lending support to government development agencies in fostering co-operation among agencies andNGOs in micro-enterprise development activities. TheKosh could also provide seeding finance for leveraging other sources of funds.

The membership of the Kosh will need to reflect the diverse constituencies it seeks to serve but in view of the pivotal role of NGOs in serving as the Kosh's field units, it is important that the Kosh be constituted as an autonomous body with due representation to voluntary sector and women's savings and loan groups.

As a national agency, the Kosh will seek to make available its services to poor women across the country. On the other hand, it is clear that the Kosh cannot try to reach its services to these women directly. Thus, a critical parameter determining the Kosh's level of activity will be the existence of NGOs and other agencies capable of assisting the women in their efforts at self-employment. According to the recent study by Friends of women's World Banking (India), in 16 states there exist about 150 NGOs (women's banks not included) actively involved with at least a total of one lakh women in group savings and lending. They are essentially rural and in almost all cases the savings activity has preceded giving loans.

The Mahila Kosh will have to be a self-sustaining one, bearing its own cost of operation and R & D. It will need Rs. 3 to 4 crore per annum, by rough estimate, for its own expenses and grant activities, and about Rs. 20 crore as lendable funds to reach about one lakh women at a time. The amount would, of course, be revolving, reaching more women. This translates into the requirement of a corpus of Rs. 25 to 30 crore and, further, long-term lendable funds on soft terms of Rs. 20 crore.

The women are ready for the credit. Now it is upto to the government to do the needful.[1]

1. *The Economic Time* April 17, 1991.

65

Women Against Women

Come International Woman's Day (March 8) scores of agencies and thousands of women (including this writer) hitch on the band-wagon to shout familiar slogans about gender parity and gender justice. There is a national mechanism that churns out fancy aspirations and deliberations in favour of motherhood and the flag. There are magnificient buildings which house those who formulate, manage and enforce magnificient development plans. The entire approach is apex-centric, and brains trust for the massive leap forward into the next century. Nothing gets articulated or enforced without this apex coterie's acceptance and involvement. The machinery is greased and oiled almost totally by men. Women are given minor physical and intellectual space in the debate that precedes development planning or conditions resource allocation and utilization.

The euphoria after a gender neutral freedom struggle has luckily persisted long enough to influence framers of our constitution to provide protective safeguards to women (for example , Article 51 A calls on every citizen to renounce practices derogatory to women). But development planning took a condescending view of all this. In the first plan and several subsequent plans, women were considered as mendicants and planners were satisfied to throw some measly scrappings their way. By equating women with social welfare, the earlier plans damaged the cause and confidence of women.

Common Lot

Some of the indignities and apathy of earlier decades were sought to be corrected in two subsequent plan periods during which, for the first time, the planners' perception of women shifted from women being charitable objects to being active participants in and contributor to development. However, this altered nuance notwithstanding, no radical change has occurred in women's status, nothing much has happened to empower Indian womanhood. Persistent factors contiune to negate her person and potential. To list some of these.

The sex ratio at 933 women per 1000 men (1981) continues to favour men. By 2000 A.D. there will be 480 million females against 500 million males.

Nearly 90 per cent of women (1981 census) work in the unorganised sector which offers no regularised basis for fair waged and decent terms of work, or for them to improve their earning potential, or reduce their drudgery through supportive services like creches, fuel, water, etc. The remaining 10 per cent of the female work-force does not necessarily have access to regulatory and protective provisions. The net access to labour laws and benefits is probably confined to about four per cent.

Women's unpaid work on the farm or in the household gets no formal recognition in computation of work at the planning level. Yet eight to ten hours, or more, could be spent daily by women in collecting fuel, fodder, water and preparing food, or in farming and animal herding.

Only 25 per cent of women are literate. In atleast 57 districts in the country, female literacy is below 10 per cent. For every 100 boys who enrol, only 65 girls are able to do so. Drop-out in school girls is estimated at 60-odd per cent at the primary level and above 75 per cent at the elementary stage.

Uncontrolled fertility continues to pose a health hazard to women as to the country. Maternal deaths on account of pregnancy or intended or unintended abortion are numerous. Modern medical technology allows parents to abort the female foetus. The female infant experiences a slow material and psychological suffocation which gets accentuated at every stage of the life--as a child, during adolescence, as a teen or a pre-teen mother, as an over-burdened, overtaxed reproducing machine, which destroys her health and that of her unborn children and the cycle of neglect and damage goes on. Meanwhile, emotional operation continues, as do violence and indignities (dowry demands, bride burning, sati, rape and even rape in custody).

Credibility Gap

Where is the meeting ground between the harsh reality and the platitudinous exuberance of national plans, and what do women themselves do to close this credibility gap ? The administrative machinery and its thinkers and enforcers continue to be mostly men, with women accounting for less than 10 per cent in any of the national services or institutions (administrative, police, judiciary, legislative bodies, etc.). Even the women who are in the system, do not necessarly see themselves as conduits for other women or their cause. There are quite a few who are in fact regressive and oppose protective provisions for women on the ground that itcompromisestheir competitive calibre, compelling them to be recognised as another backward class. Yet, without such protective safeguards, the gender gap connot be filled. Even with them, it could take several decades. It is imperative that until approximate gender parity is achieved, women in the leadership positions come down from the high horse they are riding and agree to designate themselves as 'backward'.

Another requirement is for these 'leading' women to sensitise themselves to the problems and aspirations of women who have not made it. Leadership is not only to 'serve' others but to allow others to emerge as leaders. It is symptomatic of the female psyche and insecurity that she is unable to nurture other women, or even spouses of men she may nurture and elevate to leadership roles. Mrs. Gandhi was supreme illustration of this inverse gender bias, and the tradition set by her continues.

Indifference to women by women permeates all levels of our society. If as a woman you are fighting for wage parity and promotion in a male-dominated office, you still tend to pay less to a woman than to a man for comparable jobs at home. Within the households, the assignment of tasks between male and female servants by the housewife perpetuates the economy's prejudice of keeping women confined to demeaning labour and elevating men to more dignified functions. In offices women tend to offer lower terms (for secretarial as well as professional level functions), to women than to men. The need is here to resolve our inner insecurities as women in ruling leadership positions, and to open up avenues on a preferential, and at the least equal basis to women.

A vast unutilised and insensitised human resource is represented by the urban educated women past the stage of giving birth to and caring for young children. No plan or programme has ever been devised to absorb them through job sharing, transportation assistance and minor incentives (not necessarily financial) as a cadre of extension workers to work in development programmes in cities and towns. Eye-catching slogans like ' Each One Teach One' and `Health For All' have not come anywhere near these literate women. Such women should rise and organise themselves into acting groups and divert some of their `Kitty Party' resources (time and money) to helping improve the lot of the urban slum women. Even without an organisation, each woman individually can do much to educate and empower the less fortunate woman in her immediate neighbourhood, sharing knowhow on existing facilities and how to benefit from them. This is the modest but solid foundation for a woman-to-woman development movement.

Ad hoc Approach

Organised collective dissent is known to have a dramatic effect. This is an area where women have been more successful than elsewhere. Morchas and petitions protesting dowry deaths, inflation, shortage of cooking gas, and victimisation at the hands of men are now quite common. But their impact remains superficial since very little is done by the organisers to mobilise protest on a sustained basis, or to take it down to the ground level. Whether it is voluntary agencies or political parties or trade unions, the interest in women's involvement is ad hoc, and mobilisation occurs more around personalities and instances than on concepts and long-standing issues. What is needed is to utilise the incidental protest upsurge as an occasion to commit sustained energy to fighting the injustices, governmental default or social failures that caused the incident. Thus, if sati is the issue, the women's responsibility goes beyond condemning a Roop Kanwar or the administration. Massive and continuous campaigns collecting signatures and thumb impressions are required to confirm personal commitment by women never to attempt suicide, or physically harm another woman through bride-burning or inciting her to commit sati, etc. The battle against female foeticide and infanticide, like--wise, will not be won by protesting or banning amniocentesis alone but by pregnant women themselves, and those around her, pledging to refuse to undergo or send other women for such screening.

Woman of the media have a special onus to deliver the goods vis a vis women. With a few exceptions who follow the activist line unsparingly even to their own personal cost, the media's and media women's feminist involvement is next to nil. Most women in media are metropolitanised and that takes them away from focussed analysis of ground level issues. A curious distance arises unavoidably on account of class differences. For the media, women who can sip red wine with ease in the Capital's political and cultural salons, women's movement gets to be strangely stereotyped. They see women free only when they can talk politics, denounce Americanism, oppose Rajiv Gandhi and support social and marital laxity. This section of the media is doing more harm than good to the women's cause. For example, some Bombay-centered magazines, in the last few years, have encouraged bigamy by romanticising the parallel or bigamous marital status of film stars and other celebrities. Thus, what laws have justly banned has been thoughtlessly resurrected by such media attention, to the detriment of women's cause of monogamy.

Real Answer

Another illustration of the emotional gulf between the elitist and the so-called plebian women concerns the issue of presenting the right image of the Indian woman. There are media feminists who oppose vulgarisation of the Indian woman and ask for review of the content before programmes are put across. This appears to be a self-conscious reflection of their own alienness from mainstream Indian womanhood. If we like the TV serial *Ramayana*, we are not necessarily anti-woman or anti-Muslim or anti sect or another. If by exposing the injustices inflicted on women in a gruesomely compulsive manner, a Shyam Benegal can bea comradeto an activist feminists in the media and outside, why cannot *Tamas* and *Ramayana* claim the same empathy and the same cathartic eventual outcome? Why a Shabana Azmi's death in*Nishants* is more compensatory to women than Sita's compelling end, or her refusal to commit suicide the day she was kidnapped.

The argument can go on and on, but the intent here is to allow women flexibility to see and learn from everything, yet free to choose their own role models. If an Indian woman wishes to follow Sita's example and refuse to liase with anyone other than her husband then consider that as liberated as the desire of another woman to become a co-wife in recent tradition of our glamour stars. Again, if watching Godard and Bergman liberates you and *Ramayana* or *Tamas* liberate me, then allow me the right to exercise my opinion freely. In essence then, women should not, against women. Only then can be they speak squarely - on Women's Day or any other day - of women's issues and women's predicament.[1]

1. Indian Express, Wednesday, March 16, 1988-Neera Kuckreja Sohni.

66

Women's Rights Can't be Won at Cocktail Parties

Two years ago, a young woman was forced onto her husband's funeral pyre and burnt to death in Deorala of Rajasthan. Reports of Roop Kanwar's gruesome death were splashed all over the front pages of newspapers and journalist after journalist went haring off to the site of the incident. Then all of a sudden, women's rights organisations, who had been inert until then, were galvanised into action and leapt into the fray denouncing the heinous crime from every conceivable pulpit.

Two years later, the "sati" of Roop Kanwar was commemorated with great fanfare and pomp in Rajasthan. Yet there has not been a squeak out of these groups of same woman. Where are all of them today when a horrendous crime is being celebrated? Whatever happened to all the righteous indignation of two years?

This is not the first instance when women's groups have been quick to take up an issue which is in the news, only to drop it conveniently after it has disappeared off the front pages of newspapers. It may be recalled that the same sort of thing happened when a woman called Indu Arora and her lover were accused of murdering her children in Delhi last year. For days on end, women's groups issued statements on everything about the case including the rights of women to have extra-marital alliances. But what did they eventually do for Indu Arora, where are they now? What do they do when they are not following up sensational cases of violations of women's rights?

Well, the leadership of some of these women's organisations is fruitfully employed in the business of representing the vast majority of Indian women who live the lives of unrelieved misery-oppressed and dominated by men–at various conferences, seminars and meetings at fashionable venues in India and abroad.

Whether women at large like it or not, the leaders of these women's groups are determined to do good on their behalf, and never mind if the good is mainly done unto themselves. The main thing, the need of the hour, these activists seem to suggest is to talk about the desperate situation of women in India, how they have no basic rights, how they are second class citizens in the eyes of the law and in their homes. They would have us believe that the deluge of words will somehow wash away the blot of oppression that most Indian women have to live with.

But this is not to suggest that women's organisations have done nothing at all for women. Many women who work in such organisations and this usually excludes the leadership, have done a lot for women and society. But they are the aceless ones, they hardly get noticed and, to their credit, they are more concerned about their work than seeking publicity.

But it is positively objectionable that these women leaders, far from helping their staff, do as little as possible to make things easy for them.

This sort of attitude will definitely lead to disillusionment and is not likely to attract any new workers. There will be few takers for a job in an organisation which cries itself hoarse about democratic functioning and yet is loathe to practise it.

Once upon a time, women's groups did take up issues like equal pay for equal work. It may interest them to know that in many fields, women still do not get equal pay for equal work but this issue seems to have been forgotten. What the women's rights organisations in India need to do is to address themselves these basic rights which women lack in this country. These things have to be secured first before we can talk about sexual and intellectual liberation.

To make matters worse, whenever the press has taken up issues like prostitution or rape and written about them, the first to let loose a volley of condemnation are the women's groups. This usual argument is that the media, which incidentally they use conveniently to keep themselves in the news, are being voyuristic and does not examine the reasons for this or that phenomenon. But surely, this is more their job - have they studied why women become or are forced to become prostitutes ? Have they done anything to help such women? Or have they been content to pontificate about the heart-rending plight of these unfortunate women at cocktail parties in posh colonies in the capital and five star venues abroad?.

Undoubtedly, they have taken up the issue of dowry. But has dowry decreased significantly because of this? The answer is no. Women's groups are definitely there at rallies and demonstrations condemning such evil practices, but when it comes to following up such cases and helping the victims' families, they seem to lose interest. However, they are, and I mean the leaders of these groups, right in the forefront when the media comes around for quotable quotes on the horrors of dowry.

In a field that has been so badly neglected as that of women, and where so much needs to be done, there can be no justification for these leading lights of women's groups to confine themselves to goading where they are sure to get publicity and going on lengthy jaunts abroad to create an "awareness" about Indian women and their status. Undoubtedly, these jaunts abroad are most useful in projecting themselves as the sole representatives of Indian women and perhaps pick up the latest in feminist jargon with which to convince foreign agencies and other philanthropists that they should contribute generously to the cause of women. The funds are, of course, most welcome, but it would be even better if such funds were used a little more effectively in the fields where women need help like family planning and education.

But since the women's movement is itself split on ideological policies, different groups seem to have different perceptions of what women need most and who is best qualified to give it to them. In this context, it may be mentioned that the women's movement broadly appears to comprise the bourgeois feminists and the radical feminists. Some years ago, in Bombay, a battered housewife approached some women's organisations for help. The radical feminists took up her case but, after some time, the victim found that during the period of a lengthy legal battle she would not be able to see her children. Unable to bear this, she went back to the very house where she was being abused and battered. Far from understanding her compulsions, the same radical feminists attacked her roundly for having betrayed the "cause". This utterly appalling lack of sensitivitymade life even more miserable for the already broken women.

Can the women's movement which is by no means terribly powerful in India afford luxuries like ideological differences? It would seem to judging by the amount of time they spend squabbling over the different idelogical interpretations of feminism.

It is not the intention here, to dimiss all women's groups as having done nothing at all for women. It is just to suggest that the government of the day and women at large would take these groups more seriously if they would, just for once, put aside their differences and address themselves to the realities of women's rights in a country which still has incidents of sati and child marriage every now and again.[1]

Inheritance Rights

Maharashtra Chief Minister Sharad Pawar recently announced plans to introduce a bill in the legislative assembly by which daughters would inherit an equal part of the family property. In spite of the Succession Act passed by the Indian Parliament in the fifties, most states have not enforced this law, nor have the majority of Indian families themselves volunteered to honour the law by making their female progeny recipients of equal property rights. The Maharashtra bill is as yet a mere idea according to government sources.

The chief minister has only outlined it in a speech in the assembly. But a number of state women's organisations--some 30 of them have been brought together to discuss the format in which the bill should be presented in the assembly. These organisations will meet again to argue out the case in favour of women. However, what the government sources say and what has been appearing in the media-particularly in the regional press--there is tremendous confusion. According to D.N. Choudhary, Principal secretary to the government of Maharashtra for parliamentary affair law and judiciary, there is not even a draft of the possible bill available which the chief minister is planning to put before the assembly. It is only an idea, he insists. He however confirms that women's groups and institutions have been invited to discuss the pros and cons of the issue. He also says that the 'idea' concerns married women who will have the right-if the law is passed--to ask for division

1. *The Times of India*, New Delhi, page 3 Date, 2-9-89.

of the husband's ancestral property and demand half of the property due to the husband. According to Choudhary, this demand for division ancestral property can be made during the lifetime of the parents of the husband and of course the husband himself. He further says that this law will help women who are abandoned or divorced by errant and irresponsible husbands. It is possible that this " idea" to propose a bill which entitles wives to a part of the husband's ancestral property is inspired by a recent morcha of abandoned and ill-treated wives who presented a memorandum to the government.

This interpretation of the 'idea' or the proposed legislation however is understood differently by the media. Many have taken it to mean the equal division of parental property between sons and daughters and even from this point of view, the reactions from the people have been symptomatic of the deep-rooted prejudices, the newly aggressive attitudes and the passion with which any family finance issue is dealt with in our society. One man, writing in a regional language daily got agitated enough to ask whether society expects brothers to beg after bequeathing property to girls, who, he says are fed and educated and married off, by parents. In reply, angry women have replied that such expenses, indeed on a higher level, are made for sons. In education, hobbies, vocation and even in food, male children are given preference and if daughters are expected to earn and enjoy their own earning jointly with their husband, so also sons should enjoy their own earning with their working/non-working wives. Other sections include the division of rights and responsibilities of proprietors and how the inheritance section needs to be improved in favour of daughters.

However, it is worth taking an overview of both the possibilities. First, that a woman must inherit a share of the husband's ancestral property upon marriage and second, that a daughter must inherit equal parental property with sons.

Let's take the first 'idea' that women should inherit part of the husband's ancestral property, while there is no question that more women are ill-treated and abandoned after marraige or that women suffer more during a divorce, a sweeping inheritance law such as the one planned by the Maharashtra government may cause more harm than welfare for a family. The fundamental responsibility of supporting the wife is that of the husband. Therefore, the solution may be in updating the maintenance laws. At present, if a wife asks for maintenance under her own personal law, the court in India takes almost a decade or more to finalise the case. An influential husband can misrepresent his income or manipulate it to prolong his case till the children are grown up or the wife has remarried or grown older. Women, therefore have been advised by law experts to take the easy way out and ask for maintenance under the Penal Code Section 125 which gives immediate but limited relief of a sum of Rs. 500 per child and a pittance for the wife. The answer is to demand that this section be revised to add Rs. 1,000 minimum per child and Rs. 1,000 for the wife immediately. In addition, women must keep their *streedhan* or their own earning or parental gifts safely in their own possession. If the wife takes ancestral property upon marriage as per the proposed law and then divorces the husband to marry another man and inherits his ancestral property too, our inheritance laws can cause total confusion. Then it is better that Hindu husbands to name a sum at the marriage and bequeiathit to her in case of divorce, desertion or separation.The sum may be invested in her name and she may receive its interest. In the second case, if a daughter inherits equal property from her parents, it can be only after the death of the parents. If children are to demand endowments during the lifetime of the parents, parents who have built their own security will be bankrupt in no time. The solution here too, is for families to settle certain sum, or a business or asset they can justly afford in the name of their daughters so that they can receive a regular income of their own. *Streedhan* should also be given in a form by which an income becomes a reality for every woman. Today, inspite of the succession law, daughters do not inherit their share because most families in India do not want to fragment their agriculture holdings. Business families do not want sons-in-law meddling or demanding a share in the management of their business or companies. Women being emotionally dependent on their husbands, children and their in-laws, are apt to allow husbands to take over their *streedhan* or share of property. This must be avoided at all costs.Ifdaughterscannot practically inherit land or business, parents must bequeath by a clear will, assets to her which will help to live a dignified life. It is seen today that sons and daughters-in-law do not necessarily look after aged parents. Many are parted due to work or other reasons. Sometimes daughters are closer to parents. Sons who inherit all the property too squander it on liquor, gambling and other vices. So a feasible division of property is the solution. As far as possible, a life of dignity must be ensured for all parents, sons and daughters. To achieve this, all children must be educated equally. Parents, in their capacity as guides, must encourage their daughters-in-law to earn and men must endeavour to be proper providers if they are to marry and beget children. With more and more breaking on the rocks of ego, family squabbles and financial greed, women must be alert and educated so that they are at no one's mercy [1].

Move with Men-folks

What are the issues pertaining to women which are being focussed in the current year ?

As far as the department is concerned, we are trying to focus on the implementation. Lot of new initiatives have been taken, but the actual implementation at the grassroots seems to be weak.

Why?

Various agencies are involved. To me, the focus at this crucial stage has to be on the implementation with the strengthening of the machinery at various levels.

One has heard this story before from everyone in the Government. Coming to your Department specifically, why hasn't this been done in the last four years. After all this is the end of the 5-year term.

---

1 - *Famina*, April 8, 22, 1991 ; pp. 40-41.

I agree. But there are problems. Take for instance the legislation on the family courts. In 1984, the Bill was passed but until now only six courts have been set up by the State Government. I cannot directly set up the courts. We write to the States but seem to be having one problem or the other. The other thing we are trying to do is the sensitisation of the administration itself whether it is IAS, IPS or any other because we feel that unless you sensitise them to issues they are dealt with in routine manner. The third is the new scheme for instance, the Women's Development Corporation. We have until now 11 of them functioning and three are in the process of being set up. In these cases we do the funding. We give a 49 per cent matching grant to the 51 per cent of the State. They have to find the money and we can put in the matching grant only after that. We cannot force it on them. So there have been a lot of discussions and the actual programme to take off. I am not saying that the state Government is not keen on implementing but they sometimes have their own problems and therefore the projects get delayed.

What are the specific priority issues where the focus is on implementation ?

I would say dowry and dowry atrocities, where we want every state to have a special cell for women to have a place to go. Another thing I have been interested is to have more women in the judiciary, particularly the lower courts and the police stations. These are two things which I feel will change a lot. The Home Ministry has launched a campaign for recruiting more and more women but I agree enough has not been done. Once it is done as effectively as one would like to see it, the entire atmosphere and environment will change. But issues have been getting focussed in the last four years and even middle level administrators are taking interest and coming up with projects for women. One must realise that it is only since 1985 that one has a full-fledged Department for women and therefore, many initiatives are coming from the people outside the Department as well.

What specific steps has the Government taken to push these issues to the fore and what have been its failures and successes?

It is difficult to say because the main implementing agency has to be the State Government and I cannot keep giving orders. They are as concerned as we are, but these are the usual problems of getting things going. The second problem is pushing it beyond the State capital to the smaller towns. What the State Governments say is that we cannot find people to serve in these committees at the local level. Either there is no communication between them at the local level or the State Government does not take the trouble to find the people. I cannot do it directly. My bottleneck is the state capitals. So how do I go about it ?

By penalising the State government for not treating the women as a priority area ?

You cannot penalise the State Government but I will tell you what we did. We have the working women's hostels which we fund totally and the State Government does not have to give a matching grant, but the recommedation has to come through the State Government. So what used to happen was that the State Government would just not recommend any voluntary agency. Therefore we set and deadline of three months within which if the State Government did not object we would release the grants directly. This worked and helped things to move faster but this cannot happen everytime.

It can, because if you coordinate with the planning ministry who gives them funds for development and set a pre-condition that women have to be treated as a priority area and unless there is implimentation, the money will not be released, the state Government will automatically do it.

This is exactly a recommendation we have made where we have said that all ministries must take on certain responsibility in implementing certain target oriented programmes not only of the State Governments but also the Union Ministries so when they make allot tments and draw up their plans they will put this component as compulsory which was the whole idea of bringing them into the mainstream otherwise you just give targets which are never met. And it is only when that happens that something concrete will take shape.

Will it ever happen and why hasn't it happened so far ?

I cannot tell you why it has not happened but we did realise that unless there was a new dimension given, the same old story would be repeated. We did feel that simply making money available would not help. Everytime they pleaded that *paisa nahin hai* (There is no money) Our point is that you give a share to women from whatever money you have. Why should you say that only for women you have no money. Secondly we did feel that planning and co-ordination for women's programme has to be decentralised. You can't just keep saying that for women you just have to sit somewhere and plan. They have to be involved and coordination has to be there at district level. Third, some of our existing delivery system needs specialisation. The programmes require expertise, for instance the Development Corporations should be run by technically qualified people on a commercial basis and later become self-sufficient. Everyone wants grants indefinitely so you cannot expand. I can tell you that among the recommendations we have made, we have classified them into three categories : one which can be done immediately by administrative orders; second which require legislation and the third which is long-term and have to go into long-term plans. In these we have talked of interventions - short term interventions which would be necessary to bridge the time gap and give them what has been denied to them so far.

Do you think the voluntary agencies who take up the cause of woman have done anything so far ?

They have and I believe that they can do much more. I only feel that not enough of them exist in the rural areas. The second thing which I have noticed that women social workers who have been doing voluntary work so far need to be paid. we also feel that there is need for greater coordination between the voluntary agencies. There are many groups functioning in the rural areas and doing commendable work. Of these some are known and some not very well known.

So you feel that the voluntary groups functioning in the rural areas are more effective than those in the State capitals and Delhi.

I think so. I am not saying that they are not doing anything. I am just saying that some groups are more visible and there are groups which are more involved at the grassroots and we need more and more such groups.

Does India have a successful feminist movement ?

I think it is a very positive movement and that is the reason why it has not met with the type of hostility it has in other countries.

Which are the areas where the feminists and the voluntary agencies need to be corrected ?

I think any women's movement should be balanced enough not to create sense of insecurity. You cannot change things overnight. One has to take the men along to achieve results.

Do you feel that the movement has created insecurity ?

No, in fact because it has not, the movement here has not run into problems like in other countries.

67

Rights Writing - Kali for Women

When *Kali* for women started out as a feminist publishing house, it was written off as a flight of fancy, an unviable venture doomed to a quick demise. Today, 5 years with 20 books later, it is hailed as Asia's first and only feminist publishing house (though New Delhi based 'Manushi' too publishes books), credited with bringing out quality literature. The acclaim that Vandana Shiva's *Staying Alive,* Kali's biggest success so far, has achieved, given sceptics food for second thought.

Kali's tie-ups with publishers in the U.S., Europe, South and South-East Asia and Africa are a major reason for its success. It publishes books in collaboration with radical publishing houses like Zed, Women's Press of London and Forlaget Oktober, a Norwegian publishing house, thus ensuring a good distribution network. In U.K. and the U.S., several Kali publications have sold all rights and its titles have sold even before publication.

Says David Davidar, editor and publisher of Penguin India : "Kali for women is doing wonderful work. It's one of the few redical and committed publishers around." A review of *Staying Alive* (India : Rs. 125; UK : £28.95) in *TheSpectator* hails it as : A uniquely modern Green mixture of Hindu mythology, social disquiet, dry statistical tables and assault on Western male science. " The book is an off-beat articulation of the challenges women in ecology movements are creating and an explication of their struggles.

Kali's small office has an informal, academic look. Brimming with cane furniture, indoor-plants and books, it is basically a two-women show. Frail and articulate Ritu Menon, 41 and the matter-of-fact Urvashi Butalia, 38 say their long stints in the publishing industry and involvement with women's issues have made Kali a success. Menon's years with Vikas and Orient Longman and Butalia's stints with University Press (OUP) and Zed prompted them to try and progressively alter the perspective on women through publishing. Says Menon : "Through our academic titles, we question the biases against women, through our general books we create awareness on social issues which also pertain to women and, we actually give people an alternative."

An example : Kali's non-sexist children's book in Hindi, *Ulti Sulti Mitto* (Rs. 3), by Kamla Bhasin which has sold 38,000 copies. Its central character Mitto is, unconventionally, a girl and the book refrains from stereotyped characters on a sexist basis.

Kali's primary concern is publishing Third World Studies on women, but it also brings out titles in fiction, re-prints, monographs, pamphlets and diaries, publishing in English and occasionally in Hindi.

Kali's first *Women and the Media* (Rs. 15) published in collaboration with Isis International of Italy and Pacific and Asian Women's Forum of Sri Lanka, which dealt with the negative depiction of women in media and the agitations launched by women's groups in Asian countries against it, sold 4,000 copies. *Truth Tales* (Rs.45), a collection of short stories, has also done well. Institutional buying is its mainstay but Menon says there's been tremendous response from individuals. Most of Kali's books are commissioned, but Menon also gets three to four manuscripts a month for consideration. She claims Kali has no prejudice against male authors and the fact that it's yet to publish one is a mere co-incidence. Says she: "We are activist publishers. This ensures quality and honesty in our work. "But says R. Advani, OUP's chief editor: Kali is a creditable venture though it has not yet come up in a major way in terms of number of titles and their visibility in the market."

Kali's forthcoming books include *Phaniyamma* (Rs. 45) by M.K. Indira, a novel about a child widow translated from Kannada, and *The Quilt and Other stories* (Rs. 50) by Ismat Chugtai. It is also starting a book club with "like minded" publishers. Clearly, Kali has shown an activism and publishing can be wed in harmonious and profitable enterprise.[1]

Women's Perspective Plan - Skirting the Issue

It was a document promising to free Indian women from the clutches of social oppression. But exactly a year after the National Perspective Plan for Women 1988-2000 (NPP) was presented to the Prime Minister, and 17 months after it was officially released with the attendant hoopla, little has been done to implement it.

Put together by a 14-member core group, constituted in 1987 and headed by Margaret Alva, Minister of State for Women, Youth and Sports, the NPP makes 353 far-reaching recommendations. These include : a uniform civil code, property rights to women, reservation of seats for women in elected bodies, banning of sex determination tests, and making harassment of wives for dowry as a ground for seeking divorce.

1. Sharmila Chandra, India Today, September 15, 1989, p. 150.

The NPP also talks of encouraging industrialisation of rural areas to provide employment options to women, giving credit to women, and setting up a Central maternity benefit fund.

So far, the suggestions have been confined to paper, with little or no attempt to translate them into action. Nandini Azad of the Women's Centre, National Institute of Public Co-operation and Child Development (NIPCCD) and a member of the core group disagrees. She says : " By January, 275 recommendations were sent to the ministries. Around 179 have been accepted in principle.

But leading women activists confess to being in the dark regarding the progress of the NPP. Queries a puzzled Veena Mazumdar of the Centre for Women's Development Studies : "Has the NPP been sent to various state governments and the Planning Commission? Has a feasibility report about its implementation been prepared : Is it going to be presented in the Parliament? " In fact, adds Ila Bhatt, M.P. and founder of the Self-Employed Women's Association : "I haven't heard of the plan since it was presented to the Prime Minister."

It is no surprise then that optimism is at a low ebb. What gives more strength to this view is the feeling that the NPP has bitten off more than it can chew. Says Ranjana Kumari of the Delhi-based Mahila Dakshata Samiti : " A strong back-up machinery, structural support and delivery mechanism is required to fulfil the high-sounding promises."

What is ironical is that the core group comprising government officials has recommended the adoption of a uniform civil code to the Government, a step scuttled earlier by the Government. At the same time, it has failed to consider cultural plurality and religious sensitivity of the country. Says Sushila Kaushik of Delhi University's Women's Studies and Development Centre : "The NPP displays a tendency to latch on to the propagandist bandwagorn"

And it is to be expected, some are dismissing the NPP as a pre-election stunt. Kumari goes further saying : "The plan is inherently non-implementable. " According to her, the fault lies in the fact that the authors of the plan take a sectoral view of the situation instead of an intergrated one.

Bhatt finds another ground for complaint - the steps will inevitably lead to bureaucratisation of the system. Says she : "Officially sponsored agencies like commissioners and women's development corporations, recommended by the NPP, will centralise power."

Echoing the same feeling , Madhu Kishwar, editor of *Manushi* (a bi-monthly dealing with women's rights), says the plan recommends the setting up of cells, directorates and committees without assessing the role of the existing ones. Nor does it undertake an evaluation of the failure of the existing policies and laws on women.

In the meantime, the NIPCCD has begun organising workshop and meetings with professionals to make them familiar with the document. Also initiated is a strong networking among women's organisations.

Clearly, however, an overwhelming sense of cynicism has greeted the NPP. "It is just as well if it is not implemented," says Kishwar. "It enhances the power of state to interfere in the lives of the people." Shifting from the earlier government view of women as assets of the family to that of state-owned `resources', the NPP, according to Kishwar, projects motherhood as an inevitable contribution that women, must make to nation.

But the way the things are going it will not be surprising if like the 1975 Committee on Status of Women Reports, a document on which no action was taken, the NPP becomes yet another testimonial to state apathy. [1].

---

1 - Sharmila Chandra - *India Today*, September 30, 1989, p. 71.

68

Do Women Need Part-timeJobs?

If Ashwini Marathe a state government employee, undertakes the strenuous two hour journey her office in the suburban train it is to earn an extra income for her family. Her day begins at 6.00 A. M. and ends at 11.00 P.M. Of the not less than 17 hours at her disposal, she spends ten to twelve hours outside her home, travelling to work and attending to heaps of files at the office. In the remaining time, she has to rush through the domestic and child rearing chores.

Like Ashwini, there are thousands of working women who have to walk a tightrope between the two spheres of home and work. Is part-time work for women a solution to their problems ? Will it ease their workload or increase it ? Given the responsibility that a woman has towards her family and her work-place, and the difficulties she faces trying to do justice to both her roles as a working woman and mother, the Maharashtra Government has made a proposal of part-time jobs for women. Recently, the proposal has been circulated in various state government departments to assess the opinion of women employees.

Mr. K.G. Paranjape, ex-chief secretary, Maharashtra, placed the broad outlines of the proposal before the government in 1988. In his report Mr. Paranjape has stated that financial necessities and growing urbanisation have forced women to take up jobs. As a result they have to spend hours away from their home. In cities like Bombay, women have to come to work from far away suburbs and they are away from home for ten to twelve hours. This raises several issues on the home front, the major one beinglookingafter children especially those in their growing years.

Alternative child rearing facilities are not readily available. Also, creches or daycare centres are no substitute for a mother's attention and care, the report adds. Therefore, there is a proposal before the Maharashtra government to provide partime jobs to women employees. Part-time work means division of jobs of full-time, permanent women employees, so as to create two-part-time jobs. This will enable working mothers to contribute to the family income at the same time find sufficient time to spend with their families and children.

The part-time work is optional, the report adds. Women whose children have grown up and who have help at home can continue to work full-time. Part-time work will be in two shifts. The suggested timings are 9.45 a.m. to 1.30 p.m. or 1.45 p.m. to 5.15 p.m. or 12 p.m. to 3.45 p.m. that is, four hours of work.

A major advantage of this proposal, according to the report, is the creation of two jobs in place of one. Hence, there are more employment opportunities for the needy, unemployed women.

Mr. Paranjape, in his report has quoted the example of Japan, where part-time work system for women has been a success. Once successfully implemented at the state government level, the scheme can be extended to the public sector and private sector offices. Clerks, typists and stenographers' jobs will be available on part-time basis.

Further, Mr. Paranjape has made certain proposals for working mothers with infants. The report says that women resuming from meternity leave should be allowed to work part-time for minimum of two years period. And this period will be treated as one year at the time of retirement.

The part-time work issue is a hot subject of discussion in all the state government offices, being one of everyone's concern.

Woman state government employees have expressed varied opinions, ranging from "not favourable for us" to "good on parts", i.e.for working mothers with infants. A number of top officials refused to comment on the proposal [1].

1. *The Economic Times*, New Delhi, Sunday October 1, 1989, p. 3.

69

Mahila Yojna Announcement Avoidable

Chief Election Commissioner R.V.S. Peri Sastri said it would have been better if the announcement of the Indira Mahila Yojna had been avoided at this juncture, reports UNI. On the complaints about the announcement of the Yojna by Congress (I) President Rajeev Gandhi, Mr. Peri Sastri told a news conference here that the ministry of human resource development had stated in writing that plan for uplift of women had not been drafted in the ministry.

He read out the reply received from the ministry at the press conference in which the ministry said that while an integrated programme for the development of women was being prepared by the ministry, it was different from the Congress (I) document on many counts.

Pointing out some differences, the ministry said while the Congress (I) plan visualised channelling of funds through panchayati raj institutions, the government document under preparation planned to involve agencies like the DRDA.

While conceding that some similarities could not be ruled out altogether the ministry's reply also said that the Congress (I) documentvisualiseduplift of all women whether residing in rural or urban areas, but the government plan was mainly meant for rural women.

On another complaint made to the Commission, Mr. Peri Sastri said the Commission had found that a specific reference had been made in the Congress (I) manifesto and it had also been decided that it would be announced by the Congress (I) president on November 19.

Asked persistently to clearly specify whether the model code of conduct had been violated, he said it could best be described as a " borderline case". " It would have been better if its announcement had been avoided," he reiterated.

He also stated that this was also the "consensus opinion"of the three-member commission as till now all decisions had been taken after arriving at a consensus.

70

Harnessing Women Power

The village of Markunda in Bidar district, Karantaka, on the main road linking Hyderabad to Bombay, had never seen such an invasion. A large open ground belonging to the mandal panchayat was transformed overnight into a tent village, with colourful lights giving it an air of festivity. Over 1,300 women from as far away as Mysore district to the south and from villages in Maharashtra streamed in, on buses and on foot. They had come to attend a Mahiti Mela (Information fair) organised by the Karnataka Mahila Samakhya.

A few hundred yards away from this pleasing sight were ugly concrete box-like structures, the Karnataka government's idea of ideal houses for the rural poor. These yesores, representing a complete lack of imagination, were a telling contrast to the originality of the concept of the Mahiti Mela which was about to begin next door. While in the rural housing programme both concept and implementation came from the top, the Mahiti Mela was the custome of the radically different approach adopted by the Mahila Samakhya. This is a programme designed to empower women to recognise and deal with their own problems. While a component of the programme is literacy, it is neither the main ingredient, nor the dominant one. The Mahila Samakhya programme, wholly funded by the Netherlands Government is working through the Union Education Minister in three States, Karnataka, Gujarat and Uttar Pradesh. The project is presently conceived to run for five years and could be extended to at least two more States, Maharashtra and Andhra Pradesh.

In Karnataka, where the programme has run for 20 months, it has seen a remarkable development. The Mahiti Mela in Bidar from February 1 to 3 was, in some respects a demonstration of the impact the programme has already had in the districts of Mysore, Bijapur and Bidar where it has been functioning.

The concept of Mahila Samakhya is a simple one. Instead of a top down approach, it believes in building from the bottom up. So the first step is to identify women from the communities where the programme is to be implemented, who can be the Sahyoginis (which literally means helpers, and therefore does not have any hierarchical connotations attached to it) to assist women at the village level to form Sanghas. These sanghas would then determine the issues to be tackled in their villages. The Mahila Samakhya's direct contribution is non-formal education.

A direct consequence of this approach is the way the sanghas in the three districts are formulating their own sets of priorities. In Bijapur district, for instance, the women have written plays which give the message of the importance of literacy, and at the same time highlight several other problems confronting them such as money-lending and exploitation by landlords. The State Programme Director of the Karnataka Mahila Samakhya Ms Srilatha Batliwala says, they have deliberately chosen to support the Sanghas to autonomously acquire the resources to run services for themselves rather than entering into the field of service delivery themselves.

This is the key conceptual difference between this programme and many others which use service delivery as an entry point into a community. Indeed, much of the developmental intervention even by non-governmental ground through the Sixties and Seventies relied heavily on providing services or at least being the link between communities and service least being the link between communities and service delivery agencies. Ms Batliwala says her own experience over the years, where she has worked with such groups, has revealed that this leads to a dependency syndrome where communities continue to rely on an outside source to provide them with services.

More importantly, such interventions do not pay adequate heed to the needs of women who remain marginalised because of what Ms Batliwala terms the 'patriarchal underpinnings' of such interventions. As a result, women's needs are not given priority and they feel, they do not benefit directly from such interventions. The service delivery model also fails to address the complexities of rural existence.

The idea of the Mahiti Mela was born out of a recognition of women's right to decide what they wanted to learn and how. When a representative of non-governmental groups in Maharashtra, involved in income generation activities, approached the Karnataka Mahila Samakhya for an opportunity for the women of the two States to meet and exchange views, the actual concept ofa mela', which connotes a joyful occasion, was conceived.

The process of consultation with the Sanghas lead to a widening of the subjects on which information would be provided. The choice of subjects on which information was desired shattered many stereo-types about rural women's interests. Apart from law and health, and issues relating to income generation such as credit and loan facilities, the women wanted to know about alternative rural technologies such as biogas, smokeless chulhas, horticulture and plant breeding.

They also discussed issues relating to the functioning of the Panchayati Raj with the Mandal Pradhan of Markunda, where the mela was held and spoke to the Superintendent of Police of Bidar about the role of police.

One of the most interesting 'stalls' in the mela was the tent in which law was discussed. The three days were organised to allow representatives of the different Sanghas from each of the 14 talukas from the three Karnataka districts, and the participating groups from Maharashtra to attend one session on each of the subjects.

Thus, on the day the Bijapur group went to the law session, they were able to discuss laws most relevant to them, namely those relating to the Devadasi system and to child marriage. The law session was conceived by a Delhi lawyer, Ms Ratna Kapoor, who enlisted some students from the National Law School in Bangalore to conduct the same. What was different about this session, as opposed to an academic narration of law and the rights of people, was that the resource persons interacted closely with the women to find out exactly what they thought of customs like Devadasi system and child marriage before informing them about the law. They also gave the women information on the manner in which the law was insufficient and often unfair to women. This was an important perspective to convey as there is a tendency to mystify the law and legal institutions.

When the women were asked whether they knew instances of child marriage in their villages, many hands went up. Not only had some of them married off their own children at ages ranging from one to eight years, but several women admitted that they had themselves been child brides. The team informed them about the law, the punishment it lays down for anyone endorsing such a marriage, and for the man who marries a minor. But the law does not annul the marriage. As a result, once the errant husband has served his term in jail, he is free to return to live with his child bride.

The Devadasi session was particularly revealing because of the variance of the views expressed about the morality of the whole system. While some women thought that Devadasis were immoral women, others expressed their sympathy for women caught in the system, and the Devadasis present articulated their own dilemma. As a result, they also learned to appreciate the problems of people caught in such systems.

The session with the Mandal Pradhan of Markunda demonstrated the extent of the women's involvement in their own village and taluk level institutions. A number of them were members of their mandal panchayat which covers 15 villages. But their common complaint was that despite 25 per cent reservation for women on these local self-government bodies, the voice of the women was not heeded.

One Harijan woman from Bijapur district, who was Upapradhan of her mandal, said the Pradhan would not permit her to decide on contracts for developmental works. As a result, while he gave work to people from other villages, people in her village criticised her for not getting them work.

Another woman narrated the problems she had with the mandal when she discovered that a contractor was mixing too much mud in the cement. She managed to obtain information about the exact quantity of mud and cement that is legally permitted, challenged the contractor, proved that his mix was wrong, and got the contract suspended. Such instances illustrate what the process of 'empowerment', which is the chief objective of Mahila Samakhya, has done.

A great forward

Many of the 1,300 women who attended the Mahiti Mela, had never travelled outside their talukas. For them such a step, of leaving their men folk for four days was, as Ms Batliwala said, "a great leap". It was a physical demonstration of what the process of empowerment can do. The other proof, if one must call it that, was the confidence with which the women approached the resource persons on the subjects on which information was being imparted. For hours, they sat listening attentively. Some were taking notes. Others interrupted whenever they had a question. There was no hesitation, no coyness. They conveyed in their attitude, the belief that it was their right to know.

But a question that is bound to arise, even as one views the confidence in these poor rural women, is whether it can be sustained. Mahila Samakhya, at the moment, is conceived as a five year programme. What happens after the funding from the Centre stops ? Is there not a danger in all such Centrally-sponsored programmes that they show signs of success in the initial period, and then lapse into apathy or even degenerate altogether once the funding stops ?

Ms. Batliwala is aware that the greatest danger the "movement", as she prefers to call the process initiated by Mahila Samakhya, faces if the Government decides to close it down. In preparation for such an eventuality, she and her team have endeavoured to ensure that structures that are not integral to the process can be jettisoned at any point. For instance, already the State office of the Samakhya, says Ms Batliwala, is not essential because the district coordinators are well organised. She is confident that if this can happen in just 20 months, the process has attained an adequate momentum to continue even if funding stops.

Another strategic decision she took in the early days of setting up the Mahila Samakhya in the State was to minimise the interaction of city-based people with village groups. She considers this as important because she has realised that the very presence of people from another class raised the expectations of delivery of some form of services or resources, thereby undercuting the principle of self-reliance and empowerment. She has ensured that the district coordinators and the Sahyoginis are not delinked from their own environment. For such women, there is demand for delivery of services as there is from outsiders. As a result, they can work directly on strengthening the Sanghas encouraging them to formulate programmes.

In fact, Mahila Samakhya has found it easier to form Sanghas where no non-governmental organisation has intervened. This is because NGOs start off being intermediaries between the people and the government, but end up doing the service delivery themselves. As a result, the pressure for service delivery in areas where there has been NGO intervention, is even greater than in places where such outside intervention has not taken place. "Unless you are confident, it is easy to get drawn in, because this is the easiest and quickest way of winning people's confidence. But it is the least effective in the long run," says Ms Batliwala.

These are still early days and Mahila Samakhya's efforts in Karnataka need more time. But the contrast between the colour, life and joyful spirit of the Mahiti Mela and the funeral look of the State Government's rural housing project described above is, perhaps, the most illustrative statement of two radically different approaches to development. It is already clear which has better survival chances.[1]

Towards legal literacy for women

At the recent Mahiti mela for women organised by the Mahila Samakhya, the sessions on law were intended to work with a feminist approach to legal literacy. Such a strategy rejects the information giving approach to law that does not give women an understanding of their own oppression because there is no participation in the learning process. Furthermore, information-giving in the form of pamphlets, lectures and one-day seminars does not give women an understanding of the limits of law and serves only to cultivate a dependency on law and lawyers who come to set the agenda. It creates a false consciousness about law, that it can solve one's problems, and thus further inflates the power of law without necessarily empowering women in the process.

---

1. *The Hindu*, Sunday, February 17, 1991 p. 17-18, Kalpana Sharma

Feminist approaches to legal literacy work towards exposing assumptions on which law is based, that is, the class, caste, religious and gender biases which underlie law. The approach seeks to expose the myt of law's claim as a universal, external, objective, neutral truth. It seeks to lay bare how the perspectives of those who make and interpret laws, including judges, who are predminantly male, Brahmin and middle-class, inform legal culture and the content of law.

In order to communicate to women the limits of law, it is essential that women participate in the learning process. Ideally such a process should be pursued in the context of a literacy programme over a long period of time with small numbers of women in spaces that are for women. Such a setting exists in the women's sanghas that have been developed by rural women in different Mahila Samakhya districts.

In the broader context of the Mahiti Mela, given the limitations of time and the presence of such large number of women, the possibility of having an effective participatory legal literacy process was more difficult to achieve. Yet, it was possible to stimulate different way of thinking about law, and of law's relevance in women's lives.

More specifically, it provided women an opportunity for understanding and addressing the extent to which law facilitates women's rights as well as how it undermines their rights. We looked at the patriarchal bias that pervades law and gives some women more rights than others. This understanding began with the sharing of women's experiences. That is, instead of reeling off provisions on the Devadasi law, or laws on the forests, desertion, bigamy and cruelty, women first shared their personnel experiences and their views whether such acts hurt them or caused them pain. We then looked at different legal provisions governing these actions, and talked about the extent to which they helped remedy these wrongs, or further hurt women.

For example, the issues of child marriage, Devadasi practice and prostitution were discussed. None of the laws relating to these practices necessarily helps women. Although those performing child marriages are penalised, the law itself is not rendered null and void. Thus, the girl child's rights are in no way protected. Similarly, the law continutes to reinforce the stigma attached to Devadasi and prostitute women as it penalises these women in its impact because of the nature of the work they do. The law is based on assumptions of morality and concerned with the protection of the public's rights. That is, women who offer sex because of religious practice or money are considered as immoral and/or criminal. It does not treat these women as engaging in this work because of economic necessity. Furthermore, as a result of moral preface on which the law and social responses are based, Devadasi and prostitute women become stigmatised.

Tribal women from Mysore shared their vague recollection of what life in the forests used to be like for tribals. They spoke of the changes and harms that occurred which undermined their tribal culture and way of life. The women had little understanding of why these changes had occurred. The role of the forest laws in corroding tribal culture and disrupting their lives was then discussed. That such laws were passed to promote the state's interests in revenue from forests and not to protect the rights of forest dwellers enabled women to link the violations in their lives to the broader structural causes. Such knowledge is empowering as it provides an understanding of the limits of the law and its relevance in subsequent strategies for remedying these violations.

It is thorough this interaction of women sharing experiences about their lives that the communication of law and its limits becomes at all meaningful to them. Only through such a process can law be disempowerd, the fiction that it is the truth belied and legal literacy become genuinely empowering for women.[1]

---

1. *The Hindu*, Sunday, February 17, 1991- p. 18, Ratna Kapur..

In search of a saviour and salvation

Ichhaben Shanabhai stays at Mogri village near Anand town. She was working for 20 years in a tobacco factory, popularly known as a 'khadi'. Her husband is a farm labourer and they have five children. One day a tobacco heap cascaded on her and she was buried underneath. She had to be taken to hospital in an unconscious state. Since then she has no job. Nobody is willing to give her work in a tobacco factory. Her daughter-in-law works in her place instead. She complains that even after 20 years of service, she was not given anything for medical treatment.

Kheda district of Gujrat is known for the Amul dairy and for the tobacco used in bidis. The dairy and the tobacco have made everyone rich barring the workers in the tobacco factories. Kheda produces 80 per cent of the 170-180 million kg. of bidi tobacco in the country.

The economics of tobacco

Tobacco was apparently introduced in India by the Portuguese. It now occupies an important place in the economy. About 450 million kg is produced annually. The area under tobacco is four lakh hectares - 0.3 per cent of the total cultivated land. The Government collects Rs. 1,500 crores as excise. The annual output of tobacco products is worth Rs. 2,700 crores of which Rs. 150-170 worth is exported. Nearly five million people are directly or indirectly involved in the production. The Charotar region consisting of Anand, Thasra, Petlad, Borsad and Nadiad talukas. Kheda district is the largest producer of bidi tobacco. About 65 per cent of the cultivated land in Charotar is under this crop. Bidi manufacturers from all over the country come here to purchase tobacco.

The tobacco processing industry in Gujarat was started around 1945. There are about 800 processing factories in Kheda district. About 40,000 workers, mainly women, are employed in these factories. The working condition is horrible. They are not paid the statutory minimum wage, not to speak of provident fund and other benefits. The labour laws are being flouted with impunity by the factory owners. The story of 18-year-old

Jyotika is more tragic than Shanabhai's. She was working for three years in khali and hails from a poor family. Work in a tobacco factory often brings disease. Jyotika got yellow fever and her health deteriorated. Meanwhile, she was married. Her mother-in-law often abused her for being pale and sickly. Ultimately, she was sent back to her parents. Now she does not go to the khali because of poor health. The khali ruined her marriage as well as health.

The plight of women workers

These and many untold and unrecorded tales of tears exist here. The women do not even remember how old they are-they are so illiterate. Their hard work involves 8 to 10 hours a day. Some have been working for the last 20 years. In the beginning, they used to get Re. 1 or Rs. 1.50 for 12 hours of work. After independence, the rate was raised though not much. It became a meagre Rs. 2.50 to Rs. 3 a day by 1970. After a decade, the rate went up to Rs. 5. During 1985-87, it was Rs. 7. In 1989, it was increased to Rs. 10 which they get now--far below the minimum wage of Rs. 18.

The work starts at about 8 a.m. and lasts till 6-7.30 in the evening with a lunch break of about three hours. The dried tobacco leaves from the fields are brought to the khalis and heaped. Processing involves thrashing and breaking the leaves. The leaves are then passed through sieves to get the required flakes, small or big. Then comes the mixing, grading, drying and curing. This processing converts angad (raw tobacco) into jarda (purified broken flakes) and into jardi mixture (blended). Machines are being increasingly used for processing. More sophisticated machines are being brought. That would spell unemployment for many workers. What have the women to say about their work ? Laments Shantaben, a khali worker for long. "I used to have headache, vomiting, giddiness and fever. Gradually I got accustomed to it."

Fight for women's right

A voluntary organisation, SEWA, has started organising

the women workers since 1986. Ms Renana Jabwala of SEWA says, "So far we have organised the women workers of 30 villages and have managed to get identity cards for 1,400 of them. We have also persuaded the owners to re-employ 100 sacked workers. We got the wage raised from Rs. 7 to Rs. 10. We are trying with the Government and the owners to give the minimum wage of Rs 18." In 1987, lawyer Girish Patel filed a petition in the Gujarat High Court to enforce the minimum wage. The court ordered an inquiry by a committee into the working and living conditions of the workers. The committee was asked to submit its report by June 22, 1987. The report was delayed and the committee consisting of Ms. Illa ben Pathak, social worker, Mr. Ramesh Dholakia and Mr. Jyotindra Shelat, both lawyers, and Mr. J.H. Tanna, Court Officer submitted it only on April 13, 1988. The committee visited many tobacco factories in Kheda district and met the owners and workers. In its report it said, "Appalling is too mild a word to describe the inhuman working conditions of the workers employed in these units....None of the labour laws is in practice implemented by the labour officials though on paper everything exists....The labour welfare laws are only on statute book and the Labour Department can be charged with indifference, callousness, complicity and even partnership with the khali owners." The report added : "Most women....refused to give their names, did not want to be seen near us for long, but were keen to tell us that their exploitation was acute. They said that they got maternity leave, but no payment of the period of leave."

The committee made many recommendations. But the report and the public interest petition filed by Mr. Girish Patel are still pending with High Court along with one lakh other cases for want of sufficient number of judges. The politicians have so far turned a blind eye to this 45-year-long targic tale of exploitation, including Mr. Madhavsingh Solanki, former Chief Minister, who hails from Kheda district. The owners' money and muscle power, it seems, are more useful to them.[1]

1. *The Hindu*, Sunday, February 17, 1991- p.19, Chaula Kuruva.

Women and environment : the symbiotic link

An African woman was once asked whether she understood the importance of encouraging her children to wash their hands after they had relieved themselves in answer to calls of nature, particularly after eating. She replied, "I have to carry water for my family seven miles every day. If I caught anyone wasting water by washing their hands, I would kill them." Another woman was asked what changes were noticed in her village, after taps were installed there. She said, "The babies no longer die."

Both these experiences could easily be from any developing country, so widespread is the problem of acquiring basic needs like water, food and fuel for disadvantaged women in the Third World.

Women's work often interfaces with their physical environment. They are not only nurturers and nourishers of their families, children and dependents but are also economic producers, though often in an intangible manner. Their work in food production, agriculture and farmwork, in forests - whether in afforestation of gathering forest-produce, is an area that is most often taken for granted as part of wider activities in the community.

However, rural women in Third World countries account for atleast 50 per cent of all food production. In Africa, they perform about 80 per cent of all agricultural work; in the Himalayan region by 70 per cent. Thus their involvement and interaction with their environment is intimate and immediate. Yet they have arguable access to the food they help to grow, to the water they need to cleanse their families and maintain good health, to the fuel which they must gather to keep their home fires burning, to fodder for their animals, and finally to the forest produce which they gather and sell to make a living. It is also sadly true that women have to walk farther and farther in search of these basic resources, for less and less of them with the onslaught of denudation, degradation and contamination. In the forests, they are at the mercy of the forest guards, contractors and officials.

They do not have always ownership rights to land which remain vested in a husband, father, brother or son. As women's claims are maintained through this relationship with a male, any alienation might result in the loss of rights of land use, even if they are the main cultivators. Even amongst urban women, their rights to property or assets that they might work to sustain and improve are still nebulous. This stresses the lack of space for decision-making for women. Perhaps, the time has come to examine the case for environmental resource guarantees for women.

Women and Water

Women are primarily responsible for the health, nutrition, hygiene level and comfort of their families. In this context women's access to natural resources, like water is of extreme importance. When women are facilitated, their homes and their hearths radiate with health and well-being. When they are deprived, dirt, disease and hunger are their lot.

Water influences malnutrition in two ways--its shortage reduces food production as well as the efficiency with which the food is used. Contaminated wells and pots, as wells as unclean food carry diarrhoeal diseases to children. However, merely having access to a good water source is insufficient. People must know how to use it. In this connection it has been observed that many water and sanitation problems are behavioural ones.

In agriculture, where a majority of women are involved, their productivity can be enhanced by extension services, loans, fertilizer subsidies, simple devices which can be produced locally like shoes, buckets, efficient fuelwood and stoves. Technology has permeated work practices in many ways, but does not always necessarily reach women. A simple example is that our pourakarmikas still gather up the dust of the streets with flat pieces of tin, into wicker baskets. Their tools are no more efficient today than they were years ago.

Women's status, poverty and population are all interlinked. Any relative improvement in one of them brings in its wake all-round benefits. Beyond all this, the ultimate criterion is the economics of human survival in the direst of conditions, the interdependence of the human-habitat link, and the political priority it receives from dynamic leadership. The realisation of basic needs of the majority of the population finds a place in party political manifestos not always on a government's priority list as the disadvantaged need it. This is not always due to deliberate neglect, but often due to the marginalisation of such basic issues in a nation's mounting pressure on priorities for political stability.

Women's role in the disadvantaged population en masse is of great relevance, as even within the given number they form the poorest of the poor. Their interface with their environment is determined thus by their status, their lack of it or possession. This indicate the feminisation of poverty. Can such a personalisation lead to "the personal becoming the political ?" Can women's involvement in local politics work to support people's movements and their lives such as the Chipko Andolan in 1974 when the women of Reni, North India took simple but effective steps to stop tree felling, thus saving 12,000sq km. of sensitive watershed ? Can such involvement spark off similar movements for survival of self and family in a safe environment elsewhere too ? It has, as borne out by the thousands of women's community gardens and small farmer associations that came into existence in Zimbabwe on the country's independence from colonial rule.

Similarly in Dhandhuka, Gujarat, a generation of excessive fuelwood gathering and over-grazing led to desertification, which in turn triggered off social and economic disintegration. Conflicts flared over contaminated water in brackish wells and at a point in time, some four fifths of the population had to migrate to survive. In 1981, the women of Dhandhuka who as elsewhere were traditionally procurers of water, suggested to community organisers that a permanent reservoir he constructed to store rainwater. After much debate, the community set to work in 1986, to get the job done.

Clearly from these examples, enhancing the status of women through accessing basic needs to them, results in an improvement of the human environment relationship. Female literacy, awareness and education go hand in hand with it, demystifying traditional taboos in reaching awareness of self and society to women. When women are aware of themselves, their biology, their fertility are motivated to regulate their lives through discipline, they do reach a point where through discipline they can lead their lives with imagination and creativity. The economics can be better managed as also the human-habitat relationship.

However, politicians, policy makers and bureaucrats have not always understood this link from the point of view of women. Either women alone are addressed, or environment alone. The time has come now to realise the symbiosis between the two. With a year to go before the World Conference on Environment and Development or EGO 92 at Brazil, it would be timely now to review the environment issue from the point of view of women's role as partners, inseparable from the environment. Women's partnership in development itself is yet to be assessed in total; their presence in the environment issue is barely even acknowledged. Can a beginning be made atleast now ?[1]

---

1. *The Hindu*, Sunday, February 17, 1991, p. 20. Bhargavi Nagaraja.

71

Work for Women : Need for Reviewing EGS

The Government of Maharashtra has begun to process of reviewing the scope of its Employment Guarantee Scheme which has been universally credited with keeping unemployment in Maharashtra lower than anywhere else in India. But policy planners reviewing the scheme must recognize that hundreds of thousands of women from rural Maharashtra are among the principal beneficiaries of the existing scheme. A review of the programme must focus on this core group. An effort by the Maharashtra Government to provide a gender component to such a large-scale employment programme can then be reviewed for replication in other States as well as in some centrally-funded rural employment schemes across the country.

Maharashtra is one of the State where more women than men work as agricultural labourers. Women in Maharashtra exceed women in the rest of India in work rate participation. For marginal workers the figure is 9.4 per cent while for the rest of India the figure is 7.18 per cent. For the main female workers - those working for a full day - the figure in Maharashtra is 31.39 per cent. For the rest of India it is just 16 per cent. The swing upward has been registered in the last ten years. Contrary to prevailing tradition in Maharashtra men from landholding households and not just landless labourers send their women out for manual agricultural cultivation. The last ten years have also seen a 77 per cent increase of women over 60 in agricultural labour. By far that largest number of women doing such work belongs to households just below the poverty line.

Attraction to women

The one state-administered employment programme to which such women flock in increasing numbers is the Employment Guarantee Scheme (EGS). Legislated in December 1974 the EGS was supposed to embody the spirit of one of the Directive principles of state policy in the Indian Constitution - to "provide employment to all those who seek it".

The scheme focussed on the rural unemployed and aimed to provide them with manual jobs particularly during the long dry season when any other form of agricultural production, with the exception of sugarcane, was not possible. Workers were paid daily wages according to the amount of work they completed. Their labour was supposed to create "assets" like small irrigation schemes and other development projects which in turn would spur growth and long-term employment in the rural Maharashtra. But over the years the EGS became notorious for its incomplete and haphazard work. Funds were wasted on non-plan activity and projects which collapsed as soon as they were completed. The Government is presently considering ways in which more durable "assets" can be created through the EGS which may now operate only for fixed periods of the year and be restricted to development activity around the village.

Now scores of micro-studies have established, beyond doubt, that more women than men work under the EGS. Yet, for inexplicable reasons, this fact does not figure in government reports. The planning department insists that the average female labour attendance on EGS sites is less than 50 per cent. This is the first discrepancy that must be corrected before plans for change proceed any further. It would be counter-productive for the Government to formulate a scheme without a clear profile of its target group.

There are many reasons why women use the EGS more than men. A pre-requisite for an EGS site is its proximity to the homes of those demanding such work. This suits women because it means they can rush back to their unpaid household labour from the work site. Next, to its credit, wages paid under the EGS are less unequal than elsewhere. Labourers usually work in family groups and the wage is usually given to the head of the group. So even though studies show that women receive less than men for the same work, they do not object because it all goes into the family pool.

A recent study on the EGS and women workers commissioned by the Women's Welfare Department in the Ministry of Human Resources Development was undertaken by the Institute of Social Studies Trust (ISST). It was prepared by a female trade unionist Chhaya Datar of Maharashtra and has some important comments to make on the importance of the EGS to women workers. The reserach covered several districts which have been the focus of activity under the EGS. The researcher also revisited areas which had been covered by an earlier ISST report on this scheme. Not only did it confirm the larger participation of women in EGS activity but the study also provided some important details on the importance of such work in the lives of its female beneficiaries.

First, for many women, the wages they earned through the EGS made up about 60 per cent of their total income. Men earned more through different kinds of wage labour where payment rates are higher. For women, income earned through the EGS was core income.

Next, women's income did not "supplement" the family income within the families covered by the research; men and women contributed about 32 per cent and 31 per cent of the total income. In certain cases, women working in hte EGS contributed about 75 to 100 per cent of the income. These were usually female-headed households - reportedly on the increase today, throughout the country. Women's earnings through the EGS are crucial because they keep the house-hold above the minimum survival level.

The EGS is used by two kinds of rural workers - landless labourers and those with marginal or small landholdings. Landless labourers, on the whole earn 50 per cent of their income through the EGS. Women's earnings are therefore crucial to this group particularly since most EGS participants are below the poverty line.

For marginal landholders, however, the 22 per cent of their EGS earning are also vital. The remainder of their income comes from their own farm labour. Given the fact that landholdings for such groups are one hectare or less, such earnings alone would make survival difficult. For this group too, women's earnings ensure that the family survives.

Findings of study

When the issue is survival, it is clear that any changes in the EGS must be made with caution so that women do not find themselves deprived of this major source of income. There are some changes which, however, could be incorporated into any new programme blueprint. Chhaya Datar's report underlines a recommendation made in an earlier ISST report which is to incorporate applied nutrition programmes into the EGS. Under the former, infants as well as lactating mothers given food free of cost. A criticism of this programme is that it has often failed to locate and assist the neediest women. If fitted into the EGS, the lacuna would disappear.

The integrated child development programme aims at

providing child care and maternity services to clusters of a hundred villages. Food and education is given to the children and nutrition and health care are taught to their mothers. If the purpose of the altered EGS is to provide continuous work for an entire dry season at fixed sites, then it should not be difficult to operate these programmes simultaneously at EGS sites. The 1974 EGS legislation must be rewritten to both recognise the gender component of this scheme and make it mandatory for the Maharashtra Government to ensure that the woman worker is given the dignity and the assistance that her dual role as child bearer and wage earner demands. Unless the law itself is rewritten ad hocism to this area will be the norm rather than the exception.[1]

Review Schemes for Women

In a report to the Planning Commission economists, sociologists and voluntary workers have urged a review of all existing schemes for women's employment and income-generation. The experience of implementing these schemes on the ground is that they all treat women's employment and income as supplementary and not central, to the survival of the family and the community. None of these schemes tends even to generate a minimum wage for women after 8 to 12 hours of daily hard labour. Most of the schemes are designed as supplementary activities by women, part-time here and part-time there. The same seems to be the nature of the various Intergrated Rural Development Programme (IRDP) schemes which also focus on partial and supplementary interventions in enhancing women's income and employment possibilities.

There is also need to do away with the sex-stereotyping of the nature of women's role from all the schemes. Most of the existing women's economic activities tend to focus on sewing, tailoring, home-making, etc. and not on things like agriculture, dairy, forestry, construction and masonry. Thus it is important that this kind of sex bias and gender distortion be removed from the existing schemes. Even the guidelines and illustrative examples provided should include a wide range

1. *The Indian Express*, New Delhi, August 27, 1988, p. 9, Shahnaz Anklesaria Aiyar.

of alternate occupations, work and activities. The social thinkers and policy planners who met in Lucknow under the banner of the Society for Participatory Research in Asia found one recurring scheme. It was felt that much of the women's existing work is full of drudgery and is based on primitive technologies.

Another overriding need is to recognise, and make visible the role of women as producers and workers in their own right. " It was important that women's employment, or women's contribution towards family and community income, is not seen merely in a supplementary sense. Women, through their work and production, inside the family, in the community, are today major contributors towards the survival of the family and, in many of their families perhaps the sole contributors," it was argued.

It is women's labour which produces goods and services in the household, and in the community to a substantially large extent. The reconceptualisation is important because many programmes and schemes for women's economic activities, employment and income generation are conceptualised on the premise that the women need supplementary income. This is erroneous conceptualisation and should be done away with once and for all.

It was also reiterated that while the Plan document may contain chapters and sub-chapters on different aspects of women's development, it is important to have an integrated and holistic perspective on the issues, problems and concerns of women. In particular, the perspective needs to be explicitly concerned with the problems and needs of poor women, both in the rural and urban areas.

It was argued that all the programmes for strengthening the health and nutritional status of women focus on women as mothers, either caring or rearing babies, and that is why women's health programmes are generally mother and child health programmes. There is a need to look at women's health in a broader framework, not merely in the reproductive role, but in their productive and citizendship roles as well.

Similarly, the discussion on the various current health services and programmes seems to indicate that health programmes are being increasingly equated with family planning programmes. The budget for general health programmes is decreasing in relation to the increasing budget of family planning programmes. Thus, family plannig has become a major intervention for health and nutritional aspects of women's development, because a substanitial portion of family planning programmes are focusing on terminal mothods to be used by women.

In reality, highly targeted and target-oriented family planning programmes are trying to focus on women in order to establish it as the only implementable option available with the health service delivery. This is not only inconsistent with the principles of health care, but also raises some serious questions about the status and dignity of women.

The increasing privatisation of health care is making access to health services very remote and difficult to poor - rural and urban - women while the middle class and the elite are using the private health care facilities, the study said. The status of health service delivery mechanism in remote rural areas has been worsening over the years. Thus, there is a need to ensure that Government-sponsored schemes and services in health care reach the poor women and are available on a constant basis.

It was argued that the question of implementing various programmes and schemes for women's development is essentially one of political will and the priorities that the political leadership attaches to these issues and concerns. It was not a question of resources, because resouces in any circumstances are bound to be limited and given. It is the question of fixing priorities and allocation of the available resources according to those priorities.

It has been suggested that women's organisations, voluntary agencies and others should be actively involved in ensuring the social accountability of the teachers of primary and secondary schools. It was felt that Panchayati Raj institutions, people's organisations and other mechanisms should also be entrusted with this task of ensuring continued social accountability of those responsible for education of girls and women in the country.

There was an animated discussion on media and women. There is on official policy on media with regard to women. There is policy for television in regard to women. It is important that this policy is reviewed on a regular and periodic basis in the light of the various programmes and advertisements being shown on television. It was felt that many of the commercial interests are undermining the status and concerns of women and violating the very policies that the Government has set for itself.

In the electronic media, little of women's activities are shown as news. Therefore, it is important that a balanced presentation is ensured and a variety of women's programmes presented regularly. Given the diversity and size of the country, it was urged, television and AIR should be decentralised in terms of programming and software production. It is only then that specific and local views and needs of women will get highlighted.[1]

$30m for Tamil Nadu Women Project

The International Fund for Agricultural Development (FAD) has approved a $17 million loan for a women's development project in Tamil Nadu. The Government of India will contribute $13.6 million to the project, thus raising its overall financing to $30.6 million, a United Nations release said. The seven-year project, located in three of the most impoverished districts of

1. *The Hindustan Times*, September 4, 1989, p. 9, Govind Thukral.

Tamil Nadu, offers a new approach to the problem of women and political status of women rather than on providing economic assistance along.

This will be a accomplished through the provision of a well rounded development package inducing credit, a savings and loan programme and training in activities ranging from farming and livestock raising to small business management. Through the project some 40,320 women, many of them heads households, will benefit directly with annual household incomes expected to increase from between Rs. 640 to Rs. 8,300. All the project beneficiaries currently have annual family incomes of under Rs. 4,800.

The credit feature of the project will liberate women from the clutches of the local moneylenders who currently charge upwards of $40 interest on loans. Through their groups, women will be able to receive credit individually or with other women at the national interest rate of about $10 per annum.[1]

1. *The Economic Times*, New Delhi, Thursday June 8, 1989 - p.3.

72

Role of Women in Agriculture

The population of our country, excluding Assam, according to the 1981 census, was 665.29 milion, of which 343.93 milion were males and the remaining 321.36 million were females. Of these 321.36 million females, 247.55 million or 77.03 per cent were counted in villages and the remaining 73.80 million or 22.93 per cent in cities and towns. This chapter is devoted to an analysis of data relating to 247.55 million females who were counted in villages and efforts have been made to highlight the differential between scheduled caste (SC), scheduled tribe (ST) and non-scheduled caste/scheduled tribe. (non—SC/ST) females engaged in the agricultural sector. Of the 247.55 million rural females, 42.64 million or 17.23 per cent were SC, 24.00 million or 9.72 per cent were ST and the remaining 180.85

million or 73.05 per cent were non-SC/ST.

So far as the work participation rate is concerned, of the 247.55 million rural females in the country, excluding Assam, 39.60 million or 16.00 per cent were economically active and classified as main workers. The work participation rate was the highest (28.81 per cent) amongst ST rural females followed by SC rural females (1975 per cent). The rate was the lowest (13.41 per cent) among the non-SC/ST rural females. High work participation rate among SC and ST rural females appears to be on account of their development in the agricultural sector, i.e. cultivation and agricultural labour.

Among the three segments, i.e., SC, ST and non-SC/ST rural females, as said earlier, the work participation rate was the highest among ST rural females. Of the ST rural female main workers as many as 92.05 per cent were engaged in the agricultural sector--45.27 per cent as cultivators and 46.78 per cent as agricultural labourers. In the case of SC rural female main workers, 89.69 per cent were engaged in the agricultural sector - 17.56 per cent as cultivators and 72.13 per cent as agricultural labourers. Against this, 85.05 per cent of the non-SC/ST rural female main workers, were engaged in the agricultural sector - 41.50 per cent as cultivators and 43.55 per cent as agricultural labourers.

The high percentage of agricultural labourers (72.13 per cent) and a very low percentage of cultivators (17.56 per cent) among the SC rural female main workers suggests that SC rural females had to work in the fields of others as agricultural labourers, obviously to augment their family income. Not even one-fifth among them worked as cultivators, possibly because they do not own land to cultivate. In the case of ST rural female main workers the percentage of cultivators was the highest among the three segments of population being discussed here. Though the majority among the ST rural female main workers was of agricultural labourers (46.78 per cent), the percentage of cultivators (45.27 per cent) was also the highest. This means that in comparison to SC rural female main workers in whose case only 17.56 per cent were cultivators, the percentage of cultivators among ST rural female main workers was much higher. This may be because of the fact that of the entire ST female population, 94.03 per cent was inhabited in villages and only 5.97 per cent lived in cities and towns. In the case of SC females, the percentage of those who lived in villages was 84.37 and the remaining 15.63 per cent were counted in urban areas. The non-SC/ST females were comparatively more urbanised as 26.25 per cent among them lived in cities and towns and 73.75 per cent in villages.

It is quite interesting to note that the sex ratio, i.e. female per 1,000 males, among rural SC and ST main workers was 497 female main workers per 1,000 male main workers. In the case of non-SC/ST female main workers were much less in number as compared to rural male main workers.

It is a sad story that inspite of implementing various schemes for the uplift of the weaker sections of society, not much appears to have been achieved, which inference is supported by the fact that even in 1981, 6.07 million among SC and 3.72 million among ST rural females had to work in the fields of others for remuneration.

Though it may not directly be of much relevance to the present study, yet it may be mentioned that the prevailing literacy status among SC and ST females and the present drive to fill all the vacancies reserved for STs and SCs, it appears, is not going to benefit in a big way, particularly SC and ST females who together form 26.95 per cent of the total population of the country (excluding Assam), as 91.55 per cent among SC and 93.19 per cent among ST rural females, at the time of the 1981 census, were illiterate. Even in urban areas, 75.66 per cent among SC females and 77.68 per cent among ST females were illiterate. Even among those who were literate, the percentage of those who had passed Xth standard or higher was not much.

Reverting back to the main topic of women on the agricultural front, we find that the agricultural labourers in comparison to cultivators were in a disadvantageous position and economically much weaker. The agricultural labourers form a significant strength among SC, ST and non-SC/ST rural female main workers but if we study the inter-segment variation within a state or Union territory, that may give a more clear picture. It may be that in a particular state the percentage of agricultural labourers, among all the three segments, did not vary much and in some cases it varied considerably. For instance, when we work out the indices, taking the percentage of agricultural labourers among non-SC/ST rural female main workers as 100, we find in the states and Union territories of the north-eastern region, which are predominantly inhabited by ST populaton, the indices of SC and ST rural female agricultural labourers was quite low. It means that proportionately more non-SC/ST rural female main workers were engaged as agricultural labourers as compared to SCs and STs. For instance, the indices for SCs and STs were 47 and 5 in respect of Arunachal Pradesh. In Mizoram, not even a single ST rural female main worker was engaged as agricultural labourer. On the other hand, the indices were quite high in some states and Union Territories, both for SCs and STs, while in some cases the indices were quite high for SCs and low for STs and vice versa. For instance, in Rajasthan, taking the percentage of agricultural labourers among non-SC/ST rural female main workers as 100, the indices for the SCs and STs were 273 and 230.

It is high time that we planned a strategy to tackle this gigantic problem of females of weaker sections working on the agricultural front so that their working in their own fields or in the fields of others could be minimised which will help them to devote more time and attention to the welfare of their family and bring up the children by paying the attention they deserve.[1]

Four Steps to Progress

The National Perspective Plan for Women (1988) describes the challenges ahead in the following words. "Agriculture and

1- *The Economic Times*, New Delhi, October 21, p. 5, O.P. Sharma.

allied fields provide the largest sector for women's employment. It largely determines the rural women's socio-economic status. In case of both agriculture and animal husbandry, development strategies have provided very little attention to women in comparison to their active involvement in both the sectors".

The National Commission on Self-employed women and women in the informal sector chaired by Smt. Ela R. Bhatt have also observed "Modernisation and technological changes have affected women adversely. The introduction of new technology in the long run requires new skills. Women do not have access to these skills and training. Hardly any research has been done to evolve technology which will improve the employment situation of women and alleviate their drudgery by developing tools which could make their work simple".

Having diagnosed the malady, what kinds of remedies should we apply ? I would like to suggest a four-pronged strategy in the area of research and training.

Impact of New Technologies--Specific Occupations

A careful study of the impact of new technologies should be undertaken in selected farming areas taking the family as a unit. Families witha assets (land and/or livestock) and without assets (landless labour dependent entirely on wage earnings) should be considered separately for measuring the impact of new technologies within the family, the impact on women with reference to both employment and income should be studied separately so that house-hold data can be disaggregated for analyzing the impact of new technologies on women. The impact should be measured in terms of additional jobs created and the jobs made redundant and thus lost following the introduction of new technologies, both at the production and post-harvest phases of major farming systems.

Technologies for Women

There is need for compiling an inventory of opportunities opened up by new technologies available for women belonging to (a) farming families and (b) landless labour families. What are the precise suggestions of scientists with regard to the technologies available for women and particularly for those seeking wage employment? A catalogue of the opportunities, either present or potential both at the production and post-harvest phases, should be prepared. It will be useful if the scientists could indicate whether the technologies developed by them for reducing drudgery and increasing the energy input-output efficiency ratio could lead to a diversification of labour use and income or only to the displacement of women wage labourers from their traditional occupations. Since women will benefit greatly if there is flexibility in the timing, duration and place of work, there is particular need for examining what efforts, if any, have been made by scientific institutions to introduce flexibility in time and place in jobs for women. Such inventories should be part of an on-going dialogue between scientists and users so that reasearch priorities reflect user's needs.

Women in Technology Development and Transfer

Based on an inventory of opportunities for new avenues of employment opened up by science and technology, there is need to review methods of promoting the greater involvement of women, both in technology development and transfer. Steps must be taken to provide women with managerial and organizational skills so that they are able to occupy leading positions both at the policy making and task implementation levels.

Studies on Delivery System

The delivery of production inputs like seeds, fertilizer and credit as well as new knowledge and skills often tends to have a sex bias in favour of men. Hence, the knowledge and skill transfer mechanisms adopted by extension agencies and the input supply procedures adopted by both government and non-government organizations need careful study. Similarly, the price support and marketing systems as well as the steps taken to improve the other links in the production-consumption chain will need examination from the point of view of their relevance to women farmers, farm managers and farm workers.

It has been the general experience so far that if the target group with regard to the size of a farm holding in agricultural research and development programs is the small farmer, then all farmers--whether big or small derive economic benefit from new technologies. The reverse, however, will not be true. Similarly, it is my conviction that if the target group with regard to sex in agricultural R & D efforts is women farmers and farm workers, then all members of the farm familymen, women and children will benefit. The reverse may not always be true, as the experience gained so far generally suggests. Hence, we need to give a fresh look at our agricultural and rural development strategies and programmes. [1]

Role of Women in Future Agriculture

Ever since organised agriculture has taken roots in human evolution, the culture of agriculture has been closely associated with woman. It is acknowledged that woman is the agriculturist in the world. While mere basically hunters, it was the woman who collected the grains, fruits and cooked for the man and looked after the domestic animals like cattle, sheep, goats, poultry, etc. Throughout the history of mankind till today, woman directly or indirectly influenced the course of agriculture and animal husbandry. In developing countries like India, 81 per cent of the rural women depend upon agriculture either as cultivators or labourers and participate in several activities, such as seeding, transplanting, weeding, fertilizer application, plant protection, thinning, harvesting, processing, shelling, winnowing, storing, looking after the animals, kitchen gardening, etc.

Several of these operations are exclusively carried out by women only. The role of women in agriculture varies on the

1. *The Times of India,* New Delhi, -p. 8, A sponsored feature on International Conference on Women in Agriculture (Nov. 30 to Dec. 4, 1988), M.S. Swaminathan.

socio-economic status of the families, regional differences, cropping and animal husbandry pattern, etc. The nutrition of the family entirely depends upon the vision and the activities of the woman. While woman plays most significant role in agriculture, her participation is taken for granted in the male dominated societies.

The next revolution in agriculture and animal husbandry in India has to come through increased role of women in these areas. In addition to upgrading the expertise in traditional areas of women agriculturists, such as animal husbandry, crop farming, vegetable and fruit cultivation, agricultural based village industries, fish marketing, etc. Women can take up such other activities as conducting and guiding research, conveying technologies to village women, bee-keeping and mushroom cultivation, seed production, social forestry, exploitation of biogas, scientific storage of grains, fruits and vegetables, village co-operatives, rural banking and financing, etc. The participation of women in transfer of technologies in the countryside will bring revolutionary changes in our agriculture, animal husbandry and nutrition of our people.

At present, most of our transfer of technology programmes in agriculture are carried out by men folk who often neglect 50 % of our population, that is, the woman. The woman who is culturing the agriculture and also looking after the health and nutrition of the family is not exposed to the latest technologies. As a result, many of our transfer of technology programmes are not effective or giving the desired results. It is the training of the village woman which holds the key for success of future agriculture.

Education of Women in Agricultural Field

Education of women plays a very crucial role. It will be interesting to see the level of education of women in our Agricultural Universities. There is a growing trend in recent years among women to take up agricultural education. While in some Universities, the percentage of girl students is increasing in recent years, in some Universities, the desired progress is not seen. For example, in Kerala Agricultural University, the number of girl students in B.Sc. (Agriculture) has been steadily increasing in recent years and in 1987, out of the 141 students admitted at B.Sc. (Agriculture), 90 are girls and only 51 are boys. Similar trends are seen in the case of Tamil Nadu Agricultural University, Andhra Pradesh Agricultural University, etc. where their percentage is varying from 31 to 65 per cent. The girls are not only taking to agriculture but they are also entering into Veterinary Sciences, Fisheries, Basic Sciences, Horticulture, Engineering, etc.

In contrast to the situation in South India, the admission of girl students in B.Sc. (Agriculture) and other allied subjects in North India is very low. The girl students are taking more to Basic sciences and Home Sciences than to Agriculture, Veterinary Sciences, etc. States like Uttar Pradesh, Punjab, Haryana, Rajasthan, Bihar, West Bengal, Gujrat, Madhya Pradesh, Orissa, Assam, Himachal Pradesh, Jammu and Kashmir, Maharashtra, etc. which have tremendous agricultural, horticultural and animal husbandry potentialities, may have to make special efforts to increase the number of girl students in their course curricula and also encourage more women to take to professional teaching, research, etc.

Women are admirably suited to carry on researches in Biotechnology, Genetics, Cyto-genetics, Microbiology, Mycology and Plant pathology, Entomology, Agricultural Economics, Rural Credit, Home Science and several such activities. I am sure, with the greater and enlightened role and involvement of women, the agriculture of India will further progress and prosper.[1]

Scientific Role of Farm Women

"In ancient India women have been no less than a divine status. Laxmi, Durga and Saraswati are the three great *goddesses* of prosperity, power and wisdom respectively. The ancient scriptures declare that *gods* live where women worshipped.

1. *The Times of India*, New Delhi, p. 8, M.V. Rao in sponsored feature.

However, a multitude of derogatory attributes have been ascribed to women in the post-vedic period. According to Manu, a woman must never be independent. In childhood, she must be subject to her father, in youth to her husband and when her Lord is dead, to her sons." In both these contexts, the role of women has been visualised as passive one.

The constitution of India provides for equal rights and privileges for men and women and makes special provisions for women to help them to improve their status in society. A number of social enactments have been introduced for removing various constraints which hindered their progress. No doubt that the constitution contemplates a social revolution brought out through the use of law as an instrument of directed social change. But inspite of these, there has been staggering progress in ameliorating the working conditions and socio-economic status of women, especially in the rural areas.

There has been even lack of awareness among the people about various legislations and programmes being implemented for the benefit of women. The studies sponsored/conducted by the ICSSR on status of women report (1971), "an alarming trend of continued deterioration in both their conditions and status, and even more disturbing is the fact that the process of deterioration has accelerated in the last three decades." Based on the review of Indian Studies, it could be seen that the Census of India estimated an all-India economic participation rate of 21 per cent for women and 53 per cent for men in 1981. Nearly 63 per cent of all economically active men were engaged in agriculture compared with 78 per cent of women. Almost 50 per cent of the rural female workers were classified as agricultural labourers and 37 per cent as cultivators. The respective proportions of male rural workers have been reversed with 55 per cent reported as cultivators and only 24 per cent as agricultural labourers.

The seventh five year plan document of the Planning Commission states : "Recently a declining trend has been observed in the employment of women labourers. Some of the new technologies have displaced women from many of the traditional activities - The green revolution has led to increased demand for casual labour, dispossession of small holders from their land and consequently pushing out women from such small holdings to become wage earners. Though many of the tasks performed by males are getting mechanised, the women continue to toil in labour intesnsive jobs--women get limited job opportunities in modern occupations/travels as they do not get access to the training reuired for new technologies. In many areas where multiple crops are grown, the work load of women has increased."

Since 1970s, a global concern for women's emancipation in all spheres has been expressed. In India such efforts have also been made by different Ministries/Departments and Non-Government organizations, but in a vast country like India, the impact of such reports has hardly been enough. In case of agriculturewhere involvement of women is far more prominent, the situation is no better. In fact, the agricultural development system has not yet taken farm women population seriously in the mainstream of its development processes. Therefore, it is high time that this issue is discussed and deliberated at the national and regional levels in order to sensitize people about its potentiality, prospects and obstacles, and charting the course of actions devoted to bringing women as active partners in research and development (R&D) with equal rights and privileges.

The Research system in agriculture as well has not been made deliberate efforts in tackling specific problems which confronted farm women. One argument may be that the research is gender neutral and the research results can be utilized by the farm men and women alike. Perhaps, this may be possible to some extent, but a well-guided and directed research on operations/areas in which farm women are involved can fetch added dividends. There is also a need for coupling and identifying research results in all disciplines which are readily available for the extension system for farm women. The ICAR has, therefore, launched a research study at all-India level on the subject which would involve all the agricultural universities and the ICAR Research Institutes.

Indian farming community represent a complex social system including its heterogeneous nature, economic and social inequalities, caste and class differentiation, traditional social structure and systems, regional imbalances in development, under-developed village institutions, very low level of education, and a relatively fixed and expected role of women. To cut across these barriers, a well coordinated, directed and concerted efforts by all agencies responsible for and interested in rapid development of rural women have to be made at all levels of administrative and development hierarchies.

The present International Conference of Women in Agriculture unlike several others, is not only broader in scope and size in terms of covering all dimensions of agriculture but also by way of participation where both national and international delegates from all shades are participating. The major objective of the Conference are : Sensitizing farm scientists, planners, administrators and development workers as to the role being played by farm women in agriculture, the impact of modernization in agriculture has on them, and the specific need for generating appropriate agricultural technologies keeping in view their working environment. Indentifying appropriate agricultural technologies for farm women aimed at (a) improving their work efficiency, (b) reducing drudgery, (c) creating job opportunities and (d) enhancing income status. Identifying research gaps/problems in relation to women farmers which should find a place of pride in the scheme of research programmes in the country.

The ICAR is promoting higher education for girls, especially those coming from rural areas. There are 18 Home Science Colleges and Departments in 26 State Agricultural Universities with over 800 admission capacity annually. However, there are very limited women scientists in research and educational institutions, and likewise in extension organizations of the State Departments of Agriculture. This requires augmentation really. The vocational training for farm women and young girls are being promoted by 91 Krishi Vigyan Kendras (Farm Science Centres) of the ICAR in India. As per Government of India's policy, all the districts are expected to have a Krishi Vigyan

Kendra in due course of time with a view to training farmers, school drop-outs, young farmers and farm women[1].

Farm women and the ICAR

Farm women play an important role in Agricultural development in India. They constitute about half of the rural population and about 30 per cent of them are directly engaged in farming. Their contributions in agriculture go unnoticed and they remain as invisible workers on the farms. It is commonly believed that women play insignificant and supportive role in agriculture. The customary sub-servient role of women at home is reflected in the area of farming also.

The Indian Council of Agricultural Research has made special efforts to involve women in agriculture, not only in agricultural occupation, but in agricultural profession also including research, education and extension education. In the field of agricultural education, the enrolment of women in the past years was not very encouranging. However, about 15 per cent of the total enrolment in the State Agricultural Universities now consists of girls specially from rural areas. In southern Agricultural Universities, the number of girl students has increased significantly. In the 18 Home Science Colleges located in 16 SAUs, the intake capacity per year in Home Science stream at under-graduate level is around 800 and at post-graduate level, it is 212. It is heartening to note that a large percentage of these girls come from rural areas. Thus through formal education in Home Science, the SAUs have expressed their commitment to the upliftment of farm women. In the last 25 years, about 8,000 girls have been trained in the discipline of Home Science. These girls after completing their education, engage mostly in educational and development activities in their respective states.

The ICAR has also initiated and sponsored programmes and projects in Home Science mainly with the purpose of

---

1. Dr. C. Prasad, Dy. Directer General, ICAR, International Conference on Women in Agriculture.

helping rural women overcome malnutrition, disease and socio-economic constraints involved in their development. An All India Co-ordinated Research Project on Home Science is being operated at six centres in the country viz. Ludhiana, Hissar, Udaipur, Pantnagar, Hyderabad and Dharwar. It encompasses the areas of food and nutrition and child development. The council is making active efforts to increase the number of centres in near future so that the regional imbalances in the Home Science research activities may be taken care of. Similarly, ad hoc research projects are also being funded by the ICAR for the benefit of rural women. These projects mainly concentrate on nutritional study of children of various age groups, deficiency diseases, goitre disease, anthropometric studies, cognitive lingual and social development of children, etc.... In addition to these projects, the Home Science College staff also conduct socio-economic and other relevant technical and epidemological surveys in the adjacent villages to keep watch on the outbreaks of diseases and epidemics and thereby helping the rural women in maintaining health of their families.

Mass Media and farm Women

The recent expansion of mass media network in the country has improved the chances of reaching a large part of the country with development messages. Radio which has already reached over 90 per cent of the Indian population and television with a promise to reach over 70 per cent population are the potential media of tomorrow. The print media, of course, has the limitation of having low readership in rural areas because a very large percentage of our daily newspapers are read in cities only. Only 0.2 million copies of the daily newspapers reach the rural areas. For about 2 per cent English-knowing populaiton, we print 20 per cent of our daily newspapers. The space-wise coverage of agriculture in daily newspapers is only about 3 to 4 per cent which is very low.

The main carriers of farm information in printed form are the farm magazines which are published by the Government agencies, agricultural universities, some selected voluntary organisations and private bodies. About 250 such magazines are published every month with a dismal circulation of only about 5 lakhs. Even a medium sized daily newspaper would claim this much of circulation in a city. Moreover, there is a heavy mortality among the farm magazines specially those published by private bodies. Unfortunately, due to low literacy in rural areas, these magazines have very few readers. But, the recent increase in the literacy among the younger generation in rural areas has created a class of "secondary readers" who listen while others are reading.

Social scientists believe the extent of mass media exposure is directly related to the 'modernisation of the audience. A study was recently concluded in Delhi villages which has testified this fact. It was found that higher mass media exposure result into positive changes in lifestyle of farm women. The life-style included family and community activities, interest and opinions shared by women on important socio-economic issues. Thus mass media have shown a tremendous persuasive impact on farm women. Radio and television provide them education for better living and improve their mental horizon along with entertainment.

Farm women with higher media exposure preferred to have their own opinions on many important socio-economic issues like dowry, early marriage, selecting marriage partners, women in politics, child-adoption, breast feeding, opening of bank accounts in their names, use of modern kitchen gadgets, earning for improving standards, etc.

Media Strategy

It is thus, encouraging to know the impact mass media have on the lives of rural women. However, we need to have a specific media policy to reach women with more development messages to channelize their activities in pre-determined directions. The 'urban model' which our media are following at present will have to change. Farm women who have to play more important role in agriculture, have to be exposed to new technologies through various media of communication. A happy combination of entertainment and education has to be made to carry farming messages to them with a suitable media mix. In fact, women will have to be treated as a special category. Use of second TV channel for farm information may be considered.

There is a need for an overall media strategy in the country which could take into account the mass-media together. Initial efforts in this direction were made when encouraged by Dr. M.S. Swaminathan, a couple of conventions and workshops were organised by ICAR for farm journalists and media men. However, now there are only few occasions when all media men sit together and talk on these issues. Recently formed 'FARM' a professional association of journalists is a welcome move in this direction. Besides, these non-official efforts, there is a need to have a total view of farm information system in the country in which special attention may be given to women who constitute half the audience. The Directorate of extension, Ministry of Agriculture, Government of India should take initiative in this direction and prepare a policy paper on this vital subject and hold discussions and consultations at various levels. Media strategy will be important outcome of this exercise.[1]

Farm Women : Who Determines the Needs ?

The role of women in agriculture is recognized in seminars, acedemic discussions and books on agriculture. However, in practice, the contribution of women in agriculture is minimised and her identity seen largely in the context of social norms which sees a woman as a daughter, a wife and a mother. Even in this sphere the emphasis is on continuing with the traditions followed earlier where women were required to provide fuel, fodder and water. The problems which have been added due to diminishing national resources are not adequately recognised. It is, therefore, essential that immediate efforts are made to improve her access to technology which would make her task on the home front easier.

The law recognizes the women's right to inheritance. The law however, remains on the statute books. Apart from the

1 - *Dr. P.N. Mathur, Asstt. Director General, ICAR.*

difficulty of long and lengthy legal proceedings, the social pressure exercised on women are enough to ensure that she does not get an equal share. In spite of progressive legislation, the land continues to be passed on to the men of the family. Free legal aid should be provided to ensure that land is actually passed on to farm women. Women have by traditionplayed a major ròle in agricultural operations, it is a common sight to see women helping in transplanting, weeding and other operations. Inspite of that there was not adequate emphasis on developing and popularising tools which would reduce the hard physical labour involved.

Winnowing, cleaning, storing of foodgrains is one more task assigned to women. Research and training in the field of post-harvest technology should be totally oriented towards women.

Women have over the years worked with dairy animals. The effort made in training women by some agencies has shown that women have adopted to modern technology easily. Programmes of research and development for women need to be further strengthened.

Relevance of farm Technology to Rural Women

Women in rural areas have remained excluded from a host of processes which advance human life, on ground that they are biologically unsuited to the world of science and technology. The studies have,however, shown that where females are not socialised against technology and given the same basic education, they tend to score as high or higher than boys of the same age. Needs and priorities of women are very different than those of men. Their needs also vary depending on a number of factors viz., educational level size of family, opportunity for employment, access to land and credit, social and economic standing in the community, cultural and religious norms, etc.

The reasons for which technocrats tend to bypass women are clear. Rural women's work is overwhelmingly focussed on food production rather than on the more lucrative cash crops, on subsistance rather than export market which brings foreign exchange; on nutrition and family welfare rather than on market oriented agro-industrial pursuits of the corporations.

Vast majority of farm researchers are men, who may not take account the special design needs of women. The women are physiologically different from men, their work posture is different. In addition, women often use technology in the presence of small children and are, therefore more concerned about safety. Designers should, therefore, meet their clientele in their own rural environment before finalising a design and during initial field testing.

Women have far less access to information about technology than men, both by virture of their inferior education status and their relative isolation from public life. Given their relative isolation therefore, any serious attempt to increase level of technology for rural women requires a special strategy to facilitate their access to innovations. This may include provisions of female extension workers for specific tasks in diffusing technological innovations, the use of radio and other mass media, and entertaining the co-operation of female professionals such as teachers and nurses who reach women directly.

The two main methods of transferring technology - the indirect trickle down and the direct 'sales' approach are both likely to by-pass rural women. Where a special effort is directed at women, for example by femaleextension workers, they are more likely to focus on women in their domestic roles in the home rather than on their more productive roles in agriculture, processing, marketing and storage of food, or on their entrepreneural activities in cottage and small industries and relating services.

Suitable technical innovations which are available to women to lighten their work burden, increase efficiency and quality, or raise yields and the volume of produce, can be transferred to them effectively only by strategies which reach them directly. Most methodology is dependent upon otherinfrastructureinputs and service for its own success. In the case of improved hand tools or implements, for example, local availability of scrap iron may be essential to the maintenance of supply by a village blacksmith at a price local women can afford.

Women must be involved in early discussions on the implications of new technology, especially when it has major implications for change without the household. To involve rural women directly in technology development and transfer, a big task of re-orientation on training is needed. Women and men extension workers need consci entisation and direct training in working with women farmers. Some of the initiative in this direction include curriculum changes in agricultural education.

The past decade has focussed attention on women and much has been achieved for some women. Rural women, however, have for the most part remained untouched, unaware and therefore, excluded from its benefits. Years of isolation of farm women in their world of science and technology is finding the technocrats ill-equipped to meet the challenges for development of farm women. The words of technology remains one of the bastions of male control but legislation and policy changes have begun to make this area accessible to women.

A sample survey of a village near Bhopal, within a radius of 15 kms. revealed that average size of family is 6-7 persons per family. On an average 24 per cent farm women were educated. Seventy per cent of the rural women were engaged in agriculture and 30 per cent were engaged in domestic and other allied works. The time spent by an average rural woman in agriculture-cum-demestic works was about a day. Rural women use only local methods and traditional tools to perform agricultural operations, which caused considerale fatigue and drudgery in the daily life. One of the examples of drudgery faced by farm women may be quoted as bowing behind the plough - in which the woman is supposed to walk about 48 hours to complete the sowing of a hectare.

The following tools and implements developed by the

Central Institute of Agricultural Engineering are very useful:

Seed-cum-fertiliser drills which perform the dropping of the seed and fertiliser mechanically in the rows with only one operation and no additional labour is required.

Paddy transplanter-five or six rows of IRRI type transplanters have been adopted with promising results. The machine can be operated by a woman efficiently. Also, growing of special type of nursery known as Mat type nursery has to be introduced to raise seedlings suitable for IRRI type machine.

Harvesting tools - a sickle, light-weight and 25% more efficient, has been developed. Now more than six designs of improved sickles are being manufactured and marketed in India. A tractor-drawn vertical conveyor reaper for harvesting cereals has also been developed. Efforts are under way to develop bullock drawn reaper to harvest cereal crops. Tools for post-harvest oprerations tubular maize-sheller, groundnut decorticator, cleaner, graders and storage bins designed and developed at CIAE, Bhopal have proved to be efficient and are liked by rural women.

Policy and Legislative Approaches

The archaeologists, anthropoligists and historians in general agree that it was women who domesticated crop plants and thereby initiated the art and science of farming. The fact that in developing countries, agriculture continues to absorb more than two-thirdsof female work force as compared to less than 10 per cent in the industrialised marketing economies and less than 25 per cent of the centrally planned industrialised economies is sufficient indication of what agricultural development has done to section of the population which initiated the production of food for the benefit of humanity. As regards the women's role in various sector of agriculture and estimate of the Food and Agriculture Organization (FAO) states that the percentage of women in agricultural force is 46 in Sub-Saharan Africa, 31 in North Africa/Middle East, 45 in Asia and 40 in the Carribean.

According to the I.L.O estimates, the contribution of agricultural communities is 45 per cent of the total 279 African labour communities. In this women play a major role in cultivation. In Sub-Saharan Africa, such communities constitute 53 per cent. It is imperative that women's role in agriculture had remained unacknowledged till recently because of conceptual invisibility, resulting from false assumptions of the relationship between women and agricultural activities. Nevertheless, agriculture remains a major sector where women's labour is concentrated particularly in developing countries. Modernisation and scientific development of agriculture has led to the exclusion of women as a beneficiary of this process. This is a very significant question which agencies concerned with the upliftment of farm women at various levels should ask to themselves and try to find possible answers and solutions to the problems of farm women.

Another pragmatic issue is related to an assessment of the relative importance of human labour, animals and tractors as a source of power. It has been stated that in 84 developing countries, the combined share of animal and mechanical power in agriculture in 1980 was 12 per cent for 31 African countries, 26 per cent for 15 countries in South and South-East Asia. 35 per cent for 14 countries in the Near East and 38 per cent for 24 countries in Latin America. These figures suggest that for decades in Latin America. These figures suggest that for decades to come, "live human labour is and will continue to be the principle productive force in the rural societies of many countries." Prospects of raising productivity to combat the growing hunger". depend on improving the capacity and quality of the human labour.

Mahatma Gandhi argued that women's productive abilities and mental attitudes were essential forces that need to be allowed full and free play for human and social development with justice and dignity. D.S. Kothari has argued that enhancement of women's role in public affairs is essential in today's world to save humanity's head-long rush to annhilation.

Since the beginning of the International Women's Decade,

various international conferences have debated the issues concerning women and agricultural development and sought to identify critical strategies to resolve these problems. The more important can be listed as (a) agricultural modernisation and the cleavage between commercial agriculture and subsistence food production, (b) access fo peasant women to the knowledge, training and extension services (c) gender inequality in access to resources, (d) gender discrimination in wages, credit and membership in decision-making bodies especially rural institutions, (e) gender biases in data systems note giving the due attention to women and (f) absence of essential support services to assist women.

The Community Development Programme in 1952, with its emphasis on integrated rural development did identify rural women as a target group. However, the suggestion to include an economic component in the women's programme was turned down. The emphasis on women's role as consumers and the home science extension approach not only contributed to the low profile of the programme but also resulted in its isolation from the main rural development programmes.

For historical, cultural and socio-economic reasons, there is gender differentiation in ownership of land and other productive assets, work roles and division of labour within and outside the house-holds. Several studies have collected empirical evidence of how development and modernisation of agriculture has displaced women. Land use policies, privatisation of common property resources, land alienation among tribals and forest policies have also affected peasant women's rights to land and access to forest resources.

Despite national and international recognition of rural women's contribution to food production and the links between the food crisis in African countries and the neglect of women's role as food producers and their rights to own land; attempts to increase women's access to land and other productive resources have been only marginal.

India has witnessed a paradox, where the food production has grown along with growing landlessness, impoverishment and mal-nutrition afflicting a large section of the population.

The focus on gender dimensions of poverty and landlessness has highligted the invisibility of women's work, drudgery in providing goods and services for subsistence, i.e. water, fuel, fodder, etc. The crisis of rural poverty, decline in common property resources, deforestation, rising cost of fuel and in - effective planning to meet the basic minimum needs (drinking water, shelter, fuel, health care, etc) have further extended poor women's typical work day.

A workshop held in 1987 come to the conclusion that "the stark reality of poor rural women's life to overburden of labour for family maintenance. Unless this overburden is relieved considerably, the creation of additional earning opportunities will either remain unutilized or will be met at the cost of their health other responsibilities. Relieving women of the burden should be considered a *non-variable* part of the support services such as child care, supply of water, fuel, fodder, etc.

Women issue is not an isolated issue. The development of 50% of the country's human resources will mean a qualitative change in development approaches and priorities. In view of the complexity of problems of women and their lack of equal access to assets, knowledge and resource, a multi-dimensional integrated approach needs to be adopted. It is important to recognise the farm women as an equally important participant in the programme of agricultural production and in no way she should be considered as a supplementary worker.

Legislative protection may not become effective because apart from legal and administrative lacunae, they are not always adequately powerful to break through the barriers of socio-cultural norms and unequal power relations within the community. Law and policy are acts of intervention in the social process which can and de-effect the socio-cultural norms, values and power systems. This process of change can be accelerated by changes in public consciouness and political will.[1]

---

1. Vina Majumdar, Centre for Women's Development Studies, International Conference on Women in Agriculture, *Supplement of Times of India,* New Delhi

73

Women in India : Law and Reality

A Full decade after demanding changes in the law, women's groups in India are being forced to consider whether enlightened laws in themselves are enough to enhance the status of all women. The recent Suman Rani case, in which the Supreme Court halved the sentence of two policemen convicted of rape by a lower court, is the immediate reason for this discussion. Despite a stronger law, under which the sentence forcustodial rape was enhanced to a minimum of 10 years rigorous imprisonment, there are few prosecutions even as the number of registered rape cases increases each year. From 5,298 rape cases registered in 1982, the number increased to 6,356 by 1985. These, of course, represent only the tip of the iceberg as majority of rape cases remain unreported.

The Supreme Court judgement in the Suman Rani case is distressing not just because the policemen who were convicted of custodial rape by three lower courts had their sentence reduced by half, using the proviso of " adequate and special reasons "which empowers a court to reduce the sentence, but because of the reasons given by the court for this litigation. The gist of these is that Suman Rani's character was such that she more or less asked for it and that in the circumstances, the men were not wholly to blame.

Women's Character

The question whether women's character has any bearing on determining whether she has been raped or not was one of the central issues discussed over a decade back, when women's groups demanded amendment of the rape law. In fact, the Law Commission had strongly recommended that no evidence relating to women's character or previous sexual experience should be entertained as evidence, as this had no relevance to determining whether the women had been raped. Significantly, the sessions court judge who gave an earlier ruling in the Suman Rani case had stated: "All said and done, even a girl of easy virtue is also entitled to all the protection of law and cannot be compelled to sexual intercourse against her will and without her consent. Offence of rape and other allied offences were created for the protection of fallible, earthly mortals, and not for goddesses."

It is interesting that in the US, where a rape is reportedly committed every six minutes, the issue of rape, and particularly the question of the victim's character, has also become the focus of discussion , thanks to a Hollywood film, *The Accused*. The story is about a woman who is a stereotype of the kind of "fest" girl who, people feel, invites rape. The film conveys the horror of gang rape in scene showing the girl being attacked by three men while the rest of the men in the bar cheer on the rapists. Despite being a Hollywood product, the message of the film is clear: no women "deserves" to be raped assaulted in this fashion. It is telling comment on our social attitudes that the Bombay film industry's equivalent of *The Accused*, which was *Zakhmi Aurat,* reduced the issue to a farce with a gang of raped women seeking vengeance on their rapists by castrating them.

Telling Comment

The recent discussion on this page about whether there should be an all-India law, like the statute in to enforce, and may conflict with some existing laws, it is necessary to make a statement, best done through a law, that such obviously discriminatory actions will not be permitted. They argue that many laws curbing social evils have been formulated and legislated even before a demand for them has emerged in society. Even if the more determined violate it, the law could act a deterrent. This discussion becomes especially relevant in the light of the harrowing story of the joint suicide pact by three bright young women in Chandigarh,who were distressed that their mother went to great lengths, including using eminocentesis, in order to have male child after a gap of 15 years.

The dowry law has also sparked discussion along the same lines. The minister of state for home affairs admitted in Parliament that there had been a steady increase in the number of dowry deaths, while the minister of state for women, Mrs. Margaret Alva, stated on television that, despite the amended dowry law, there had been few convictions in the last four years.

There are those who argue, such as the *Manushi* editor, Madhu Kishwar, that the issue is not dowry but inheritance. Until ways are found to ensure that women get a rightfulshare of their parental property, the dowry problem will not end because women themselves will not cooperate in fighting against it. Kishwar argues that when women get so little, how can we ask them to give up even the few things they can carry with them to their marital home as part of dowry. She suggests that there should be a law invalidating a will which disinherits a daughter after marraige.

But just as a dowry law has not stopped the practice of dowry giving, or bride-burning, and the Supreme Court judgement in the Mary Roy case on the inheritance rights of Syrian Christian women did not stop their fathers from making special wills disinheriting them, how will another such law fare?

Rising Fundamentalism

It is not insignificant that coinciding with the rising religious fundamentalism in the country, issues concerning women are also being communalised. Whether it is sati, or maintenance for divorced Muslim women, or inheritance rights, or a uniform civil code, the crucial issues of the rights of women as human beings are getting tangled in arguments supporting either religion or tradition. People who support change, but do not want to appear out of touch with the dominant reality, are bending over backwards to "explain" traditionssuch as sati. Inadvertently, they are playing into the hands of those who would like to perpetuate every tradition that relegates women to a secondary status. Those who attach these traditons, are now being dubbed as either "western" or "armchair activists", and dismissed for their ostensible lack of understanding of something called the "Indian reality".

These reactions to any criticism of so-called tradition are but one aspect of the tremendous resistance to change, especially when it touches on a patriarchal system that is accepted as an inviolable norm. Yet, without a change in this system, even the best of laws will fail to make a difference to the lives of women.

74

Sweating for Freedom

The scene is the large, increasingly urbanised but droughtprone region of Mashvar in Satara western Maharashtra. Our narrator is a young woman Chetna Bhalla who has spent long years fighting for women's rights in the slums of Bombay and villages of Bihar and who is presently closely involved with the women's wing of the Shetkari Sangathan. What Chetna has to say about this corner of India is nothing less than startling.

Each month, for the last one year now, an average of some 15 women have been contacting Chetna, for advice and assistance in divorce litigation. Indeed, litigation over divorce (and land) is growing so fast that otherwise itinerant lawyers from nearly Pune are 'migrating' to Mashvar for a better living. These women are suffering no more (or less--how do you compute pain ?) than thousands of women all over the world who are trapped in unhappy marriages.

State intervention, however, through the Employment Guarantee Scheme, which enshrines an individual's right to work, means the women in this region are reasonably ensured of work and a wage. It has brought them liberation.

The main issues facing women in this area are wife-beating and bigamy. Perhaps, because it is a drought-prone region where survival is a harsh struggle. Mashvar has a tradition of bigamy. There is nothing unusual for a man to contract a second 'marriage' without ending the first. The first wife's inability to produce a son was in the past, common reason for a second relationship described as a Gandharva marriage.

In the past, women mutely accepted some of the sops thrown their way to ensure compliance with system. The first wife for instance, was given her due share of 'respect' (after her "worthlessness" as a procreator was proclaimed to all the world) by a tradition which ensured that the son born to the second was usually married to a member of her family. The second "wife" then and now has no legal rights, but she was "respected" because she could produce a son. Poverty, the premise of a shelter, food and protection were reason enough, in the past, for women to accept such a system.

It continues today. Since women continue to see marriage as crucial to their status and survival, men have made dowry the new but unstated reason for such Gandharva marriages. In the past the second 'wife' usually came from a poor family bringing very little, but herself to her new home. Today, the second `wife' is often under 20-semi-literate; but her parents are willing to pay upto Rs. 6,000 to send their daughter to a married man, if he has a farm and full-time employment.

The two communities, where bigamy is unknown are the tiny Muslim community (of some 25 families) and Dalits where the first wife will usually marry someone else if her husband wants another.

The good news is that women are now standing up to say "stop" and when their refusal to be treated as chatter falls on deaf ears, when the beating becomes too frequent, women are walking out of such marriages. In Mashvar it is possible because they are wage earners. Most women work on their own farms, as they did in the past. Such labour, however, does not bring them personally any monetary returns as the earnings from the farms, however, meagre, are taken away and apportioned out by the males.

Today women are earning an independent income working on the Employment Guarantee Scheme (EGS) work sites. A large-scale rural employment programme legislation enacted by the Maharashtra Assembly in 1977, makes it mandatory for the State to provide employment to needy rural adults whenever they approach the village tehsildar in a group for jobs. Since Mashvar is a drought--prone area with farm holding averaging about five acres, most farm families need the additional income they can earn on EGS sites which although it frequently does not provide the mandated minimum wage still pays more than private farms.

Women working on EGS sites earn a daily wage that averages between Rs. 150 and Rs. 200 a month. Whereas in most families, most of the day's earnings are handed over to the male household "head", women know that EGS will permit them to survive independently and with some dignity should they leave their marital homes. After divorce, many are accommodated in the parents' homes where they are not seen as additional mouths to feed. Many women are already heads of households in which the male has usually migrated to look for employment. Their children are also employed, with girls below 18 put into saris, and passed off as adults to work on EGS sites.

Clearly, in this region the social barriers against leaving your husband, began discussing your private marital problems publicly, approaching a law court, have been broken finally. The district court, usually responsive to maintenance request, takes into account the husband's earnings both on the farm and at the EGS work site. The amount most frequently decreed is about Rs. 180 a month for wife and child. Women on the whole, are not displeased with such sums. Whether the court's "responsiveness" is due to the presence of the women's wing of the Sangathan, or whether it is usual response of a "liberated" section of the judiciary is not clear. Suffice it to say that women have enough confidence in the courts (and in themselves) to litigate in growing numbers today.

Meanwhile, the State dithers over passing legislation which would enshrine the concept of a matrimonial abode - which in effect would grant a wife equal share over poverty jointly used with her husband after marriage. For in Mashvar, after years of litigation women also find that men prefer spending 4 months in jail as defaulters on decreed maintenancepayments.

Next, despite bigamy being illegal, the practice is flourishing in the region. So cumbersome is this law and so difficult its execution, that it is impossible to deal with it here. Suffice it to say that bigamy is not a "minority" issue nor is it a relic of the past. It is flourishing and thriving in one of the most prosperous States in India - a reality sombre enough for us to sit up and deal with[1] .

Changing Goals of a Women's Group

In both the depth of its understating of the women's question and in the spread of its reach amongst rural women, the Mahila Aghadi, the women's wing of the Shetkari Sangathan, born three years ago at a convention at Chandwad, Nasik district has moved a long way. This was evident from the participation in the second women's convention of the Mahila Aghadi held in the town of Amravati in Vidarbha on November 8,9 and 10, 1989. More than 5,000 women delegates made their way across Maharashtra to the convention. Most of the women participants at Chandwad were in some way related to the male members of the Shetkari Sangathan. Also the real motives

---

1. *Indian Express*, New Delhi, August 29, 1989, 1989 p. 8, Shahnaz Anklesaria Aiyar.

of the Sangathan leader, Mr. Sharad Joshi, were questioned by women's groups. Had his campaign for remunerative prices for agricultural produce run dry ? Was the womens' issue a new ploy to widen his reach ? Did he have a genuine understanding of the burdens of rural women?

One had to acknowledge that Mr. Joshi spoke at Chandwad a language rarely heard from the lips of Indian males. He spoke of the double burden women carried, the under-valuation of their contribution to agriculture and how women were treated no better than male property. Despite the correct lanuage, his understanding, however, appeared limited and certainly did not percolate to other male members of his organisation. Also, despite its being termed a women's convention, Mr. Joshi's presence was ubiquitous. He sat on the platform, spoke at every session, briefed the press and authored the main document for the convention.

In contrast, Amravati was markedly different. Only women sat on the platform. Only a handful of men, representing the Shetkari Sangathan and other farmers' organisations, attended as observers. Mr. Joshi did speak at most of the sessions, but his intervention consisted mainly of a synopsis of what had already been stated by other women.

Heart-searching

In content too, the convention went several steps beyond Chandwad. In the intervening three years, there has been considerable heat-searching and discussion amongst women leading the Mahila Aghadi. Although the men of the Shetkari Sangathan, including Mr. Joshi, have been part of these discussions, the new formulations on issues such as property rights of women and work are almost exclusively the effort of these women. Some of their initiatives have not been fully supported by the Shetkari Sangathan: for instance, the battle against alcoholism in the villages. In villages where they were well organised, the Mahila Aghadi launched an anti-liquor or *daru bandi* campaign. They would demonstrate in front of liquor shops, demand their closure and often break liquor bottles in front of these shops as a form of protest. They admit that the campaign has not been entirely successful because the shops tended to re-open as soon as their campaign died down. But the issue has galvanised the women.

What is significant, however, is that even as the women campaign against liquor, they will not admit publicly that the reason the issue has drawn such a response from rural women is because of the undeniable link between alcoholism and wife-beating.

For strategic reasons, say the Mahila Aghadi activists, they do not want to emphasise any issue that will lead to a confrontation with the men whose support they need for their agitations.

Another issue that has been approached with some caution is that property right. In Chandwad, a resolution was adopted which held that "every female", by virtue of birth in the family, should obtain rights to property on equal terms with the male issue . In the three years since then, no progress has been made on this count.

Property is an important factor for the kind of women the Mahila Aghadi has managed to enlist because the majority of them come form the ranks of small and medium landholders. Unlike tribal women and landless agricultural labourers, inheritance and property rights are a central concern for these women. Their membership of these classes also means much greater confinement within the house for them than women of the lower classes. Therefore, their participation in conventions like the one at Chandwad and Amravati constitutes a significant break with the tradition.

Women Campaign

The women who have been assisting in formulating both the understanding on the issue of property rights and the strategy to be adopted - including *Manushi* editor, Ms Madhu Kishwar - have come to the conclusion that a gradual approach is best as the issue is far too complex. Existing laws are not being implemented because of entrenched social attitudes. However, while one cannot wait till such attitudes change, an attempt has to be made to make the prospect of women inheriting property acceptable to a conservative rural society. In this reasoning that has prompted the Mahila Aghadi to adopt what they term the "Hingoli" plan, which evolved out of a discussion held in that town in Maharashtra. Mr. Joshi has appealed to all Shetkari Sangathan activists to set aside a small part of their plot of land so that the income from it can go directly to their wives who should be given independent control of this income. The investment for that plot, however, would still need to be borne by the men.

The Mahila Aghadi activists are of the view that even though such a plan is far from adequate, it could start a process of change in dominant male attitudes. They emphasize that this is just an intermediary step. Indicating his awareness of the resistance even such a minor step could face, Mr. Joshi, when he made the appeal to the male members of his organisation, emphasised that he was asking them only to earmark a part of their land not to hand it over to the women.

From a purely theoretical standpoint, such an approach seems inadequate, because it fudges the main issue of power. property represents power and control. If you are not willing to acknowledge that, and try and skirt around it with a few concessions, then the problem will never be solved.

At the same time, it is difficult to dismiss the attempt made by this rural women's group to bring about change in something to fundamental. Such an approach could work, at least in some restricted areas where the organisation has the strength to enforce its writ. No judgement can, however, be made without watching the programme over a period of time.[1]

---

1. *The Times of India*, New Delhi, Saturday, November 25, 1989, p. 8

75

Women and Population

This critical evaluation of the researches on the effect of population policy on women examines the interconnection of the demographic, developmental and women's problems and identifies gender gap in the health issues. The sycophants are concerned with population control by hook or by crook. Unlike, in this study the authors are bothered about the population policy that does not exploit vulnerability of women.

In the introduction, the authors (Malini Karkal and Divya Pandey) give basic demographic information such as high maternal and child mortality rate as well as morbidity rate. They succinctly bring out that women are looked upon as only reproductive machines whose only worth is in their motherhood. The women's movement supports the birth control methods as a basic democratic right to be exercised by women without any socio-political compulsions. Moreover, these should not be other health hazards related to these contraceptive methods.

What happens in India and the other third world countries is irresponsible state-intervention in this most 'private' area. Hence we have mass sterilizations without proper follow-up, harmful oral and injectible contraceptives thrust upon the poor women without informed consent, material incentives and disincentives to avert births, obsession with target fulfilment with its associated corollaries such as bribing, cheating, corruption by the family planning officials and ultimate victimisation of the poor-helpless people.

Due to anti-women social values the sex-ratio continues to be adverse. It was 972 in 1901 and 935 in 1981.

While examining the socio-cultural dimensions, the authors highlight the fact of reinforcement of the modern industrial system over the age old patriarchal system making women's subjugation acute and generalised. The desire for male child has now been expressed in the spread of centres for aminocentesis that is followed by female foeticide". Review of literature on women and health delineate the survival struggles of women's right from birth to reproductive age and to death.

While examining the literature on impact of reproduction on health, the authors are repeatedly struck with the fact that "women have very little choice in decision-making. They have no control over their fertility. In addition, due to lack of knowledge and access to contraceptive information and services, their pregnancies are too closely spaced and more than desired." Pregnancy before 18 years was 50-58 per cent in Madhya Pradesh, 26 to 38 per cent in Uttar Pradesh and around 48 per cent in rural Karnataka. In the slums of Bombay, tribal Orissa and urban Karnataka, it was around 29 to 33 per cent.

The fourth chapter, "Women's issues and population policy in India" is quite exhaustive. The studies on "Maternal and

Child Health (MCH)" service show that majority of women are still unaware of immunisation , need for feeding during illness such as diarrohoea or measles among the children. In their critical appraisal of family planning in India the reviewer, Ms. Veena Poonacha states "there was a clear shift in the family planning programme: from a programme for the health and welfare of population to a programme of population control. It introduced time and target oriented approach to family planning. The evaluation of the programme became in terms of birth averted". Excesses during emergency rule (1975-77) that boomeranged and the orientation of family planning made a drastic shift from male as a target to female as a target.

Scathing scenario emerges when the authors describe an evaluation of vasectomy camp in Gujarat which "brought out that 39 per cent of the men sterilised included (1) men whose wives had attained menopause (18.9 per cent), (2) those who were secondarily sterile and therefore not using any family planning methods (12.4 per cent), (3) those who were either unmarried or separated or widowed (3.8 per cent), (4) men whose wives were in the age group of 45 and over (2.1 per cent) in whose case no pregnancies could occur or reproductive performance could be very low (5) cases were reported where either of the spouse had been sterilised earlier (1.8 per cent)."

Inspite of repeated requests and protests by the feminist groups in India, the government has introduced Net-0-En and other long-acting contraceptive which are banned in the west. Multi-national pharmaceutical companies have big stake in this. Against which, the authors feel that the population policy will be more appealing and effective only when it changes for better factors that affect adversely an individual family. This is corroborated by knowledge,, attitude and practice (KAP) studies.

Inspite of legislation of abortion in India only one million out of the 5 million abortions performed are safe. Another danger is the use of Medical Termination of pregnancy Act as a means of contraception. Due to repeated criticism of the government in the post-emergency period by the feminists, the government has changed its stance and in its new strategy it "gives family planning the broadest dimensions of social engineering, including not only health and family welfare, but also child survival, women's status, employment, literacy and education". Now the National Perspective Plan (1988-2000 A.D.) which aims to achieve NRR wants to involve voluntary organisations in this drive.

This highly informative analytical and sensitively examined study will be useful for all development activities, women's groups and researchers pursuing population studies and women studies.[1]

Why the Female Ratio is Falling

The 1991 census has recorded a population sex ratio of 929 fémales per 1000 males, which is seven points lower than the 1981 census into of 934. It is not clear whether a trend can be inferred. In absolute terms, the change in the population sex ratio is not as large as it appears. If it had remained unchanged at 934, we would have had 20 million fewer women than men as compared to 31 million now. The two figures are almost equally bad and there is, therefore, not enough ground to believe that the position of women has worsened considerably. Of course, the fact that it has not improved considerably is in itself a bad sign. But it is worthwhile in examining the reasons for the estimated fall in the sex ratio between 1981, if only to desensationalise the issue. The reality is more complex than the media have tended to suggest. A decline in the sex ratio does not imply a worsening of the absolute condition of health and survival for women. What it means is that the gap between male and female survival may have increased. Absolute levels of female health and survival may still have (and in all probability actually have) improved considerably.

Censuses tend to underestimate both females and males. There are probablyno large differences in the underestimation

1. *The Economic Times*, New Delhi, August 27, 1989, p. 6, Vibhuti Patel.

of males and females at a gross national level. However, when one disaggregates the population, female underestimation is greater in some cases. For example, the 1981 census found the greatest gap in enumeration was in the central and northern zones of the country. Even if there has been no further increase in the gap in these two regions, there could be an apparent fall in the overall sex ratio, if the share of population of this region has increased.

Census Data

The recent census data show that these two regions now account for 94.9 per cent of the total population as compared to 34.1 per cent in 1981. Similarly, the 1981, post -enumeration check found a greater gap in male-female under-enumeration for older persons, especially those above 60 years. The population projections of the Registrar General's office, which come so close to census estimates suggest that the population over 60 may have increased from six per cent in 1981 to 6.6 per cent in 1991.

So on the whole, it appears that changes in the structure of the population may explain a small part of the apparent decline in the sex ratio between 1981 and 1991. This explanation assumes 'no fundamental change in enumeration trends. However, with increased education and modernisation, one could expect that the gap between male and female underestimation will narrow.

Until recently one could state with some confidence that there was no real evidence that the sex ratio at birth in India was any different from, that in other parts of the world (104-108 male births for every 100 female births). Retrospective surveys in several parts of (especially northern) India found the sex ratio of children at birth to be abnormally high, but on the whole this appeared to be due to a greater under-reporting of dead daughters by women. Direct analysis of hospital-based births found nothing unusual in the sex ratio.

But in the last few years, we have seen the unanticipated interference of a technological advance. The increasingly easy availability of amniocentesis to detect the sex of the foetus as well as the MTP procedure, in some localised areas at least, has led to a rush to aborted female foetuses and consequently, possibly an arificial rise in the sex ratio of births. According to the departments of family welfare, about three million medical terminations of pregnancies have been performed since 1984-85 by government-recognised institutions in the country. If one (somewhat generously) assumes that a quarter of these followed sex-determination tests, they would count for about 0.75 million of the estimated 31 million females shortfall in the country.

Medical Evidence

Medical evidence suggests that as yet amniocentesis cannot accurately predict the sex of the foetus in the earliest weeks of pregnancy. So a significant proportion of the abortions that follow the test may actually be male. Moreover, to the extent they were female, it is not clear that all these aborted foetuses would otherwise have been born or would have survived until the census. We may get a clearer idea of the magnitude of the change once we have detailed tables on age specific fertility rates as well as the age breakdown of the population from the 1991 census. These changes are unlikely to be significant on any large scale.

Female mortality may be dropping more slowly then male mortality. One can look at two ways in which this may have occurred; first an increase in the gap at all levels and, second, no general change in the gap but a change in the distribution of certain socio-economic groups in the total population.

How likely is the first explanation? This hinges not on a rise in absolute levels of female mortality but in relatively slow declines in female as compared to male mortality. This is a distinct possibility given the strong preference in the country and steadily falling morality levels. Given such a combination, it would not be surprising, if the gains in survival accrued disproportionately more to males so that even if female mortality declined as well, the gap between the two became wider, leading to a further fall in the population sex ratio.

The second explanation also has some force. Female education tends to reduce absolute levels of child mortality, but may initially be accompanied by an increase in gender differences in mortality, as the increased resources available for child health are used disproportionately in favour of boys. Female literacy and education have risen over the last decade.

On the whole, it appears that a small but significant increase in the sex differential in mortality may have taken place at the national level, and may account for at least a part of the decline in the Indian population sex ratio.

However, to appreciate the female disadvantage in life and eventually in survival more effectively, one needs to highlight the large male-female differential in absoulte numbers rather than harp on minor fluctuations, which are essentially what the last 20 years have witnessed.

76

IndianWomen—Endangered Species

Indian women seem to be heading towards becoming an 'endangered species' in another 100 years if the misuse of medical techniques like amniocentesis is not stopped. Though female infanticide. The practice of killing of female infants - had been legally banned, in practice it still takes place here and there. One hears about it happening particularly in Rajasthan. Pre-natal annhilation of the female species is being resorted to in many parts of the country under the guise of medical determination of genetic abnormalities. This is known as aminocentesis. It is a medical technique to detect serious mental and physical abnormalities in an unborn baby. Fluid is drawn from the mother's amniotic sac and the cells in the fluid are cultured and tests done. Such a test can be done around the sixteenth week of pregnancy. If any abnormality is detected, the foetus can be treated or aborted. What is atrocious, however, is that this medical advancement has now more often not come to be used as a device to opt for one gender and discard the other. If the test shows a female foetus, it is often aborted.

Choose your Child - a Criminal campaign

Our socio-religious- cultural ethos gives undue importance to a male child. A daughter is an unwelcome addition in most of the families, even now. Advertisements and hoardings in newspapers, magazines and at strategic points by which say "choose your family", "boy or girl ? " and so on are a common sight. Couples aspiring for a male child are tempted to go to these clinics in order to take no chances. Recently, there have been sharp protests against it. Meetings, rallies and demonstrations have been held and demands made to close down these clinics and punish the doctors who perform these tests. In fact, such clinics are thriving in many parts of the country.

It is believed that there are courier services to send samples of the amniotic fluid of pregnant women from Rural Health Centres in some states to big towns and cities. Between 1978-83, 18,000 female foetuses are reported to have been aborted in the country after sex-determination test. According to some reports, in Bombay alone, there are 16 laboratories and 40,000 tests are carried out in a year. A survey conducted in 1983 reveals that out of 8,000 abortions done in six Bombay hospitals, 7,000 foetuses were female. Responding to public agitations and demands, Maharashtra has, however, passed a law banning the practice, the Regulation of Use of Pre-natal Diagnostic Techniques Act, 1988.

There is now a strong demand for a central legislation to ban sex-determination and pre-selection sex tests as state laws, obviously, cannot achieve the desired results. People who want to have this test done may very well go to other jurisdictions which do not have lawagainst it. Such a practice is to be attacked on many counts.

It is a legal offence, constitutionally it is *ultra vires*, morally it iscontemptible,socially it is atrocious and ecologically it is inexpedient and disastrous.

The following provisions in the Indian Penal Code are relevant in this context, Section 312 says, "Whoever voluntary body causes a women with a child to miscarry shall, if such miscarriage be not caused in good faith for the purpose of saving the life of the woman to be punished with imprisonment of either description for a term which may extend to seven years and shall also be liable to fine." Section 316 says, " Whoever does any act under such circumstances that if he thereby causes death, he would be guilty of culpable homicide and does by such act causes the death of an unborn child, shall be punished with imprisonment which may extend to ten years and shall also be liable to fine."

Under the Medical Termination of Pregnancy Act, 1971, a pregancy may be terminated under certain conditions in the following circumstances viz.-

> Where the continuance of the pregnancy involves a risk to her physical or mental health.

> Where there is substantial risk the child, if born, would suffer from such physical or mental abnormalities as to be seriously handicapped.

> Where the pregnancy is a result of rape or failure of contraceptive device and causes great anguish to the woman.

Even for medical termination in these circumstances, the opinion of one medical practitioner in the case of a pregnancy upto 12 weeks, and of two medical practitioners in the case of a preganancy between 12 to 20 weeks testifying that these circumstances exist, is needed. Doing away with a foetus subsequent of a sex-determination test is not covered by any of the laws. Thus abortions resorted to simply because the gender of the child-to-be is not of the choice of the parents is clearly an offence under the law.

It is also clearly against a constitutional mandate. Article 51 A(e) of the Constitution says that it is the fundamental duty of every citizen "....to renounce practices derogatory to women." Surely a practice or device which permits or seeks to do away with a foetus simply because it is a female is derogatory and very much against human dignity. The practice is inexpedient as the destruction of female foetuses will create an imbalance in the male-female ratio in the population. Rape, illicit relationships, polyandry and so on, will be the by-products of this phenomenon.

Besides, this practice is not devoid of risks to the mental and physical health of the mother, who after undergoing the test resorts to abortion, and also of the child who is born after such a test.[1]

Do Indian Women Face Extinction ?

Trouble began for Sunita Chaturvedi (21) mother of two daughters when she became pregnant again. Her husband Girdhari and her in-laws decided that she should not deliver another daughter this time. It has to be a boy, or else she will have to get the foetus aborted. In our male-dominated society, Sunita had no choice. She was taken to Bombay when she was four-and-a-half-months pregnant. Dr. Meenaxi Merchant at Opera Nursing Home performed amniocentesis - a sex determination test (SDT) - on her. The result : Sunita's foetus was female. Next, Dr. Merchant performed Sunit'a abortion under Medical Termination of Pregnancy Act (MTPA) by suction (or dilation) and evacuation method. Sunita was discharged within 12 hours and advised to take ampicillin and pain killers. But within four days Sunita was dead. The cause: penetration (blunt injuries

---

1. *The Times of Inddia,* New Delhi, December 27, 1988, p. 3 Agenda, Kusum.

to the abdomen associated with post-operative rupture in that region) or due to injury while doing amniocentesis.

Sunita's case has how become cause celebra for women groups in India. Bombay's Mahila Dakshata Samiti has filed a writ petition in Maharashtra High Court seeking to prohibit ameniocentesis, or any other SDT from being carried out and selective abortion of female foetus. Further, a bill seeking a ban on amniocentesis, leading to selective abortion of female foetus has been moved in Maharashtra State Assembly by the well-knownwoman activist and opposition legislator, Mrs. Mrinal Gore.

The technique of discovering the sex of the foetus (amniocentesis) was first introduced in India in 1974 using costly equipment imported from Europe and USA. The test involves withdrawing a sample of the amniotic fluid, which surrounds the foetus by inserting a needle throughthe skin, uterine walls and the aminiotic sac. The fluid in the sac contains living cells sloughed off from the foetus. Tests on the fluids show the sex of the foetus, its maturity and deformity, if any. Amniocentesis was intended to discover the presence of Darwin's syndrome - a type of congenial mental retardation which occurs more commonly in children borne by women over 35 than by younger mothers. But amniocentesis is being abused by many doctors to make a fast buck.

Bias Against Girls

Hundreds of clinics, charging Rs. 500 to Rs. 5,000 for amniocentesis test have sprung up across the country. Mr. Vibhuti Patel , a leading activist of the Women's Centre (WC), Bombay says, " If SDTs followed by abortion of female foetuses continue, it would soon render women in India an endangered species".

She is not wrong. What began as trickle five years ago is now threatening to become a torrent. Figures bear this out. According to WC, around 11,000 couples took SDTs between 1974-79 in Bombay. But between 1979-82 this figure jumped to

78,000. While no one has come out with figures after 1982, but estimates of people taking SDTs, followed by abortion of female foetus are estimated at 100,000 a year in Bombay alone.

An observer says the figure for the entire country is expected to be alarming. And they are going to worsen as SDT clinics spread to rual areas. At present they are restricted to major cities only. India is one of the four countries in the world where an already adverse male-female ratio has been getting worse over the last 60 years. Today, there are some 936 women to every 1,000, men. Infant mortality in India, specially of females, is one of the highest.[1]

Strong Bias Against Female Children

An earnest young "townie" went to a small village called Amawar in Uttar Pradesh, just a few hours drive from Varanasi. He was sent from the city to gather local population statistics. So, how many children do you have, he asked each adult. The answer varied from one to four. Quite small, thought our perplexed young man. Family planning must be working at last. Suddenly a loitering youth asked the confused townie, "Do you want to know about children or boys ?" Children, of course, stammered our indignant friend. His now amused audience, their disdain for townfolk confirmed, laughed and suggested the double his numbers. For the daughters of Amawar were only "guests" in their native village.

Literally and figuratively, little girls do not matter. Describing this incident Razia Ismail, the chief progrmme committee information officer in South Asia for UNICEF, wrote in 1986 that one of the great ironies of the women's decade is that even women's organisations and women Scholars had not woken up to the specific needs of female children until 1985. While 42 per cent of the country's population is under 15, and half of these youngsters are girls, yet, more than 11 years after

---

1. *The* Pioneer, May 10, 1987 - A.S. Negi

India formulated a national strategy for women's development and two years after the climax of the International Women's Decade, said Ismail, millions of little girls remain "our unseen Indians".

The position is not very different today, claim women from the nations of south Asia meeting at a conference of the South Asian Association for Regional Co-operation (SAARC) in Delhi, on the girl child. Initially, like several other international bodies, the SAARC technical committee on women and development did not focus on the girl child. It looked at the needs of adult women. It was only after its 1986 conference on children that SAARC gave itself a mandate to examine the specific problems of children in every technical committee.

What's new about the female child, you may well ask. We know female infant mortality is higher than male. That mothers breastfeed infant girls for much shorter periods than boys to start ovulating quickly and conceive again - this time, hopefully a boy. We know this pattern of malnourishment continues through life - so what else is new ? Quite a bit, says recent researchı. It suggests we also focus on the girl. She is a person not just a phase between infant or woman. There are some important details and new statistics emerging from such rasearch which must be noted by our planners and law-makers. Existing legislation must bring the girl-child into its purview.

'Prepared' for Womanhood

Before puberty, from the age of five onwards, she is 'prepared' for womanhood by being initiated into a series of house-hold tasks which quickly extend into "assisting" her mother in low-paid, unskilled jobs. After puberty the child becomes woman. A study by Ranjana Kumari titled "Growing up in Rural India" focuses on this abrupt "metamorphosis". Once a girl has attained puberty, she has immediately "acquired" the capacity to reproduce. So, her entire life changes - abruptly her mobility is restricted, she is rebuked for jumping or running she becomes periodically "impure" and "untouchable", the few privileges she enjoyed as a "pure" child are suddenly snatched away. Pulled out of school, given a series of additional household tasks, these new burdens on her underdeveloped body meant to prepare her for marriage. The child is woman. Which means the family, particulaly father, is under tremendous pressure to get her married or else he will be accused of "Bhruna Hatya" (embryo murder) if he "wastes" her fertility. With the average age of puberty in India being 13 - 14 obviously marriage by then is a common event. Where, then, is the time or space for the growth and development of the personality, the body and the spirit that adolescence is all about ?

What use serves a law which forbids child marriage and insists the legal age of marriage for a girl is 18 ? Today, India has one of the lowest female mean ages at marriage in the world. Given the religious, social and economic compulsions behind child marriages, the mean age for marriage for girls has increased by just five years in eight decades. In several States, the marriage age varies from 15 to 16 - well below the legal prescription. Nonetheless, there is some change. Census figures state that between 1971 and 1981 mean ages on the whole increased more in rural than in urban India. Ranjana Kumari's study described some 48 per cent of the rural girls she interviewed expressing their dislike for an early marriage and preferring marriage after 18.

The Child Marraige Restraint Act was passed some 10 years ago. Not once has it been reviewed with the needs of the girl child in mind. If it were, we would not have kept the Registration of Marraige Act pending, refusing to enact it for unfathomable reasons. We have laws ensuring the registration of births and deaths and there are numerous ways the State can insist on marriage registration, particularly in conjunction with the registration of births and deaths.

But then - the girl child is the unseen Indian. We often discuss child labour, we know it is nonsense to see it as synonymous with male child labourer. Yet we know little about the kind of work a female child performs and care even less about her rights as a worker - which she certainly is. A "Status Report on Indian Women from Birth to 20" produced by

Dr. Meera Chaterjee for the National Institute for public Co-operation and Child Development and presented at SAARC meet, makes the following points:

-While the percentage of rural working boys aged 5 - 14 actually fell from 11.37 per cent in 1971 to 10.05 per cent in 1981, that of girls doubled - from 4.6 per cent in 1971 to 7.8 per cent in 1981.

-1971 to 7.8 per cent in 1981.

-Overall there was a four fold increase in the percentage of working girls. The figures for boys remained constant.

-As they grow older into the 15 - 19 group, the highest growth rate is for female children. While this has increased by 17 per cent for girl workers, it has actually declined by eight per cent for boys. The largest growth rates in the female workforce were in Haryana, Punjab, Orissa, Tamil Nadu and Karnataka. The lowest were in Uttar Pradesh, Kerala and Bihar.

Age-wise, girls enter the workforce earlier than boys. While eight per cent of female child workers come from the 0-14 age group, the percentage for males is four per cent. About 20 per cent of girls under 20 are full-time or main workers while for boys the figure is just 14 per cent.

Of course, we have read in ealier columns one consequence of all this - the level of illiteracy among female workers is 84 per cent while that of males is 50. Boys are now permitted to remain in school longer than girls. Another paper "Out of Sight out of Mind: The Female Working Child in India " by Neera Burra describes the kind of jobs that girls are in by the time they are 14. Here too, their "invisibility" is ensured. Large numbers of female child workers are in home-based piece-rate industries where they often do not get separate wages because the adult female worker - usually their mother - is paid such a low rate making agarbattis or beedis that she enlists her female children to work with her and thus increase her output.

The female child is rarely seen as a worker either by the employer, the parent or the State and is exposed to cumulative inequality.

The Government has enacted the Child Labour (prohibition and Regulation) Act of 1986. It is meant to protect children under 14 from hazardous employment. But it is useful only for children who go out to work. The premise of labour legislation is that there must be identifiable employer and identifiable employee whose working conditions can he regulated and wages fixed. It explicitly denies protection to children working as part of family labour.

According to Ms Sujaya, Joint Secretary in the Department of Women's Development, Ministry of Human Resource Development, a bureaucrat who is part of an energetic team within the ministry, "Many diehards still refuse to look at gender in child development". Ten years ago, she recalled, when we began to look at women's issues, we were told to look at the family and at women within that context. Today, there are many educationists nutritionists and development activists who continue to insist that it is wrong to focus on female children; it is much more relevant to examine the caste and class factors that lead to property is the enemy to be attacted. But, whatever we know women and girls clearly shows that while poverty cripples, gender bias, in addition, destroys. It is time those concerned about human development threw away their blinkers and responded to the special needs of the female child.[1]

Female Foeticide-Gujarat

Though an official campaign wants the people to treat a son and a daughter alike, the message is not sinking in . The female is condemned even before she is born - thanks to sex-determination tests. Thousands of "women"vanish even without

1. *Indian Express*, New Delhi, September 24, 1988 -p.9 - Shahnaz Anklesaria Aiyar.

as much as a cry. Most on social grounds, a few on medical grounds. The estimated 1988 toll of female foetuses in Gujarat is 41,000. On an average, 250 to 300 sex-determination tests are conducted daily in the state. In nearly half the cases, pregnancy is terminated if the results show a female foetus. According to a rough estimate, last year alone, sex-determination tests in the state reached the staggering figure of 1,08,000. However, Ahmedabad tops in the state with 18,000 female foeticide out of approximately 35,000 sex-determination tests. These figures confirm the findings of a recent survey conducted by the Forum Against Sex-Determination, a city unit of a national body, fighting this crime against women. Even leading pathologists and gynaecologists of the city who are in this "business" killing female foetuses "reluctantly" agree to these figures.

Dubious Distinction

If today Gujarat has the dubious distinction of having highest number of female foeticide in the country, it is not an overnight development. It is a culmination of a trend set in nearly 15 years ago. The Forum against Sex-Determination has determinedly sought to end this obnoxious practice all over the state. The government even promised to pass a legislation on the lines of Maharashtra where pre-natal sex-determination tests are banned. A forum delegation, which had met the health secretary, Mr. K. Ramamoorthy last year was given a promise that in the monsoon session itself a legislation would be tabled before the assembly. But now the forum leaders feel that the government is just not inclined to appreciate the enormity of the problem.

Mr. Babubhai Vasanwala, Janata Dal leader, had in the last session of the assembly presented a private members Bill, which stated that between 1978 and 1982 as many as 78,000 female foetus were destroyed and that the government was duty bound to take immediate steps to ban pre-natal sex-determination tests in the state. However, after the assurance given by the chief minister, Mr. Amarsinh Chaudhary, that the government itself would bring forth an appropriate Bill.

Mr. Vasanwala had withdrawn his Bill as a gesture of goodwill. Soon thereafter, the health minister, Mr. Vallabhbhai Patel, had, while inaugurating a sonography unit in a government hospital at Rajkot, condemned sex-determination tests in no uncertain terms and announced the government's intention to take stern action against those engaged in pre-natal sex-determination and in selective abortion. According to the forum leaders, the government has yet to match these words with action.

Government Determined

However, Mr. Ramamoorthy reiterates that the government is determined to put a ban on sex-determination tests and legislation has already been formulated and had been referred to a committee of three experts. In the meantime, the central government has sought Gandhinagar's opinion on the proposed legislation that will effectively ban sex-determination tests all over the country. That is why the delay, asserts Mr. Ramamoorthy. But Dr. Lata Shah, convenor of the forum, alleges that a powerful "business minded" lobby of pathologists and gynaecologists has brought pressure on the government to delay the legislation. If the state government is keen to pass the legislation, why should it wait for the Union government to pass a Central law ? She asks. Dr. Shah is not impressed with Mr. Ramamoorthy's contention and even point out that the Maharashtra government did not wait indefinitely for a Central law. The forum at Bombay had succeeded in putting pressure on the government to adopt its own law. The Gujarat government is well aware that the passage of a Central law is a time consuming process.

Referring to Maharashtra's Regulationof Use of Pre-Natal Diagnostic Techniques Act, 1988, Dr. Shah says that as per this law no generic counselling centre, laboratory, clinic, gynaecologist, medical practitioner or any other person is allowed to use the per-natal ultra-sonography, for the purpose of indicating the sex of a foetus - with of without the possible object of female foeticide. The Act also bars any laboratory or clinic from giving any advertisement regarding facilities of per-natal prediction of sex.

Theoretical Position

Of course, this will be the theoretical position when sex tests are banned. Actually the tests will continue illegally, because there is one perennial truth about themarket place : if a demand for an item or a service exists, somebody is bound to supply it. Sex-determination tests are ridiculously simple. They are of two kinds, amniocentesis and ultra sound. In aminocentesis, a gynaecologist inserts a needle and takes out fluid from the womb of a women 16 weeks pregnant. This is sent to a laboratory which takes three weeks to pronounce if the embryo is a boy or girl. If the sex of her unborn child is not to her liking, the mother can have an abortion, this being safe till 20 weeks after conception. Aminocentesis predicts a child's sex with total accuracy.

The second sex-determination test, ultrasound, relies on a sopisticated machine which costs anything between Rs. 2 lakh and Rs. 20 lakh. The machine takes a picture of the foetus when the mother is 16 weeks pregnant, and the picture tells the sex of the child, though only with 90 per cent accuracy.

Aminocentesis costs a couple of thousand rupees, and an ultra-sound costs two or three hundred. Is it conceivable that a mere law will end these sex tests? If laws could change societies and attitudes, the practice of untouchability would have ended years ago. The same is the case for dowry deaths and so many other evils in the society. Let us see what happened in Maharashtra. In May, 1988, the state government banned pre-natal tests to determine a child's sex. But in Bombay, you find any number of clinics doing these tests clandestinely. Because these tests are illegal, the clinics charge whatever they wish. If the tests were legal, the competition between doctors for business would bring the price down.

Centre's Decision

In fact, the Centre's decision to ban sex tests will hit the poor hardest. Affluent Indians will still be able to afford the high fees charged by private doctors. But where will the poor go ? Government hospitals will not offer sex determination tests. So the poor will have two equally hard choices : (a) spend money they cannot afford in private clinics, or (b) end up with a daughter they do not want. Ultimately, the poor will have larger families than they wanted.

Of course, it is shameful that women should want to have female foetuses aborted. In any civilised society, a girl should be wanted as much as a boy. This is so in affluent western democracies, and it is true about well-to-do Indians also. But there is no denying that among many Indians, a son is seen as an asset and a daughter as a liability.

When sex tests were legal in Maharashtra, one line from clinics grabbed people's attention : "Better to spend Rs. 500 now than Rs. 50,000 later on". This meant that Rs. 500 spent on aborting a female foetus would save the parents Rs. 50,000 in dowry later on. The prejudice against daughters is shameful, but legislation is no way to erode it. What is needed is education and the social awareness which comes with it. Why do we not hear dowry deaths in Kerala ? The answer is that because it is India's most literate state.

India is not the only country where women occupy a subordinate position. In Saudi Arabia, women are forbidden from driving cars. In Muslim Sudan, a women cannot go abroad without permission from her husband, brother or father. In Israel, 10,000 women cannot get a divorce because Jewish law says they have to get their busband's consent. All over Asia, infant girls have been fed poison; they have been smothered after birth or simply not fed. In South Korea, male births exceed female births by 14 per cent, in contrast to a worldwide average of five per cent. In one province of China, men between 30 and 45 outnumber women by 10 to 1. In fact, female infanticide is widely practised in China.

But it's irrational to think that legislation can end sex-determination tests. A ban cannot keep technology away from people. Our censors frown on kissing on the Hindi screen. But thanks to VCRs and foreign films which can be freely duplicated, children sitting in their homes can see torrid love scenes.

If we want the abortion of female foetuses to end, we have to concentrate on spreading female literacy, we have to give women inheritance rights[1] .

Sex Determination or Extermination

Amidst all the chaos evident in the New Delhi, with walk outs in parliament, the Central Government has announced its intention to introduce a bill in the current session of parliament regulating the use of sex determination technologies. The bill has not yet been finalised by the Law Ministry. It will be based on the recommendations of a committee set up two years agowhich relied heavily on the experience of drafting a similar law in Maharashtra. The prospect of a Central law to regulate the use of sex determination technologies, raises many of the same questions that arose when the Maharashtra law was formulated. The basic question then as now is whether the law can ever deal with such a problem.

The issue is simple. Technologies that were developed half a century ago to detect genetic deformities in the foetus, and whic incidentally could also reveal the sex of the foetus, have been blatantly and rampantly misused in India for the selective elimination of the female child. The problem caught media attention when Dr. Bhandari in Amritsar advertised his ante-natal sex determination clinic in 1979. Subsequently, activist groups in Bombay noticed a proliferation of such clinics which openly advertised the service. At that time, the main technology being used was aminocentesis, which involves removing amniotic fluid from the pregnant women after 90 weeks of pregnancy. The test can reveal any genetic abnormality as well as the sex of the foetus. On discovering that the foetus was female, an abortion was conducted.

---

1. *The Times of India*, January 25, 1991 - Arvind kala.

The campaign against the misuse of aminiocentesis and other sex determination tests was launched by a group in Bombay, the Forum Against Sex Determination and Sex Pre-selection, which feared that if the practice continued unchecked, it would seriously affect an already negative male-female sex ratio. The forum collected information which proved that scores of gynaecologists in Bombay and in smaller towns in Maharashtra, were openly advertising and doing the tests. Furthermore, a liberal Medical Termination of Pregnancy Act (MTP) allowed women to give contraceptive failure as the reason for undergoing an abortion, if they did not want to give birth to another girl.

One of the studies, that resulted from the campaign, and which was officially sanctioned by the Maharashtra Government which had begun considering the feasibility of a law to check female foeticide, found that 42 out of 50 doctors questioned, that is 24 per cent, performed sex determination tests. The study, by Dr. Sanjeev Kulkarni, calculated that these doctors averaged 270 sex determination tests a month. With more than 1,000 gynaecologists practising in the city of Bombay, the extent of the problem could well be imagined. The majority of the doctors also believed that they were performing a humane service for women who did not want daughters. In other words, they felt no guilt, nor did they consider this an illegal act, although the technology was being clearly used for a purpose other than the one for which it had been invented.

The impact of the continued misuse of sex-determination was also evident from the statistics gathered by three sociologists of two villages in Bijnore District, Uttar Pradesh. They found that sex ratio in the district was 863 females to a 1000 males, even lower than the national average of 935. Sex determination clinics had been operating in the district for several years prior to the survey.

It was acombinationof outrage and such facts that led to the campaign demanding for a ban on sex determination technologies. The discussions on the law, which were initiated by the health ministry of Maharashtra are relevant today with the Centre considering a national law. The questions raised then have yet to be fully answered.

First would it be right to ban a technology just because it is being misused ? After all, aminocentesis or chronic villi biopsy, another such test, is a vital one which can be alert parents about renetic abnormality in the foetus, thereby giving them the option of resorting to an abortion if they did not wish to be burdened with an abnormal child.

Seondly, could a law check a pratice that arose out of social conditionwhereby the value of a woman was so low that parents were reluctant even to give birth to a girls? Would merely preventing people fromdiscoveringthe sex of the child stop, the practice ? Would it not push it underground and raise the rice ?

The very nature of the test made its control extremely difficult. Amnioentesisdoes not require sophisticated equipment. A qualified gynaecologist can remove the amniotic which can then be tested in any pathology laboratory by geneticst. How could one catch a doctor in the act of conducting a sex determination test ? The activists who were associated with the formulation of the Maharashtra law, insisted that the only way to check the growing misuse of the technology was to prohibit private practitioners from conducting it. They held that if the test was restricted to government medical institutions, its misuse could be checked even if not completely eliminated.

This, however, was not accepted by the Government which feared that such a regulationcould be challenged under Article 19 of the Constitution.

The Maharashtra Experience

The Maharashtra Regulation of Use of Prenatal Diagnostic Techniques Act, 1988, which came in to effect on May 10 of that year, was the product of many months of intense discussions between government bureaucrats, activists, doctors, like Dr. Pal who opposed the law, and lawyers. Although at the outset the law was welcomed as Maharashtra became one of the first states to take such a step, subsequently it has been criticsed both for the obvious loopholes that exist in it and its lackadaisical implementation by the Government.

The act regulates the use of sex determination technologies but does not ban them. It also does not touch on the aspect of sex pre-selection technologies, which the Forum felt should have been part of the law. The act provides for a State Appropriate Authority (SAA) which is enjoined to register institutions conducting these tests and state and regional vigilance committees which supposed to keep an eye on these institutions and follow up are complaints. It also lays down that sex-determination technologies can only be used on women over 35 years with either a history of two or more abortions, or who has been exposed to teratogenic drugs, radiation, injection or hazardous chemicals or with a family history of mental retardation or physical deformities. Under no circumstances is the doctor permitted to reveal the sex of the foetus. The Act also prohibits advertisements about pre-natal sex-determination tests.

Several months after the law passed by the Maharashtra legislature, there was no sign of SAA or the vigilance committees being constituted. It took the State Government more than seven months to start moving on the law. When it finally took some steps it did not demonstrate sufficient alertness or urgency. For instance, soon after the constitution of the state vigilance committees, activists discovered that the Government had appointed a gynaecologist who had been performing sex-determination tests. Following their protests, she was asked to step down.

Since then, the implementation of the law has been practically non-existent. The state vigilance committee received two complaints in 1989, about two private hospitals which were advertising sex-determination facilities. The complainants sent photographic proof of this. The committee did not move with any alacrity. Instead, it handed over the task of investigation to an official of the Bombay Municipal Corporation, and by the time the team went to these hospitals, the boards had been removed.

Even the SAA has not been effective. Despite knowing that there are literally thousands of private nursing homes and clinics in the state with facilities to conduct sex-determination tests, the SAA received only 11 applications for registration from the Bombay Circle, which consists of Bombay, Thane, Raigad,Ratnagiriand Sindudurg districts. Of these nine have been registered . To date some 16 clinics in Maharashtra have been granted permission to use the technology for detecting genetic abnormalities.

Dr. S.R. Salunkhe, joint director of health services, admits that there is no way in which the clinics that have not applied to the SAA for registration can be forced to do so. Nor does the Government have the machinery to check whether unregistered nursing homes are conducting these tests or not. In fact, Government officials privately admit thatcheckingthe misuse of aminocentesis is a relatively low priority area when there are far more pressing problems in the area of health care.

Dr. Pritam Phatnani, a medico-legal expert, however, says that the law has not curbed the practice at all. Instead of conducting the tests in the nursing homes, doctors are now sending the samples of the amniotic fluid just across the border to Gujarat, where laboratories proliferate. The test results merely states 'favourable', which means a male foetus, or 'unfavourable' meaning the converse. The law has also raised the price of the test. While this could have constrained a few, it was unlikely to deter the more determined. And as medical practice is increasingly regarded as a business, only the more principled doctors would deny themselves the opportunity of making a few more rupees.

But health officials given the task of implementation claim helplessness in the absence of a machinery to check clinics and powers to question and inspect such institutions. At present the vigilance committees can inspect a registered clinic if a complaint against it is filed. But they can do nothing about unregistered clinics which are suspected of conducting the tests. In fact they have no power to demand information from these clinics in order to ascertain whether they are conducting sex determination tests covertly.

In the final analysis, given the experience in Maharashtra, it is clear that legislation in itself is inadequate in an area which requires social reform. The same attitude that has led to bride-burning, or justification of 'sati', governs the cold-beded decision of parents to abort female foetus. Until Indian society grants women equal status to men, and values them as human beings, such practices as female foeticide or infanticide will continue. At the same time, it is evident that a government and a society that is made aware of an illegal and immoral practice like female foeticide cannot condone it. And merely because it is difficult to check this evil practice without a fundamental change in social attitudes, does not obviate the need for a law. Indeed, the very fact of a law can be used to generate awareness on the issue.

The advantages of a Central law are evident. It would prevent the undercutting of State laws, such as the one in Maharashtra, by neighbouring States that allow the practice. It would also constitute a statement that the Central Government regards the problem as serious enough to require a law. However, before finalising Central law the union Government should learn from the shortcomings of the Maharashtra law. For instance, the state especially mentions the sex-determination technologies now in use. But it is more than likely that new techniques will be devised in the future which are also safer than the present ones. The Central law should ensure that such future technologies are also covered by the law.

The powers of the appropriate authority and the vigilance committees also have to be reassessed and probably enhanced to ensure that they can fulfil the function for which they have been appointed. For instance, just as the Federal Drug Administration has inspectors, the State vigilance committees should be provided with permanent staff who could carry out surprise checks on clinics suspected of conducting these illegal tests.

At the same time, regardless of the extent to which the law is tightened, it is evident that only a continued campaigning by the groups concerned to create awareness and to pressure the States to implement the law, will make a difference in the long run. The only people who will monitor clinics suspected of performing sex-determination tests and report them to vigilance committees and also ensure that theircomplaintsare, followed up, are the individuals and groups who are aware of the problem and concerned that it should not continue. The existence of a law will assist them in the task of creating awareness and restricting the abuse of the technology. They connot, however, sit back and rest.

This is the reality with regard to all social laws in this country. They can be translated into reality only if enough people demand it[1].

1. *The Hindu, Sunday,* January 6, 1991 - Weekly Edition-2-Kalpana Sharma.

77

Demography : The Declining Sex Ratio

As in poor countries, in India, too, we have a record deficit of women over men. What causes concern in India, however, is the fact that the women-to-men ratio has been continuously declining over the last few decades. In the 1901 census, there were 1,072 females for every 1,000 males. Since then the ratio of women to men gradually declined and today we have only 929 females for every 1,000 males.

The decline in number of females to males has never been uniform. Sociological and biological reasons reinforce each other for a declining sex ratio. Inter-state variation is quite high -- 861 in Arunachal Pradesh and 1,040 in Kerala. Females outnumber males in very few districts. But there are at least 44 districts which have a women-men ratio below 850. Half of these districts fall in U.P. Almost all the districts in MP, UP,

Haryana and Rajasthan form a sort of continuous grid with a belt of sex ratio below 850. However, a favourable sex ratio is observed in the compact tribal tracts of MP, Orissa and AP.

In Europe, 105 male births take place for 100 female, whereas in India this ratio is 108 to 100. This marginal preponderance of males over females at the time of birth does not wholly account for the large deficit of females in India. Similarly, though there is omission of females in the total count of population, it is not high enough to account for the declining ratio. Other reasons like higher infant mortality of females, maternal mortality, etc., appear to carry more weight. As a matter of fact, it is the social and biological environment in India which has really very little to offer. The preference to male children is writ large in Indian customs, in the de facto operation of laws of inheritance, in marriage and in everything else that happens in society.

An All-India Family Planning study by the Operation Research Group finds that an overwhelming majority of the couples believed that one must have a son mainly to carry on the line and support the family; three-fourth preferred 2-3 sons.

Do the 1991 census statistics on women-men ratio indicate that female infants are subject to greater risk of mortality in the northern states of Haryana, Punjab, Uttar Pradesh and Rajasthan, etc. ? The sex ratio is adversely marked for Haryana (874); UP (882); Punjab (888). On the other hand, southern states have slightly lower female mortality during infancy, compared with males in other states. Some studie reveal higher age specific death rates for females in the 0-4 rather in all 0-14 age groups in India. In terms of age specific mortality rates, it is seen that in a few states like Kerala, HP and AP, female death rates are lower than those for males. So, the figures of sex ratio are also favourable - 1,040 (Kerala); 996 (HP) and 972 (AP) i.e., quite above the all-India average of 929 females per 1,000 males. Survey findings also reveal that the percentage of ailing males given medical treatment is higher than the percentage of females getting such treatment, implying neglect of the female.

An ever widening gap between male and female education also reveals the relatively low status of women.

Early marriages have subjected Indian girls to the risk of motherhood at a tender age. Data analysed by population research centres reveal that two-third of female marriages occur before the girls are 15 years old. Studies have shown that incidence of maternal mortality is high among mothers under twenty. To reduce female mortality and halt the diminishing number of women, increase in age at marriage is must. The declining sex ratio in India is not merely biological phenomenon; it is the cumulative effect of social practices and preferences which are inseparable from each other. No doubt, a higher mortality among male children is visible upto the first month. Soon after, male children begin to receive preferential treatment. The relatively low mortality rates of 10 - 14 years old girls in all states may be explained by a relative advantage enjoyed by living daughters in their parental homes compared with those 15 -19 years who tend to be exposed to the social and biological risk of early marriage and child bearing. The female death rate is about one third higher than that of males in the reproductive age group 15 - 44 as revealed by National Sample Survey and other studies. This too can be attributed to the comparatively low economic status of women. Too early, too close, too frequent, too late (till late) child bearing are also evidence of the low status of Indian women.

A WHO study directed by Ramalingaswami and others has revealed that prevalence of anaemia is the highest in India. An ICMR bulletin also says that about 70 per cent of our pregnant women suffer from anaemia which contributes to nearly 40 per cent of maternal deaths. Protein deficiency and anaemia are quite common. This is more true to expectant and nursing mothers, who are prone to high mortality.

In almost all developing countries including India, for women, the incidence of morbidity and accessibility to health care, nutrition are governed by economic and social factors. Ignorance and low utilisation of health services and non-use of the right type of food are expressions and bye products of sex-specific economic deprivation. Even increases in the price of items of daily consumption affect dramatically the health of women in a family.

In this context, those who have studied the reasons underlying the low-status values accorded to daughters and the relative preference for sons in several Asian societies opine that where a women's productivity is high or higher than that of the male and when and wherever there is a high demand for female labour force in agriculture, the undervaluation of women and girls are relatively less. So, in the southern parts of India which have a 'rice-based' agricultural organisation system, high demand for female labour gives women greater economic and social autonomy and less discrimination than in the 'wheat-areas'. This is not the sole reason for the differences in the sex ratio between southern and northern states but holds true in the general economic framework.

Again, a study of rural households from all over India on the allocation of family resources proved to some extent that where the expectation of employment for the woman is relatively high, female children receive a higher share of household resources (than in places where female employment levels are low). The difference in the expected economic productivity of adults due to sex dominates the difference in health care or education level in accounting for variations. Current sex ratio differentials in this context need to be examined.

Some studies show that economic factors play a basic role in the neglect of female children, in terms of their health and educational levels. A comparative study of demographic difference between north and south India includes that son preference and better care for males is far more acute in the northern region where the `kinship structure' is such that there is 'low female autonomy for economic matters' than in south India. There are other studies from India which attempted an in-depth economic analysis of the causes of malnutrition among young children in the villages of Punjab. Sex was found to be the most significant determinant of nutritional status, more consistently accounting for variations in nutritional status than any of the other variable. This variation in nutritional was far greater among the low caste, on the lower end of the economic spectrum. This in turn leads to differential morbidity conditions. A single study may not explain everything but in castes' light on sex ratio in Punjab (888) and Haryana (874).

A survey of a south Indian village revealed that the expenditure on treatment of first born girls was approximately 35 per cent of that on first born boys. A comparison of sex and birth order with medical expenditure found a virtual absence of medical treatment of girls down the order. Among families cross-classified by expenses, most money was spent on first born or second born children. Female children, although high valued in some families, received almost no medical attention. Chandlers on 'Investment in children' gives an account of survey findings in rural Karnataka, that breast-feeding of boys lasted longer. Although no sex discrimination was noted in terms of regular food, preference was noted in distribution of 'more nutritious food'. Also, some were given better quality medical care than daughters and treated at an earlier stage, regardless of the number of boys in the family. Girls were shown to less qualified doctors and seldom to city doctors. If their illness persisted they were hardly attended. With equal proportions of illness, the health centre saw 74.1 per cent male children and 26 per cent females. Even doctors were described to be reported showing discriminatory behaviour specially in families with many girls. Many mothers observed that they wanted to obtain treatment for the daughter but due to low status in the family and ignorance, had no power to seek health care.

Food distribution patterns recorded showed that men and children were given food first and women are what remains thereafter. Studies in food affected West Bengal suggest that in times of crisis girls suffer from malnutritution more frequently and more adversely than boys. In another situation, again in West Bengal, the boys fared better than the girls consequent to land reforms and an overall improvement in nutritional status. Available data on dietary consumption among 1-18 year olds show that girls consume much less than boys. This situation has a link with unfavourable consequences on health status of young mother. This nutritional deprivation may run through the period then they are in the family way and lactating.

Studies like this are micro in nature and therefore limited in their scope but they speak volumes about the status of women in India. Given the nature of the data it is difficult to draw conclusions about the factors responsible for the 'vanishing' Indian females. However, the fast deteriorating situation calls for serious analysis, debate and, most importantly, some concrete action[1].

---

1 - *The Economic Times*, April 19, 1991.

78

Female Foeticide Undemocratic

Dharma Kumar's advocating aminocentesis for sex-determination (Times of India, December 9) is not a reflection of the idiosyncracies of an isolated individual. What has appeared in newspapers by way of 'debate' on women's issue this year, almost takes one back to the days of the 'Age of Consent Bill'. But it must be noticed that all this is not a simple renewal of the debates of the 19th century, which our nationalist leaders thought they had settled once and for all. There is a systematic and orchestrated attempt by a section of our intelligentsia to intervene at the present conjuncture of social and political crisis to put forward solutions which are essentially right wing. One can remember that not long ago there appeared in the columns of the Indian Express an article by an equally well-known intellectual, Ashish Nandy, giving sympathetic social sanction to Sati. Dharma Kumar's article against a central legislation on aminocentesis belongs to the same category. She argues that since there is a widespread and deep-seated prejudice against women, their marriages are so expensive and they cannot provide the economic security or the ritual usefulness that a son can for their futures. She then goes on to give a number of facts regarding different aspects of discriminatory practices against female children, and draws from them his 'logical' conclusion that if their lives are so bad it would have been better if they had not been at all. As a matter of further consideration she points towards the high incidence of female infanticide in this country. Since a large number of female children are going to be killed anyway, she says, why waste the nation's resources and emotions in nurturing new female members. Let the society concentrate on those who have survived.

As an eminent social scientist she must know that it is nothing but social Darwinism in its crudest form. In the name of "raising the social status and life expectancy of those who are born", she is prepared to sanction not only that many more be disallowed to be born at all, but also that society continues to want them. There is no reason otherwise for her very categorical statement or why one should "force poor people to have daughters they so strongly do not want and may ill-treat or neglec? "

Close look

A close look at this statement reveals yet another aspect of her reactionary perspective. It is, according to her the poor who most grudge the birth of a girl. This is nothing but ignorance of a social reality, that among the really poor a girl is as much a source of labour as a son, and their marriages are not so 'expensive' nor rituals among them taken so seriously as to create such a social pressure against the birth of a female child. In any case the percolation of the prejudice, to the extent it has reached the poor, does not find indulgence for the simple reason that they cannot afford the high price it entails. She is, however, even prepared to take her argument to far more dangerous dimensions when she says that sex determination tests are increasingly being used by precisely those classes whom the family planners want to reach." And she is quick to link it up with "abortion" as a means of birth control which is a "national policy". This is nothing but the justification of elimination of those whom the society considers unwanted. One shudders at the social and political implications of such a justification. One must tell her to learn a little more about the artisan families she refers to. How do artisan families make two ends meet, if they do not transmit their skills to daughters also? More concerned with their "rights over their bodies", she has not bothered to know how much of craft production in India is dependent on women of the artisan families.

Wonderously the selective destruction of the foetus seems different to her from the right of a woman over her own body! Right wing radicalism precisely thrives on the confusion and perversion of democratic rights to advocate solution which are essentially anti-social. Women are to be made ready tools in destroying their own species by presenting female foeticide as an exercise of their democratic rights.

The contempt that Dharma Kumar shows for progressive legislation is equally reflective of her neo-right radical perspective. "The widespread and deep-seated prejudice against women" is too deep-seated, according to her, to be wiped out by legislation. It would, by banning the practice, drive all such evil social practices underground. Presumably what she then wants is that discriminatory practices against women be not considered crimes at all, so that they may be all carried on above board and, for that reason, be easily commitable and without fear of retribution. Granted that legislation is not *sufficient* to curb any social evil but then why have laws against Sati Cutsom or child marriage, or female infanticide, or dowry, or specifically against deaths related to dowry ?

Not Mere Evil

She deliberately refuses to consider the fact that Sati, system, female infanticide and child-marriage are not merely 'evils' to be condemned, but they are crimes. And they are crimes precisely because they are against the *law* of our land, or of any civilized society for that matter. The legislation of any society is a reflection of the values cherished by that society, it is also an indication of the direction towards which the society wishes to advance. Law is an instrument of social transformation, and particularly in backward societies, it is a pre-requisite, a condition for social change. Interestingly, at a time when the left and democratic circles of this country are clamouring for progressive social legislation protecting the rights of the oppressed sections and minorities, and for governmental responsibilities for implementing all such legislations, here is our 'modern' intellectual, Dharma Kumar, not just sanctioning the non-implementation of legislation, but also absolving the government of all responsibility for discriminatory practices against women, by not having them designated as crimes in the first place.

The celebrated intellectual that she is, she must surely know what a high percentage of the world's people live below the poverty line. She must also know that a bigger percentage than that lives in despair of ever having a fair future. Following her central argument that those who have no bright future to look forward to may not be allowed to be born, will she permit a logical extension of her argument to advocate mass sterilization of all the poor of the world ? Will she advocate genetic engineering and selective breeding in the procreation of only what is considered the best and most wanted, and the elimination of those unwanted ? She further asks very morally, "is female infanticide preferable to female foeticide," as if at least one of these we are bound to sanction and accept By her logic not only are women to bear the brunt of the country's family planning programmes, but the women among the poor must doubly bear it so, because they have even less to offer to their female child. How is that different from the Jews to bear with the weight of Nazi Germany's social and political crisis.[1]

1. *The Times of India*, New Delhi, December 26, 1988, p.4- Nalini Tane,ja

79

Female Foeticide : Census Pointers

No civilised Indian can have read without a sense of shock and foreboding that the sex ratio according to the 1991 census has declined to 929 females per 1,000 males, that is, 71 females less per 1,000 males than at last count in 1981.

Comparatively speaking, women would appear to have been better off at the turn of the century, when the country was not so " advanced " technologically, for the sex ratio then was 972 females to 1000 males. The census commissioner and certain officials in the family planning department have warned us to treat census figures announced as provisional. However, the final count, while it may reveal under-enumeration, will not change the sex ratio unless only women have been under-enumerated .

Medically Proven

It is a well-known and medically proven fact that the female foetus is harder than the male one and that, all things being equal, women live longer than men. The sex ratio in the advanced countries of the West, therefore, is overwhelmingly in favour of women. Against this background, it becomes clear that we are actively killing women in frightening numbers. The ways we do so are through malnutrition, lack of health care and general neglect.

A study of pre-school children conducted in seventies in Narangwal, Punjab, showed that, whereas the female to make ratios for pre-natal deaths and still birthswere 73:90 and 51:82 respectively, they became rapidly unfavourable to female the moment nurture passed from nature to human hands. Thus the ratio for infant deaths from the first day to one month and from one month to one year for females to males were 65:55 and 55:35 respectively. It is interesting to study, against these figures, statistics compiled by Care (Co-operative children in Punjab suffering from severe malnutrition. The findings showed that 29 per cent of the cases were male and 71 per cent female.

It was to be expected that, in a society with such an overwhelming preference for male children, more active methods elimination than undernourishment and neglect would be employed as soon as they were made available. Thus, the amniocentesis test used for the detection of genetic abnormalities in the foetus, acquired its new application a little over a decade ago when doctors blatantly began to advertise it as a test to determine the sex of the foetus. Sex detection could lead to abortion if the foetus were reported to have been aborted after sex-determination tests. Given our poor infrastructure for detection and monitoring of such phenomena, we can safely assume that the number of cases was much higher.

So outwardly "clean " was this method of foeticide, that, when feminist groups demanded that banning of sex determination tests and the Maharashtra government responded with the enactment of the Maharashtra Regulation of Use of Pre-natal Diagnostic Technique Act in April 1988, there was a sizeable "responsible" opinion arraigned against it. Detractors of the law were right in their prediction that the enforcement of the law, (if indeed an efficacious enforcement was at all possible, given in and wants) would drive sex-determination tests underground into the hands of the unscrupulous making them, in the process, many times more expensive. Added to this was fact that the test continued to be available in neighbouring Gujarat.

However, where this school of thought erred was in arguing that in a country where abortion had been legalised, and was being used as a family planning method, female foeticide was perfectly legitimate. This argument is sure to be put forward again when the demand for central law against sex determination tests gathers momentum once again. It is, therefore, necessary to point out the fallacy inherent in the argument.

Under the Medical Termination of Pregnancy Act, 1971, a pregnancy may be terminated only where its continuance involves a risk to a woman's physical or mental health; where there is substantial risk that the child, if born, would suffer from such physical or mental abnormalities as to be seriously handicapped; where pregnancy is the result of rape or failure of contraceptive device and causes great anguish to the woman. To extend the last clause to include any other nature of pregnancy likely to cause a woman anguish is deliberate and mischievous to distort the sprit of law. Abortions carried out under the law do not upset the sex ratio whereas selective abortions, as we have seen, do and are, therefore, ecologically and socially disastrous.

A central law govern the use of sex determination technologies has to be made not because one is so naive as to expect it instantly to curb female foeticide, but because legislation is supposed to point the way in which a society believes it should move, and because the existence of law helps those who are involved in bringing about attitudinal changes. The major area in which attitudinal change has to be brought about is in the increasing incidence of dowry. Advertisements for sex-determination tests pose the choice between daughters and dowry crassly and succincty: "Better pay Rs. 500 now," they advice, "then Rs. 5 lakhs later".

Whopping Increase

With dowry, as with sex-determination tests, legislation has not curbed the evil. Despite the Dowry Prohibition (Amendment) Act of 1984, reported dowry deaths have increased by a whopping 32 percent between 1985 and 1987. In 1987 a group of senior social workers and social scientists who had been regular guest lecturers at the Lal Bahadur Shastri National Academy of Administration, Mussoorie disclosed that a majority of IAS probationers who married after joining service, demanded dowries ranging from Rs. 15 lakh to Rs. 50 lakh. Boys from other professions are known to have their rate cards too. It has been a commonly held notion that the key to all social problems in India is education. But dowry and its attendant evil, female foeticide, occur more widely among the educated middle class than among the under-privileged and unlettered. And herein lies the rub. Who will educate the educated?[1]

1. The Times of India, April 12, 1991, Shanta Gokhale.

80

Are Women Indifferent To Health?

Well Woman Programme launched by Apollo Hospitals, Madras analysed 1,000 woman who had availed themselves of this health check, has served to emphasis several basic truths women should give serious thought to. Of the 1,013 women whose data were analysed, 752 were from Tamil Nadu; 251 from other states and 10 from other countries. Most of them were educated and from the urban middle-class. Age wise, 109 were below 30, 408 in their 30s, 316 in their 40s and the rest over 50. A fact that stood out was that just 23 of the vast majority had health problems of one kind or another. This leads to one or both of two conclusions.

> Women who feel well do not think it necessary to have a preventive health checkup.

Women who feel unwell think nothing more is necessary than a quick remedy, often self-administered and sometimes by a doctor.

Awareness of the importance of preventive health checkup what the Well Woman Programme seeks to promote, is sadly lacking even in the educated middle class. A second fact thrown up by the analysis was a sizable number of women believed themselves to be in normal or near normal health, with nothing more than what they thought to be passing indispositions. Many of them were found to have problems, some serious and even life threatening, like diabetes mellitus, hypertension and ischaemic heart disease. A majority of the women of course, had problems of which they were aware and, in many cases, had lived with for varying periods. These instances only confirmed that they had come for the check up not because they thought it desirable to have a preventive health check, but because they had inconvenient and persistent problems. Most of them, however, were unaware of how easily their problems could have been prevented.

The Spectrum of Problems

The spectrum of problems that were uncovered in all the women ranged from the simple to the serious. But one common feature characterised most of the women, inadequate awareness and indifferent attitudes and practices in respect of the factors that tilt the scale from good health to ill-health.

Over-weight and obesity, for instance, were found in 20 per cent of the women. Many assumed obesity to be natural, or even a sign of good health. Obesity means not only a loss of form and figure, of youthful appearance and of physical fitness (in themselves--substantial losses), but it is the starting point of many health problems. There is great need for women to recognise how easily within reach the disciples and rewards of dietary control and exercise are. Once the conscious maintenance of the preventive defenses of the body is slackened, the door is open to disease in a bewildering variety and degree of seriousness. The 206 obese women suffered from a variety of concurrent problems like diabetes mellitus, ischaemic heart disease and obsteoarthrosis. The 181 women with anaemia were unaware that a regular intake of iron-rich greens in their diet could easily have prevented this debilitating condition which takes away so much of the rest for life.

Lack of awareness and indifference exact far more extensive and severe health penalties than is generally realised. Nowhere is this more striking than in the high incidence of diseases originating from indifference to environmental and personal hygiene. Amoebiasis was found in 139 women on routine motion examination. They had to be taught to give more serious consideration to two simple precautions :

"Drinking boiled water as the simplest way to guard themselves against this insidious disease with a potential for serious complications.

Adequate hand-washing after toilet, an important safeguard that removes the faecal-oral route of infection.

More complex factors were seen at work in the 84 women with diabetes mellitus and 81 with hypertension. A strong family history of both these diseases did not prompt them to be on the guard. In the case of diabetes mellitus, remaining slim, staying on a balanced diet, exercising on a regular basis and having health checks could have certainly reduced the magnitude of the problem. A disturbing feature in established diabetics was lack of awareness of the disease, of the importance or content of diabetic diet and the need for regular medical checks. Instances of high blood sugar levels were seen in women who had abandoned allopathy in favour of other systems of medicine. Surely it is not advisable to abandon the diagnostic test regimens of the allopathic system.

In established hypertension, it was refreshing to see that in all but a few instances blood pressure was under control with medication. Staying slim and active and restricting the salt load in the diet could have certainly contributed such in their well-being.

Specific Problems

Moving on to women-specific problems, 128 were found to have diseases of the uterus and ovaries on ultrasound scans necessitating gynaecological surgery, major or minor. A total of 168 women had menstrual disorders and were under sporadic hormone treatment without complying with the basic safeguards-regular checking of weight and blood pressure, monthly self examination of the breasts and annual pap smears (to detect cancer of the cervix). A rather frightening habit of self-medication with hormones for postponing periods during religious and social functions was noticed. A similar casual approach to the use of hormones was seen in 94 women who had taken the contraceptive pill. Women should realise that hormones are a powerful tool of modern medicine. Just as there are documented benefits from their judicious use, there are dangerous side effects, sometimes threatening life.

It was surprising that 447 women admitted to have had one or more abortions. Of them, only 160 admitted to some form of contraception involving themselves (contraceptive pills, IUCD, or tubal ligation). A few indicated the use of alternative methods (abstinence, safe period, condoms and vasectomy). It seems unfortunate that women should opt for medical termination of pregnancy in such large numbers rather than practice reliable methods of contraception, especially when there is such large scale effort to popularise the various methods of family planning.

Lake of Hygiene

The horrifying consequences of neglect of personal hygiene were striking in 396 women with varying degrees of inflammation of the cervix evinced from pap smears. While the daily bath is considered a must in the country by reason of both climate and religious tradition, it seems strange that personal hygiene should be so neglected. Several facts emerged from discussions with women in the group:

Thorough washing of the genitalia during bath or at other times of the day was not a matter of habit among the couples.

Douching with plain water or simpler alternatives were largely unknown.

Washing before or after intercourse was not practised by couples even in cases where genital or urinary tract infections were present.

Women were unaware of the link between chronic infections of the cervix and abnormal pap smears and also of the importance of having repeated pap smears after the infections were eradicated.

None of the 1,013 women had had a pap smear test in her sexually active life.

In India the incidence of cancer of the cervix is high because of personal and socio-economic factors. It therefore becomes imperative for responsible couples to practise stringent personal hygiene, undertake treatment for genital infections and realise the importance of annual pap smears. The smear is the only method available to detect cancer of the cervix in its incipient stage when cure is possible. Till these precautions and practices become widespread, cancer of the cervix will continue to be a major killer of women in the country.

It is obvious from this study that education, affluence and ready access to medical help in urban areas are largely neglected by indifference to and ignorance of health matters. There is an erosion of traditional lifestyles particularly relating to food habits. And, finally, there is the unrealistic expectation that modern medicine can undo the harm one brings upon oneself[1].

Pollution Exclusive to Women

When we talk about pollution, the immediate thing that comes to one's mind is the smoke emitting automobiles, factories

1. Dr. Uma Krishnaswamy.

and similar things. But then, there is another little known type of pollution, to which our women folk has been exposed from time immemorial. It is known as domestic pollution and it emanates from our kitchens. Though a lot of study and research are yet to be done in this field, whatever little had been done gives ample evidence to show that domestic pollution causes many a lethal diseases - especially to women, the reason being obvious.

Various Factors

Ninety per cent of the Indian household uses firewood, cowdung and crop residues as fuel. Burning of these fuels produce highly carbonated smokes: continuous respiration of which causes or help to cause many diseases including cancer. The harmful elements from the domestic smoke are the total suspended particles and Benzo (a) pyrene. The recommended limit of the total suspended particles during cooking is 120-150 microgrammes/cubic meter. However, in an average rural Indian household, it is about 7,000 microgrammes/cubic meter during cooking hours, which varies from three to six hours a day.

Various factors enhance, the density of total suspended particles in the household, the main factors being the size of the kitchen. Most of the houses in the rural areas are small and the provision for ventilation is very negligible. The result it that smoke remains within the dwelling unit for a long time. The other reason is the use of multi-mouthed stoves.

Climatic conditions also act as an impediment in the release of smoke from the cooking place. During winter and rainy season, mostly all openings are kept closed as a result of which, the smoke gets blocked within the dwellings. Moreover the temperate inversion prevents the smoke from rising.

Harmful Effects

The effects of inhalation of smoke are many. Evidence of heart disease called 'Pulmonate' has been traced in persons who are exposed to smoke/inhale smoke, which has been found in cigarette smokers only. Studies in the northern part of India and Nepal indicated that persons exposed to such pollution are susceptible to chronic bronchitis. It also has an adverse effect on children and infants. One of the main reasons for the high morbidity and mortality rate in infants were found to be acute respiratory infection. It is partially due to irritation caused by such indoor, smoke filled conditions, in the rural areas and urban slums.

Another smoke emitting fuel used extensively in the rural area of India is biomass. Biomass release carbon monoxide and formaldehyde when burned. Carbon monoxide is a toxic gas, which reduces the haemoglobic content in blood. Inhalation of carbon monoxide continuously also leads to heart diseases and impair foetal development.

It is well known fact that the immunity power of anaemic persons is very less. In India, it is estimated that 40 - 50 per cent women in reproductive age and almost 50 per cent pregnant women are anaemic. The harmful effect of carbon monoxide on our rural women and children can be roughly gauged from the above data.

Formaldehyde too is highly harmful. It causes irritation in the eyes, nose and throat. It poisons the lung tissues and would exacerbate skin wounds. As exposure to cigarette smoke during pregnancy increases the risk to mother and child, women using biomass as cooking fuel also are exposed to similar health hazards. Excess and continuous exposure to wood smoke would also increase the chances of chronic obstructive lung diseases, heart diseases like car-pulmonate, cancer, particularly lung and nasopharyngeal, acute respiratory diseases.

Smokeless Chulhas

The first and foremost solution to this problem is to minimise usage of fuelwood and biomass for cooking. An additional benefit of such a measure would be lesser pressure on our already depleted forest lands. Kerosene, liquid petroleum gas and electricity should be supplied to our rural areas without any disruption.

Another important and feasible solution is to popularise the smokeless stoves. Smokeless chulhas have been made and further improved upon by many energy conservation and research institutions like the Tata Energy Research Institute, Pondicherry; Central Power Research Institute, Bangalore, etc.

Alongwith extensive use of smokeless chulhas, the kitchens of our rural areas should have to be slightly improved upon to incorporate proper ventilation, so that whatever smoke forms inside the kitchen should be freely released outside. Installation of biogas plants in rural houses is another step which should be popularised. It is economical too, as biogas plants could provide electricity, cooking fuel and manure.[1].

---

1. *The Ptoneer*, Lucknow, June 9, 1989, p.9, N. Bhadran Nair.

81

Women-The Key to Family Planning

It was about three decades ago that President Habib Bourguiba of Tunisia said on the national radio : "We are a small country with poor resources. If we continue to have such a high population growth rate, we will not be able to feed our people. Many husbands however, continue, to think that to have lots of children is proof of their manhood. That is manhood, but rabbithood. A true man is a father who provides for his children, puts food in their mouth, shoes on their feet, love in their hearts, and education in their heads. If you cannot provide all these for your children, you cannot and must not have more children ".

The key to economic prosperity in the developing countries is their ability to control the population growth rate. Nowhere is the situation as grim as in India. Of the 90 million added to the world population each year, 17 million are born in this country. The birth rate has been almost constant at 32 per thousand for some years now.

Elsewhere in South Asia, population growth has reached critical proportions in Pakistan, Nepal and Bangladesh, Though all these countries started family planning programmes long ago, they have been outpaced by other developing countries which introduced them later. In India, apart from a lack of political commitment, the programme has been handled in a ham-handed manner. The quality of health care, so vital for effective family planning, has been poor. The UNFPA is doing a special study on these four South Asian countries to see how the population can be controllrd says the turn of the century.

Prime Minister Mitchell of Barbados, the sunny, cricket-loving Caribbean country, was so distressed by the high rate of teenage pregnancies in his country that he warned, "Bat as much as you want, but be careful of the number of runs you score". Such political comments on excessive population growth by national leaders are unfortunately few. Most heads of government of developing countries in Asia, Africa and Latin America are chary of saying anything at all, because fertility control is such a personal matter and because in many cases talking or doing anything about it entails high political costs.

Religious sentiments, too, are easily provoked. Both Catholics and Muslims have reservations on the subject. In Iraq, the mullahs castigate families with less than five children for not doing their duty by their nation and religion. According to a recent report in a newspaper, the use of contraceptives has even been banned.

Demographic Trends in Third World

Demographic trends in other third world countries are equally distressing. The world is at critical juncture and what we do over the next decade will determine the pattern of world population growth for much of the next century. If we fail to control explosive population growth, there will be 14 billion people on earth in 2,100, almost thrice the population today. of the population increase will be between 90 and 93 per cent in the poor countries. These additions, Dr. Nafisa Sadik, executive director of UNFPA, has warned, will not only cripple the development process, but create enormous potential for violence and social upheaval by millions of unemployed youths. The impact of a burgeoning population on the environment is mind-boggling.

Governments of high-fertility countries are already spending increasing amount on essentials and have no money left for any other investments. Kenya spends a third of the total government budget on education, health and water supply and urban housing. If fertility rates remain high, the amount would have to increase nine-fold to maintain current standards.

The ravages of unplanned population growth are evident in many third world countries. In the last four years, 37 of the poorest nations have cut their health funds by 50 per cent and their education budgets by 25 per cent. In Sub-Saharan Africa, which has the highest population growth rate (three per cent annually), agricultural production per capita actually fell by 15 per cent between 1965 and 1985. Nutritional levels, too, are dropping. It is estimated that 40 to 45 per cent of the women and children in the developing world are getting less than the minimum 2,000 calories per day specified by WHO. The drop in nutrition levels means that the infant mortality rate, which has been going down in most countries, may shoot up again. The social and economic structure may also be bettered. In some poor countries, the patient/doctor ratio is already 35 times higher than in Europe or North America and it is rising.

Unplanned Growth

Ironically individual families as well as governments in developing countries which have recognised the importance of planned parenthood and population control are asking for financial assistance. But the UNFPA does not have that kind of money. As against the present budget of 510 million, UNFPA feels an investment of 2 billion dollars is needed annually over the next decade, if family planning targets are to be achieved. Two billion dollars may sound like a huge amount, but it is less than the U.S. tobacco industry spends on advertising in North America alone or than the cost of a nuclear submarine. It is a mere two per cent of total global development aid. With individual assistance of just $ 10 $ to 20 a year, a woman can control her fertility and safeguard her health and that of her children. For women in poor countries who are caught in the destructive maelstrom of fate and fertility, assistance could be a lifeline.

Third-world nations will have to invest in women, for they hold the key to the future of these countries. They are crucial not only to containing population growth but also to sustaining development. There is concrete evidence of the linkages between female education, fertility and mortality, between gainful employment for women and patterns of family formation, and between women's participation and the success of population programmes and of economic development. Social and economic self-determination are a natural sequel to women's control over their fertility[1].

---

1. *The Times of India,* New Delhi, Saturday 27, 1989 P.6, Usha Rai.

82

Complex Problems That Women Face Today

Roudalph Ellison had taken up the cause of emancipation of women, perhaps he would have written 'Invisible woman' exposing the state of a woman forced to live in a society where she is marginalised to the point of invisible although many women have been able to take it to the top, several are left to swim the turbulent waters to reach the harbour; many still have to find that gleams and flickers at the other end seems ever so distant that one is always moving towards it.

The trauma faced by every woman is quite beyond a man's imagination. A woman, who has entered into the world of men, is bound to lose herself in the overwhelming crowd unless she has an iron will to keep striving and moving forward. She faces various trials and tribulations and, for her to be accepted, it is not enough if she is as good as a man, she has to be even better. The thought she is inferior is sown in her mind by society which is goaded on by the belief that women are soft and practise docile blind obedience to gratify men.

I do agree that man and woman are different from each other. They are two different beings unique in their own ways, special and important for any society to function. They serve complementary functions and it is necessary that a man recognises a woman's indispensability in a society and vice versa. We will be striking discordant notes if we feel that man can run the affairs of the world alone without the assistance of woman--that is why they are created for -- to do things together -- not to consider women as inferiors and make slaves of them.

Psychological Problems

Today's man seems to be Rousseau's acolyte, he revels in perverted pleasure. He likes to see woman suffering. He would rather be a good father than be a good husband. Therefore, the problem is basically a psychological one - one that lies deep in the minds and hearts of men. The man who tortures his wife feels quite pained if the same happens to his daughter after her marriage. That is why women's problems cannot be solved by laws alone imposed by the State. The attitude and thinking have to change. No law can possibly say that a man has to treat his wife this way or that. It is conscience that has to govern one, not law, in fact, laws have not solved women's problems in India.

Limitations of the Law

Take for instance the Sudha Goyal case in Delhi in 1983. The Sessions Judge gave death penalty to Laxman, the husband and his mother, for killing Sudha for not bringing substantial dowry. This did not have any effect at all as they were released by the High Court. But when the Supreme Court reversed the judgement sending the two behind bars, Laxman had already married a second time. Today no law has curbed dowry deaths and bride burning. Roop Kunwars and Shalinis are ever on the increase and dowry hunters have not stopped lusting for money. This being the case, the recent Act giving a right to daughters in the share of family property will neither aggravate the problem nor solve it. Aminocentesis and female foeticide may be on the increase as parents may not be willing to spend for the marriage of daughters and also gave them their share of family property. Now the law that allows a daughter an equal share in the property does not take into account the amount spent by her parents for her marriage include dowry, jewellery, etc.

Having spent huge amounts on her marriage, parents will be unwilling to give an equal share of property when there may also be sons in the family. As the girl after marriage goes and lives with her husband in his house, she enjoys a share of her husband's responsibility. Moreover, the man perhaps has married the girl for her property. This law will fail in our society. Ours is a caste ridden, fanatical and narrow-minded society, and such laws will more harm than good. Any reform has to start at the very basic level. Men's attitude has to change. More and more women have to come out of their shells and make themselves educated and financially independent. A time will come when marriage does not become a business bargain and then surely this law will prevail.

Another area, where the law has not helped women, is rape. Take the Mathura case in 1979 in which two policemen, who were convicted on charges of rape of tribal girl, were released by the Supreme Court which held that as there was no evidence that the girl resisted, she must have consented. What is even more disheartening is that even 11 years after the rape law was amended and a new offence - that of custodial rape - was included, the court reduced the sentence on two Haryana policemen, convicted of custodial rape, from ten years to five on the ground that the victim (Suman Rani) was a person of easy virtue. Even if the law has helped women in exceptional cases, the judgement came a little too late, as in the case of Maya Tyagi who could get justice only after ten years.

What about the Shah Bano case ? That courageous woman was mocked at by religious fundamentalists and the State, that should have safeguarded the rights of women, succumbed to the outcry of the community and passed the Muslim Women's Bill exonerating Muslim husbands from the responsibility of maintenance of their wives after divorce. That which is detrimental to women's interests is allowed to continue in order that the minorities - consisting of men--are not offended. Thus the law have not helped women. It is always the poor women who have to put up with such injustice and they are cheated because they are uneduated and quite unaware of the laws. Even if they are awere of them, the gruesome procedure that leads them to court and an equally gruesome are cheated because they are uneducated and quite unaware of the trial make them lose heart. Moreover, they have hardly any financial or moral support and without the women's organisations, they will hesitate even to register a case.

Women's problems in India attains its complexity because of the various degrees of degradation that we find here. The upper class woman may be said to be emancipated, for in most cases she is educated and financially independent and will not hesitate to walk down her husband if he treats her badly. Moreover, marriage for her is not a necessity. The middle class woman presents a complex dimension, because she is educated, knows laws for women, but yet is pinned down by convention. In most middle class families, it is a woman's job," he would say, and the wife would unquestioningly do it. This is perhaps because the man has raised an impregnable ego barrier and the wife has to dance to his whims and fancies. Marriage, therefore, enable a man to go on a long ego trip whereinhe can come to believe in his own assumed superiority and the woman become his hobby-horse.

Two Syndromes

The position is not any better even in families where women work, for here too there are certain conditions. She shall not be more influential than he. She shall not be more educated than he and shall not earn even a paisa more than he. This is no exaggeration but the whole truth. It is also disheartening note that in many cases women are struck by a before-marriage syndrome and an after-marriage syndrome. The former makes them speak of their own role in society and condemn male chauvinistic attitudes while the latter makes them feel that they are after all inferior, and male chauvinism assumes an added attraction as they are themselves on the verge of becoming mothers-in-law. This is pathetic.

The lower class woman on the other hand, is exploited because she is uneducated. But in most cases she does not suffer psychological trauma as the middle class woman, for the latter is educated and is aware of her deprivation while the former is not. Also the lower class woman is very much influenced by third-rate films which glorify in depicting women as inferiors and waiting to be trod on by men. Cinema, being their chief entertainment, should instruct at least to some extent, which it does not. Conversely, it works to encourage religious dogmatism and maudlin sentimentality.

Man or woman, one is basically a human being and this should be the substratum for the ever-growing tree of humanity in which case it is bound to give the best fruits. Today a woman is just allowed to remain, so that she performs her duties as wife, mother and so on. She has been made a 'goddess' or a 'devil'. She is the personification of love and compassion, greed and evil, she is creator and destroyer, she is 'Shakti', she is 'Kali', she is anything but a human being. Also a woman wants to marry because of compulsion. An unmarried woman is looked down upon by society. She is told all the time: "You have got to marry some day and bear children." This advice is given by no less than her mother and the yolk of blind obedience is handed on to the next generation. Why should anybody think that a woman wants to marry, that she has to marry ? Why should we think that she has to have children and participate only in the process of procreation ?

Just because the woman is at home it does not mean that she eats and sleeps and does nothing. Both man and woman have to realise that marriage means 'commitment' and it calls for efforts from both of them to keep the marriage going. If either of them feels disinclined to get entangled in this life-long commitment, it is better to stay single rather than applying for divorce later on flimsy ground which often wreck the life of their children, if they have any. A balance of attitude is what one should try to achieve, an equilibrium, the absence of which is causing havoc in the western society. Without sacrifices or compromises, there cannot be a happy married life; but it is unfair to expect woman to make these all the time.

The issue has attained its complexity due to various categories of women that we have. At one level, we have women facing ill-treatment and injustice craving to find dawn of justice and independence. At another we have those, having achieved independence, becoming the target of growing market strategies and Western customs and practices. Sandwiched in between, there are women dynamic and successful, who are very much aware of their rights and privileges, but even as they are on their way to achieving equilibrium, they find themselves, rather unconsciously, pinned down by traditional beliefs and convention. At this critical juncture education seems to be the password.

Educating the economically backward women will make them send their daughters to school which, in turn, will help women coming from the lower strata to join the mainstream. Valuebased education might also solve the problems of dowry deaths and bride-burning. Going into its psychology one would come to understand that mothers-in-law torture their daughters-in-law only because of their sense of insecurity and deprivation. In such cases education will make these women think rationally and see things in the right perspective. Though no society can be without dissenting opinions, an educated society will at least treat tolerance as its sterling virtue.

The key to such a society lies in our hands. Both sexes could realise that each is indispensable to the other. Extreme chauvinistic attitudes will not help anybody. What if women started thinking "The whole of humanity rests on our hands.

We create and if we choose not to, we can obliterate the whole of human race". FCPs, you think ? It may sound absurd but in the absence of a humanitarian approach, the rise of this brave new world cannot be totally ruled out.

83

Tribal Woman's Power

The struggle for the land rights of the Ho tribal women of Singhbhum in Bihar has yet to be resolved. What started as a letter of petition sent to the Supreme Court in 1982 by Madhu Kishwar, editor of Manushi a journal about women and their problems in society - still awaits a final hearing in the courts. The letter was admitted a writ petition on August 20, 1982; by justice P.N. Bhagwati, as public interest litigation. A formal writ petition was latter filed by Maki Bui; a tribal woman; her daughter Sonamuni; and Madhu Kishwar. The writ petition challenges the validity of the customary law prevalent amongst Hos, which, by restricting land inheritance rights to, 'male heirs in the male line', flouts the constitutional prohibition of discrimination on grounds of sex alone.

The petition points out that Ho women do most of the agricultural work including sowing, weeding, reaping, threshing and marketing of grain besides work like gathering and marketing of forest produce to supplement the family income. The village economy revolves around women's labour. Men do a few tasks like ploughing which are traditionally taboo for women. As men frequently migrate to urban areas, it is women who hold together the family and the tribal way of life. Yet, women are not allowed to inherit or own land in their own name. Only sons have the right to inherit the right to cultivate and live off her father's land. This is known as a usufructory right. But she loses even this limited right as soon as she marriage. As a wife she does not acquire any independent right to her husband's land. This lack of control over the land keeps women vulnerable and insecure, despite their crucial contribution to the family economy. Since the land belongs to the husband, he has the upper hand and may throw the wife out at any time.

A woman who is thrown out by her husband is at the mercy of her brothers who may or may not allow her to return to the parental home. she no longer has any rights over the parental land. An unmarried woman who is rape or seduced by a non-tribal also loses her usufructory right to the parental land. As a widow, a Ho woman has a usufructory right over her husband's land. She can cultivate it during her lifetime, but cannot sell or mortgage it. But as the petition emphasises, this right exists in theory rather than in practice. In practice, only when a widow has sons, espacially adult sons, is she able to safeguard her right to cultivate the land. This is because the sons, who are the real heirs, can defend their rights more easily than the widow alone. A widow who has no sons can rarely retain her hold over the land. Her husband's male agnates usually succeed in pressuring her through threats of violence, into giving up the land to them and migrating from the village or remarrying.

Purpose Behind Murder of Women

The petition also points out that 'there are several cases of murder of single women, unmarried or widowed, by their own relatives. The petitioners purpose for killing women is that they are witches. The petitioners, however, say that the real reason appears to be to eliminate women so that their limited rights over the land can be taken away.'

In a study published in the Economic and Political Weekly in the issues of January 17, 24 and 31, 1987 - 'Toiling without Rights : Women of Singhbhum', based on an intensive survey of villages in Singhbhum, Madhu Kishwar elaborate on the link between witch-killing and land hunger:

"Violence against women often takes the form of witch-killings. No systematic study has been made of this phenomenon. Most commentators attribute it to superstitious ignorance. However, it is important to remember that it is usually against women that so-called superstitiousness erupts. My study suggests that often the real motivation for witch-killing is the desire to eliminate the women and take away her land. I came across several such cases in Chaibasa court.'

Another significant phenomenon which the study links to the discriminatory land inheritance law is the large proportion of single women among the Hos : 'According to the 1972 census, approximately 11 percent of all Ho women 45 years of age and above had never married. A similar figure has been reported ever since the census operations in India began. This is an incredibly high percentage for any community in India.' (The all-India figure for all communities is less than one per cent).

The Study suggests that one reason for this phenomenon could be the fact that as unmarried daughters women have atleast a right on their own behalf to cultivate their natal family's land throughout their lifetime, whereas as wives they have no independent right over the husband's land and also lose the limited right on the father's land. Therefore more women prefer to stay unmarried and set up house separately with their parents after their brothers marry and separate from the parental family. However, brothers often try to pressurise sisters to marry so that they do not have to give them a portion of the land to cultivate.

The petition asked for he following reliefs :

1. Declaration of the alleged customary law disinheriting Ho tribal women is unconstitutional and therefore null and void;

2. Mandatory order to the state of Bihar to reformulate land records showing Ho tribal women as equal sharers in land;

3. Mandatory order to the state of Bihar to provide free legal aid to tribal women;

4. Interim order restraining Maki Bui's husband's male agnates from interfering with her usufructory right over her husband's land.

Although the petition is based on the Ho Women's situation which has certain distinct features, it has implications for other tribal women too (tribals constitute seven per cent of India's population and also for peasant women generally).

The study goes on to say that although Hindu women under the Hindu Succession Act of 1956 have the right to equal inheritance on their father's self-acquired property, in practice, property is almost always willed or given away to sons alone, and daughters are ipressurised into surrendering their rights. The study concludes that this vulnerability is in fact greater for women of non-tribal peasant groups in North India, for example, peasant women, unlike tribal women, are not allowed to openly undertake productive work in the fields and markets. Though they may work at household duties they are viewed as unproductive, their only utility being as bearers of sons. Having no control over land and related assets, they have almost no say in decisions regarding their own lives such as education, employment and marriage.

Such practices as strict seclusion of women, rigid controls over their mobility, early marriage, heavy dowry payments, denial of education, strong son preference, testify to the low status of these women. The low sex relation (low proporation of women to men in the population) in these peasant communities is another indicator of the devaluation of women, because of their visibly more productive role in the economy, have relatively greater bargaining power in their society. They are not viewed as expendable nor are daughters unwanted the way they often are in Hindu peasant communities. This is reflected in the fact that the sex ratio in the Ho tribe is in favour of women (1041 women per 1000 men), whereas the all-India figure is 935 women per 1000 men, India being one of the very countries in the world with a sex ratio biased against women.

Tribal Women relatively

The tribal women's relatively better position is reflected, not just in the sex ratio but in their greater mobility, relatively greater freedom to decide whether to marry and whom to marry, whether to take employment and where, and a greater access to divorce and to remarriage as widows and divorcees. These women are much more assertive and able to make the best of options available to them than are most non-tribal women - rural or even urban.

This strength typified in Maki Bui, the old tribal woman of Konjo village in Singhbhum, who is one of the petitioners in the and Geeta Luthra who are handing the case, filed a petition on behalf of Maki Bui, accusing the respondents of committing contempt of court and requesting that the matter be heard expeditiously, since she was living in fear for her life. The Supreme Court once again directed the state government to ensure Maki Bui's personal safety, but this order continues to be flouted.

The state government seems to have adopted a policy of dragging its feet in the case. Although repeatedly pulled up by the court for this attitude, it has repeatedly sought adjournments. The court has again and again asked the state governement to say whether it is willing to amend the law so as to give inheritance rights to tribal women but the state government's has, on one pretext or another, evaded giving an answer, so a resolution seems nowhere in sight.

The case has dragged on for over five years owing to the state governments tardiness and also due to the backlog of cases pending in the Supreme Court. Maki Bui has no way of knowing when the case will finally be decided. although she continues to hope against hope that she will live to see the day. She is anxious to come to Delhi for the final hearing and on one occasion actually managed to make the trip - when the case was not even heard even though it was listed for the final hearing. Ever since, Maki Bui has continued to write and enquire after the progress of the case. Those who have intervened on her behalf are unable to give her any satisfactory reply. They also wonder whether even if a favourable judgement is delivered, it will be implemented - given the Bihar government's general indifference to the plight of tribal women.

One positive outcome of the case has been the generation of a debate on the question of land rights for women. Other women have been inspired to take up the demand in different ways. For instance case. She a widow with only one child, a daughter named Sonamuni (also a petitioner) who is married lives in Uliguttu village. Maki Bui's husband was employed as a police constable and she accompanied him to postings to places as distant as Madras. After her husband died, his male relatives, of whom the most powerful is the village headman, began to harass her. Since she had no son. they wanted her to hand over the land to them and depend on them for food. When she refused, they began to forcibly cultivate her land. Since Lonjo is her husband's village, his blood relatives live there, not Maki Bui's No village would like to oppose the powerful and influential headman who has connections with the local government administration and police. Therefore, no one came to Maki Bui's rescue when she was threatened with violence by the headman and his broke sons. On one occasion they down her door in attempt to murder her.

She even heard that they were planning to get her killed as a witch. On several occasions she had to take refuge in her daughter's house. But when she heard that it was possible not only to assert her legal right to use the land but also to demand a further right to give the land to her daughter, she was eager to go ahead and file the case for a change in the law, despite the risks involve. Ever since the position was admitted in the Supreme Court and notice issued to the respondents (the state of Bihar and Maki's husband's male agnates), the threats and hostility to her in the village naturally escalated. she, her daughter, son-in-law and two grand children were forced to live in mortal fear.

Delayed Justice

In 1982, the Supreme Court, while admitting the petition, passed interim order directing the state government to ensure the safety of life and property of the petitioners and non-interference with Maki's usufructory right in the land. But this order was openly violated by the village headman, with the collusion of the local administration and police. Three years after the petition was filed, lawyers Pinky Anand Mary Roy of Kerala challenged the Travancore Christian Succession Anand, under which Christian women in some parts of Kerala were denied inheritance rights. Her petition to the Supreme Court was successful - the act was overruled and Christian women in Kerala now have equal inheritance rights in parental property.[1]

---

1. The Illustrated Weekly of India, August 7, 1988, p. 40-41, C.P. Rajasthan.

Index

A Better Deal for Rural Women, 658
Abortion—Index of Immorality, 84
About Marriage System Comments, 294
Academic Interest, 112
A Cry in the Wildness, 30
Active Law Enforcement, 491, 536
Active Vigilance, 490, 535
Additional Rape Trauma—Symptoms, 187
Adhoc Approach, 675
Adiseshiah, S., 662
Administrative Duties, 563, 629
Adultery, 248, 491, 509
Advertisements of Rooms, 80
Afshar, Haleh, 44
Against Guideline, 276
Age of Consent, 92, 139, 381
Old Practice, 418
Agnipurana, 1
Agra, 196, 199, 234
Aggrawal, R.N., 446, 455
Aggrawal, S.M., 446, 455, 456
A Great Forward, 704
Ahmad, Dr. C.N., 6
Ahmedabad, 15
AIDS, 346
Air Force Act 1950, 605
Aiyat, 54
Ajanta, 3
Alarming rise in rape cases, 167
A Less Stressful, Less Costly alternative, 356, 406
Ali, Syed Amir, 26
Allahabad, 50, 196, 199
Allah, 5
All are Combatants, 611
Allauddin, K., 661
All Conflicts can be Solved, 485
All India Institute of Medical Science, 286
All India Muslim Personal Law Board, 56
All India Women's Conference, 12, 637
Alva, Margaret, 296, 692
Ambedkar, Baba Saheb, 10, 402
Amendment in C.P.C., 422
Amendment in Cr. P.C., 432
Amendment in Indian Evidence Act, 422, 432
Amendment in I.P.C., 421, 432
Andhra Pradesh, Agricultural, University, 733
Anti-Vice Squad, 136
A Police Woman in a man's World, 599
Apollo Hospitals, Madras, 82
Apple of Discord, 367
A Private Grief-Suharabi's Tale of Woe, 38
Arabi Kalyanam, 33
Aray, J.P., 443
Army Act, 1950, 604
Arora, Dr. Shakuntala, 468
Arthasastra, 556
Arul, F.V., 571
Arunachalam, Jaya, 639
Arunachal Pradesh, 326, 353
Arya Marriage Varidity Act, 1937, 14

Arya Samaj, 15
Arhoka, 556
Assam, 57
Attack Engineered, 588
Attraction to Women, 717
Attray, J.P., 453
Awaking amongest women, 15
Awareness of Rights, 239
Ayodhya, 196, 199

Babior, Sharmon, 360
Bajaj, Rupa Deal, 108
Banatwala, G.M., 55
Banning the Bra-case Histories, 125
Bano, Shah, 5, 27, 35, 54, 60, 438, 471, 476, 553, 817
Bano, Shakila, 372
Bansbara, 8
Batliwala, 704, 705
Batta, Mayadevi, 572
Battered, 361
Bedi, Kiran, 576, 588
Beevi Avva Ummal Pathumma, 29
Begum, Safdari, 48
Behavioural Pattern of Women Prisoners Released on Bail, 517
Being the Bread Winners of the Family does not Protect Women against Marital violence, 463
Belgium, 78
Besant, Annie, 95
Be Willing to Fargive, 482
Bhagwati, P.N., 821
Bhutto, Benazir, 243
Bias against Girls, 770
Bibi, Chand, 26
Bible and Women, 66
Bihar, 168, 326, 327, 733
Birla, K.K., 646
Bloch, Dr. Iwan, 83
Blue Films, 136
Bombay, 15, 122, 285, 438
Bombay Municipal Corporation, 783
Borak, Dr. D.L., 494
British Government, 81
British Raj, 255
British Standard for Censorship in India, 81
Buddhism, 19

Calcutta High Court, 63, 589
Calcutta, 9, 119, 122, 248, 261
Calicut, 35
California, 388
Call to help women's Self-employment, 656
Canada, 388, 560
Can Amendment to Act Education Dowry 2, 449, 459
Cars, 425
Case Law, 129, 172
Cases of Death, 350
Cases of Divorce, 438, 475
Causes of Dowry, 418
Census Data, 763
Central Board Film Certificate, 276
Centre's decision, 778
Chaddha, Kumkum, 640
Chandigarh, 326
Chandrachud, Y.V., 52, 165, 378
Changing Goals of a Women's Group, 755
Changing Life Styles, 259
Changing Moral Line the Society, 381
Changing Pattern of Women in India Society, 7
Changing set Values and Moral Turpitude in the West, 139
Chatterji, Soma, A., 322
Chattopadhyay, Kamla Devi, 15
Chaturvedi, Sunita, 769
Chawla, Damyanti, 644
Chawla, Dr. H.M., 286
Chet Ram, 472
Chicago Police Department, 156
Chief Judicial Magistrate, 29
Chief Justice, 160, 318
Child Abuse, 509
Child Labour Act. 1986, 775
Child Marriage Restraint Act, 773
China Shop, 10
Choose your Child—a Criminal Campaign, 767
Choudhury, D.N., 682
Choudhury, Sushma, 113
Choudhury, Kanchan, 599
Christianity and Women, 6
Christian Women, 67
CID, 283, 284, 443, 559, 624

— role of, 543
Cinema, 364
Civil Code, 9
Clergy's Role, 44
Clientele, 199
Close look, 794
Clutches of *Sati*, 3
Code of Criminal Procedure Sec. 174-sub-section (3):, 27, 426, 437
COFE POSA, 122
Columbia, 388
Come out Fighting, 583
Common Civil Code, 5
Common Criminal Code, 27
Common Lot, 672
Common Wealth Confronts Violence against Women, 390
Conclusion, 192
Condition of Muslim Women in India, 5, 27, 553
Condition of Women after Independance, 9
Connivance, 588
Constant threat, 533
Contemporary Scene, 486
Correctional Service Canada, 408
Corrupt System, 528
Court Vs Censors, 275
Craft on Show, 645
Credibility Gap, 673
Crime and Punishment, 530
Crime and Punishment of Women Criminals, 513
Criminal Laws, 426, 436
Criminality amongest Criminal Tribes Women, 497
Criticism, 59
Cúltural Climate, 166

Dadra & Nagar Haveli, 326
Daman & Diu, 326
Das, C.R., 86
Das, Jatin, 299
Defective Law—Infective Law Enforcement agency and Opening of Law Dispensing Agency, 137
Dehradun, 196, 199
Delayed, Justice, 827
Delhi, 50, 168, 169, 261, 326, 353, 438
Delhi High Court, 10, 117, 402, 635
Delicate of Mediation, 354, 404
Devi Lal, 160
Democratic Party of Afghanistan, 42
Demographic Trends in Third World, 811
Deorala in Rajasthan, 20
Deputy Chairman of Rajya Sabha, 56
Desai, D.A., 52
Determined recruits, 619
Dev Raj Radhakant, 8
Dharma Shastras, 9
Dhansa, 370
Different Meanings, 240
Different Training, 580
Difficult task, 574
D.I.G., 443
Dirty picture, 123
Discuss It Now, 482
District Magistrate, 456
Divorce, 437
Does Research on Men Apply to Women?, 346
Do India Women face Extinction?, 769
Domestic Discord and consequent Work Inefficiency, 595
Dowry, 419
— cruelty against women, 422, 432
— consultation committee, 450, 459
— deaths, 442, 452
— prestige & prejudice, 419, 429
— prohibition, 420
— act 1961, 420, 456
— act 1968, 425, 436
— act 1984, 638
DTC, 142, 143, 146, 147
Dubious Distinction, 776
Durgapur, 619
Duties of a Wife, 25
Duties of Women Police, 548

Early Beginnings, 556, 623
Early to Marry and Early to Die, 307
Economic Disparity, 418

Economic of Tabacco, 709
Economist, 7
Education and Earning Capacity does not Save a Women from Humiliation an Cruelty, 464
Education Inequality, 418
Education of Women in Agricultural Field, 732
Effective Policing by Women for Women, 597
Effects towards Reformation, 247
'Ek Chadar Maili Si', 291
Eleborated Training, 574
Elizabeth, 413
Ellora, 3
Elusive Laws and Protracted Legal Proceedings, 478
Emerging from Purdah to fight the Veil, 42
Equal Remuneration Act, (ERA), 1976, 638
European, 86
Eve-teasing, 142, 488
Evidence Destroyes, 240
Excessive Sex Indulgence in West, 82
Exemplifying Virues, 277
Exhibitionism, 134
Expensive Law, 32
Expension of Judicial System, 36

Factors Leading to Prostitution, 203
Factors of Sexual Offences, 99
Fallacy, 216
Family Courts Act. 1984, 553
Family File, 607
Farm Women and the ICAR, 737
Farm Women: Who Determines the Nuds?, 740
Farooqui, Vimla, 306
Father-a sanction Ligitimely, 323
Favourite Victim of Homefires, 446
Fearless, 590
Female Criminality, 497
Female Foeticide—Gujarat, 775
Female Infanticide Outlawed, 313
Feminism Sans Fire and Brimstone, 339
Few facilities, 360
Fight for Women's Right, 710
Finding of Study, 719
First Class Judicial Magistrate, 6, 28, 34, 37
First Indian Police Station Staffed by Women, 569
First Women Police, 568
Flesh Trade: Report and Recommendations, 190
Focus is on Women Artists, 643
Formicatory Dolls, 79
Forum against Rape, 178
Functionaries of the Trade, 194
Fundamentalism has not Stopped Pakistan Women, 241
"Fundamentalism", 19
Fundamentalists Spouses Storigent Step, 19
Future Perspectives of Crime and Women, 510

Gandhiji, 344, 346
Gandhi, Dr. Mahesh, 248
Gandhi, Indira, 161, 550, 569, 597
Gandhi Mahatma, 86, 745
Gandhi Rajiv, 58, 59, 588, 676, 698
Ganga Ram Hospital, 217
Gang Rape, 154
Garibi Hatao, 524
Geeta, 395
Geoff, Dr. Sanders, 336
George, K.N., 579
George Nagent, 227
Germany, 78
Ghos S.K., 596
Gill, K.P.S., 108
Girdle and Bra, 125
Girl-runners of Basal, 231
Glenn, Dr. Wilson, 332
Glittering Light and Show Business, 134
Global Rise in Crime against Women, 170
Goa, 168, 326
Godse, M.G., 284
Godse, Nathuram, 124
God, 37
Goel Kanwalzit, 448, 458
Goel, Sudha, 457
Gokhale, Namita, 299
Good Mediation is often Invisible, 357

Good Prospects, 621
Good via Media, 608
Gopalan Dr. C., 280
Gopi, 636
Goswami, N.N., 587
Government Determined, 777
Government of Andhra Pradesh, 206
Government of Maharashtra, 716
Granfeldt, Hele, 658
"Gree Form Scheme", 383, 384
Green Land, 409
Growing Need for Women Police, 538
Guidelines, 552
Gujaral, Satish, 295
Gujarat, 20, 51, 57
Gujarat High Court, 711
Gulf War, 22, 23
Gully, Radha, 232
Gupta, Neena, 322
Gupta, S.C., 214

Handling of Women Criminals, 521
Haq, Gen. Zia-ul, 20
Harijan, 542
Harmful Effects, 807
Haryana Chief Minister, 160
Haryana, 168, 370, 377
Hassan, Dr. Zoya, 62
Heart Searching, 756
Heavy Odds, 117
Hecker, 91
Heptullah, Dr. Najama, 56, 295
Hetero-Sexuality, 134
High Court, 29, 453
High-profile Meet, 278
"High-tech", 22
Hindu Code Bill, 10, 402
Hinduism, 19
Hind Marriage Act. 1955— 240, 315, 424, 435, 633
Hindu Minority and Guardianship Act. 1956, 315
Hindu succession Act. 1956— 436, 824
Hindustan Times, 119
Hindu Widow, 16, 316
Historical Case, 108
Holi, 143, 144
Holy Bible Lays down, 66
Home Rule, 11
How fair is the Law to the Fair Sex, 552
How the other Half Lives, 646
Hussain Shahnaz, 299
Hussain, Shamim Bano, 239

Iddat, 52, 53, 59
Identity Crisis, 217
Illegal Custody Extension, 529
"I' MA comeback Girl", Kiran Bedi, 586
Immoral Traffic Act. 1956, 549
Impact of New Technologies Specific Occupations, 729
Important of Dowry, 417
Importance of Dowry, 429
Important Time and Place, 482
In a Violent Environment even a Violent Husband is Protection, 469
Inderjit, 297
Indian Constitution, 8
Indian National Congress, 12
Indian Penal Code, 351, 378, 768
Indian Scene, 85
Indian Union Muslim League, (IUML), 35
India Today, 61, 119, 120, 349
Indira, M.K., 692
In Havelock Ellis' book we read:, 83
Inheritance Rights, 682
Injunction, 126
In Search of a Saviour and Salvation, 709
Institution of Hindu Marriage: A Legal History, 311
International Criminal Police Organisation Interpol and Women Police, 628
Introduction of Jury System, 138, 381
Introduction Personal Security System, 380
Institution of Marriage, 3, 17
Investigational Work, 548
Investigation of Rape Cases, 156
Iraq, 23
Ireland, 492
Islamic Introduction in India, 26
Iyer, Krishna, 422, 433, 524

Jabwala, Renana, 711

Jackson, V., 91
Jagdish, 370
Jain, Ashok Kumar, 236
Jain, J.P., 3, 64
Jain, P.K., 584
Jain, S.C., 449
Jammat-e-islam, 36
Jammu & Kashmir, 168, 619
Janak Puri, 148
Japan, 122, 359, 492, 561, 627
Jauhar, 400
Jawaher Lal Nehru University, 62, 169, 284
Jehan, Noor, 26
Jharoda Kalan, 619
Joshi, Sharad, 756
Judicial Magistrate, 6
Judicial View, 443, 453
—Legislation on Bride Burning at the Cross Roads, 448, 458
Juicy Story, 542
Junejo, Mohammad Khan, 243
Justice Delayad is Justice denied, 288
Justice Pratap, S.C., 277
Juvenile Delinquents-self Multilation in Adolescent Female Offenders, 518

Kabul, 42
Kabul University, 41
Kahaniyan, Manohar, 212
Kakkar, Dr. Sudhir, 291, 292
Kama Sutra, 255, 636
Kamlesh, 231, 232, 233
Kanpur, 519
Kapoor, H.L., 584
Karajia, R.K., 125
Karan, Vijay, 148
Karnataka, 326, 327, 353
Karnataka Mahila Samakhya, 700
Karodhar, 131
Karunakaran, K., 570
Karunanidhi, M. 654
Karve, Maharishi, 16
Kashmiri Bazar, 234, 235, 236
Kasturba, 346
Kaur, Arveen, 460
Kaur, Raj Kumari, Amrit, 9, 10, 635
Kaur, Shanni, 443, 453, 472
Kautilya, 556
KAVAL, 192
Kerala, 14, 326, 327, 353
Kerala, Agricultural University, 733
Kerala High Court, 28
Khadi, 709
Khajuraho, 113
Khan, Amjad Ali, 296
Khan, Arif Mohammed, 56
Khanna, Vinod, 114
Khan, Sir Sayed, 26
Khan Sultan, A., 620
Khomeini, 43, 44
Khomeinini's Decrel, 45
Kick in back at eve-teasers, 146
Kishwar, Madhu, 395, 397, 750, 757, 821, 823
Konark, 636
Koop, Dr. C. Everett, 388
Koran, 43, 64
Kothari, D.S., 745
Krishi Vigyan Kendras, 736
Krishna, 10, 636
Krishna, V.R., 224
Kuchh to Kiya hoga, 367
Kulkarni, Dr. Sanjeev, 781
Kumari Pratibha, 579
Kumari Ranjana, 772
Kumari Sambhog, 113
Kumar, Suresh, 130
Kumata, 2
Kunju, Gafoor, 28, 29
Kuputra, 2
Kurta-Pyjama, 217
Kuwait, 465

Lack of Hygiene, 805
Lack of Information, 23
Lack of Systematic Work, 271
Lal Vikram, 647
Law, 171
—logic, 52
—obscure defination, 127
Learning from the Queen, 484
Legal Aid Act. 1974, 383
—inforcement, 380
—lacunal, 227
Leitner, Dr. G.W., 319
Liberal thinking, 605
Licensed prostitution, 271

Limitations of the Law, 815
Liquor poverty, 386
Listen to your Mate, 483
Living with out Violence, 413
Lock-ups Worst Equipped, 528
Lok Sabha, 397, 442
Loopholes abound in Rape Laws, 158

Mahabharata, 2
Mahanirvana Tantra, 3
Madhya Pradesh, 169, 168, 219, 326, 327, 353
Madoka, Yoriko, 361
Madras, 122, 207
Mahabharat, 556
Maharaja, 112
Maharashtra, 131, 752
Maharashtra Experience, 782
Mahila Dakshata Samiti, 240, 284
Mahila Kosh, 665, 670
Mahila Samakhya, 706
Main Demand, 273
Maintenance Act. 1956, 315
Malai Yowani, 113
Malayalam, 36, 113
Male Chauvinism, 164
Malhotra, Jagdish Lal, 449
Malhotra, Kanchal, 645
Malik, Suman, 461
Malka Bazar, 234
Mamta, 113
Mance of Eve-teasing, 132
Mandsaur, 219
Manipur, 326, 353
Manju, 232, 395
Mantagu, E.S., 11
Manu, 7, 419
Manushi, 365, 750, 757
Manusmriti, 1
Marital Crimes, 500
Marriage Laws Amended Bill, 1978, 638
Marriage, 3, 4
Married Women's Property Act of 1982, 419, 632
Martist Ideology, 189
Mass Media and Farm Women, 738
Mass Rapes-a-Manifestation of Caste, 288
Mathura, 196, 199
Mayo, 78, 82, 86, 87, 88, 89, 93, 180, 207, 208, 308, 309, 317, 321
Mazumdar, Veena, 693
Max well House New York, 510
M. Bureau, 77, 84, 85
Measures, 537
Measures to Prevent Crime Against Women, 177
Media and Women, 10, 28, 7, 636
Mediation and Family Violence, 408
Media Strategy, 739
Medical Evidence, 764
Medical Proven, 799
Medical Termination of Pregnancy Act, 1971, 768, 769
Meghalaya 326, 353
Mehmood, Tahir, 58
Mehra, Vimla, 239, 283
Mehr, 52, 54
Mehta Hans, 10, 402, 635
Mehta, Vinod, 117
Memories of a Marriage Marred Man, 292
Menon, Achyuta, C., 570
Menon, N.R. Madhava, 225
Marchant, Dr. Meenaxi, 769
Method, 192
Mishra, Rangnath, 52
Mithlesh, 232
Mitra Manusi, 639
Mode of sustenance, 664
Madi, C.K., 656
Modi, Yogender Kumar, 648
Mohammad, 24
Mohamedan, 87, 112
Moihuddin, 32
More Varied Duties for Police Women in Bombay, 568
Moulvi, Dr. C.N. Ahmed, 28, 36
Movement Against Rape, 155
Move with Men-folks, 685
M. Paul Bureau, 74

Nagaland, 168, 326
Nagpur, 125
Naidu, Sarojini, 11, 12, 95
Naik Girls Protection Act, 1929, 267
Nair girls, 14

Namaz, 55
Namboodari Brahman, 14
Nariman, F.S., 590
Nari Niketans, 508, 541
Nasik, 755
National Cadets Corps, 618
National Cancer Institute, 347
National Institute of Public Co-operation Child Development, 280, 693
National Rural Police, 562, 627
Native Perspective, 411
Nautch Girls' Fantasy, 227
Navy Act, 1957, 605
Nayak, 113
Nayar, Kavit, 645
Nechi Training Centre in Alberta, 411
Need for special fund, 666
Nepal, 122
Netherland, 7
New Delhi, 114
New India, 9
New Jersey, 388
New thinking, 36
New Trends in Criminality, 504
New Wave, 256
New York, 84, 94, 410, 559, 625
Nishter, Jamil, 49
Nitish, 212
Not Corrupt, 597
Not mere Evil, 796
No more a man's world, 640
No-Government organisations, 389
Not with a Criminal History, 534
Nude therapy, 124
Nudity, 128

Obscare, Laws, 116, 135
—legar reforms, 378
Obscenity Laws, 378
Offences Against Women, 163
Offence Relating to Moral Turpitude, 97
Oneness of Proof, 381
Onus of Proof, 139
Orissa, 57, 207, 326, 327, 386, 596, 733
Other Cases of Harassment, 351
Ottawa, 408
Our first "conflict", 480
Our Successful out come, 481
Out dated Adultery Laws, 249
Outrageous Pornography, 80

Painful Awakening, 593
Paisa Nahin Hai, 688
Pakistan Women Gain Confidence, 48
Pandits of Nadia, 8
Panwar, Sury, 645
Parajape, K.G. ex-chief Secretary Maharashtra, 696
Patel, Vallabhbhai, 777
Pathak, R.S., 160
Pawar, Sharad, 682
Perceptive, 645
Purpose behind Murder of, Women, 822
Petition asked for he following reliefs, 824
Phaniyamna, 692
Phatnani, Dr. Pritam, 784
Plight of Muslim Women, 440, 477
Place of Women in the Indian Constitution, 1947, 13
Police and Women, 550
—norms conduct, 54
Police by Women Police in Foreign Countries, 556
Police Women are as Good as Men, 592
Police Women of Delhi: Less brown, Equal Skill, Morce grace, 571
Police Women Sore at Promotion policy, 579
Police Rule and Performance in Dowry Death Cases, 447, 456
Police Role in Dowry Burning Cases, 447
Policing by Women, 550
Policy and legislative Approaches, 744
Police and Pornography, 118
Political Patrons, 225
Political Rapes, 154
Political will Must to Women's Studies, 342
Pollution Exclusive to Women, 806
Pondicherry, 326, 327

Poonal, Roshini, 143
Poor-civic Anenities, 530
Porn Power, 113
Portrait of a Women Offender, 498
Position of Indian Women, 88
Position of Women in Europe, 89
Position of Women in Hindu Society, 94
Post-Traumatic Stress Disorder, 182
Poverty Drives Tribe and Nepali Girls to Prostitution, 219
Power and Control, 409
Pregnancy Tests, 612
Pre-marital and Extra-marital sex, 70
Pre-Natal Diagostic Techniques Act. 1988, 777, 782
Prepared for Women Hood, 772
Preventing Pros-titution, 380
Prevention and Control of Trade, 204
Preventive Duties, 563, 629
Preventive Measures, 489
—Against Sexual Crimes, 137
Preventive Measures Against Sexual Crimes, 380
Principles of Mohammedan Law, 54
Privacy and Security, 607
Private Enquiries, 80
Problems of Keeping Women in Jail, 514
Procedure, 541
Professor, Gray, Jeffery, 331, 336
Prof. Max Muller, 17
Progressive Legislative of the Protection of the rights of Women, 8
Prohibition of Dowry Act. 420
Prolif-erating Rape Cases, 289
Prompt Registration, 490, 536
Property and Inheritance, 14
Prostitution, 487
Prostitution as Profession, 508
Protective Homes, 237
Protest Against Shariat Laws, 34
Psychological Reaction, 156
—problems, 815
Punishment of Women Criminals, 514
Punjab, 733

Quran, 28, 477

Radha, 467, 468
Radio, 364
Rafimarg, 143
Rajasthan, 168, 326, 327, 733
Rajkot, 15
Raj Kumar, 116
Ramamoorthy, K., 776
Ramaswamy, Cho, 124
Ramayan, 556, 676
Ram Janmabhumi Temple Babri Masjid, 57
Ranpur, 619
Rao Betty, 466
Rao Nagmani, 639
Rape and Need for Women Police Officers, 546
Rape as Weapon of War, 154
Rape of Minors, 286
Rape Victims—Reasons, Responses and Reforms, 105, 165
Rasna, 113
Ravana, 164
Ray, Sayajit, 323
Ray, Sukumar, 323
Reaction of a Women Police, 540
Real Answer, 676
Recommendations of the Bureau of Police Research and Development, 177
Reddi Dr. Muthulakhami, 95
Reddy , O, Chinnappa, 52
Refrigerators, 425
Relevance Off Arm Technology to Rural Women, 741
Reluctance to the Victims to Report Cases and Police Apathy, 136
Remarriage Act of 1856, 16
Repression of Women, 300
Research Centre for Women's Studies, 637
Resource Hand-book, 412
Restriction of the Freedom of Women, 4, 17, 36
Review Scheme for Women, 720
Rights of Muslim Women, 5, 27
Right of Property, 91
Rise of Women Police and International Criminal Police

Organisation Interpol, 562
Rising Climes Against Women, 392
Rising Fundamentalism, 751
R.K. Puram, 148
Robrigues, S.F., 602, 604
Role of Brahma Samaj, 15
Role of Judiciary, 236, 381
Role of Procurers Brothel-Keepers Pimps and Touts, 200
Role of the Press, 380
Role of Women in Future Agriculture, 731
Role of Women Organisations, 381
—Policing, 628
—Freedom struggle, 15
Role of women in Terrorism, 494
Raman Law, 4
Roy, Kamal, 118
Roy, Raja Ram Mohan, 8, 15, 313, 400, 633
Roy Somnath, 218
Rule of Women in Policing, 562

SAARC, 772
Sadhana, 233
Sadik, Dr. Nafisa, 812
'Saheli', 455
Sait, Aziz, 58
Seksena, N.S., 519, 550
Sally Ranne, 346
Salunkhe, Dr. S.R., 784
Sandhu, Harbhajan, 645
Santosh, 370, 371
Saraf, Prabhat Kumar, 123
Saraswati Ramadevi, (1958-1922), 8
Saraswati, Swami Dayanand, 15
Sarda's Rai Sahib Harbilas, 14
Sarkar, S.K., 49
Sastri, Peri, 608
Sati, 20, 400, 678, 794
Satyam Shivam Sundaram, 130
Saudi Arabia, 23
Saena, Sunil, 576
Scientific Role of Farm Women, 733
Sculpture of *Khjuraho,* 3
—Konark, 3
—Rajasthan, 3
—and South Indian Temples, 3
Second World War, 22
Security of State, 11
—India, 11
—Madras, 11
Sec. 294 IPC, 490, 536
—354
Sec. 497 IPC, 536
Sec. 509 IPC, 409, 536
See your Part in the Problem, 483
Seminar of Calcutta, 12
Sentence of Guilt, 126
Sesant, Annie, 12
Session Judge, 29. 438
Sethi, Rajeev, 298
Sex Determination or Extermination, 780
Sex, 3, 124, 217
Sex Roles and Criminality, 496
Sexual Offences-categories, 101
—Classification, 98
Sexual Revolution, 255, 263
"Sexy", 113, 135
Shahabuddin, 57, 58
Shah, Dr. Lata, 777
Shah, R.L., 144
Shah, Zahir, 41, 42
Shame and Torture, 170
"*Shantia* Kand", 519, 551
Shanti, 233
'*Shariat bachao'*, 55
Shariuddin, Malik, 155
Shariat, 62
Sharma, Amita, 372
Sharma, N.K., 238
Shastri, Lal Bahadur; National Academy of Administration, 801
Sheela, 233
Shetkari Sangthan, 752, 755
Shiva-Parvati, 125
Short R., 521
Shusheela, 395
Sikh, Hindus and Hashai Hazaras, 42
Sikkim, 168, 169, 326
Singh, Bharat, 591
Singh, Buta, 158

Singh, Khushwant, 295
Singh, Rajinder, 291
Singhvi, Dr. L.M., 3, 297, 305
Singh, Narinder, 460, 461
Sita, 164, 556
Skin flicks, 121
Smokeless Chulhas, 808
Smuggling of Blue Films, 122
Social Fightout Against Sexual offenders, 380
Social Security Scheme, 537
Sodhi, Dr. Roshan Singh, 233
Sofa-sets, 425
Sojaya, C.P., 529
Solution, 176
Some form of Outside Support can Embolden a Women to Fight Back, 462
Soyal, Sudha, 815
Spain, 78
Special Cell, 283
Special Marriage Act. 1954, 8, 633
Spectrum of Problems, 803, 805
Speedy Justice, 450, 459
Sri Lanka, 603
Srivastava, Tej, 237
Start Fighting, 142
Steps to Combat Discrimination Against Women, 374
Steps towards Reformation of —Female Offenders, 516
Stop Magazines Syndicate, 115
Stridhan, 417, 684
Strict Discipline, 614
Stringent Safeguards, 109
Strong Bias Against Female Children, 771
Strange Customs in South, 14
Studies on Delivery System, 730
Sudha Goels Case, 446, 455
Suharabi, 38
Suicide Attempts, 387
Suicide by Women, 400
Suicide, 400, 444, 454
Suicide Case and Role of Law Enforcing Agencies, 403
Sujaya, C.P., 662
Sultan, Razia, 26
Sunna, 64
Supervise Duties, 563
Suppressive Duties, 630
Supreme Court, 6, 27, 29, 31, 35, 36, 60, 129, 237, 440, 453, 827
Surya, 113

Taking on the teasers, 148
Talak, 53
Talaq, 638
Talaq-pidit, 59
Talwar, Dr. P.K., 216
Tamil Nadu, 50, 113, 168, 326, 327, 353, 469, 572, 802
Tamil Nadu Agricultural University, 733
Tamil Nadu Report, 570
Tamil Nadu Women Project, 723
Tanna, J.H., 711
Techniques for Interviewing Rape Victims, 187
Technologies for Women, 729
Television, 425
Telling Comment, 750
"Thai Kulam" (women folk), 654
Thailand, 492
Their numbers have grown Alarmingly Over the Last Few years, 220
Theoretical Position, 778
Third National, 538
Three Faces of Eve, 264
Times of India, 59
Tippu's Story, 532
Tokyo, 359, 561
Toronto, 388
Toughening, 620
Towards Legal Literacy for Women, 706
Trade-Elements and Management, 201
Trainers Experience, 616
Training, 559, 624
Treatment of Women Convicts in the Courts, 512
Treatment Programme Profiled, 414
Trend Obscene Literature, 77
Trends in Female Criminality, 503

Tribal Women Relatively, 825
Tripura, 326, 327
Trivandrum, 28, 619
TV, 364, 367, 443
Two Syndromes, 817
Tyabji's Muslim, 53
Tyagi, Maya, 816

Unnatural Offences, 133
University of Bradford, 44
University of California, 360
United States of America, 559, 626
Unplanned Growth, 812
U.P., 168
U.P. Tops in Crime Against Women, 352
Urge for Sex Change, 223
U.S.A., 492
US Supreme Court, 127
Uttarakhand, 387
Uttar Pradesh, 326, 327, 353, 733
Uttar Pradesh Export Corporation, 50

Varanasi, 196, 199
Various Factory, 807
Vasanwala, Babubhai, Janata Dal Leader, 776
Vashist, Shakuntala, 572
Vasudev, Uma, 298
Ved Marwah Defends Kiran Bedi, 587
Veera Raghavan, Dr. V., 169, 284
Verghese, Jamila, 298
Venkataraman, R., 275
Venugopal, K.K., 584
Verdict, 52
Verma, Meera, 579
Very Low Wages, 529
Victims, 194
Vidyasagar, Ishwar Chandra, 8, 16, 313, 323, 633
Vijifdar, K.A., 118
Violence Against Women, 424, 434
Violence Against Women Rising, 388
Vinay Nagar, 148
V.I.P., 549
Vishwa Hindu Parishad's, 63
Vouchsafing of Women's Rights, 633

Walking out of a Violent Marriage can be the Difference between Life and Death, 466
War and Women, 22
Wars Multiply Women's Woes, 21
West Bengal, 57, 168, 326, 327, 353, 733
West Germany?, 492
What is Obsence and what is not, 136
What is Rape, 151
Who are these Rapists?, 284
Who is a Rapits?, 153
Whom is she Offending?, 509
Whom is she Offending?, 496
Whopping Increase, 801
Why do Men Rape Women?, 153
Why Infanticide?, 502
Why the Female Ratio is Falling, 762
Why Women are Driven to Kill?, 501
Why Women in Policing?, 545
Why Women Join Force, 613
Wider Concept, 130
Widow Re-marriage, 16
Widow Remarriage Act., 1956, 424, 435
Wife and Beating Still Rampant, 385
Wife Beating Syndrome, 423, 433
Women and Environment: the Symbiotic link, 712
Women and Girls Act. 1956, 508
Women and Police, 547
Women and Prostitution, 507
Women and Sexism in Drug Abuse, 494
Women and the Media, 691
Women and Water, 713
Women are Virtual Slaves in Iran, 43
Women As Equals, 344
Woman as Shakti, 3
Women Campaign, 757

Eldering & P. Liseman (Eds.), *Early intervention and culture.* The Netherlands : UNESCO.

Kagitcibasi, C., Sunar, D., & Bekman, S. (1989). *Psychological education project.* Ottawa : IDRC.

Kamin, L. (1974). *The science and politics of IQ.* Hillsdale, N.J. Erlbaum.

Kanfer, F.H., & Karoly, P. (1982). The psychology of self management: Abiding issues on tentative directions. In P. Karoly & F.H. Kanfer (Eds.). *Self management and behavior change.* New York: Pergamon Press.

Kapadia, S., & Fantuzzo, J. (1988). Effects of teacher and self administered procedures on the spelling performance of learning handicapped children. *Journal of School Psychology,* 26, 49-58.

Katona, G., & Strumpel, B. (1978). *A new economic era.* New York: Elsevier.

Kaul, K.K., Sundaram, K.R., Rajput, V.J., Mukherjee, V.J., Khurana, U., Phadnis, R.V., Lele, A.K., & Puri, V.S. (1982). Influence of socio-economic deprivation on physical and sexual growth during adolescence in school and college boys. *Indian Journal of Medical Research, 75,* 624-631.

Kaul, S. (1991). *Assessment of impact of nonformal preschool education of integrated child development services on children's specific abilities.* Unpublished doctoral thesis, M.S. University of Baroda.

Kaur, B., Linda, K., Razorio, M., & Maheshwari, P. C. (1992). *A follow up study of children of Bastar* (1982-1990). Unpublished report, Department of Human Development and Family Studies, M.S. University, Baroda.

Kaur. H.,Singh, S., & Malhotra, D. (1985). Malnutrition and cognitive development. *Journal of Personality and Clinical Studies, 1,* 23-25.

Kazdin, A. (1982). Current developments and research issues in cognitive behavioral interventions: A commentary. *School Psychology Review, 11,* 75-82.

Kazdin, A. (1987). Treatment of antisocial behavior in children: Current status and future directions. *Psychological Bulletin, 102,* 187-203.

Kazdin, A., Bass, D., Siegel, T., & Thomas, C. (1989). Cognitive behavioral and relationship therapy in the treatment of children referred for antisocial behavior. *Journal of Consulting and Clinical Psychology, 57,* 522-535.

Kazdin, A., Esveldt-Dawson, K., French, N., & Unis, A. (1987). Problem-solving skills training and relationship therapy in the treatment of antisocial child behavior. *Journal of Consulting and Clinical Psychology, 55*, 7685.

Kelley, H.H. (1971). *Attribution in social interaction.* Morristown, N.J. : General Learning Press.

Kendall, P.C. (1985). Toward a cognitive behavioral model of child psycho-pathology and critique of related interventions. *Journal of Abnormal Child Psychology, 13*, 357-372.

Kendall, P.C. (1991). Guiding theory for treating children and adolescents. In P.C. Kendall (Ed.). *Child and adolescent therapy: Cognitive-behavioral procedures* (pp. 3-22). New York: Guilford Press.

Kendall, P.C. (1993). Cognitive-behavioral therapies with youth: Guiding theory, current status, and emerging developments. *Journal of Consulting and Clinical Psychology, 61*, 235-247.

Kendall, P.C. (1994). Treating anxiety disorders in youth: Results of a randomized clinical trial. *Journal of Consulting and Clinical Psychology. 62*, 100-110.

Kendall, P.C., & Braswell, L. (1982). Cognitive-behavioral self control therapy for children: A component analysis. *Journal of Consulting and Clinical Psychology, 50*, 672-689.

Kendall, P.C., & Braswell, L. (1993). *Cognitive-behavioral therapy for impulsive children* (2nd Ed.). New York: Guilford Press.

Kendall, P.C., & Finch, A.J. Jr. (1979). Developing non-impulsive behaviour in children: Cognitive-behavioral strategies for self control. In P.C. Kendall & S.D. Hollon (Eds.). *Cognitive-behavioral interventions: Theory, research and pocedures.* New York: Academic Press.

Kendall, P.C., & MacDonald, J.P. (1993). Cognition in the psychopathology of youth and implications for treatment. In K.S. Dobson & P.C. Kendall (Eds.), *Psychopathology and cognition* (pp. 387-432). San Diego: Academic Press.

Kendall, P.C., & Morris, R.J. (1991). Child therapy: Issues and recommendations. *Journal of Consulting and Clinical Psychology. 59*, 777-789.

Kendall, P.C., & Panichelli, S. (1995). Cognitive-behavioral treatment. *Journal of Abnormal Child Psychology, 33*, 107-124.

Kendall, P.C., & Wilcox, L.E. (1980). A cognitive-behavioral treatment for impulsivity: Concrete versus conceptual training with non-self controlled problem children. *Journal of Consulting and Clinical Psychology, 48*, 80-91.

Khattri, P.K., & Gupta, P. (1981). Reduction of abusive language in socially disadvantaged children: Its transfer and maintenance. *Child Psychiatry Quarterly*, 14, 145-153.

Kohs, S.C. (1923). *Manual for Kohs Blocks Design Test.* Chicago : Stoulting.

Kohli, Atul (1987). *The state and poverty in India: The politics of reform.* Cambrdige: Cambridge University Press.

Kosiewicz, M.M., Hallahan, D.P., Lloyd, J.W., & Graves, A.W. (1982). Effects of self instruction and self correction procedures on handwriting performance. *Learning Disability Quarterly, 5,* 71-78.

Kothari, Rajni (1989). *Politics and the people.* New Delhi: Ajanta.

Koul, L. (1986). *A study of the effects of mastery learning strategies on achievement motivation and task anxiety of socially disadvantaged group in Himachal Pradesh.* Unpublished report, Department of Education, Himachal Pradesh University.

Krishnan, L. (1990). Deprivational environment and psychological services : Applying social psychological information. *Seminar on deprivational environment and psychological services.* Department of Psychology, Gorakhpur University.

Kumar, A., & Tripathi, A.K. (1986). Locus of control of disadvantaged adolescents. *Psychological Reports, 59,* 933-934.

Kumar, P., & Mehta, M. (1983). Socio-economic deprivation and differential personality development. *Asian Journal of Psychology and Education, 11,* 21-27.

Kuppuswamy, B. (1982). *Social change in India.* New Delhi: Vikas.

Labov, W. (1973). The logic of nonstandard English. In N. Keddie (Ed.), *Tinker tailer : The myth of cultural deprivation.* Harmondsworth: Penguin.

Lam, D.J., & Palsane, M.N. (1997). Research on stress and coping : Contemporary Asian approaches. In S.R. Rao, & D. Sinha (Eds.), *Asian perspectives on psychology* (pp. 265-281). New Delhi : Sage.

Lapierre, D. (1986). *The city of joy.* London : Arrow Books Ltd.

Lave, J. (1977). Cognitive consequences of traditional apprenticeship training in West Africa. *Anthropology and Education Quarterly,* 18, 117-177.

Leacock, E.B. (Ed.) (1971). *The culture of poverty: A critique.* New York: Simon.

Ledwidge, B. (1979). Cognitive-behavior modification or new ways to change minds: Reply to Mahoney and Kazdin. *Psychological Bulletin, 86,* 1050-1053.

Leon, J.A., & Pepe, H.J. (1983). Self instruction training for remediation of arithmetic deficits. *Exceptional Children, 50,* 54-60.

Lewin, K. (1951). *Field theory in social science.* New York : Harper & Row.

Lewis, O. (1961). *The children of Sanchez.* New York: Random House.

Lewis, O. (1966). *La Vida: A Pureto Rican family in the culture of poverty.* New York: Random House.

Lewis, P. (1991). *Social action and the labouring poor: An experience.* New Delhi: Vistar.

Lidhoo, M.L., & Khan, M.A. (1990). Bright underachievers among the socially backward : Counselling and remedial measures. *Indian Journal of Clinical Psychology, 17*, 28-32.

Lochman, J.E., & Lenhart, L.A. (1993). Anger coping intervention for aggressive children: Conceptual models and outcome effects. *Clinical Psychology Review, 13*, 785-805.

Lochman, J.E., White, K.J., & Wayland, K.K. (1991). Cognitive-behavioral assessment and treatment with aggressive children. In P.C. Kendall (Ed.), *Child and adolescent therapy: Cognitive-behavioral procedures* (pp. 25-65). New York: Guilford Press.

Loera, P.A., & Meichenbaum, D. (1993). The "potential" contributions of cognitive-behavior modification to literacy training for deaf students. *American Annals of the Deaf, 138*, 87-95.

Lukes, S. (1973). Methodological individualism reconsidered. In Alan Ryan (Ed.), *The philosophy of social explanation* (pp. 119-129). London : Oxford University Press.

Machado, L.A. (1980). *The right to be intelligent* (translated by M.C. Wheeler). Oxford : Pergamon.

Mahn, C.S., & Greenwood, G.E. (1990). Cognitive-behavior modification : Use of self-instruction strategies by first graders on academic tasks. *Journal of Educational Research, 83*, 158-161.

Mahoney, M.J. (1974). *Cognition and behavior modification.* Cambridge, M.A. : Ballinger.

Mahoney, M.J., & Nezworski, M.T. (1985). Cognitive-behavioral approaches to children's problems. *Journal of Abnormal Child Psychology, 13*, 467-476.

Majeed, A., & Ghosh, E.S.K. (1983). Effects of ethnicity, social class and residential background on cognitive differentiation. *Psychological Studies, 28*, 13-17.

Mal, S., & Jain, U. (1990). Effects of prolonged deprivation on learned helplessness. *Journal of Social Psychology, 130*, 191-197.

Manning, B.H. (1990). Cognitive self-instruction for an off task fourth grader during independent academic tasks : A case study. *Contemporary Educational Psychology, 15*, 36-46.

Mascie-Taylor, G.C.J. (1984). Biosocial correlates of IQ. In C.J. Turner & H.B. Miles (Eds.), *The biology of human intelligence* (pp. 99-127). Nafferton : Nafferton Book.

Mata Prasad, Dwivedi, C.M., Kumar, S., & Rastogi, S.N. (1988). Mental subnormality and social class. *Journal of Personality and Clinical Studies, 4*, 183-186.

Mathur, S.S., & Kalia, A.K. (1984). Values as a function of caste. *Journal of Education and Psychology, 45*, 64-67.

Mayers, R.G., & Hertenberg, R. (1987). *The eleven who survive : Toward a reexamination of early childhood development program options and costs* (Report No. EDT69). Washington D.C. : World Bank.

Mead, G.H. (1958). *Mind, self and society : From the standpoint of social behaviorist.* Chicago : Chicago University Press.

Mehta, M. (1992). Level of school performance of backward and nonbackward Rajasthani higher secondary boys. *Journal of Psychological Researches, 36,* 64-67.

Mchta, P. (1994). Empowering the people for social development. In R.N. Kanungo & M. Mendonca (eds.), *Work motivation models for developing countries* (pp. 161-183). New Delhi: Sage.

Meichenbaum, D. (1977). *Cognitive-behavioral modification : An integrative approach.* New York : Plenum Press.

Meichenbaum, D., & Genest, M. (1980). Cognitive-behavior modification : An integration of cognitive and behavioral methods. In F. Kanfer & A. Goldstein (Eds.). *Helping people change : A textbook of methods* (2nd edition). New York : Pergamon Press.

Menyuk, P. (1963). Syntactic structures in the language of children. *Child Development, 34,* 407-422.

Miller, D.R., & Swanson, G.E. (1958). *The changing American parents : A study in the Detroit area.* New York : Wiley.

Miller, J., & Eller, E.B. (1985). An examination of the effect of tangible and social reinforcers on intelligence test performance of middle school students. *Social Behavior and Personality, 13* 147-157.

Miller, P.J., & Moore, B.B. (1989). Narrative conjunctions of caregiver and child : A comparative perspective on socialization through stories. *Ethos, 16,* 428-449.

Minhas, B.S. (1974). *Planning and the poor.* New Delhi: S. Chand.

Minocha, A.C. (1990). Planning for poverty reduction in India. In G. Misra (Ed.), *Applied social psychology in India* (pp. 85-100). New Delhi: Sage.

Mishra, A. (1992). *Role of age, school related differences and contextual change in recall and organization.* Unpublished doctoral dissertation, Banaras Hindu University, Varanasi.

Mishra, B., & Tripathi, L.B. (1991). *Some aspects of language development among Hindi speaking children in deprivational and non-deprivational environment : A psycholinguistic study.* Unpublished report of NCERT sponsored research project, Department of Psychology, University of Gorakhpur, Gorakhpur.

Mishra, C. (1987). Locus of control and creativity across SES and subculture. *Jounral of the Indian Academy of Applied Psychology, 13,* 57-63.

Mishra, G. (1991). *Cognitive processing of tribal and non-tribal children.* Doctoral dissertation, CAS in Psychology, Utkal University, India.

Mishra, P.S. (1988). *Development of organizational processes in verbal learning.* Unpublished doctoral dissertation, University of Gorakhpur, Gorakhpur.

Mishra, R.C. (1976). *Perception and comprehension of certain types of pictorial materials.* Unpublished doctoral thesis, Allahabad University, Allahabad.

Mishra, R.C. (1982). Perception and comprehension of some pictorial symbols as a function of familiarity and nature of depicted objects. *Perceptual and Motor Skills, 55,* 59-62.

Mishra, R.C. (1990a). Cognitive stimulation, training and perceptual - cognitive task performance by socially deprived children. *Indian Journal of Current Psychological Research, 5,* 1-11.

Mishra, R.C. (1990b). Society, ecology and competence. In G. Misra (Ed.), *Applied social psychology in India* (pp. 41-60). New Delhi : Sage.

Mishra, R.C. (1996). Caste, education and urban contact as factors in pictorial perception and interpretation. *Indian Educational Review, 3,* 17-30.

Mishra, R.C., & Sinha, D. (1991). Acculturation, cognitive changes and interpersonal adjustment : A study of some changing tribes of Bihar. New Delhi : ICSSR Project Report.

Mishra, R.C., Sinha, D., & Berry, J.W. (1996). *Ecology, acculturation and psychological adaptation : A study of Adivasis in Bihar.* New Delhi : Sage.

Mishra, R.K., & Mishra B. (1992). Acquisitional hierarchy of words: Impact of family types. *Psycholingua, 22,* 7-16.

Mishra S. (1992). *Ecological disadvantage and skill for pictorial perception and classification.* Unpublished doctoral dissertation, Banaras Hindu University, Varanasi.

Misra, G. (1982a). Motivational structure and prolonged deprivation. *Indian Journal of Social Work, 43,* 11-18.

Misra, G. (1982b). Deprivation and cognitive competence. In D. Sinha, R.C. Tripathi, & G. Misra (Eds.), *Deprivation: Its social roots and psychological consequences* (pp. 151-175). New Delhi: Concept.

Misra, G. (1982c). Experiential deprivation and development of representational competence. In R. Rath, H.S. Asthana, D. Sinha, & J.B.P. Sinha (Eds.). *Diversity and unity in cross-cultural psychology* (pp. 70-77). Lisse: Swets & Zeitlinger.

Misra, G. (1983). Deprivation and development : A review of Indian studies. *Indian Educational Review, 18,* 12-32.

Misra, G. (1984). Effects of disadvantage on attainment : The Indian experience. *Bombay Psychologist, 5*, 102-116.

Misra, G. (1985). Situational and personal determinants of attributions for achievement outcomes in India. *Indian Journal of Community Guidance Service. 2*, 1-18.

Misra, G. (1988). Social disadvantage and achievement attribution. In A.K. Dalal (Ed.), *Attribution theory and research* (pp. 60-80). New Delhi : Wiley Eastern.

Misra, G. (1990). Psychology of deprivation. In G. Misra (Ed.). *Applied social psychology in India* (pp. 119-140). New Delhi : Sage.

Misra, G. (1990a). Deprivation research and its policy implications. *Indian Journal of Current Psychological Research, 5*, 61-68.

Misra, G., & Jain, U. (1988). Achievement cognitions in deprived groups: An attributional analysis. *Indian Journal of Current Psychological Research, 3*, 45-54.

Misra, G., & Misra, S. (1986). Effect of socio-economic background on pupil's attributions. *Indian Journal of Current Psychological Research, 1*, 77-78.

Misra, G., & Shukla, A. (1984). Recognition of pictorial material as a function of experiential deprivation and age. *International Journal of Behavioral Development, 7*, 95-103.

Misra, G., & Shukla, A. (1986). Experiential deprivation and the development of spatial representation in children. *Psychologia, 29*, 115-122.

Misra, G., & Tiwari, B.K. (1986). Environmental correlates of cognitive development. *Indian Journal of Applied Psychology, 24*, 41-52.

Misra, G., & Tiwari, B.K. (1990). Environment and cognitive development. In U.K. Bevli (Ed.), *Resarches in child development: A book of readings* (pp. 251-270). New Delhi: NCERT.

Misra, G., & Tiwari, B.K. (1992). Psychological differentiation in Indian children: Role of ecology, quality of schooling and home environment. *Indian Educational Review, 27*, 23-35.

Misra, G., & Tripathi, K.N. (1993). The concept and context of human development. In T.S. Saraswathi & B. Kaur (Eds.), *Human development and family studies in India: An agenda for research and policy* (pp. 90-103). New Delhi: Sage.

Misra, G., & Tripathi, K.N. (1998). Cognitive development. In A.K. Srivastava (Ed.), *Child development : The Indian perspective.* (pp. 75-111). New Delhi: NCERT.

Misra, G., & Tripathi, L.B. (1977). The concept of prolonged deprivation and its measurement. *Indian Journal of Behaviour. 1*, 48-60.

Misra, G., & Tripathi, L.B. (1978). Prolonged deprivation scale. *Indian Journal of Pscyhology, 53,* 65-76.

Misra, G., & Tripathi, L.B. (1980). *Psychological consequences of prolonged deprivation.* Agra : National Psychological Corporation.

Mistry, V., Kaul, S., & Dhar, H. (1986). *In-depth study of non formal preschool education component in Baroda urban ICDS Block.* Baroda: Department of Child Development, M.S. University.

Moghaddam, F.M. (1990). Modulative and generative orientations in psychology : Implications for psychology in the three worlds. *Journal of Social Issues, 46,* 21-41.

Mohan, V., & Gill, N. (1988). Personality differences of socially deprived and non-deprived school children. *Journal of Psychology, 1,* 23-27.

Mohan, V., & Nalwa, K. (1992). Delinquency proneness as related to deprivation. *Indian Journal of Criminology, 2,* 93-98.

Mohan, V., & Verma, S. (1990). Social deprivation, intelligence and personality correlates. *Indian Journal of Community Guidance Service, 7,* 25-36.

Mohanty, A.K. (1987). *Social psychological aspects of assimilation/ integration in a language contact situation.* Paper presented in the thematic panel on Language and National Integration, XII Indian Social Science Congress, Mysore, India.

Mohanty, A.K. (1990a). *Language of the disadvantaged and the disadvantage of language.* Presidential address in the thematic panel on Language and Poverty, XV Indian Social Science Congress, Berhampur, Orissa, India.

Mohanty, A.K. (1990b). Psychological consequences of mother tongue maintenance and multilingualism in India. In D.P. Pattanayak (Ed.), *Multilingualism in India.* Clevedon, England: Multilingual Matters.

Mohanty, A.K. (1990c). Social psychological aspects of languages in contact in multilingual societies. In G. Misra (Ed.), *Applied social psychology in India.* (pp. 61-84). New Delhi: Sage.

Mohanty, A.K. (1990d). Psychological consequences of mother-tongue maintenance and the language of literacy for linguistic minorities in India. *Psychology and Developing Societies, 2,* 31-51.

Mohanty, A.K. (1992). Bilingualsim and cognitive development of Kond tribal children: Studies on metalinguistic hypothesis. *Pharmacopsychoecologia, 5,* 57-66.

Mohanty, A.K. (1994a). *Bilingualism in a multilingual society.* Mysore: Central Institute of Indian Languages.

Mohanty, A.K. (1994b, July). *Bilingualism in a multilingual society: implications for cultural integration and education.* Keynote address in the International Congress of Applied Psychology, Madrid, Spain.

Mohanty, A.K. (1994c, December). *Language socialization in a multilingual society: analysis of some preliminary data.* Paper presented in the International Conference on Early Childhood Communication, Bhubaneswar, India.

Mohanty, A.K., (In press). Language behavior and processes. In J. Pandey (Ed.), *Fourth Survey of research in psychology.* New Delhi : Sage.

Mohanty, A.K., & Mohanty, M. (1985). Intellectual and linguisitc abilities of children in an early education programme. *Psychological Studies, 30,* 92-96.

Mohanty, A.K., Panda, S., & Mishra, B. (1999). Language socialization in a multilingual society. In T.S. Saraswathi (Ed.), *Culture, socialization and human development.* New Delhi: Sage.

Mohanty, A.K., & Parida, S. (1993). *Bilingualism and attitude towards language and cultural maintenance and integration in a tribal - nontribal contact situation.* Unpublished manuscript, Utkal University, Bhubaneswar.

Mohanty, A.K., & Perregaux, C. (1997). Language acquisition and bilingualism. In J.W. Berry, P.R. Dasen & T.S. Saraswathi (Eds.), *Handbook of cross-cultural psychology: Vol. 2 Basic process and human development (2nd ed.).* Boston: Allyn & Bacon.

Mohanty, B. (1980). Effects of sociocultural disadvantage on intelligence and short-term memory. *Indian Psychological Reivew, 19,* 17-24.

Montagu, A. (1975). Introduction, In A. Montagu (Ed.). *Race and IQ.* New York : Oxford University Press.

Moseley, M.J. (1990). Mother child interaction with preschool language delayed children : Structuring conversation. *Journal of Communication Disorders, 23,* 189-203.

Moulik, T.K. (1981). Psychology of poverty. In Udai Pareek (Ed.), *A survey of research in psychology-1971-1976 (Part-II)* (pp. 635-681). Bombay: Popular Prakashan.

Moscovici, S. (1976). *Social influence and social change.* New York : Academic Press.

Mukherji, S. (1997). Poverty index and high fertility and mortality in Indian states : Crucial policy implications. *Social Science Abstract* (Indian Academy of Social Sciences), *21,* 96-98.

Mukherjee, M., Chatterjee S., & Gupta, R. (1991). Factors of prolonged deprivation, intelligence level and academic achievement. *Psychological Studies, 36,* 20-24.

Muralidharan, R. (1970). Home stimulation and child development. *Indian Educational Review, 5,* 43-51.

Muralidharan, R., & Banerjee, U., (1973). An exploratory study of intellectual development of kindergarten children in relation to their paternal occupations. *Educational and Psychological Research Journal, 1*, 1.

Muralidharan, R., & Banerjee, U. (1975). Effect of preschool education on the school readiness of underprivileged children of Delhi. *International Journal of Early Childhood Education, 7*, 188-191.

Muralidharan, R., & Kaur, B. (1987). A study of the relationship between physical development, language and cognitive development of tribal school children. *Bombay Psychologist, 9*, 7-17.

Murthy, C.V., & Panda, S.C. (1987). A study of intelligence, SES and birth order among children belonging to SC, ST and non SC, ST groups. *Indian Journal of Behaviour, 11*, 25-30.

Muthayya, B.C. (1988). Dynamics of rural development. In J. Pandey (Ed.), *Psychology in India: The state-of-the-art* (Vol. 2) (pp. 225-278). New Delhi: Sage.

Myrdal, Gunnar (1960). *Asian drama: An inquiry into the poverty of nation*. London: Penguin.

Nagar, D. (1989). Socio-psychological problems and personality patterns of deprived children living in destitute homes of Rajasthan. *Indian Educational Review, 24*, 91-94.

Nair, S.B. (1980). *Acquisition of mother tongue in different social groups (Malayalam)*. Unpublished doctoral dissertation, Kerala University, Trivandrum.

Nanda Biswas, U., & Pandey, J. (1996). Socio-economic mobility and perception of status among tribal and caste groups. *Journal of Cross-Cultural Psychology. 27*, 200-216.

National Institute of Public Cooperation and Child Development (1992). *National evaluation of integrated child development services*. New Delhi: Author.

NSS Report. *National Sample Survey of India*, (1982). New Delhi.

NSS Report. *National Sample Survey of India*, (1991). New Delhi.

Ojha, S.K. (1991). Effects of deprivational factors on achievement motivation of women. *Psychological Studies, 36*, 52-56.

Ommen, T.K. (1988). *Protest and change*. New Delhi: Sage.

Omprakash, S. (1993). Psychological symptoms amongst untouchable students of IITs. *Journal of Educational Planning and Administration, 7*, 165-180.

Oyen, E. (1992). Some basic issues in comparative poverty research. *International Social Science Journal, 134*, 615-626.

Padhy, M. (1992). *Assessment and training of cognitive skills of Nolia children through play methods*. Unpublished doctoral dissertation, Utkal University.

Pal, A., Verma, P., & Vasudeva, P. (1989). Sex and SES differences in competition and cooperation. *Psychological Studies, 34,* 160-165.

Pal, R., & Dixit, S.K. (1983). Development of level of aspiration in relation to grade and sex. *Asian Journal of Psychology and Education, 12,* 1-4.

Pal, R., & Tiwari, G. (1984). Self concept and level of aspiration in high and low achievement secondary pupils. *Indian Psychological Review, 27,* 17-22.

Panda, B.N. (1991). Academic achievement and selected demographic factors: A study of urban-rural high school adolescents. *Journal of Education and Psychology, 49,* 49 53.

Panda, K.C. (1988). Social psychology of education. In J. Pandey (Ed.), *Psychology in India : The state-of-the-art,* Vol. II (pp. 279-337). New Delhi : Sage.

Panda, K.C., & Das, J.P. (1970). Acquisition and reversal in four subcultural groups generated by caste and class. *Canadian Journal of Behavioral Science, 2,* 267-273.

Pandey, N., & Tripathi, R.C. (1982). Scheduled caste children in high caste school: Some motivational consequences. In D. Sinha, R.C. Tripathi & G. Misra (Eds.), *Deprivation: Its social roots and psychological consequences* (pp. 218-234). New Delhi: Concept.

Pandey, J. (2000). Socio-cultural dimensions of poverty. (This volume).

Pandey, J., Kakkar, S., & Bohra, K.A. (1982). The functional perception of poverty in India. *Journal of Social Psychology, 117,* 144-150.

Pandey, J., & Singh, A.K. (1985). Social psychological responses to perceived and objective indicators of poverty in India. In I.R. Lagunes & Y.H. Poortinga (Eds.). *From different perspectives: Studies of behavior across cultures.* (pp. 148-156). Lisse: Swets & ZeitLinger.

Pandey, J. Sinha, Y., Prakash, A., & Tripathi, R.C. (1982). Right-left political ideologies and attribution of the causes to poverty. *European Journal of Social Psychology, 12,* 237-331.

Pandey, K. (1988). Environmental influence and all round development of the child. *Child Psychiatry Quarterly, 21,* 23-28.

Pant, P. (1974). Perspective of development: 1961-1976. Implications for planning for a minimum level of living. In T.N. Srinivasan, & P.K. Bardhan (Eds.), *Poverty and income distribution in India* (pp. 9-38). Calcutta: Satistical Publishing Society.

Pareek, U. (1970). Poverty and motivation : Figure and ground. In

V.L. Allen (Ed.), *Psychological factors in poverty* (pp. 330-317) Chicago : Markham.

Pareek, U. (1994). Interventions to deal with poverty. In U. Pareek (Ed.) *Beyond management* (pp. 118-128). New Delhi: Oxford & IBH.

Pathak, M.P., Saxena, N.K., & Mishra, L.S. (1983). Some psychosocial factors associated with mental retardation. *Child Psychiatry Quarterly, 16,* 116-122.

Pathak, P., Ranganathan, H.N., & Deshpande, A. (1994). Development of social maturity during infancy and contributing influence of environmental components including motor and mental development: An exploratory study. *Psychological Studies, 39,* 66-72.

Patnaik, N., & Rath, R. (1982). Effects of cognitive training on the achievement of socially disadvantaged low achievers. In R. Rath, H.S. Asthana, D. Sinha, & J.B.P. Sinha (Eds.), *Diversity and unity in cross-cultural psychology.* Lisse : Swets & Zeitlinger.

Patra, S., & Babu, N. (1999). Role of second langauge as the medium of instruction. In U.N. Dash & U. Jain (Eds.), *Perspectives on psychology and social development.* New Delhi: Concept.

Pattanayak, D.P. (1984). Language policies in multilingual states. In A. Gonzalez (Ed.), *Panagani (language planning, implementation and evaluation).* Manilla: Linguistic Society of the Philippines.

Payne, M., & Furnham, A. (1985). Explaining the causes of poverty in the West Indies: A cross-cultural comparison. *Journal of Economic Psychology, 6,* 215-229.

Pinto, M.A. (1980-81). Analyse de certaines capacites logico-verbales dans deux quartiers socioeconomiquements differencies de Rome. *Bulletin-de-Psychologie, 34,* 725-730.

Poortinga, Y. (1993). Orientation on culture : Some comments on intervention progrmas. In L. Eldering & P. Liseman (Eds.), *Early intervention and culture.* The Netherlands : UNESCO.

Powell, M.B., & Oei, T.P. (1991). Cognitive processes underlying the behavior change in cognitive-behavior therapy with childhood disorders : A review of experimental evidence. *Behavioral Psychotherapy, 19,* 247-265.

Prillettensky, I. (1989). Psychology and the status quo. *American Psychologist,* 44, 795-802.

Punithambal, M. (1990). A comparative study of adjustment problems of disadvantaged and non-disadvantaged children in relation to their academic achievement. *Journal of Educational Research and Extension, 36,* 148-152.

Pushpa, M. (1990). Social deprivation and cognitive style. In U.K. Bevli (Ed.), *Researches in child development: A book of readings* (pp. 194-202). New Delhi: NCERT.

Quraishi, A., & Hussain, A. (1982). Socio-economic status difference in patterns of aggression among school children: A porjective study. *British Journal of Projective Psychology and Personality Study, 27,* 1-6.

Radha, D. (1984). Future prospects of employment of women in India. *Indian Journal of Social Work, 45,* 287-296.

Raina M.K. (1993). Perspective on the gifted and talented disadvantaged in India. In B. Wallace & H.B. Adams (Eds.), *Worldwide perspective on the gifted disadvantaged.* (pp. 304-329). Oxford: Academic Press.

Rainwater, L. (1970). Neutralizing the disinherited: Some psychological aspects of understanding the poor. In V. Allen (Ed.), *Psychological factors in poverty.* Chicago: Markham.

Ram, N. (1990). Marginalization and social mobility in urban India. In G. Misra (Ed.), *Applied social psychology in India* (pp. 233-244). New Delhi: Sage.

Rangari, A. (1987). Caste affiliation, sex, area of residence and SES as source of variation in intelligence of students. *Indian Psychological Review, 32,* 43-47.

Rangari, A., & Palsane, M.N. (1982). Relative Intelligence of Schedule and Non-schedule caste college students. *Bombay Psychologist, 34,* 112-119.

Rao, S., & Singh, S. (1981). Sex type, income level and age in relation to reaction to frustration: An Indian study. *Zeitschrift Psychologia, 189,* 206-213.

Rastogi, A.K., Srivastava, V.K., Dutt, K., & Singh, J.V. (1987). Pattern of development in pre-school children of a rural community. *Indian Journal of Clinical Psychology, 14,* 29-31.

Rath, R. (1972). *Cognitive growth and the class room learning of culturally deprived children in the primary schools.* Paper presented at the East-West Centre for Cross Cultural Studies: Honolulu.

Rath, R. (1982). Problems of integration of the disadvantaged to the mainstream. In D. Sinha, R.C. Tripathi, & G. Misra (Eds.), *Deprivation: Its social roots and psychological consequences* (pp. 239-259). New Delhi: Concept.

Rath, R., Dash, A.S., & Dash, U.N. (1979). *Cognitive abilities and school achievements of socially disadvantaged children in primary schools.* Bombay : Allied Pubilshers.

Rath, R., & Patnaik, N. (1979). Effects of training on some cognitive abilities. *Journal of Psychological Researches,* 23, 81-92.

Rath, R., & Sircar, N.C. (1960). Inter-caste relationship as reflected in the attitudes and opinions of six Hindu caste groups. *Journal of Social Psychology, 51*, 3-25.

Rath, S. (1992). Cognitive-behaviour interaction with disadvantaged tribal school children: An empirical study. *Indian Psychologist, 19*, 4-9.

Rath, S. (1995). Verbal self-instructional remedial training with tribal and non-tribal low achievers : Issue of differential treatment efficacy and generalization. *Psychologia, 38*, 182-191.

Rath, S. (1996). Effects of modelling and self-instructional training on Santal tribal children. *Indian Psychologist, 8*, 39-46.

Rath, S. (1998). Verbal self-instructional training : An examination of its efficacy, maintenance and generalisation. *Europian Journal of Educational Psychology, 13*, 399-409.

Rathore, A.R. (1990). Adjustment among middle school students in relation to SES and social structure of the school. *Indian Educational Review, 25*, 25-31.

Reddy, A.N.V. (1992). *The impact of deprivation awareness on some dimensions of self.* Unpublished doctoral dissertation, Gulbarga University, Gulbarga.

Reddy, G.B. (1987). *Language development in socially disadvantaged and socially non-disadvantaged children.* Unpublished doctoral dissertation, Sri Venkateswara University, Tirupati.

Reddy, N.Y. (1991). Psychological strategies for the educational development of socially disadvantaged group. *Indian Educational Review. 26*, 143-155.

Reddy-Sujatha, B.N. (1986). Analysis of some of the socioeconomic status scales developed in India. *Indian Journal of Behaviour, 10*, 1-10.

Rede, L.R. (1990). Nature, character and dimensions of rural poverty in India. *Asian Journal of Economic and Social Studies. 9*, 280-305.

Richardson, K.S., & Bryner, J.M. (1984). Intelligence: Past and future. In P. Fry (Ed.), *Changing conceptions of intelligence and intellectual functioning* (pp. 199-226). Amsterdam: North Holland.

Rodman, H. (1971). *Lower-class families: The culture of poverty in Negro Trinidad.* London: Oxford University Press.

Rogoff, B. (1990). *Apprenticeship in thinking.* New York : Oxford University Press.

Rosenthal, R., & Jacobson, L. (1968). *Pygmalion in the classroom.* New York : Holt, Rinehart & Winston.

Rosnow, R.L. (1981). *Paradigms in transition : The methodology of social inquiry.* New York : Oxford University Press.

Rosnow, R.L., & Georgoudi, M. (1985). *Contextualism and understanding in behavioral science.* New York : Praeger.

Rowntree, B.S. (1901). *Poverty : A study of town life.* London : Macmillan.

Roy, Ajit (1972). *Politics and economics of Garibi Hatao.* New Delhi: Peoples Publishing House.

Roy, R. (1982). The meaning and measurement of poverty. In D. Sinha, R.C., Tripathi, & G. Misra (Eds.), *Deprivation: Its social roots and psychological consequences* (pp. 5-16). New Delhi: Concept.

Rudolph, L., & Rudholph, S. (1987). *In pursuit of Lakshmi: The political economy of the Indian state.* Chicago: University of Chicago Press.

Sachidananda (1983). Reaching the rural poor. *Journal of Social and Economic Studies*, 1, 79-92.

Sahu, S. (1979). Effect of social disadvantage on verbal competence and language achievement. *Psychological Studies, 24,* 66-71.

Sahu, S. (1989). Verbal competence of socially disadvantaged children. *Journal of Social and Economic Studies, 9,* 59-65.

Sahu, S., & Devi, B. (1982). Role of home environment in psycholinguistic abilities and intelligence of advantaged and disadvantaged pre-schoolers. *Indian Journal of Psychology, 57,* 61-68.

Sahu, S., & Jena, A. (1983). Psycholinguistic abilities of socially disadvantaged children. *Psycholingua, 13,* 25-30.

Sahu, S., & Patnaik, S. (1987). Reading proficiency and strategies of disadvanataged children. *Psycholingua, 17,* 39-34.

Sahu, S., & Sahu, S.K. (1981). *Cultural influences on language achievement and psycholinguistic competence of second graders.* Paper presented at 5th IACCP Congress, Bhubaneshwar.

Sandeep, P., & Pushpa, M. (1981). Deprivation and cognitive development in children. *Child Psychiatry Quarterly, 14,* 47-54.

Sans, M.C. (1982). Rendimiceto intelectual endos groups de sujetos de deferente nivel socioeconomico, *Revista-Latinoamericana-Psicologia, 14,* 223-234.

Saraswathi, T.S., & Dutta, R. (1988). Current trends in developmental psychology: A life span perspective. In J. Pandey (Ed.), *Psychology in India: The state-of-the-art* (Vol. I) (pp. 93-152). New Delhi: Sage.

Saraswathi, T.S., & Dutta, R. (1990). Poverty and human development: Socialization of girls among the urban and rural poor. In G. Misra (Ed.), *Applied social psychology in India* (pp. 141-170). New Delhi: Sage.

Satyarthi, M.K. (1982). A study of the effect of economic status on students' attitude towards school experience. *Asian Journal of Psychology and Education, 9,* 7-9.

Scanlon, P. (1977). A study of some environmental influences on language development. *Child Care, Health and Development, 3,* 149-164.

Schiff, M., & Lewontin, R. (1986). *Education and class : The irrelevance of IQ genetic studies.* Oxford : Clarendon Press.

Scribner, S., & Cole, M. (1973). Cognitive consequences of formal and informal education. *Science,* 182, 553-559.

Sen, A. (1988). *Psycho-social integration of the hadicapped: A challenge to the society.* New Delhi: Mittal Publications.

Sen, Amartya, K. (1982). *Poverty and famines: An essay on entitlement and deprivation.* Oxford: Clarendon Press.

Sen, Amartya. K. (1985). *Commodities and capabilities.* Amsterdom: North-Holland.

Sen, Anima, (1992). *Mental handicap among rural Indian children.* New Delhi: Sage.

Sen, Arun. K., & Sen, Anima, (1984). *Cultural deprivation and mental retardation.* Delhi: Northern Book Centre.

Senger, K.S., Singh, K.D., & Srivastava A.K. (1985). Personality traits of scheduled and non scheduled caste adolescents: A comparative study. *Child Psychiatry Quarterly, 18,* 48-52.

Sharma, P., Michael, A., Reddy, M.V., & Gehlot, P.S. (1985). Migration and mental illness. *Indian Journal of Psychological Medicine, 8,* 47-52.

Sharma, R., & Tripathi, R.C. (1988). Teachers' expectations and attributions : The self-fulfilling prophecy cycle. In A.K. Dalal (Ed.), *Attribution theory research* (pp. 33-59). New Delhi : Wiley Eastern.

Sharma, S., & Ahuja, T. (1990). Antecedents of psychological differentiation. *Journal of Personality and Clinical Studies, 6,* 211-215.

Sharma, V.P. (1983). Academic performance as a function of prolonged deprivation. *Journal Psychological Researches, 27,* 48-53.

Shotter, J. (1980). Action, joint action and intentionality. In M. Breuner (Ed.), *The structure of action.* Oxford, England : Blackwell.

Shukla, A. (1990). Experiential deprivation and development of shape coding in children. *Psychological Studies, 33,* 62-68.

Shukla, S. (1988) *Effect of some environmental factors on individual differences in language development.* Unpublished doctoral dissertation, Utkal University, Bhubaneswar.

Shukla, S., & Mohanty, A.K. (1986). Development of syntactic ability among Hindi-speaking children. *Social Science International, 2,* 44-50.

Shukla, S.N. (1991). *Learning and memory among socially deprived groups : A developmental study.* Unpublished doctoral thesis, Avadh University, Faizabad.

Shukla, Sandhya, Mishra, U., & Singh, T. (1994). Relative deprivation and reaction to frustration. *Journal of Personality and Clinical Studies, 10,* 45-51.

Shyamlal (1992). The Jain movement and socio-religious transformation of the "Bhangis" of Jodhpur, Rajasthan. *Indian Journal of Social Work, 53,* 59-68.

Sigel, J.E. (1990). Psycho-educational intervention : Future directions. *Merrill Palmer Quarterly, 26,* 159-172.

Sigman, M., Newman, C., Jensen, Ake A.J., & Bwibo, N. (1989). Cognitive abilities of Kenyan children in relation to nutrition, family characteristics and education. *Child Development, 60,* 1463-1474.

Silva, P.A. McGee, R. Thomas, H., & Williams, S. (1982). A Descriptive study of socio-economic status and child development in Dunedin five year olds. *New Zealand Journal of Educational Studies, 17,* 21-32.

Singh, A. (1987). *Certain deprivational factors in language development in children.* Unpublished doctoral dissertation, University of Allahabad, Allahabad.

Singh, A.K. (1983). Parental support and academic achievement. *Social Change, 14,* 21-24.

Singh, Amar, K. (1976). *Social disadvantage, intelligence, and academic achievement.* Paper presented at the 14th annual conference of the Indian Academy of Applied Psychology, IIT, Kharagpur.

Singh, Amar, K. (1980). Social disadvantage and academic achievement. *Social Change, 10,* 15-18.

Singh, Amar. K. (1983). Parental support and academic achievement. *Social Change, 13,* 9-14.

Singh, Anoop, K. (1991). *The social psychology of poverty.* New Delhi: Mittal Publications.

Singh, Anoop, K., & Pandey, J. (1985). Dimensions of coping with socio-economic problems. *Social Change, 15,* 51-54.

Singh, B.G. (1995). *Development of the Bastar tribes.* New Delhi: Classical Publishing Company.

Singh, L.B. & Sinha, B. (1983). The Santal students : Their intelligence and achievement motivation. *Indian Journal of Social Work, 44,* 167-173.

Singh, N.P., & Aggarwal, P. (1987). Effect of nutrition on intellectual development. *Perspectives in Psychological Researches, 10*, 25-29.

Singh, R. (1988). Relationship between achievement motivation, intelligence, introversion-extraversion, SES and achievement in mathematics. *Indian Educational Review, 23*, 99-102.

Singh, R. (1992). Socio-economic status and psychogenic needs. *Perspectives in Psychological Researches, 15*, 108-110.

Singh, R.R. (Ed.) (1980). *Social work perspectives on poverty*. New Delhi: Concept.

Singh, S. (1983). Perceived self-efficacy and intellectual performance of socially disadvantaged students. *Journal of Social Psychology, 125*, 267.

Singh, S., Kaur, H., & Dubey, R. (1986). Malnutrition and cognitive development among deprived and non-deprived children. *Indian Journal of Clinical Psychology, 13*, 29-34.

Singh, S., & Misra, G. (1985). Effect of competence manipulation on cognitive performance and persistence in relation to socio-economic deprivation. *Psychological Studies, 30*, 12-26.

Singh, S., & Misra, G. (1988). Attribution of performance as a function of deprivation and ethnicity under competence and helplessness conditions. *DEI Research Journal of Psychology, 6*, 1-7.

Singh, S., & Sinha, A.K. (1986). Relative importance of social deprivation, intelligence, punctuality and ethnicity in predicting educational achievement. *Psychologia, 27*, 23-25.

Singh, Tarlok (1969). *Poverty and social change*. New Delhi: Orient Longman.

Singh, T., & Dwivedi, C.B. (1993). Deprivation, context, and processing of textual materials. *Journal of Genetic Psychology, 154*, 73-83.

Singh. T., & Dwivedi, C.B. (1994). Relation of text structure to context-processing during reading. *Journal of General Psychology, 121*, 157-168.

Singhal, R., & Misra, G. (1992). Meaning of achievement: The role of socio-cultural background and social class. *Psychologia, 35*, 42-49.

Singhal, S. (1969). Environmental variables and intellectual performance of young children. *Indian Journal of Applied Psychology, 6*, 74-81.

Sinha, D. (1969). *Indian villages in transition*. Bombay : Allied.

Sinha, D. (1976). Study of psychological dimensions of poverty : A challenge and necessity. *Journal of Social & Economic Studies, 4*, 167-220.

Sinha, D. (1977). Some social disadvantages and development of certain perceptual skills. *Indian Journal of Psychology, 52*, 115-132.

Sinha, D. (1980). Some cognitive and motivational concomitants of poverty. *Social Change, 10*, 3-8.

Sinha, D. (1982a). Socio-cultural factors and the development of peceptual and cognitive skills. In W.W. Hartup (Ed.), *Review of child development research*, Vol. 6. Chicago : Chicago University Press.

Sinha, D. (1982b). Towards an ecological framework of deprivation. In D. Sinha, R.C. Tripathi, & G. Misra (Eds.), *Deprivation : Its social roots and psychological consequences* (pp. 25-35). New Delhi : Concept.

Sinha, D. (1984b). *Manual for story-pictorial EFT and Indo-African EFT.* Varanasi : Rupa.

Sinha, D. (1985). Cognitive and motivational correlates of deprivation and their implications for the education of scheduled caste children. *Journal of Personality and Clinical Studies, 1*, 11-16.

Sinha, D. (1990). Intervention for development out of poverty. In R.W. Brislin (Ed.), *Applied cross-cultural psychology* (pp. 77-97). Newbury Park: Sage.

Sinha, D. (1994). Some cognitive consequences of deprivational environment and their policy and action implications. *Trends in Social Science Research, 1*, 43-57.

Sinha, D., (1997). Some social disadvantages and development of certain perceptual skills. *Indian Journal of Psychology, 52*, 111-132.

Sinha, D., & Mishra, R.C. (1982). Some socio-environmental disadvantages and skill for perception of pictorial symbols. *Personality Study and Group Behaviour, 3*, 111-121.

Sinha, D., & Mishra, R.C. (1988). A developmental study of psychological differentiation among rural and urban tribal children in relation to quality of schooling and religion. *Creative Psychologist, 1*, 17-25.

Sinha, D., & Mishra, R.C. (1993). Some methodological issues related to research in developmental psychology in the context of policy and intervention programmes. In T.S. Saraswathi & B. Kaur (Eds.), *Human development and family studies in India.* New Delhi : Sage.

Sinha, D., & Misra, G. (1982). Deprivation and its motivational and personality correlates. In D. Sinha, R.C. Tripathi, & G. Misra (Eds.), *Deprivation : Its social roots and psychological consequences* (pp. 195-215). New Delhi : Concept.

Sinha, D., & Misra, G. (1989). *Coping strategies of socially disadvantaged students in a new environment: Some observations.*

Unpublished manuscript, Department of Psychology, Barkatullah University, Bhopal.

Sinha, D., & Shukla, P. (1974). Deprivation and development of skill for pictorial depth perception. *Journal of Cross-Cultural Psychology, 5*, 444-450.

Sinha, D., Tripathi, R.C., & Misra, G. (Eds.) (1982). *Deprivation : Its social roots and psychological consequences*. New Delhi : Concept.

Sinha, J.B.P. (1998). Poverty syndrome: Personal communication.

Sinha, R.R. P. (1980). *Tribal and nontribal intelligence*. New Delhi: Classical Publications.

Sinha, Y. (1988). Causal explanations of poverty. In A.K. Dalal (Ed.), *Attribution theory and research* (pp. 115-128). New Delhi : Willey Eastern.

Sinha, Y., Jain, U., & Pandey, J. (1980). Attribution of causality to poverty. *Journal of Social and Economic Studies, 8*, 349-359.

Skutnabb-Kangas, T. (1986). Who wants to change what and why : Conflicting paradigms in minority education research. In B. Spolsky (Ed.), *Language and education in multilingual settings*. Clevedon: Multilingual Matters.

Skutnabb-Kangas, T. (1988). Multiculturalism and education of minority children. In T. Skutnabb-Kangas & J. Cummins (Eds.), *Minority education: From shame to struggle*. Clevedon: Multilingual Matters.

Slavenburg, J. (1993). Critical issues in the evaluation of preschool intervention programmes. In L. Eldering & P. Liseman (Eds.), *Early intervention and culture*. Netherlands : UNESCO.

Slavin, R., & Madden, N. (1993). *Success-for-all prevention and early intervention in elementary schools*. Netherlands : UNESCO.

Sood, N. (1992). Preschool education in ICDS: An appraisal. *NIPCCD Technical Bulletin*, 5.

Southworth, F.C. (1980). Functional aspects of bilingualism. *International Journal of Dravidian Linguistics, LX(1)*, 74-108.

Spivack, G., Platt, J.J., & Shure, M.B. (1976). *The problem-solving approach to adjustment*. San Francisco : Jossey-Bass.

Spolsky, B. (1986). Introduction. In B. Spolsky (Ed.), *Language and education in multilingual settings*. Clevedon, England: Multilingual Matters.

Srinivas, M.N. (1978). *The changing position of Indian woman*. Delhi : Oxford University Press.

Srivastava, A.K. (1989). A study on field dependence-independence among Mizo children. *Psychological Studies, 34*, 55-58.

Srivastava, A.K., Banerjee, J., & Tripathi, A.M. (1996). *Role of acculturation in the development of values among children: Ma-*

ternal views. New Delhi: National Council of Educational Research and Training.

Srivastava, A.K., & Lalnunmawii (1989). Cooperative-competitive behaviour and conflict resolution style among Mizo children: A cultural perspective. *Psychology and Developing Societies, 1,* 191-205.

Srivastava, R.S. (1988). Social change and social violence in India: A contemporary perspective. In K.S. Shukla (Ed.), *Collective violence: Genesis and response (pp. 234-243).* New Delhi: Indian Institute of Public Administration.

Srivastava, S. (1990). *Effects of experiential deprivation and anxiety on episodic-semantic distinction.* Unpublished doctoral Dissertation, Banaras Hindu University, Varanasi.

Stanovnik,T. (1992). Perception of poverty and income satisfaction. *Journal of Economic Psychology, 13,* 57-69.

Stark, K.D., Rouse, L.W., & Livingston, R. (1991). Treatment of depression during childhood and adolescence cognitive-behavioral procedures for the individual and family. In P.C. Kendall (Ed.). *Child and adolescent therapy : Cognitive-behavioral procedures* (pp. 165-206). New York : Guilford Press.

Stone, L.J., & Church, J. (1972). Some representative theoretical orientations in developmental psychology. In W.R. Looft, (Ed.). *Developmental psychology : A book of readings* (pp. 35-59). Hindale : Dryden.

Suar, D., & Chand, S.K. (1991). *A baseline study of MCH/WEANE project.* Ranchi : Xavier Institute of Social Service (mimeographed).

Suar, D., & Prasad, S.K. (1995). The vital role of NGOs.*Social Welfare, 41,* 16-17.

Sudhir, M.A. (1989). A study of achievement motivation in relation to selected personality and socio-educational factors. *Journal of Educational Research and Extension, 25,* 198-205.

Sukhatame, P.V. (1981). On measurement of poverty. *Economic and Political Weekly, 16,* 1928-1935.

Tendulkar, S.D. (1998). Indian economic policy reforms and poverty: An assessment. In I.J. Ahluwalia & I.M.D. Little (Eds.). *India's economic reforms and development.* (pp. 280-309). Delhi: Oxford University Press.

Tharakan, P.N.O. (1987). The effect of rural and urban upbringing on cognitive style. *Pychological Studies, 32,* 119-122.

Tharakan, P.N.O. (1992). Calicut socio-economic status scale. *Indian Journal of Community Guidance Service, 9,* 231-242.

The Daily Statistics Canada (October 13, 1992). *1991 Health Activity Limitation Survey,* p.1.

The United Nations Development Programme. (1991). *Human development report.* Oxford : Oxford University Press.

Tikoo, P.N. (1985). *Indian Woman : A brief socio-cultural survey.* Delhi : B.R. Publishing Co.

Tiwari, A. (1987). *Achievement motivation in a deprived society.* Agra: National Psychological Corporation.

Tiwari, B.K. (1986). Development of memory in relation to some socio-cultural factors. *Psycholingua, 16,* 31-36.

Tiwari, P.S.N. (1990a). Achievement motivation among beneficiaries and nonbeneficiaries of IRDP in relation to their perceived poverty. *Psycholingua, 20,* 87-93.

Tiwari, P.S.N. (1990b). *Attributional analysis of agricultural productivity and perceived poverty in deprivational environment.* Paper presented at Seminar on Deprivational Environment and Psychological Services, University of Gorakhpur, Gorakhpur.

Tiwari, P.S.N., & Mishra, N.L. (1988). Study of causal perception in relation to perceived economic status of rural poor. *Advances in Psychology, 3,* 61-68.

Tiwari, S.K. (1994). *An empirical study of learned helplessness in deprivational environment.* Unpublished doctoral dissertation, University of Groakhpur, Gorakhpur.

Townsend, P. (Ed.) (1970). *The concept of poverty.* New York: American Elsevier.

Townsend, P. (1979). *Poverty in the United Kingdom.* Hardmondsworth: Penguin.

Tripathi, A.K. (1993). *Some aspects of social cognition and perceived environment among villagers of eastern U.P.* Unpublished doctoral dissertation in psychology, University of Gorakhpur, Gorakhpur.

Tripathi, L.B. (1982). Some methodological problems of deprivation studies. In D. Sinha, R.C. Tripathi, & G. Misra (Eds.), *Deprivation : Its social roots and psychological consequences* (pp. 49-71). New Delhi : Concept.

Tripathi, L.B. (1986). *Prolonged deprivation and psychological functions.* UGC National Lectures, Department of Psychology, Banaras Hindu University, Varanasi.

Tripathi, L.B. & Misra, G. (1975). Cognitive activities as a function of prolonged deprivation. *Psychological Studies, 21,* 54-61.

Tripathi, N.M. (1991). *Family experiences and cultural background as factors in the development of pattern reproduction skill.* Unpublished doctoral dissertation, Banaras Hindu University, Varanasi.

Tripathi, R.C. (1988). Applied social psychology. In J. Pandey (Ed.), *Psychology in India: The state-of-the-art (Vol. 2) Basic and applied social psychology* (pp. 95-158). New Delhi: Sage.

Tripathi, S.K., Bhusan, B., & Pradhan, P.N. (1990). The economic impact of the IRDP. *Indian Journal of Social Work, 51*, 100-106.

UNDP - United Nations Development Program (1997). *Human development report.* Oxford: Oxford University Press.

Upadhyaya, S.K. Saran, A., Agarwal, D.K., Singh, M.P., & Agarwal, K.N. (1992). Growth and behavior development in rural infants in relation to malnutrition and environment. *Indian Pediatrics, 29*, 525-606.

Upadhyaya, U. (1986). Construction and standardization of a tool to measure sense of deprivation. *Indian Psychological Review, 30*, 29-37.

Upadhyaya, S. (1980). Social disadvantage, academic adjustment and scholastic achievement. *Social Change, 10*, 23-30.

Vagrecha, Y.S., & Gon, M. (1985). Economic stress and protest social behaviour. *Indian Journal of Social Psychiatry, 1*, 275-281.

Vahn, W.J. (1988). Cognitive-behavioral group counselling : An introduction. *School Counsellor, 135*, 43-52.

Vajpayee, A. (1995). *Training and cognitive task performance : A comparative study of high and low caste children.* Unpublished doctoral dissertation, C.C.S. University, Meerut.

Valentine, C.A. (1968). *Culture and poverty.* Chicago: University of Chicago Press.

Vance, E.T. (1973). Social disability. *American Psychologist, 28*, 498-511.

Vashisht, S. (1990). *Enabling mothers of infants (0-3 months) affected by cerebral pals, mental retardation to foster infant development by planning a stimulation programme.* Unpublished Master's dissertation, M.S. University of Baroda.

Vazir, S., & Kashinath, K. (1995 April). ICDS and psychological development. *Nutrition News, 16*, No. 2.

Vazir, S., Bhogle, & Naidu, N. (1988). Influence of psychosocial factors on the nutritious status of pre-school children. *Journal of the Indian Academy of Applied Psychology, 14*, 1-18.

Venkatamma, P. & Rajamanickam, M. (1984). A study of prolonged deprivation among tenth standard students. *Indian Journal of Community Guidance Service, 9*, 35-50.

Verma, B.P., & Sheikh, G.Q. (1992). Learning styles of advantaged and disadvantaged students. *Indian Journal of Psychometry and Education, 23*, 61-68.

Verma, M. (1992). *A developmental study of perceptual skills in children.* Unpublished doctoral dissertation, Banaras Hindu University, Varanasi.

Index

Abraham Lincoln, 274, 276
Absolute poverty, 93
Achievement attribution, 173-74
Ackerman, P., 281
Administrative definition, 73
Affluence effect, 282
Afforestation, 247
Agarwal, A., 123, 124, 131, 189
Agro-economic development, 85
Ahluwalia, M., 48
Ahuja, R., 135
Alam, K., 138
Allen, V.L., 74
Alripu, 198
Amartya Sen, 55, 262, 278, 281
American psychology, 23
Anandalakshmy, S., 46, 57, 98, 124, 194
Anandamaya Siksha, 104
Anganwadies, 190, 194
Anglicization, 108
Anjali, S., 35, 107, 149
Annunciation, 193
ANOVA, 153
Antecedent, 96
Anti-poverty programmes, 184, 186, 188, 199, 249
  types, 187
Antyodaya, 184
Argentina, 158
Atal, Y., 279
Athwale, Pandurang Shastri, 198
Attribution, 169-70
  changing, 175-76
  generality of, 170-72
  studies, 70

Barbadian adolescents, 85
Basic Interpersonal Communication Skills (BICS), 115
Beck, T.C., 48
Beggars, 42
Behavioural manifestations, 122
Bernstein B., 149
Berry, J.W., 112, 165, 225
Bevli, U.K., 142
Bharatiya Sanskar Nigam Samiti, 190
Bhargava, A., 149
Bhatia, M.S., 126
Bhogle, S., 56
Bhoodan movement, 187
Bilingual education programme, 116
Bilingualism, 109, 110, 111
Binoba Bhave, 187
Birhors, 126
Biswas, Nanda, 53
Black-white dichotomy, 23
Block-Design Test, 160, 220
Block Pramukh, 233, 234
Bohra, K.A., 86
Breaking mental barriers, 236
Broomstick effect, 68
Bronfenbrenner, U., 62, 98, 165

Caloric intake, 48
Caplin, N., 97
Caste hierarchy system, 78
Caste and mobility, 81-82
Cash crop cultivation, 247
Causation, 30
Causes of poverty, 43, 83-85
Challanges, 39, 100, 108, 188
Chatterjee, B.B., 89, 147
Chaturvedi, M.G., 105
Child labour, 56
Child poverty, 56
Childhood malnutrition, negative effect of, 125
Childhood nutritional status, 124
Childhood blindness, 230
Chronic stress, 126
Cini Asha, 197
Codd, J.A., 162
Cognitive Academic Language Proficiency (CALP), 115
Cognitive Behaviour Training (CBT), 200, 201
  common features of, 203-204
  interventions, 207
    efficiacy of, 206
    programme, 209-13
  multi-faceted intervention programme, 208

promises of, 205-206
Cognitive competence, 148-50
Cognitive functions, 135
impact on, 66-67
Cole, M., 28, 223, 225
Common Property Resources (CPRs), 250
Command Area Development programme (CADP), 242
Communications, 150
Community based initiatives, 197-98
Community based intervention Programme, 230-32
Community Based Rehabilitation (CBR) programme, 231-233
Community Development programme, 187
Conceptual issues, 30
Consentization, 193, 273
Constraints, 98, 128
Controllability, 168
Copestake, J.G., 188
Corruption, 135, 199
Coward, B.E., 74
Criticisms, 160
Cube Construction Test, 160
Cultural deprivation, 50
Culture of poverty, 46, 74, 121
Cummins, J., 115
Cumulative deficit, 222
Current Psychological Research, 127

Dalal, A.K., 38, 230, 264
Dalits, upliftment of, 56
Dandekar, V.M., 48
Danzinger, K., 99
Das, J.P., 136, 147
Dash, A.S., 136
Dash, Uday N., 37, 183
Data collection techniques, 145
Dayal, E., 49
Defining poverty, problem in, 94-95
Demonstration, 27
Deprivation, 22, 26, 42-50, 69, 93, 101, 132, 169, 267, 283
awareness of, 52
effects explanations of, 144-45
degrees of, 269
Indian Researches in, 265-66
interaction of, 173
kinds of, 214
paradigm, 33, 252
specific features of, 51
Deprivational factors, 142
Destitutions, 47, 93
Development of Women and Children in Rural Areas (DWCRA), 187, 244
Deviations, 90
Disabilities, 230
survey, 234
Disadvantage-advantage, dichotomies of, 23
Disadvantage children, cognitive development of, 214-20
Disadvantage Rural People (DRP), 244
behaviur characteristics, 245-46, 250-52
critical awareness, 256-57
economic characteristics, 249-50
self-reliant development of, 241-45
social characteristics, 248-49
Disciplines, 31, 41, 261
Dreze, J., 47, 263, 264
Drought Prone Area Programme (DPAP), 242
Dubey, S.N., 129
Dwivedi, C.B., 138
Dysfunctional coping strategies, 270

Economic deprivation, 50
indicators, 73
liberalization, 195, 278
poverty, 22
Programme Committee, 185
resources, 23
Economistic fallecy, 280-81
Education, 230, 256
Education for All, 104
Educational achievement, 143
failure, 34
resourcefullness model, 192
Edwards, J.R., 55, 106, 108
Eighth Five Year Plan, 186
Eklavya, 198
Elementary education, universalisation of, 104
Embedded Figures Test (EFT), 139
Employment, 41, 186, 189
opportunities, 29
Entwistle, H., 155

Environmental awareness, 65
conception of, 164-65
deprivation, 50, 146, 268
factors, 166
Eotous, L.U., 159
Euro-American Model, 266
Experimental deprivation, 52
Expressive Skill Test (EST), 153

Facilitating cognitive functioning, interventions of, 215-16
Fatalistic attitude, 245
Feagin, J., 84
Feather, N., 84
Fifth Five Year Plan, 186
First Five Year Plan, 185
Five Year Plans, 184, 185
Fisher, R.A., 165
Food poverty, 44
Fourth Five Year Plan, 186
Frustration, 13
Furnham, A., 84, 87

Gangwar, H.N.S., 143
Garibi hatao (eradicate povety), 59
Genetic factors, 145
Gergen, K.J., 99
Gewirtz, J.L., 90
Ghosh, S., 56
Ghurye, G.S., 221
Ginsberg, H., 161
Goodwin, N.R., 281
Gottesman, I.I., 165
Gram Sabha, 257
Grammar Comprehension Test (GCT), 152
Giriappa, S., 188
Gross National Product (GNP), 43
Gyan-Prabodhani, 198

Hanumantha Rao, C.H., 188
High School Personality Questionnaire (HSPQ), 129
Himmelweit, H.T., 98
Home Intervention for Pre-Primary Youngesters (HIPPY), 226
Homogenization, 108
Human Develop Index (HDI), 44
Human Poverty Index (HPI), 45
Hungary, 159

Illiteracy, 26, 150, 155, 200
Immediate Need Gratification, 247
IMF, 242
Immunization, 230

Inamdar, N.R., 279
Income Generation Activities for Women (IGAW), 242
Indian Acadamy of Applied Psychology (IAAP), 59
Indian Context, disadvantaged children, 208-210
Indira Gandhi, 59
Indira Rozgar Yojna, 187
Individual environmental complex, 93
Indo-African Embedded Figures Test, 220
Industrialisation, 55
Inequalities, 107,150
Integrated Child Development Services (ICDS), 190, 226, 244
Integrated Rural Development Programme (IRDP), 187,242
Intellectual abilities, 163
Intellective functions,141
Intelligence, genetic bases of, 163-64
Intelligence Quotient (IQ), 158, 217
Intelligence Research, 162
Intelligence Test, 35, 160, 161-162
scores, 141,142
Inter-generational Socio-economic mobility, 79
International Labour Organization (ILO), 73
Intervenetion programmes, 37
cultural implications, 25
evaluation of, 228
Intervention Studies,Key issues of, 220-22
Intervening variables, 150
Invulnerable Deprived People, 274-75
Irvine, S.H., 227
Issues, 21, 36,40

Jachuck, K., 141. 196, 217
Jain, Uday, 32, 33, 36, 89, 101, 132, 168, 174
Jaipur, 126
Janabandhu, 130
Jawahar Rozgar Yojna (JRY), 187, 242
Jayant, K.R., 129
Jensen, A.R., 163
Jodha, N.S., 41

Kagitcibasi, C., 158
Kakkar, S.,86
Katona, G.,77
Kaul,K.K., 123
Kendall, P.C., 206
Koli's Block Design Test, 218
Kond tribes, 78
Koul, L., 193
Krishnan, L., 92
Kui language, 113
Kui-Oriya bilinguals, 110
Kwashiorkar children, 12

Language, disadvantage of, 105 108
  varieties, 106
Leacock, E.B., 74
Lewis, Oscar, 46
Lewin, K., 98
Liberalisation, 186, 195
Linguistic abilities, 154
Linguistic deficit hypothesis, 140
  environment, 151
  investory, 151, 153. 154
  minorities, 113
  performance, 145
  skills, 140
Linguisticism, 114
Literacy, 279
Lochman, J.E., 206
Lotus of Mud, 275, 276
Low Self-Esteem, 245
Lukes, S., 99

Machado, Luis A., 157
Macro-Level intervention, 277-78
Malnutrition, 25, 65, 123, 124
  problems of, 34
Mata Prasad, 141
Maternal and Child Health Programme (MCH), 244
Methodological individualism, 99, 100
Middle income protestants, 87
Migrant slum-dwellers, 42
Mill, J.S., 99
Minimum Needs Programme (MNP), 244
Minocha, A.C., 191
Misra, G., 21, 31, 40, 50,52, 130, 132, 133, 136, 137, 138, 145, 168, 176, 183, 192, 202, 216, 274
Misra, B., 140
Mishra, P.S., 137
Mishra, R.C., 37,139, 214
Mobility, 77
Mobile creches, 197, 198
Modernization, 108
Modified Threshold hypothesis, 147
Moghaddam, F.M., 92
Mohanty, Ajit K., 21, 33, 92, 104, 106, 109, 110, 111, 11, 114, 115, 117, 140, 159, 263
Monolingual programme, 115
Monolingualism, 111, 114
Moscovici, S., 99
Moselay, M.J., 155
Monlik, T.K., 40
MRTP Act, 194
Mukherjee, M., 142
Mukhiyas, 245
Multilingual education, 34
Multilingual multicultural society, 113
Multilingualism, 109, 116
Muralidharan, R., 66, 149, 194
Muthayya, B.C., 40

Nagar D., 129
Napolean Bonaparte, 275, 276
National Institute of Nutrition, 124
National Institute of Public Cooperation and Child Development (NIPCCD), 191
National Minimum expenditure, 48
National Rural Employment Programme (NREP), 187, 242
National Sample Survey, 48, 230
Nature-Nurture Controversy, 162
Nauroji, Dadabhai, 185
Nehru, Jawahar Lal, 185
Nelson, S.D., 97
Newman Kaul's Test, 153
New Zealand, 158
Ninth Five Year Plan, 186
Non-Government Organisation, 90

Occupation, 42, 52
ODA, 242
Ojha, S.K., 132
Omprakash, S., 126
Operation Blackboard, 104, 105
Oraon tribes, 78, 126
Orissa, 104, 189, 196
Oriya monolinguals, 110
Oyen, E., 74

Panchayati Raj, 188
Act, 253
institutions, 242
model, 241
Panda, B.N., 40, 69, 143
Panda, S.C., 141
Pandey, J., 32, 54, 72, 75, 85, 86, 134, 275
Pandey, K., 53
Pareek, U., 92, 131, 193
Parental deprivation, 50
Participatory Rural Appraisal (PRA), 253, 254-255
critical awareness, 256-57
Passalong test, 160
Pattanyak, D.P., 109
Paynes, M., 88
Perceived Poverty, 52, 75-76
Perpetuating inequality, 104-110
Personality and motivational development, 127
Phulbani, 112
Physical amenities, 50
Physico-economic deprivation, 52
Physical facilities, 155
Picture Interpretation Test, 220
Pinto, M.A., 158
Planning Commission, 48, 49, 185
Political movements, 135
Pollution, 281
Poor academic achievement, 143
Poor education, 56
Poor less intelligent, 157-60
Poverty-alliviation, government interventions for, 184-85
issues of, 191
Poverty-allivation programmes (PAP), 70, 18, 195-96, 268, 278,
failure of, 91
implementation of, 94
Poverty 42
ameliorative programme, 63, 135
causal explanation of, 87
conceptualization of, 40
problems of, 33
condition of, 63
causes of, 43, 83-84
cycle, 26
deficit hypothesis, 271
eleminating programme, 44
explanation of, 97-98
fluctuations, 49
indicators, 73
integrated approach to, 75-76
measurement of, 93
mobilization stage, 235-36
National agenda, 183
negative aspects of, 61
parameters of, 24
perception of, 72-76
planned interventions, 185-86
policies and programmes, 21
problems of, 183-85
psychological dimensions, 263-64
research on, 61, 89-93
public expenditure, 48
scenario, 48
social-psychological measure of, 74-75
syndrome, 24, 191
Poverty and deprivation, 265-66
Poverty and disadvantage, 22
condition of, 126
consequences of, 121-30
contextualisation of, 26, 32
current interventions, 30
motivational concomitants, 36
problems of, 24
processes of, 25
psychological analysis of, 261
correlatesof, 269-70
research on, 283
schemes and programmes, 29
Poverty and deprivation, psychological research on, 65-66
Privatization, 195
Proféssional poverty, 41
Prolonged deprivation, 51, 92, 128, 144
Prolonged Deprivation Scale (PDS), 52, 62, 169, 176
Protein Energy Malnutrition (PEM), 123
Psycho-phsiological problems, 126
Psychological characteristics, 24
deficits, 92
deprivation, 50
interventions, 25, 29, 37, 91, 184, 191-92, 264-65
research, 93
Public Distirbution System, 195
Punarmusko Bhaba, 66
Punithambal, M., 126
Pushpa, M., 137

Quadrants, 82
Quality of Life, 29, 44, 91, 183
Quareshi, A., 129, 137
Queens' University, Canada, 238

Radha, D., 155
Rainwater, L., 46
Raina, M.K., 142
Rajamanickam, M., 53
Rajiv Gandhi Foundation, 236, 237, 238
Rangari, A., 126
Rao, V.K.R.V., 60
Rastogi, A..K., 124
Rath, R., 37, 136, 154, 209
Rath, Sudhakar, 200
Rathore, A.R., 126
Raven Progressive Matrices (RPM), 158
Reddy, A.N.V., 128, 130
Reddy-Sujatha, B.M., 51
Relative deprivation, 94
poverty, 93
Reservation policy, 226
Reynell Development Language Scale, 158
Rickshawpullers, 85
Rodman, H., 47
Rogoff, B., 224
Roy, R., 43
Rural Landless Employment Guarantee Programme (RLEGP), 187, 242
Rural poverty, 49

Sachidananda, 190
Sahu, S., 140, 149
Sambhavana, 236, 237, 238
Sanskritization, 108
Saraswathi, T.S., 98, 127, 128
Scheduled Caste and Scheduled Tribes, 26, 200, 214, 266
improving of, 186
Second Five Year Plans, 185
Self-employment, 235, 236
Self-esteem, 171
Sen, A.K., 41
Sequence Perception Test, 220
Seventh Five Year Plan, 186
Shanumugam, T.E., 66
Sharma, P., 125
Sharma, Sridhar, 126
Sharma, R., 133
Sharma, V.P., 143
Shukla, A., 52, 133, 138
Shukla, S., 140, 220
Shukla, S.M., 137
Singh, Amar K., 53
Singh, Anoop K., 41, 52. 144, 157
Singh, Ashok K., 128
Singh, S., 130
Singhal, R., 132
Sinha, D., 27, 32, 33, 59, 68, 93, 107, 134, 136, 139, 149
Sinha, A.K., 143
Sinha, Y., 70
Siruthu Project, 232-34, 239
Sixth Five Year Plan, 186
Small Farmers Development Agency (SFDA), 187, 242
Social causation, 125, 134
Social deprivation, 50
Social disadvantage, 42, 54
Social discrimination, 117
Social security programmes, 56
Socialization, 127, 150
patterns of, 135
Socio-economic mobility, 76-77
Socio-Economic Scale (SES), 27, 45, 72, 154, 158
Southworth, F.C., 110
Spolsky, B., 105
Srinivas, B., 105
Srinivas, M.N., 150
Srivastava, A.K., 129, 130, 138, 139
Stability, 168
Standard Progressive Matrices (SPM), 160
Stanford-Binet Intelligence Scale, 158
Stanovnik, T., 76
Stimulation programmes, 218
Stone, L.J., 97
Strategies, 36
Suar, Damodar, 38, 241, 253, 264
Swadhyaya, 198
Swati Patra, 116

Tara Singh, 32, 89
Telecommunication facilities, 232
Tendulkar, S.D., 195
Test of Scholostic Abilities (TOSCA), 162
Test sophistication, 225
Third Five Year Plan, 185
Tikoo, P.N., 150
Tiwari, B.K., 53, 138, 139, 196